GENDER AND GENRE IN THE FOLKLORE OF MIDDLE INDIA

A volume in the series

MYTH AND POETICS

edited by Gregory Nagy

A list of titles appears at the end of the book.

GENDER AND GENRE IN THE FOLKLORE OF MIDDLE INDIA

JOYCE BURKHALTER FLUECKIGER

CORNELL UNIVERSITY PRESS

ITHACA AND LONDON

Cornell University Press gratefully acknowledges a grant from Emory University
that aided in the publication of this book.

First published 1996 by Cornell University Press.

Printed in the United States of America

♾ The paper in this book meets the minimum requirements
of the American National Standard for Information Sciences—
Permanence of Paper for Printed Library Materials, ANSI Z39.48-1984.

Library of Congress Cataloging-in-Publication Data

Flueckiger, Joyce Burkhalter.
Gender and genre in the folklore of Middle India / Joyce Burkhalter Flueckiger.
p. cm. — (Myth and poetics)
Includes bibliographical references (p.) and index.
ISBN 0-8014-3206-5 (alk. paper)
1. Folklore—India—Chattīsgaṛh (India). 2. Women—India—Chattīsgaṛh—Folklore.
3. Folklore—Performance. 4. Chattīsgaṛh (India)—Social life and customs.
I. Title. II. Series.
GR305.5.C46F58 1996
398′.0954′3—dc20 95-50444

with thanks to

my parents, Edward and Ramoth Burkhalter,

and the performers and audiences of Chhattisgarh

Contents

PERFORMANCE TEXTS

Illustrations and Maps

ILLUSTRATIONS

MAPS

Foreword

GREGORY NAGY

Gender and Genre in the Folklore of Middle India, by Joyce Burkhalter Flueckiger, demonstrates the necessity of defining any given genre as a part of a system of genres as they exist at a given time and place within a given community. Thus we cannot speak of, say, epic as a "genre" of and by itself until we establish how the form that we call "epic" fits into a system of other forms that are complementary to it. Moreover, we cannot expect a genre such as "epic" to be a constant—let alone a universal—since different communities are marked by different systems of complementarity. Even a single community may have had different systems at different phases of its existence, so that the nature of a genre like epic may change over time.

Together with another book in the Myth and Poetics series, Dwight Reynolds's *Heroic Poets, Poetic Heroes: The Ethnography of Performance in an Arabic Oral Epic Tradition,* Flueckiger's work will force a radical revision of the concept of epic. In Reynolds's book, epic is seen as crossing class boundaries. In Flueckiger's we see epic crossing gender boundaries as well. Such shifts, Flueckiger argues, can be understood only within an overall system of genres.

From earlier studies of the occasions of public performance in the living epic traditions of India there arose the scholarly consensus that epic is performed almost exclusively by male singers. The rarely found "exceptions," however, are particularly revealing, and Flueckiger has been a pioneer of research in such crossovers of gender and genre. Moreover, her discoveries of "exceptional" epic crossovers in the repertoires of women performers provide a major impetus for comparative study. We can now see in a new light, for example, the song of Sappho about the wedding of Hektor and Andromache, considered exceptional in the history of Greek literature: that song, composed in a meter cognate with but distinct from the epic dactylic hexameter, treats in a nonepic manner themes that are otherwise characteristic of epic.

Flueckiger's book, the result of fieldwork conducted over a period of fifteen years on the oral traditions of the Chhattisgarh region of Middle India, describes in detail six genres that typify this community. These genres define themselves through their interrelationships in performance traditions and, implicitly, in the repertoires of individual performers. By closely studying these interrelationships, the author has succeeded in capturing the essence of what is known as a song culture, that is, a kind of social setting in which the performances of songs are not distinguished from the performances of rituals that happen to be basic to that setting. To the extent that a community identifies itself by way of its rituals—and by way of the myths to which they are connected—a song culture is the sum of its myths and rituals. The six genres studied in this book illuminate a new way to look at poetics, that is, through the lens of an indigenous song culture.

Preface

This book examines the indigenous principles of genre identification and intertextuality within a folklore repertoire of middle India and proceeds to use these principles as an entry into the interpretation of six performance genres selected from that repertoire. This focus for the study of the folklore of the Chhattisgarh region of Madhya Pradesh took shape only gradually over the course of fifteen months of original fieldwork and numerous return trips to Chhattisgarh over the last fifteen years.

I first went to Chhattisgarh in the fall of 1980 on a Fulbright-Hays Dissertation Research Grant with a plan to look for regional variants, particularly women's performance traditions, of the pan-Indian epic tradition of the Ramayana. My motivating question was whether and how the performance of a particular Ramayana tradition might define a cultural region and/or social groups within that region. Given the ritual dominance of the Hindi written version of the Ramayana, the *Rāmcaritmānas,* in the Hindi-speaking belt of northern and middle India, I expected that specifically regional and gender- or caste-based variants and interpretations of the epic story would be embedded in nonepic forms, such as folk songs and tales or devotional songs. So, I began my fieldwork by taping a wide spectrum of ritual and festival performances that occurred in the villages in which I lived and visited. After several months in the field, I came to a realization that while many Chhattisgarhi folk traditions offered alternative narrative variants, emphases, and worldviews to that of the Hindi *Rāmcaritmānas,*[1] the performance

[1] See Flueckiger 1991a for a discussion of the feminization and localization of the Ramayana narrative in women's Ramayana *maṇḍalī* in the Chhattisgarh plains.

genres in which these were embedded were both more interesting to me and more significant to those who performed them than was the Ramayana tradition per se.

I shifted my focus to a consideration of this folklore repertoire as a *system of genres,* listening to performers' and audiences' articulations of the boundaries of what they perceived to be a "Chhattisgarhi" repertoire and making an effort to identify its internal organizing principles and categories. I found the question I had brought to my original research topic of regional Ramayanas still relevant, although now significantly expanded: could a region or social groups within that region be identified by the performance of particular genres, and if so, how; what were the relationships between genre and community? In the course of my fieldwork, it gradually became apparent that a central organizing feature of the repertoire of Chhattisgarhi folk genres *is* the social identity of the group to whom the genre "belongs"; performers and audiences categorize genres on the basis of this social identity more frequently than on the basis of form or thematic content. Performance of these genres both identifies and contributes to the identity of the Chhattisgarh folklore region and social groups within it.

Western scholars have conducted few ethnographic studies in Chhattisgarh,[2] perhaps, in part, because of its geographic distance from major urban centers and the Hindi heartland of the Gangetic plains.[3] Because Chhattisgarh lies on the southeastern borders of the Hindi-language belt, this region and others of Madhya Pradesh are assumed to share north Indian cultural and religious patterns in the north-south axis frequently drawn in South Asian academic discourse. Yet while much of what I read in north Indian ethnographies resonated with what I had experienced during my childhood in Chhattisgarh, I felt that Chhattisgarh was somehow distinctive and that assumptions for north India could not always be applied to the

[2] After Verrier Elwin's substantial collections of the folklore of Chhattisgarh and the Maikal Hills in the 1940s (Elwin 1946; Elwin and Hivale 1944) with which he provided extensive ethnographic notes, the next ethnographically based scholarly work to be published in English was Lawrence Babb's excellent study of popular Hinduism in the Raipur plains of Chhattisgarh (*The Divine Hierarchy,* 1970). Edward Jay has also conducted ethnographic fieldwork in the region, first in Bastar District and then in the Chhattisgarh temple town of Rajim (1970, 1973). Most Indian anthropologists based in Chhattisgarh have done their own fieldwork in the tribal district of Bastar, to the south of Raipur; in my visits to the Department of Anthropology of Ravishankar University in Raipur, many of the faculty did not understand my interest in nontribal Chhattisgarh and urged me to join them in their studies of Bastar.

[3] In 1980, it was a two-day train ride from Delhi to the Chhattisgarhi city of Raipur and then another three hours by bus to the town of Basna in Phuljhar; from there, one had to make arrangements for transportation via private car, bicycle, or oxcart to outlying villages. Today, the city of Raipur is serviced by several airlines and is, therefore, more easily accessible from other urban centers.

region.[4] This was perhaps the primary motivation for my return to Chhattisgarh as a field site—my desire to understand within an analytic framework this region of middle India which I had come to know on some intuitive level as a child and which remains an important part of who I have become.

I began my fieldwork by living for several months in the village of Patharla, on the eastern borderlands of Chhattisgarh, ten kilometers from the village where my parents, Ramoth and Edward Burkhalter, were Mennonite missionaries and where I had numerous friends and contacts from my childhood. Here, I gradually internalized the rhythms of village life I had previously known only from a distance and observed the ways in which performance both creates and reflects those rhythms. I became aware of a wide spectrum of Chhattisgarhi performance genres, their rules of usage, and Chhattisgarhi "ways of talking" about performance and eventually decided to make this regional repertoire the focus of my study.

The village in which I first lived was primarily an Oriya-speaking village in the subregion of Phuljhar, with several Chhattisgarhi-speaking villages close by. Even within the latter, however, many genres identified as "Chhattisgarhi" were not uniformly available (such as the *candainī* epic tradition). To make a study of a regional repertoire would require a wider geographic field. So after several months I moved to the more centrally located town of Dhamtari in the plains of Chhattisgarh, from where I could more easily locate and access Chhattisgarhi performance genres not available in the region's borderlands.

In the village of Patharla, I lived with the only Christian family in the village, that of a pastor for whom the church had chosen this village as a central location between several small congregations that he served. Habil and Kamolini Nand, along with their two young daughters and baby son, had recently moved to the village and were living in a new home with an empty corner in one of its two rooms. The village headman and others in the village with whom I had discussed housing concurred that it would be best for me to live "with my caste [*jāti*]" and, more specifically, with persons who knew my parents. I was reluctant to live with a Christian family, but it was a situation that served me well. Living with them, I was free to visit homes and participate in the rituals of both high- and low-caste Hindu families. The family was not yet directly aligned in village politics and was unrelated to anyone in the village, and so they became the confidants of many. Located at the edge of the village, their home became a conversational

[4] This was particularly true in my readings about purdah (female veiling) and the position of women in the Gangetic plains of north India. It was these kinds of imprecise generalizations for middle India, based on north Indian ethnography and experience, that led me to expect the Ramayana tradition to have greater significance in Chhattisgarh than it does.

way station for many village women as they "went to the fields" in the evening. Not living as a young daughter-in-law in an extended family, Kamolini had fewer household obligations than she might have had otherwise and was freer to accompany me to neighboring villages and to houses within our own village; she was an invaluable companion. Both she and Habil were genuinely interested in my work and served as constant teachers about Oriya / Phuljhar culture, language, and folklore. Habil also transcribed several performances for me from Oriya into Devanagari (Hindi) script and made initial translations into Hindi.

In Dhamtari, I lived on the Christian hospital compound where my husband was working for a three-month rotation as a medical student. There was a tribal (*ādivāsī*) Gond settlement (*pārā*) right across the street, where many of the "unskilled" hospital workers lived, that I knew would be fertile ground for fieldwork. But after a week of living on the compound, I had not yet been able to decide how to make my entry into this neighborhood. Then one afternoon I heard singing and ran out to the road, where there was a large procession of women accompanying a new bride on her first entry into the *pārā;* I joined in their procession.

A woman with the name of Rupi Bai tattooed on her forearm pulled me aside and began to give me a running commentary about what was happening, instructing me at the appropriate moment to give the bride at least a rupee as my part in the community's gifting to her. This gifting tangibly identified me as an "honorary member" of the *pārā* I had just entered; there followed several other such ritual affirmations of my identity as fictive kin in the community. When I told Rupi Bai of my interests in Chhattisgarhi festivals and rituals, she begged me to return the next day, saying, "Why stay over there [the hospital compound]; this is where you'll learn." Thereafter, I spent many long hours sitting with Rupi Bai as she rolled her quota of hundreds of leaf cigarettes (*bīṛī*), was invited to their ritual celebrations, and was introduced to the life of a Gond community that in many ways typifies what inhabitants of Chhattisgarh identify as uniquely "theirs." Rupi Bai has since moved to another settlement on the opposite side of town, and I lived with her for several days when I returned to Dhamtari in the summer of 1993; the *paṇḍvānī* performance analyzed in Chapter 7 took place in her front courtyard.

Initially, I had deep reservations about beginning my fieldwork so close to "home," in the rural area where my parents had worked for over thirty years. I feared that their identity as missionaries would have a dampening effect on my access to and relationships with Hindu villagers with whom I lived and whose performances I would be recording. In fact, this fear was an indication of how little I really "knew" about the villagers' perceptions of boundaries of religious and social identification and the implications of these from a Hindu point of view. My own religious background came up only when I was asked what was my caste (*jāti,* with the implications of what was I born/how did I live, rather than what did I believe). I realize that the implications of that *jāti* were not the same as they would have been had I been an Indian woman; I had a freedom of movement, access, and action that an Indian female colleague might not have been granted so readily. To what extent and how I should take advantage of this, to acknowledge the degree to which it was not always my decision, was a process of continual negotiation for me in fieldwork.

The primary effect of the proximity of Patharla to the village in which my parents lived and the fact that I was born and raised in India was that I entered the village with an identifiable context; I was readily accepted as a Chhattisgarhi "sister."[5] In numerous conversations during those early days in Patharla and surrounding villages, I found myself, quite naturally, explaining why I had come to live in a village. At first, I framed my responses by explaining that I hoped to teach about India in an American university and wanted to learn more about Hinduism and village life by actually living in a village, attending their festivals, listening to their songs, eating their vegetables,[6] bathing in their rivers. After all, I frequently said, "What is the use/benefit [*kyā phāydā hai*] of living in a bungalow?" This one comment, often drawing gales of laughter, seemed to be, finally, explanation enough. When I moved to the Raipur plains and I had already experienced acceptance as a Chhattisgarhi "sister," I began to refer to Chhattisgarh in such "explanatory" conversations as my "mother's place" (*maikā*), to which I had returned for a visit (and nurture) from my home of marriage (*sasurāl*), the United States. I was rarely asked to give further justification for my interest in recording Chhattisgarhi songs, stories, and ritual celebrations.

This insider/outsider dual status affected what I observed, the kinds of questions I felt I could ask, and the nature of the answers I received. It was

[5] In Patharla (and in Chhattisgarhi society more generally), proper names are rarely used; in the village I was called, in Chhattisgarhi/Oriya conversation, the English term "sister." Hindi terms for sister distinguish between older and younger sister; however, my actual age did not concur with cultural expectations for a woman that age. For example, the wife of the family with which I lived was, in 1980, twenty-four years old and the mother of four children; I was in my late twenties, married, but with no children. It would have been awkward under these circumstances for me to call her "younger sister" or for her to perceive me as her elder. The English term "sister" solved that problem; and even most village elders, who certainly perceived me as "daughter," called me "sister." In other villages and urban neighborhoods I visited, however, speakers *did* try to identify my age and use the appropriate fictive kinship term of daughter, older/younger sister, or father's sister.

[6] A common greeting in the village was, "What vegetable did you eat?" or "What is your vegetable today?"

often assumed by the villagers with whom I lived, audience members, and performers, that I knew more about their performance repertoire and its cultural contexts than I actually did, partly because of a certain intuitive cultural knowledge reflected in my body language, dress, and speech patterns;[7] and this became more noticeable as I gradually picked up some of the basic "ways of talking" about performance. This assumption opened to me numerous situations that otherwise might have been closed to an "outsider"; it raised the complexity of many conversations since the speakers did not feel that they always had to "start from the beginning." However, the expectation that I "knew" often kept me from asking certain elementary questions; I was reluctant to break the flow of conversation by asking something that the speaker may have thought should be obvious to me. I usually found the answers to these questions in other contexts or conversations, but some remained unanswered. I have since become much less hesitant as a fieldworker to admit what I do not know and to be more direct with my questioning.

A similar shift has occurred in another aspect of my fieldwork methods. I first went to the field with the ideal (gleaned in graduate school folklore classes) that I should tape performances only in their "natural" (that is, unelicited) performance contexts. During my first year in Chhattisgarh, I attended rituals, performances, and festivals that I heard about in my own or in neighboring villages, often quite literally following the call of a distant drumbeat; but I did not serve as the primary patron of and rarely elicited performances, with the exception of that of the *kathānī kūhā* of Chapter 4 (which was at the "insistence" of some of the villagers with whom I lived). As a result, my recordings from that year reflect a wide breadth of performance traditions and less "depth" in any given genre than I may have wanted (particularly since the performance of many genres are tied to the agricultural cycle and annual festivals). Nevertheless, this period of fieldwork was crucial to learn the general contours of the repertoire and Chhattisgarhi "ways of talking" about performance before I began to elicit more performances (outside their ritual or spontaneous contexts) and commentary about them on return visits to Chhattisgarh. I found that these latter contexts often provided more "space" for talk about the genre than their "natural"

[7] I think of a specific example of this in my interactions with a Brahmin family in Raipur, whose son taught at the university and whose daughter was writing her Ph.D. dissertation. I had visited the family many times when the daughter told me that I was the first foreigner whose polluted cup her orthodox mother had not passed through the fire after it had been used. When I asked why, the elderly mother replied that it was because I became appropriately modest/"embarrassed" (*tum ko śarm ātī hai*) when I spoke of my husband and did not use his given name in conversation.

contexts and helped to delineate significant categories of performance context. For example, it was only when I asked a woman to sing *ḍālkhāī* songs in a village courtyard that I learned that it was a genre that should not be sung inside the village but only outside its boundaries (where I had first recorded them during the *ḍālkhāī* festival). The analyses of individual performances in the chapters that follow are drawn primarily from those I recorded during that first year of fieldwork (with the exception of the *paṇḍvānī* performance recorded in the summer of 1993 and discussed in Chapter 7), but much of what I learned about the genres through indigenous commentary is drawn from generative conversations around elicited performances and direct questioning that followed on return visits.

The field of folklore and performance studies, as well as ethnographic writing styles, has changed significantly in the fifteen years since I began this project; I, too, am a different fieldworker than I was when I began. Were I to begin another long-term project in Chhattisgarh, it would surely take a different shape. Knowing what I now do about the complexities of the repertoire and the differences manifest within performances of its genres over geographic distances in the Chhattisgarhi countryside, I would, however, perhaps not be so bold as to attempt a multigenre project and thus would lose a primary contribution of the present book.

My research in Chhattisgarh was supported by a Fulbright-Hays dissertation grant in 1980–1981 and the early stages of the writing by a University Fellowship from the University of Wisconsin. Two subsequent trips were supported by the University of Wisconsin Albert Markham Traveling Postdoctoral Fellowship (1985) and Emory University's University Research Council Summer Grant (1993). I returned to Chhattisgarh numerous times in between to visit family and friends, and each journey gifted new performances, enlightening conversations, and friendships.

Parts of this book have appeared in earlier publications: a version of Chapter 2 as "*Bhojalī:* Song, Goddess, Friend," *Asian Folklore Studies* 42 (1983):27–43; a version of Chapter 4 as "Land of Wealth, Land of Famine: The *Suā Nāc* (Parrot Dance) of Central India," *Journal of American Folklore* 100, no. 395 (1987):39–57; parts of Chapter 6 in "Caste and Regional Variants from an Epic Tradition: The Lorik-Canda Epic," in *Oral Epics in India,* edited by Stuart H. Blackburn et al. (Berkeley: University of California Press, 1989); and parts of the discussion in Chapter 8 in "Genre and Community in the Folklore System of Chhattisgarh," in *Gender, Genre, and Power in South Asian Expressive Traditions,* edited by Arjun Appadurai et al. (Philadelphia: University of Pennsylvania, 1991). I am grateful to the publishers involved for permission to reprint parts of this material.

I was invited to participate in a conference on Indian oral epics in June 1982, sponsored by the Social Science Research Council, shortly after returning from my first lengthy research trip to Chhattisgarh. I thank my South Asian folklore colleagues who participated in that conference for their welcome to me as a new colleague in the field and the continuing encouragement and responses to my work that I have received from this expanding community over the years. I am particularly grateful to Peter Claus, Margaret Mills, Kirin Narayan, Laurie Sears, David Shulman, and Susan Wadley for their early and ongoing support. My advisor at the University of Wisconsin, Velcheru Narayana Rao, first introduced me to the world of South Asian folklore as a legitimate field of academic study; his contagious enthusiasm and love for this world are reflected in his continual search for creative approaches to its study. Without his energetic intellectual challenges and interactions, rare friendship, and unfailing support over the years, I might not have persevered.

In the final stages of writing this book, when the end goal was sometimes obscured by necessary details, I benefited greatly from the vision, encouragement, and enthusiasm of Gregory Nagy, editor of the Myth and Poetics series in which this volume appears. Bernhard Kendler, executive editor at Cornell University Press helped me contextualize the book within the broader field of academic publishing and make subsequent difficult decisions. Nancy Malone copyedited the manuscript with care, and I thank her for her close reading. Finally, Kay Scheuer, managing editor, patiently guided the manuscript into publication.

I am particularly grateful to Emory University for providing a subvention that made possible the publication of the two full-length translated performance texts in this book. Full translations of these kinds of "mid-length" performances in South Asia have not commonly been published. They broaden our horizons of types of narratives performed in India, as well as break gender stereotypes (both in length and content) of those men and women perform.

In Chhattisgarh, I was affiliated with Ravishankar University in Raipur in 1980–1981. I particularly thank Saroj Bajpai of the Department of Anthropology for his time and energy in helping me to establish contacts in the Raipur area and for accompanying me to several villages. Dr. and Mrs. H. S. Martin in Dhamtari first gave my husband and me accommodation on the hospital compound in 1981, but since then have always held open a door to their home and a seat at their table whenever I have returned to Dhamtari. In Phuljhar, Kamolini and Habil Nand, Ibrahim Nand, and Shradhavati Sona were wonderful friends and conversation partners in discussing the performance traditions and culture of Phuljhar. Campa Bai was a dear companion, a spark of energy, and the source of numerous songs, narratives, and commentaries.

My husband Mike Flueckiger and my children, Peter and Rachel, have been more than patient with my frequent trips back to India and the impact of my continuing relationship with India on our family, which makes us, as my daughter once said, "not quite like other families." I thank them for their love and growing understanding. Finally, my parents, Edward and Ramoth Burkhalter, first instilled in me a love and respect for India; they created a home in Chhattisgarh in which grew deep roots that continue to nurture unexpected flowerings. They provided unconditional support to me during my numerous sojourns in Chhattisgarh, from creatively listening, responding to equipment failures and the latest adventure or misadventure of fieldwork, to meeting numerous trains and buses as I made my way back home. I sorely miss their presence when I now return to my *maikā*. It is to them and the performers and audiences of Chhattisgarh, who so graciously shared their traditions with me, that I dedicate this book.

JOYCE BURKHALTER FLUECKIGER

Atlanta, Georgia

Note on Transliteration

Italicized Hindi and Chhattisgarhi words have been transliterated using a conventional system of transliteration. Proper nouns, including names and place names, appear without diacritics and thus in the form that most closely approximates their English pronunciation. Hence, the Hindi श and ष appear as *sh* (Kauśalya = Kaushalya, Kṛṣṇa = Krishna); च appears as *c* and appears छ as *ch*. According to this system, the spelling of the name of the region under consideration in this volume should appear as "Chattisgarh" rather than "Chhattisgarh." I have retained the latter spelling, however, since it appears thus in the Census of India, on most maps, and elsewhere in print. Hindi and Chhattisgarhi differ from Sanskrit in that the final *a* is not usually pronounced, and hence I have not retained it in transliteration except for words and names to which Hindi speakers add an attenuated final *a*, such as Shiva, or in words and names that have become familiar to English readers in their Sanskrit forms, such as Ramayana and Mahabharata.

GENDER AND GENRE IN THE FOLKLORE OF MIDDLE INDIA

CHAPTER I

Introduction: Region, Repertoire, and Genre

Two vignettes from my earliest fieldwork in the Chhattisgarh region of middle India stand out as interactions that set into play what became the central questions of this study. I spent the first month on the field visiting villages on the Phuljhar borderlands of Chhattisgarh in search of a fieldwork base. Realizing not all villages would be "equal" in the number of performance genres available, the festivals celebrated, and the castes represented, I planned to ask for general performance repertoires by gender, caste, and village and take these into consideration in my choice.[1] Seated in the courtyard of a high-caste, Aghariya Chhattisgarhi village headman (*gauṇṭiyā*) in the first village I visited in September 1980, surrounded by a large crowd of household and neighborhood women, I tried out my survey strategy by rather simplistically asking "what kinds of songs they sang" (using the Hindi words *gīt* and *gānā*); drawing blank stares, I tried again, this time being more specific by asking if they sang songs at their weddings. Their categorical answer of "no" was surprising, since I had found numerous appearances of women's wedding songs (*vīhā gīt*) in printed collections of Chhattisgarhi folklore available in the library at the University of Wisconsin. It was only several days later that I began to realize that Chhattisgarhi usage of the word *gānā* (to sing), without being placed in relationship to a particular genre of song (such as *vīhā gīt*), is limited to male, professional singing—and this the women did *not* do. I realized that while I knew the Chhattisgarhi *terms* for

[1] I was still naïve at that point about the weight in making that decision that would be carried by more logistical practicalities such as finding a household in which there would be an empty corner for an extra bed, typing table, and tin trunk.

"song" and "to sing," I did not know the indigenous rules of *usage* for these terms; inappropriate usage had resulted in miscommunication. I did not yet know the indigenous "ways of talking" about folklore, genre, and performance.

The second vignette also began on this initial tour of potential field sites, but it reached closure only several months later. This time, the village was a primarily Oriya-speaking one. I had learned by now that I needed to be more specific in my enquiries about repertoire, so I asked the women of a high-caste Kolta family whether they sang *vīhā gīt* at their weddings. They enthusiastically assured me that they did: "Of course we sing them at our [*hamar*] weddings." This was the village in which I eventually chose to live for four months before moving to the town of Dhamtari in Chhattisgarh's heartland. I had already left, however, when the wedding season began five months later; and I traveled six hours by bus to return to the village for the wedding of the daughter of this same household. After a full day of ritual, beginning with the turmeric anointing (*haldī lagānā*) of the bride and now close to ending with her *vidā* (ritual of farewell, sending her to her in-laws), there had not yet been a single women's song. I reminded my friends of their earlier assertion, with what I'm sure was a note of exasperation, "I thought you said that you sang *vīhā gīt* at your weddings." They laughed, and one explained, "When we said *we*, we didn't mean *our* caste, we meant *Oriya* women."

This initially frustrating fieldwork experience images the complex ways in which folklore genres help to identify, delineate and give identity to folklore groups and communities. The assertion that "we sing at our weddings" was made to me as a newcomer to the region and an outsider to the village. The speaker was identifying on a general level with the Oriya-speaking community of Chhattisgarh, even though it is women from *ādivāsī* (tribal) castes, and not her own, that sing these wedding songs. Close to five months later, the same speaker found it humorous that I had interpreted the "we" so specifically, by caste; however, it is probable that she would not have made such a broad identification between community and genre when speaking to me after I had lived in that same village for several months and had become more familiar with the indigenous terminologies of the system of Chhattisgarhi genres and their rules of usage.

Over the initial weeks of looking for a village in which to live and the months that followed during which I visited many other villages, my questioning regarding performance repertoires became more refined. I began to frame the questions with a phrase I had heard in many of the initial responses I had received, "Here in Chhattisgarh." I would follow this with a question such as, "What kinds of festivals do you celebrate/observe (*kyā kyā tyohār manāte hai*)?" or I would give specific examples of the kinds of performance genres with which I had heard other villagers respond, such as *candainī* or the *suā nāc.* A core repertoire of genres gradually emerged from the varied responses, one that was repeatedly identified with the region Chhattisgarh. If conversations continued further or if we started to talk more specifically about one of the individual genres, the genres often began to be identified with smaller social groups (according to caste, gender, or age). The Oriya Kolta women mentioned above were not alone in identifying with Chhattisgarhi or Oriya genres on a sliding scale of inclusive identity, depending on the context and identities of conversational partners.

The focus of my study consolidated around this indigenously identified repertoire of Chhattisgarhi performance genres. I became interested in the repertoire as a *system of genres,* in its boundaries, terminologies, and internal organizing principles. As I listened to what performers and audiences talked about most when discussing or commenting on particular genres and performances, it gradually became apparent that a central organizing principle of the repertoire is the social identity of those to whom a genre "belongs"; genres are categorized on the basis of this social identity more commonly than on the basis of form or thematic content. I have used these principles of indigenous repertoire and genre as an interpretive frame through which to enter the analyses of six representative genres performed in the central plains of Chhattisgarh and in the border region of Phuljhar.

The first three genres considered in this book are female ritual traditions, and the last three are male-performed narrative genres in which female characters are central. The bounded regional repertoire of which these are a part presents to us a strikingly female-centered world. Female performers and/or characters are active and articulate and frequently challenge or defy brahminic (frequently male) expectations of gender. In this performance world, men, too, confound gender roles: a male storyteller assumes a mother's voice in noticing the subtle early signs of her daughter's pregnancy; a male character takes on female disguise to protect himself in an all-female kingdom in which he is seemingly helpless; men appropriate a particular female genre to displace its defiant voice. This play of gender and genre in the Chhattisgarhi repertoire contributes to the construction of a particular regional cultural ethos and is key to its understanding.

Chhattisgarh as a Geographic and Historical Region

Modern Chhattisgarh is a geographic, historical, cultural, and linguistically defined region of eastern Madhya Pradesh, bordering Orissa, made up

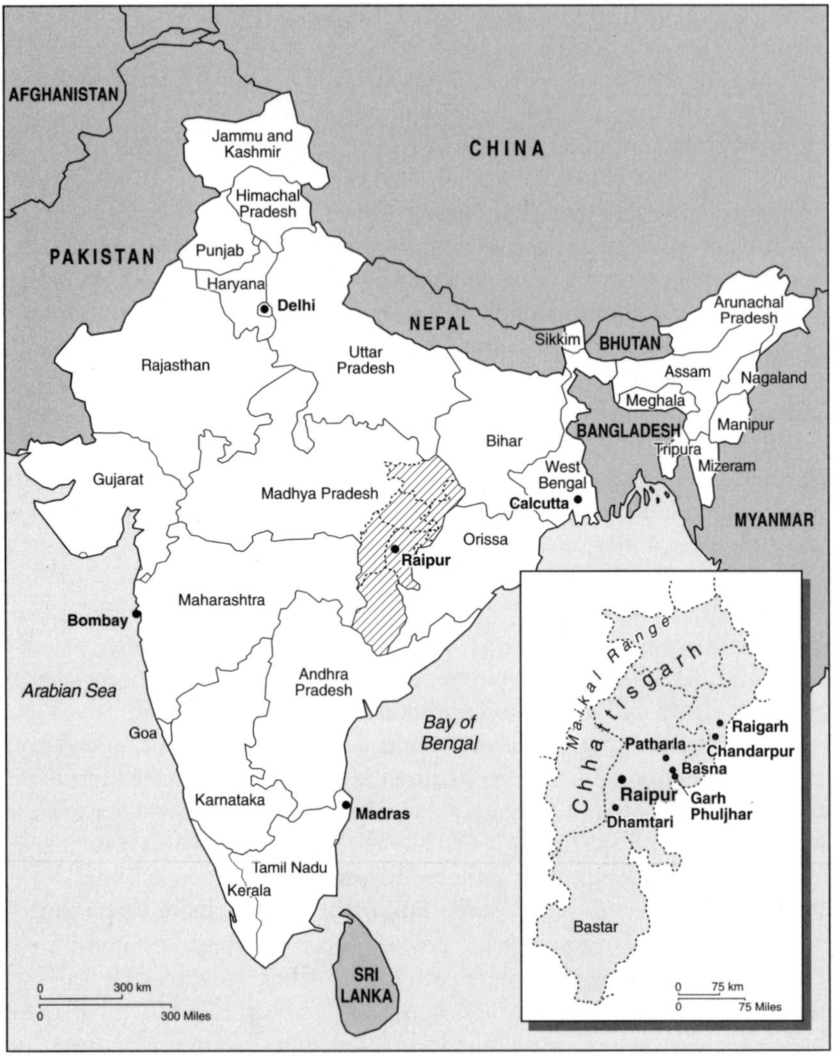

Map 1. Chhattisgarh, Madhya Pradesh

of five districts.[2] My own fieldwork was confined to Raipur District, in two distinct areas, one in the district's heartland and one on the periphery of both

[2] These include Bilaspur, Surguja, Raigarh, Durg, and Raipur Districts. Bastar District is sometimes added as a sixth district of Chhattisgarh but has always retained a distinct identity and is more often excluded from the Chhattisgarhi districts because of its unique history and its more purely tribal population.

the district and the region. Chhattisgarh consists of a large rice-growing plain, watered by the Mahanadi River and its tributaries, and the surrounding hill regions. To the northwest, the plain is bounded by the Maikal Hills, to the west by the Satpura mountain range, to the south by the hills marking the border of Bastar, and to the east by the hills separating Chhattisgarh from the province of Orissa. Historically, the geographic barrier of these hills has helped to isolate Chhattisgarh from surrounding regions and has been a contributing factor in the development of Chhattisgarh as a politically and historically defined region. Obviously, the strength of these hills as boundaries has been minimized by modern transportation systems and popular-media channels such as radio, television, and film.

The Chhattisgarhi plain is a heavily populated, fertile agricultural area. The construction of a canal system from the Mahanadi River has made possible double rice crops in many parts of the plain. The boundary hill areas are both less populated and less fertile, the original home of much of the tribal population of Chhattisgarh. Today, however, a high percentage of the tribal population lives in the plain and has been integrated into the local Hindu caste hierarchy, as independent castes.

Before Indian independence in 1947, the plains and hills were also differentiated on the basis of land revenue and tenure into the *khalsā* and *zamīndārī* systems, respectively (Weaver 1968:153–155). Under the *khalsā* system, every village and its surrounding land was controlled by a *mālguzār*, who was responsible to the central ruling power. The *zamīndārī* estates of the hill and forest regions were often as large as several hundred square miles and incorporated many villages. Each village was under the administrative power of a *ṭhekedār*, who was responsible to the *zamīndār*, who in turn paid revenues to the central power. The *zamīndār* were often quasi-independent from the central ruling power and were themselves called kings (*rājā*). In 1951 the *khalsā* and *zamīndārī* systems were merged for purposes of revenue administration (Verma 1973:4).

The early history of Chhattisgarh reveals a characteristic pattern of minor kingdoms whose kings were often from junior branches of major ruling families to the north but who had gained semi-independence from centers of ruling power, partly because of the geographic distance from those centers. This history indicates that, although centrally located in middle India, Chhattisgarh was under primarily northern political influence, rather than under the domain of southern ruling powers.

The name Chhattisgarh is popularly believed to mean "the land of thirty-six forts," *chattīs* meaning "thirty-six" and *gaṛh* meaning "fort." A. E. Nelson finds inscriptional support for this popular conception in a Khalari inscription that states that King Simhana, the second ruler of the junior Ratanpur branch, conquered the eighteen forts of the enemy. Presumably, this was half the territory ruled by the Haihayas in Daksina Kosala; therefore, the entire territory would have included thirty-six forts. But Nelson acknowledges that in all probability this was not the original derivation of the name, for the name Chhattisgarh does not appear in a single inscription. He believes the more likely derivation is from "Chedisgarh," or "the forts of the Chedi lords," since the Haihaya rulers were a younger branch of the Chedi dynasty who continued to be proud of the name (1909:49).

C. U. Wills has reconstructed, on the basis of the scant evidence left after the Maratha invasion, a Haihaya administrative political organization that also accounts for the concept of thirty-six forts (1919:197–262). He speculates that the system was five-tiered, beginning with the smallest unit of the village. Twelve villages formed what was called a *barḥon*, derived from the Chhattisgarhi word for "twelve." Seven *barḥon* formed a *caurāsī* or *garḥ* (*caurāsī* means "eighty-four"; every *garḥ* or *caurāsī* consisted of eighty-four villages). The next tier was the northern and southern branches of the Ratanpur dynasty, each ruling over eighteen *garḥ*. Finally, the entire kingdom would have consisted of thirty-six forts under the dominion of the senior ruling family at Ratanpur. Wills contends that while the precise numbers were probably more theoretical than actual, these named administrative units were functional during the Haihaya rule of the region from the eleventh to the eighteenth century. What is most significant for our purposes, however, is the concept of thirty-six forts as an important *indigenous* characterization of the region, although not all are historically documented and rarely can many (or even most) of them be named by local inhabitants.

Chhattisgarh as a Linguistic Area

Language is perhaps the most tangible identity marker of the region. In 1901, 85 percent of the population of Raipur District claimed the dialect of Chhattisgarhi to be their mother tongue. By the 1961 census, that percentage had decreased to 54.06 percent, with 31.6 percent citing Hindi (Verma 1973:101). Most of the Hindi claims came from urban areas, however, with the majority of the rural population maintaining a Chhattisgarhi identification. Oriya was the language with the next highest percentage of mother-tongue speakers in Raipur District, 8.83 percent in 1961, a number that has continued to increase in recent years as more and more day laborers and household workers have been imported from Orissa.

Chhattisgarhi belongs to the eastern Hindi language branch, along with the dialects of Awadhi and Bagheli. One primary distinguishing feature of these eastern dialects is the verbal past tense being formed with the ending *īs*. Hence, "he said" is *kahīs* instead of the standard Hindi *kahā*. These eastern dialects also use *o* instead of *e* for the genitive form of personal pronouns: *mor* and *tor* for "mine" and "yours" instead of standard Hindi *merā* and *terā*. Perhaps because of its geographic isolation, Chhattisgarhi has also developed some characteristics unique from Awadhi and Bagheli. For example, the plural is formed with the suffix *man*: *laikaman*, "the boys"; the instrumental is formed with the suffix *an*: *bhūkhan*, "with hunger"; and when a postposition follows a noun, the noun does not decline as it does in Hindi: *laikaman ke*, "belonging to the boys"; *laikā ke*, "belonging to the boy." Further, no difference exists in the conjugation of Chhattisgarhi transitive and intransitive verbs in the past tense, that is, the Hindi *ne* following the subject of a transitive verb in Hindi is lost. Finally, few Chhattisgarhi speakers use feminine verbal forms.

Language is also a primary defining feature of the Phuljhar subregion on the borders of Chhattisgarh and Orissa, where I conducted my first four months of fieldwork. That is, Phuljhar is said to be that place where both Oriya and *laṛiyā* (that form of Chhattisgarhi directly influenced by Oriya) are spoken. Surely other linguistic and cultural crossroads, similar to Phuljhar, exist on other of Chhattisgarh's borders.

When I began to read about Chhattisgarhi as a linguistic dialect and returned to the region as an adult, I found some justification for what had otherwise seemed like arbitrary grammatical "mistakes" I made (such as dropping both the use of feminine endings and the use of *ne* with the past tense of transitive verbs) and my seemingly idiosyncratic vocabulary usage in Hindi classes at the University of Wisconsin.[3] I grew up speaking colloquial Hindi, first in Chhattisgarh and then in the foothills of the Himalayas where I spent nine months each year in boarding school; I remained functionally "nonliterate," however, until I began graduate school and studied Hindi formally for four years. I found that when I began my fieldwork in Chhattisgarh, I reverted to many old childhood patterns of *dehātī* (village) Hindi, which seemed to be more easily understood (or at least created fewer barriers) than what my Chhattisgarhi friends called the *śuddh* (pure) Hindi. When I lived in an Oriya-speaking village in Phuljhar, I spoke Hindi with Oriya intonations, incorporating many Oriya vocabulary items, and was easily understood; likewise, I had few problems understanding everyday

[3] I remember feeling both confused and a little humiliated when the first-year Hindi teacher asked me during the first week of classes where I had learned my Hindi, saying I sounded "just like a servant." See Kavyopadhyaya 1890 for the most complete Chhattisgarhi grammar I have found available in English, one that includes samples of several Chhattisgarhi folk texts.

Oriya conversations, which, in this area, are heavily influenced by Hindi and Chhattisgarhi.

Chhattisgarh as a Cultural Region

Just as important as geographic, historical, and linguistic factors to the definition of Chhattisgarh are cultural characteristics considered by its residents to be unique to the region. These include dress, jewelry, social institutions such as ritualized friendships, local festivals, and both verbal and nonverbal folklore traditions. Other social and religious institutions and festivals that are, in fact, pan-Indian are also frequently identified as "Chhattisgarhi" or are associated with the region through a phrase such as "here in Chhattisgarh," as if they may not exist outside the region at all. For example, an elderly woman prefaced her question to me regarding my *jāti* (caste) with, "Here in our Chhattisgarh, we follow the *jāti* system [*jāti mānte hai*]."

A major factor contributing to this Chhattisgarhi cultural ethos is the high percentage of tribal (*ādivāsī*) population (15.6 percent in Raipur District in the 1961 census); scheduled castes formed 14.94 percent of the population in this same census.[4] Members of these tribal castes living on the Chhattisgarhi plain are now mostly cultivators or agricultural laborers, have acquired caste attributes, and have been integrated into the local caste hierarchy.[5] They have adopted many pan-Indian Hindu practices, including the worship of major Sanskritic deities and celebration of pan-Indian festivals such as *holī*, *daśharā*, and *śivrātri*. Nevertheless, members of the *ādivāsī* population have also retained many of their own traditions, including certain marriage practices, jewelry and tattooing traditions, festivals, and verbal and material folklore. This population has had a strong impact on the wider Chhattisgarhi cultural ethos and sense of identity. Both *ādivāsī* and non-*ādivāsī* inhabitants of Chhattisgarh identify *ādivāsī* traditions more than any others as being uniquely "Chhattisgarhi," whether or not they directly participate in them. A lecturer of Hindi literature at a community college in Dhamtari went so far as to say that *only ādivāsī* traditions can be called truly Chhattisgarhi; he asserted that all others are imports from the Hindi-speaking north (Narayanlal Parmar, 1981, oral communication).

For someone familiar with north Indian (particularly, those of the Gangetic plain) social patterns and practices, the status and role of women in

[4] The principal scheduled tribes of Raipur District are the Gond, Kawar, Binjhwar, Sawar, Halba, Bhunjia, and Kamar (Verma 1973:114–115).

[5] See Bailey 1960 for a fuller discussion of this process.

Chhattisgarh is particularly striking, differing even from that of women in central Madhya Pradesh.[6] Increased freedom and status are most noticeable in the absence of strict physical veiling or purdah (*pardā*) and face covering (*ghūṅghaṭ*); these are generally not observed except among wealthy members of the highest castes (whose families are/were most often immigrants into Chhattisgarh). The physical seclusion of women that coincides with veiling is also practiced much less than it is by north Indian brides in their villages of marriage (*sasurāl*).

Although the majority of Chhattisgarhi women do not observe purdah per se, they do differentiate between public and household space and hold an ideal that women should not spend any more time than necessary in public space. So that even though many lower-caste women work in construction and road building, transplanting and harvesting rice, and selling vegetables and other goods in the bazaars, for example, they do not have freedom available to men of "loitering" unnecessarily in public spaces such as tea stalls, bus stands, or bazaars.[7] In the Oriya villages of Phuljhar, too, women observe a certain degree of conceptual purdah by not lingering in public, male space. In the village in which I lived, for example, women were quite free to walk (most often in pairs) on the village main street or to the village tank to bathe and wash clothes—and often visited several friends on the way—as long as they had some destination and purpose in their outings.[8]

The greater degree of freedom and the associated perception of greater status of Chhattisgarhi women in comparison with their northern sisters may be related to the influence of the *ādivāsī* population and both the higher percentage of female labor participation and the female-to-male sex ratio in Chhattisgarh (Dange 1973). In a 1981 study, Barbara Miller mapped out, by district, the percentage of working females in rural India according to the statistics of the 1961 census. Chhattisgarh stands out on her map as one of the few regions in which the percentage is as high as 85–100 percent (see also Verma 1973:91). She suggests that in those regions where a high percentage

[6] For a comparison of women's roles, rituals, and status in north and central India (west of Chhattisgarh), see Jacobson and Wadley 1977.

[7] See Sharma 1980 for a discussion of the differentiation between public and private space for women in South Asia.

[8] I myself felt the boundaries of this freedom when I had a latrine and bathstall built onto the small house in which I lived at the edge of the village. I sorely missed the built-in daily contact with many of the village women when I stopped bathing in the river, and I soon gave up the indoor bathing to rejoin them. One evening, a close friend of my hostess came by our house on her way to "the fields" and asked her if she would accompany her, saying that she missed her company and the chance to talk. They returned a half hour later, my hostess having been filled in on some significant village "gossip." Thus, while indoor plumbing may simplify a village woman's life, it may also isolate her from other women.

of women are included in the work force, primarily rice-growing areas, there will be a more balanced sex ratio than in those areas where the percentage is lower, such as the wheat-growing areas of the north and northwest. Rice is a labor-intensive crop in whose cultivation women participate in both the transplanting and harvesting phases, whereas wheat growing requires less labor. Census statistics confirm Miller's hypothesis. Since first reported in 1901, a preponderance of females to males has existed in Raipur District. The 1961 census reports 1,037 females for every 1,000 males; a similarly high sex ratio was maintained in the 1971 census report. This statistic stands out as a unique regional feature when compared with that for the rest of Madhya Pradesh, whose overall ratio was 953:1,000, and the all-India ratio of 943.7:1,000. In 1961, the province of Punjab in northwest India had the lowest female-to-male ratio in the country at 864.3:1,000 (Miller 1981:116); this province also has a low percentage of females in the labor force. In those areas where women are active participants in the labor force outside the household, the birth of a daughter is not considered the high liability that it is in those areas where women's labor is primarily limited to the household. In the former, bride-price rather than dowry is often common practice, as is true among the lower and *ādivāsī* castes of Chhattisgarh.

There are, of course, limitations in relying too heavily on these kinds of census and survey-based statistics, not the least of which is the problem of definition of "female labor participation," but they do give us some basis on which to draw a number of generalizations about the comparative position of women in various regions of India. According to these, Chhattisgarh seems to fit more closely with the south Indian pattern of rice-cultivating areas, where the percentage of female labor participation is high, rather than with the wheat-growing areas of the north.[9] A daughter becomes more economically valuable in these regions and therefore may hold a position of higher status than her sisters in the north. Further, where women are active in the public work force, in agriculture, construction, and so forth, physical purdah is more difficult to maintain.

The relative freedom and independence of women in Chhattisgarh is reflected in such social/cultural practices as divorce and remarriage, as well

[9] This supports the suggestion that a northeast-southwest axis is perhaps more reflective of pan-Indian cultural patterns than the more frequently articulated cultural, geographic axis between north and south India. The latter more precisely refers to the northern Gangetic plain and Dravidian-speaking south; the placement of Gujarat, Maharastra, Orissa, and parts of Madhya Pradesh (including Chhattisgarh) is ambiguous in this divide. See Sopher 1980 for an extended discussion of the geographic patterning of culture, including Bernard Cohn's proposal of an east-west cultural axis for India.

as in the frequency of bride-price instead of dowry among the lower castes. Although the high castes of Chhattisgarh do not favor these practices, they are permissible and common among such middle and low castes as the Teli, Kurmi, Rawat [Raut], Panka, Dhobi, Nai, Kewat, and *ādivāsī* castes (Verma 1973:121). The census village survey of Bendri village in Raipur District reports that in practically all cases of separation and divorce in the village, it was the woman who left her husband rather than the other way around; and if she did return to her husband, there was little stigma attached to her for having lived with another man (Verma 1973:37). My experience in the Gond neighborhoods of Dhamtari in which I spent time supports these findings. In the several cases in which women had left their husbands to return to their maternal villages (*maikā*), although there was some neighborhood discussion about them, they were not stigmatized. In the chapters that follow, we will see that this relatively higher status of women in Chhattisgarh is reflected in the performance context and textual content of the folklore genres under consideration.

Chhattisgarh as a Folklore Region

In my conversations with male and female respondents from a wide spectrum of caste levels over the early months of my fieldwork, there gradually emerged a core repertoire of performance genres that was specifically identified as "Chhattisgarhi," a repertoire contributing to the perception of a unique regional cultural ethos. Audiences and performers articulated a relatively consistent listing of what belonged in this repertoire—what genres typified the region—even if they themselves did not participate in them directly as audience or performers. Among the genres most frequently mentioned were:

suā nāc — the parrot dance; an *ādivāsī* female harvest dance and song tradition
gaurā — an *ādivāsī* festival celebrating the marriage of the god and goddess Shiva and Parvati (Gaura/Gauri)
bhojalī — a song and festival tradition celebrating ritual friendships and worshiping the goddess as wheat seedlings; observed by women only
javārā — a goddess festival similar to *bhojalī* but celebrated by both men and women
bā̃s gīt — songs sung by the cowherding caste (Rauts) to the accompaniment of large bamboo flutes (*bā̃s*, meaning "bamboo or flute")
rāut dohā — couplets sung by Raut cowherders, often at the Raut festival of *mātar*
dadariyā — rhyming couplets sung primarily as field songs but also when walking to the bazaar and so on

candainī	the Chhattisgarhi regional epic
paṇḍvānī	a narrative genre based on episodes from the pan-Indian Mahabharata epic

Pan-Indian verbal traditions performed in Chhattisgarh primarily by castes relatively high in the social hierarchy are only rarely included in the "Chhattisgarhi repertoire." These traditions include the north and central Indian tradition of *rāmlīlā* (dramas based on the pan-Indian Ramayana epic), *vrat kathā* (narratives told at fasting rituals), *kissā* (mythological narratives not associated with specific rituals or festivals), and *bhajan* (religious devotional songs not associated with specific festivals). Also excluded from this indigenously articulated repertoire are, with perhaps the exception of *dadariyā* couplets, what I call "private" performance genres, such as nonprofessional, domestically performed folktales and lullabies, and genres embedded in everyday speech, such as jokes and proverbs. In a complete ethnography-of-speaking analysis of the performance genres of a given village or region, one would include both pan-Indian and private performance traditions as part of the performance repertoire. However, members of the folklore communities in which I lived and traveled differentiated between a repertoire that characterized the region and the repertoire of genres performed *in* the region. This indigenous identification places the genres marked as "Chhattisgarhi" in a particular intertextual relationship within a bounded subset of the much wider, *unnamed*, unbounded repertoire that might be identified by a folklorist. So I begin by looking first within the "marked" repertoire identified by the folklore community itself as "Chhattisgarhi," asking what characterizes this repertoire.

Phuljhar as a Subregion on the Boundaries

I began the fieldwork on which this study is based by living in a village in a subregion of Chhattisgarh called Phuljhar, which lies on the boundaries between Chhattisgarh (Madhya Pradesh) and Orissa. Phuljhar is one of the oldest and largest former *zamīndārī* estates in the modern Raipur District of Chhattisgarh, reported in the 1909 Raipur District Gazetteer to have been ruled by the same Raj Gond family for twenty generations;[10] the Phuljhar

[10] "Gond" is a generic term describing a large group of unhomogeneous tribes living in middle India. "Raj Gonds" refers to those Gonds who were once traditional rulers in what has been called Gondwana. See Furer-Haimendorf and Furer-Haimendorf 1979, chapter 1, "The Gonds in History and Literature," for an overview of the geographic spread and history of tribes that have been called Gonds. In contemporary Chhattisgarh, the term "Raj Gond" is

zamīndār was long recognized to be the head of the Raj Gonds (Nelson 1909:319). Many of the thirty-six forts of Chhattisgarh that can be identified were the headquarters of large *zamīndārī*, and Phuljhar is one of these. In what is now "jungle" near the town of Basna stand the ruins (which the villagers who showed me around said are 250 years old) of Garh Phuljhar. The headquarters of the Phuljhar *zamīndārī* were moved from Garh Phuljhar to the town of Saraipali, where descendants of the former ruling family still live in a run-down palace.

Although former *zamīndārī* estates such as Phuljhar are considered to be part of the region of Chhattisgarh, the larger ones have retained a separate identity as well. Even today, if asked where they are from, residents of modern Phuljhar frequently answer with the name of Phuljhar first, rather than Chhattisgarh. In fact, not all residents of Phuljhar want to be identified with Chhattisgarh. The *zamīndārī* originally belonged to Sambalpur District to the east, in modern Orissa. In 1906 Sambalpur District was ceded to what was then Bengal Province, but the Phuljhar *zamīndārī* was joined to Raipur District. Some Oriya speakers of Phuljhar still feel that the *zamīndārī* should have remained part of Sambalpur District, hence modern Orissa province, partially so that they would benefit from the large Hirikud Dam that irrigates so much of Orissa immediately to their east. But because of current political boundaries and structures, residents of Phuljhar are drawn primarily to the city of Raipur to their west, rather than Sambalpur to the east, as an economic, legal, educational, and transportation center.

Phuljhar is more than an administrative unit, however; it is also a cultural and linguistic subregion. The name "Phuljhar" literally means "where flowers fall," deriving from the impression voiced by residents that flowering trees exist in the jungles of Phuljhar throughout all the seasons of the year. And, in fact, this borderland of Chhattisgarh is less heavily inhabited, more "jungly" than the Raipur plains, and lies in what are called the hills of Chhattisgarh. The most common characterization of Phuljhar by its inhabitants is that it is that part of Chhattisgarh where people speak both Oriya and a variant of the Chhattisgarhi dialect called *laṛiyā*. Oriya is the dominant language of Phuljhar, but most Oriya castes speak, or at least understand, some form of Chhattisgarhi, and vice versa. One village headman called Phuljhar the "*khicṛī* [literally, a cooked mixture of rice and lentils] of Orissa and Chhattisgarh."

As one might expect by observing the linguistic patterns of Phuljhar, the subregion's inhabitants also articulate a "*khicṛī*" repertoire of performance

most frequently used to refer to landowning Gonds, who presumably were once "rulers" or *zamīndār* of greater or lesser political domains.

Village women of Phuljhar.

genres, drawing from both what is identified as the Chhattisgarhi repertoire and that identified as the Oriya repertoire. The Phuljhar repertoire includes *suā nāc*, *bhojalī*, and *gaurā* (and, interestingly, leaves out the epic tradition of *candainī*) but then adds Oriya genres such as *ḍālkhāī* (a verbal and festival tradition of reversal for unmarried girls), *homo* (a girls' song-game tradition), the tradition of *bāhak* performers (professional dancers-singers who perform at "each of the thirteen Oriya festivals"), and the festival of *rath yātra* (honoring the god Jagannath). Of significance to us is how the rules of usage change for a particular Chhattisgarhi genre (such as *bhojalī*) when performed within the context of the Phuljhar repertoire, on the regional boundaries.

When I began my fieldwork in Phuljhar, I was not fully aware of the complex ways in which the Oriya and Chhattisgarhi castes—their dialects and oral traditions—interacted. My choice of this area as a preliminary field site was more pragmatic: it is the area where I had lived as a child, my parents still lived there, and I had numerous contacts and friends in the area and access to transportation to remote villages. In retrospect, however, Phuljhar's location at the boundaries, and its characterization as a crossroads of linguistic and performance traditions, added a dimension to this study that would not have been available had I lived only in Chhattisgarh's heartland. To live on the periphery provided comparative materials that helped to delineate what I have called the Chhattisgarhi folklore region (communities sharing a repertoire or parts thereof) and the various folklore communities within that region (distinguished by the rules of usage for shared genres within the repertoire).

Indigenous Genres and Repertoire

While distinct, but overlapping, repertoires of genres can be identified for the Phuljhar borderland and central Raipur plains, the repertoires share key principles of genre identification and organization. That is, there is a Chhattisgarhi "way of talking" about performance, a system of indigenously articulated genres, that provides both us and indigenous audiences with frames for interpretation.

Influenced by the methodologies of the ethnography of speaking (Gumperz and Hymes 1972; Hymes 1974a, 1974b), performance-centered folklore scholars have reoriented the definitions of folklore genres from those of classificatory labels based primarily on form or content for the convenience of archivists and comparative folklorists to "orienting framework[s] for production and interpretation of discourse" (Bauman 1992b:53). With this new perspective, genres become "practice-centered" categories, rather than "item-centered" (Bauman 1992b:57)—active cultural categories, rather than static classificatory items. So conceived, genres are not objective categories but become "part of a politics of interpretation in which meaning and the authority to propose and ascribe categories is contested" (Shuman 1993: 71). The boundaries and interpretations of such indigenous genres are flexible and shifting within changing historical and cultural contexts. A central task of the folklorist, then, becomes that of determining not only what the repertoire of available genres is within a particular culture or community and the *indigenous* categories and organization of that repertoire but also *who* is articulating these categories.

Dan Ben-Amos made a crucial distinction between analytic categories and ethnic genres (what I am calling indigenous genres) in an early but continuingly influential essay written in the late 1960s and republished in *Folklore Genres* (1976). He distinguishes the terms as follows:

> Whereas ethnic genres are cultural modes of communication, analytic categories are models for the organization of texts. Both constitute separate systems which should relate to each other as substantive matter to abstract models. Yet this relationship has not materialized. . . . We attempted to construct logical

> concepts which would have potential cross-cultural applications. . . . In the process, however, we transformed traditional genres from cultural categories of communication into scientific concepts. . . . as if they were not dependent upon cultural expression and perception but autonomous entities which consisted of exclusive inherent qualities of their own. (215–216)

> The ethnic system of genres constitutes a grammar of folklore, a cultural affirmation of the communication rules that govern the expression of complex messages within the cultural context. (225)

Ben-Amos suggests that ethnic genres are distinguished from each other *in paradigmatic relationship one to the other*, often identifiable by sets of "contrastive attributes" (235), thereby affirming the importance of contextualizing individual genres with a *system* of genres and encouraging this as a direction for future folklore research. In the examples he explores in this essay, however, Ben-Amos looks primarily at the relationship between two contrastive genres rather than the larger repertoire of verbal folklore of which they are a part and the principles of its organization.[11]

Since the publication of this essay, most of the creative activity of folklore studies has centered on performative approaches to the study of *individual* genres, the interaction of verbal texts and performative contexts, and the emergent quality of performance, with less attention being paid to the context provided by the repertoire in which a particular genre is situated. However, a handful of excellent multigenre studies have sampled the variety of intertextual relationships between genres of a given repertoire. Gary Gossen has taken on perhaps the broadest study of a folklore system within a specific culture, that of the Chamula Indians in Mexico (1974). He elicited an indigenous taxonomy of folklore genres and searched for its organizing principles, which he found to be that of time and space. His interest was how the organization of genres reflects a worldview; he provides generalized descriptions of performers and performance context, with representative texts, rather than analyses of individual, situated performances. Another multigenre study, with a more specifically ethnography-of-speaking, linguistic approach, is Joel Sherzer's *Kuna Ways of Speaking* (1983). Charles Briggs juxtaposes a range of genres available in Mexicano verbal art (1988) to examine the differential roles of individual creativity and competence in the performance of individual genres. Richard Bauman has analyzed intertextuality on several levels, both in the relationships among several narrative

[11] See also Roger Abrahams and Richard Bauman's similar study of two contrastive genres, sensible speech and talking nonsense, in Vincentian speech taxonomy (1971).

genres in Texas (1986) and genres as they are embedded within other genres in the tradition of Icelandic legends of *Kraftskald* (1992a).

Within South Asian folklore scholarship, again, the number of multigenre studies are few (excepting collections of folklore "texts," such as those made by colonial folklorists). Susan Wadley (1975) published an early survey of the folklore repertoire of a single village community in north India in which she lists thirty-one indigenous categories of song. She suggests that the terminology for folklore genres tends to correlate with some aspect of their performance context, but she does not expand further on indigenous principles of their organization, for the purpose of the article is to provide a landscape of genres rather than their analysis. In her more recent work on the north Indian epic tradition of Dhola-Maru (1991, 1989), Wadley approaches intertextuality between genres in a manner similar to that of Bauman's study of embedded genres. She has worked closely with an individual Dhola singer and has elicited interesting commentary about the ways in which he "constructs" a performance and uses embedded genres. She finds that Dhola singers incorporate numerous nonepic song styles to create the moods of the seasons or occasions in which those songs are traditionally performed.

Ethnomusicologist Edward Henry has also sampled a range of song traditions in his study of the north Indian Bhojpuri-speaking region (1988). Again, his purpose is to provide a landscape of musical genres and to generalize about the role of music in village life; he is less concerned with indigenous categories and repertoire and other elements of performance context. He draws generalizations of the general shape and "ground rules" of, for example, women's wedding rituals or the celebration of the festival of *holī,* against which the emergent nature of individual performances could be analyzed; but he himself does not follow this line of analysis.

Peter Claus has approached the issue of genre and intertextuality (1989) by examining performative variation of what he identifies as a single genre, that of the *paḍdana* multistory tradition of southwest India (Tulunad). The indigenous terminology *paḍdana* classifies "loosely connected" stories together, although their performance contexts and styles vary significantly. Claus calls these varying styles/contexts for the *paḍdana* "subgenres." He is interested in the covariation between the "story" and its variable social contexts of performance, concluding that "different versions serve to distinguish social groups and establish relations between them" (72). The theme of performance identifying and giving identity to social groups is also central to this study of Chhattisgarhi genres. Because the social identity of the performers of the different contexts/styles of *paḍdana* vary so significantly, it is likely that according to Chhattisgarhi principles of genre identification and organization, within *this* regional repertoire, they would be categorized as discrete genres (see Chapter 6 for a discussion regarding the *candainī* narrative as performed in the *suā nāc*, where context supersedes narrative content to determine genre classification).

Finally, A. K. Ramanujan's 1986 essay "Two Realms of Kannada Folklore" encouraged South Asian folklorists to begin thinking about folklore repertoires as performative *systems* of meaning, in which each genre is related to and distinguished from other genres. He draws on an early Dravidian distinction between the paradigmatic categories of domestic (*akam*) and public (*puṟam*), a distinction of types articulated in commentary on early classical Tamil poetry, to look at the ways in which these contrastive settings are also relevant in Kannada folklore (particularly narrative). The categories help to distinguish contrasted pairs of folktales, myths, and ritual within the repertoire, distinctions that affect the performative text and style of each category.

A Chhattisgarhi System of Genres

In this study of Chhattisgarhi performance genres, I approach intertextuality—the play of genres—by seeking to understand principles of indigenous genre identification and organization within a marked repertoire. The specific ways in which the framework of genre and repertoire affects audience reception and interpretation of performance becomes apparent only in the juxtaposition of genres within the larger system. Consciously acknowledging "genre" as a frame for interpretation, then, I use these principles as entry into the analysis of individual performance traditions and specific performances of those genres. Although the categories through which I approach my analyses are based on indigenous principles of genre and repertoire, the analyses go beyond this entry and are not in any way "indigenous" themselves. Chhattisgarhi performers and audiences are much more articulate about the performance contexts ("exteriors," if you will) of their verbal and ritual folklore genres than about their textual "interiors." I have had several occasions to "try out" some of my conclusions in conversations with Chhattisgarhi friends and performers over the last few years; on the most part, they have been only vaguely interested in the implications of what they perceive to be quite obvious. As the female performer of what she framed as an explanatory narrative for the festival of *ḍālkhāī* (Chapter 3) said when I pressed her for further commentary, "Well, that's the story."

Indigenous genres are identified by a combination of formal, thematic, and contextual features (Ben-Amos 1976:225), but the degree to which one

Chhattisgarhi woman of the Raipur plains.

or the other of these is foregrounded within a given cultural repertoire and individual genre varies significantly. Ben-Amos suggests that one entry into the criteria according to which genres are distinguished and associated is to look at their names, "which often reflect their symbolic value in the network of formal communication and their position in the cultural cognitive categories" (1976:235). Like the traditions named in Wadley's survey of the folklore of a north Indian village (1975), many of the names of Chhattisgarhi verbal performance are contextually derived: the names of the festivals during which the song genres are sung, the terms of address for the performers, or the instruments used in performance. For example, *bhojalī* are the songs sung during the festival of *bhojalī*, *kathānī kūhā* literally means "storyteller;" and *bā̃s gīt* are the songs of the bamboo flute. Several long narrative genres, on the other hand, such as the regional epic *candainī* and the local Mahabharata performance genre of *paṇḍvānī*, are named after their heroines and heroes. The names of these genres provide one frame for interpretation by indicating whether it is primarily the ritual and/or the social context, content, or form of the genre that is foregrounded in the reception of its performance.

In conversations with and informal commentaries by Chhattisgarhi villagers about particular genres, however, another principle of organization emerged within the repertoire which is not directly reflected in the terminology of particular genres but which provides the central frame of indigenous interpretation and basis for intertextuality: the association between genre and community.[12] When members of Chhattisgarhi folklore communities voice associations between individual performance traditions within their repertoires, it is most often on the basis of this social organization and only secondarily by their ritual contexts. Although form is acknowledged by the usage of the Chhattisgarhi and Hindi words for song (*gīt*) and story (*kathā* or *kahānī*), their usage is fluid, and strict boundaries between these formal categories are not maintained (both in performance itself or in the usage of these terms in everyday conversation). Further, genres to which the term *gīt* may be attached are not necessarily associated with one another (such as *bhojalī gīt* and *bā̃s gīt*); and if they are, it is because of the social category into which they fall or the ritual contexts in which they are performed, not because of their form.

Thus, a verbal dueling game, identified by form as *khel*, and a festival-song genre, identified as *gīt*, performed by unmarried girls will be more frequently associated with each other than will song with song, or story with story, *across* social categories such as Oriya men, *ādivāsī* women, and unmarried girls. The regional epic *candainī* is performed in both a *gīt* (sung recitation) and *nācā* (dance-drama) style. Both, however, are categorized together simply as "*candainī*," unless the speaker wants to differentiate a particular performance. *Candainī nācā* is rarely associated with other *nācā*, and *nācā* troupes who perform *candainī* do not traditionally perform other *nācā*. Further, in local commentary and conversation, *candainī gīt* would not be associated with the *gīt* sung by unmarried girls in their formation of *bhojalī* ritual friendships. In Chhattisgarhi language usage, the terms *gīt* and *kathā*/*kahānī* have not traditionally indicated indigenous interpretive frames of reference but rather more closely approximate analytic categories that are rarely invoked by performers and audiences.

[12] This association between genre and community is not, of course, unique to Chhattisgarh and has been analyzed in numerous folklore studies (see, for example, Dundes 1983; Claus 1989; Badone 1987). What may be "unique" is the social categorization of genre as an indigenously articulated principle of identification and organization.

No single Chhattisgarhi term is equivalent to the English-usage term "genre."[13] Thus, in the following chapters, several different English words make reference to a single *indigenous* genre: festival, ritual, song, narrative. Further, we will also notice that little or no distinction is made between religious/nonreligious, ritual/nonritual genres in the social categorizations of the regional repertoire. Because form and content have been foregrounded in our Western usage of "genre," perhaps in the Chhattisgarhi context "tradition" would more accurately reflect what is meant when the name of a particular performance genre is used. When *bhojalī* festival participants talk about the festival, they rarely articulate a distinction between the rituals they perform and the songs they sing; the entire performance complex is "*bhojalī*." Or, if the girls talk about "seating *bhojalī*" (forming the ritual friendship), the ritual soaking of the goddess and her service through song are implicit in that friendship formation.[14] However, "tradition," too, has English-language connotations that I do not wish to invoke here, so I have retained "genre" as it has come to be used in contemporary folklore scholarship: a cultural framework for interpretation that sets up certain expectations, orientations, and "interpretive procedures" (Bauman 1992b:58).

Recognizing indigenous systems of genre as a source for a folklore community's commentary about its own traditions, then, I have taken the social organization of the Chhattisgarhi repertoire as a point of entry into the analyses of individual genres. A guiding question has been, What does it mean for a particular performance genre to be identified with, to "belong to," for example, unmarried girls, tribal (*ādivāsī*) castes, or the region itself? With what other genres does this designation put the selected genre into conversation or opposition? What are the interpretive frames constructed by this social organization of genre and the resulting intertextual relationships?

Although these questions have taken shape by listening to Chhattisgarhi conversations, verbal commentaries, and metafolklore—and it is there that I begin to look for their answers—these direct articulations are not "all" that the performer or audience member "knows." Much of what she or he knows about rules of folklore usage, especially the flexibility of those rules, is accessible only through ethnographic observation of performance.[15] I found Ro-

[13] I was once called on to give a lecture in Hindi on the subject of indigenous genres and drew a blank when I tried to think of a Hindi equivalent for "genre" with the implications that the word holds in Western literary and folklore scholarship. Finally, in desperation I called a Hindi professor at the University of Wisconsin, a linguist and native speaker, who immediately responded with the suggestion "genre."

[14] Gregory Nagy (1994) suggests a similar phenomenon for the genre of epic: "The genre, the set of rules that generate a given speech-act, can equate itself with the *occasion*, the context of this speech act. To this extent, the occasion *is* the genre." See also Nagy 1990:362.

[15] I thank Amin Sweeney for his critique (letter to author, May 1987) of my early essay on

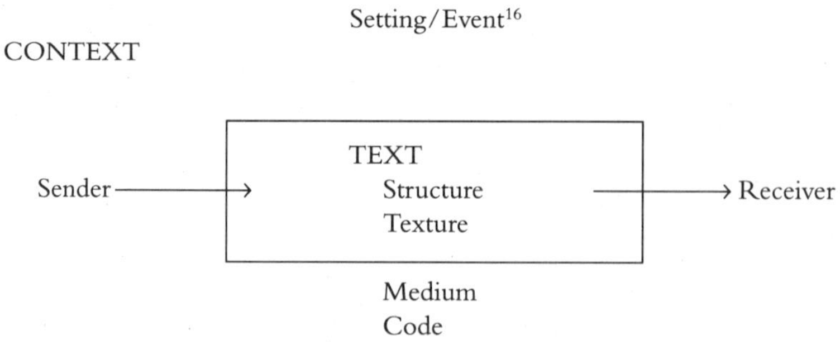

man Jakobson's model for communication (adapted by ethnographers of speaking such as Hymes and others) to be useful in sharpening my own ethnographic observation, identifying units for analysis, and in thinking through the performative implications of the social organization of genre. Jakobson identified key components of the communicative act to be addresser, addressee, context, message, contact, and code (1960). A. K. Ramanujan frequently drew on this model when he served as a discussant for conference folklore panels in the 1980s and diagramed it as shown in the schematic. The model sets up the variables of context and text as interdependent components of a system, so that any one of the components may shift depending on the identity or content of any one of the others. The model becomes dynamic, the emergent nature of performance more readily identifiable, when applied to comparative data—the "same" genre performed in two different cultural areas or two settings (for example, Phuljhar and the Raipur plains, or a ritual and nonritual setting), different performances of the same genre observed over a period of time, or the variation of components when two genres from a given repertoire are compared. I base the analyses of the genres chosen for this study, at some level, on such comparative data.[17]

To analyze all the variables of what is identified here as "context," both

---

the *suā nāc* (1987) that helped me to articulate *action* itself as a form of indigenous knowledge, as well as commentary *about* that action.

[16] Charles Briggs distinguishes the "setting/event" level of context from a broader cultural context with the term "situational context" (1988:13).

[17] In a proseminar on folklore methods held at the University of Wisconsin shortly after I returned from my first field study (spring 1982), Alan Dundes stated categorically that "the study of folklore is necessarily comparative." At the time, I thought he meant cross-culturally comparative (illustrative in the historic-geographical school of folklore studies); it was only when I began to examine individual performances of the genres I had taped in contrastive settings that I understood that comparison could be on more subtle levels and was able to agree with him.

cultural and situational, would be not only an ethnographic impossibility, but its attempt would be to throw up a screen of false objectivity (Briggs 1988:13). However, indigenous systems of genres, oral commentary, and performances themselves provide what Briggs has called "contextualization cues" (1988:15; see also Goodwin and Duranti 1992:4), cues that direct us to those aspects of context that the participants in the performance event themselves foreground. These cues, many of which in Chhattisgarh are articulated through the social identification of the genre, serve as an entry into understanding the textual "interiors" of the performances we will look at in this book.

In chapter 2 I examine a female festival tradition called *bhojalī* that is celebrated in both the Raipur heartland of Chhattisgarh and the Phuljhar periphery. The primary festival participants in Phuljhar are unmarried pubescent girls who form ritual friendships by exchanging the wheat seedlings they worship as the goddess for the duration of the nine-day festival. In the Chhattisgarh heartland, however, the festival is celebrated by married women, who become possessed by the goddess they serve, and the ritual friendships formed are secondary. The differences between the festival as celebrated in the two contexts are so dramatic that participants in the Raipur plains hardly believed my descriptions of what I had seen in Phuljhar only eighty miles away. I examine the implications of the shift in this social identification of genre, the intertextual relationships in which it places *bhojalī*, and the resulting frames of interpretation created.

Chapter 3 looks at another Phuljhar festival tradition for unmarried girls. *Ḍālkhāī* is consistently identified in everyday conversation as a "*holī* [festival of reversal] for unmarried girls." By the time I began my fieldwork in the fall of 1980, the festival was a dying one; I witnessed what I believe to have been the last celebration of *ḍālkhāī* in Phuljhar. The song tradition, however, is still creative and vibrant, sung outside the festival context by men and women alike, of all ages. These songs are characterized as "*burī gīt*" ("bad," vulgar songs). In my effort to understand the implications of these two characterizations—a festival of reversal for unmarried girls, but one whose songs are "bad"—I began by looking at the shifting frame of the performance contexts, the identities of the singers, as the festival has died. Crucial to my understanding of what the festival may have meant when it "belonged to" unmarried girls is a long sung narrative performed for me by a village wise woman as the "story of the festival," an indigenous commentary that illustrates the subtlety with which "interiors" of texts are understood. Even as the festival context for performance of *ḍālkhāī* has been lost, it is retained in cultural memory and continues to inform the interpretation of the genre as it now exists.

The *suā nāc* of Chapter 4 is spoken of as a harvest-dance genre performed by *ādivāsī* female land laborers in the courtyards of landowners, a performance that transforms the harvested paddy into ritual wealth, the goddess Lakshmi herself. However, it is a genre "claimed" by members of a wide spectrum of social groups within the folklore community as typifying Chhattisgarh. The *suā nāc* establishes a temporary performative channel of communication between two social groups for whom such a channel does not normally exist; and the focus of the performance becomes that channel itself—the auspicious dance and its nonverbal, iconographic message. The sung narratives accompanying the dance are also performed outside of the dance context, sung by women to other women of their own class and caste status. I examine the shifts in interpretive frames when the identity of performers and audience shifts in these two contexts. Outside the dance, the communicative channel is assumed to be present, and the focus of the *suā nāc* performance falls on the sung verbal text, in which the sadness of a young bride's new life in her *sasurāl* (home of marriage) is imaged.

The genre of the *kathānī kūhā* of Chapter 5 stands apart from the others I consider because there is no bounded social group with which it is regularly identified. Rather, it is belongs to individual performers who, through their storytelling, mold an audience into a performative community for a few brief hours; the audience is given the active role of "responder" to the *kathānī kūhā*. The genre is an example of the space given within the Chhattisgarhi/Phuljhar repertoires for individual creativity. The *kathānī kūhā* is known as a *professional* storyteller, one who takes folktales normally performed by nonprofessionals in private settings, "joins them one to another," and adapts them for public performance. What distinguishes his performances is not the content of the narratives but the style in which they are told, the ways in which he is able to create and hold an audience. Thus, the focus of this chapter is the performative style of the *kathānī kūhā*.

The regional epic *candainī* and the Mahabharata performance genre called *paṇḍvānī* are the two genres that have the widest social identity in Chhattisgarh, that is, they are consistently identified with the region itself, rather than by caste, gender, or age. In Chapter 6 I look at what it means for an epic to be so identified by comparing it with the "same" epic tradition as it is performed outside Chhattisgarh, in the northern Gangetic plains, where it is a caste-identified tradition. The regional identity of *candainī* and *paṇḍvānī* places them in the same generic category within the Chhattisgarhi folklore repertoire; they are regularly spoken of in tandem in indigenous commentary about the repertoire itself. The performances of *candainī* contribute to the interpretive frames through which performances of *paṇḍvānī* are received and vice versa. And so in Chapter 7, I consider this relationship, asking what it means for *paṇḍvānī* to be a Chhattisgarhi genre rather than a Hindi, pan-

Indian genre such as the Ramayana is perceived to be. When I asked what the difference was between *paṇḍvānī* and the recently televised serial production of the Mahabharata, one Chhattisgarhi villager answered that the latter was shastric (textual), whereas *paṇḍvānī* is "sung from our hearts."

The second section of the book is comprised of texts that are translations of two full performances: the Song of Subanbali (Chapter 3) and the *kathānī kūhā*'s performance (Chapter 5). Both typify South Asian performance genres for which full translations are not yet available: long, nonepic narratives. The first translation is of a one-and-one-half-hour performance by a semiprofessional female singer, and the second, a three-hour narrative performed by a professional male storyteller who weaves together discrete folktales, "line by line." My goal has been to provide translations that reflect the oral composition and performance of the texts. I have retained the line integrity of the performance texts; at times this has required a more literal, rather than "smooth," translation. The *kathānī kūhā*'s performance, in particular, catches the ethos of Chhattisgarhi village life and language. Part of this ethos, as mentioned earlier, is the strong and often defiant voice of women, which is heard clearly, but distinctively, in these two performance texts.

If indigenous folklore genres and the principles of their organization within a given repertoire are socially constructed, historically situated frames of production and interpretation, then shifting cultural and historical contexts will affect the shape of those frames and the meanings generated through them. This flexibility and transformation have been addressed for individual genres, where applicable, in their individual analyses. The conclusion of this volume looks more generally at the shifting boundaries of genre identification and classification under the influences of increasing literacy and mass media technologies in Chhattisgarh. These changes have begun to affect the principles of organization within the Chhattisgarhi folklore repertoire, the communities with which certain genres are associated, and thus the ways in which they are interpreted by members of the folklore regional community. Even while the social organization and identification of genre are reconfigured, retaining the principles of Chhattisgarhi indigenous genres, a coexisting system of classification, based primarily on form (song, narrative, dance), is emerging in such contexts as radio and television programming, print media, and folklore festivals and performance competitions. Finally, I return to the Chhattisgarhi principle of social organization of genres to look more closely at the ways in which performance identifies and gives identity to various levels of community: the folklore region that shares a repertoire, the folklore community that shares rules of usage for that repertoire, and the folklore group whose members are the performers themselves.

CHAPTER 2

Soaking the Goddess, Celebrating Friendship

Bhojalī

It is significant, perhaps, that the context for the first performance I taped for this study of Chhattisgarhi folklore was that of a festival honoring the deity Ganesh, remover of obstacles, who is worshiped before beginning any significant undertaking, journey, or public performance—an auspicious beginning for a neophyte fieldworker about to embark on what, at the time, loomed ahead as a rather intimidating journey. I returned home late that night with several hours of tape in hand but, as was repeatedly true to the nature of the years of fieldwork that were to follow, unaware, until months later, of the many obstacles that *had* been removed and the significance of other factors which that evening looked to be only annoying obstacles.

It was a late rainy season night in early September (the light half of the month of *bhādon*), and I was still looking for a village in Phuljhar in which to settle, when a friend came to my family's bungalow to call me out to hear some men singing in front of the temporarily installed Ganesh *mūrti* (image) in a nearby Chhattisgarhi-speaking village. He thought that they might know something about the Ramayana traditions in which I had stated my research interests to lie. I hesitated to go out in the night rain when, at this point early in my fieldwork, I had consciously decided that I did not want to elicit materials directly, seemingly out of context. However, I felt I should show my appreciation for the friend's interest and knew that I might need and want his cooperation in the months ahead (which I did, indeed), so I reluctantly followed him.

What we found was, as expected, a clay Ganesh *mūrti* sitting on the verandah of the home of one of the large landowners of the village in celebration of the festival *gaṇés caturthī*, which honors the elephant-headed

Ganesh. With roots in the province of Maharashtra, this festival has spread all over north and central India and has been absorbed into the Chhattisgarhi festival cycle in many large villages and urban areas. Often neighborhoods or entire villages take up a collection to support the purchase of the Ganesh *mūrti*, which then sits out on a platform in public space for all to take *darśan* (auspicious sight) of, before it is immersed at the end of the week in the local tank. In this village, there were, as reported, a group of men sitting around the image, smoking *bīṛī*, talking, and singing *bhajan*. We talked with the men for a while and eventually, with the prodding of my friend, I rather uncomfortably asked them about the Ramayana traditions that might be performed in their village.

What had caught my attention and interest, however, was a row of small baskets filled with bright green seedlings lined up in front of and underneath the platform on which the god was seated. When I asked what these were, the men said they were *bhojalī*, seedlings planted by young girls. The girls were said to worship the *bhojalī* as the goddess as she grew for nine days and then, upon immersing the seedlings in the village tank, to form ritual friendships by exchanging the seedlings as *prasād* (sanctified offerings distributed to worshipers).

Before I could ask anything further, the village headman had called the girls who had planted the *bhojalī* to sing the songs they had sung early in the evening to the goddess, this time for my tape recorder now set up near the *bhojalī* baskets. They sat in pairs, the ritual friends, and took turns leading out in a verse, with the rest then joining in, frequently bursting out in embarrassed giggles. The men who had become their audience then suggested that they sing *homo*, another song genre sung by unmarried girls as a kind of repartee game. At the time, I was frustrated with losing control of the "research situation"; the call for the performance of song genres outside their "natural" context, elicited rather than "spontaneous" performance, went against all the "ideal" methods of folklore fieldwork methods with which I had come to Chhattisgarh.

Only much later, after I had heard *bhojalī gīt* sung by married women, in a village nearly one hundred miles away from the above-mentioned Phuljhar village, did I realize that the call for the performance of *homo* was an indigenous Phuljhar contextualization of and commentary on *bhojalī*; it positioned the two genres in an intertextual relationship of which I might not have otherwise been aware. This interpretive framing was indicative of a performance context quite different from that in which *bhojalī* is performed in the Chhattisgarhi plains near Raipur. In Phuljhar, although *bhojalī* is a ritual genre honoring the goddess and *homo* is a nonritual genre of "play," they are categorized together within the broader folklore repertoire as "unmarried girls' traditions." In Raipur, on the other hand, *bhojalī* is primarily spoken of as a goddess festival, associated with other goddess festivals, particularly those whose songs are sung by married women. The rest of this chapter looks at the ways in which placement within these categories affects both the performance of the genre and its interpretation.

The Genre Defined

The word *bhojalī* has several referents: a female festival, the accompanying verbal song tradition, the goddess worshiped and honored during the festival in her form as wheat seedlings, and the ritual friendship formed by exchanging the "cooled" seedlings at the end of the festival as *prasād*.[1] The term makes no distinction between ritual and verbal tradition; the indigenous genre encompasses both. In both the central plains and the Phuljhar hills of Chhattisgarh, the festival centers around the planting of wheat or barley seeds in small shallow baskets, the sprouts of which are the goddess.[2]

The timing of the festival is somewhat flexible but should coincide with an auspicious day in the rainy season months of *śrāvaṇ* (July–August) or *bhādon* (August–September), usually a festival day. In the Raipur area, it is common to plant the *bhojalī* on *rakśā bandhan*, a festival celebrated on the full-moon day of the month of *śrāvaṇ*. On this day, sisters tie tinsel-decorated threads (*rākhī*) on the wrists of their brothers, thereby "binding" brothers to protect them.[3] If *bhojalī* are planted on this day, they are immersed nine days

[1] The immersion of a clay *mūrti* at the end of a festival (such as that of Ganesh at the end of *gaṇés caturthī*), or in this case the seedlings, is called, literally, "to cool" (*ṭhaṇḍā karnā*). With this act, the deity leaves the form; the clay becomes only clay, the seedlings only seedlings, although they are considered to be auspicious/blessed because of the earlier presence of the deity (see Babb 1975:234–235).

[2] See Gold 1988:198–199 for a description of a ritual in a Rajasthani village in which millet sprouts (called *juvārā*) are similarly planted as part of the framing rituals around pilgrimage. They are cared for by those left at home: "Those who remain at home feel that if the sprouts are flourishing through their steady care, so are their pilgrim kin" (199). The *juvārā* are also planted for the ritual in which the Ganga water that has been brought back from the pilgrimage is opened and distributed: "As a vivid sign of new life and growth, they certainly connote fertility" (199).

Hiltebeitel (1991:53–78) analyzes a similar "sprouting rite" (*navadhānya*) in the context of the Draupadi cult festivals of Tamil Nadu as an "expression of the 'essence' of the sacrifice," still associated, however, with the goddess and her energy (*śakti*), fertility, and growth.

[3] The association of *rakśā bandhan* with *bhojalī* on the Raipur plains, an articulation of the importance of the sister-brother relationship, is reflected in the commentary provided by a female village elder that the *bhojalī* baskets must be lifted on and off of the girls' heads by their brothers. A *bhojalī* verse recorded in this village asserts that only a brother, and no other male kin, can be trusted to fulfill this obligation:

later on the festival day celebrating the birth of the god Krishna, *janmāṣṭamī*, in the month of *bhādon*. In Phuljhar, *bhojalī* has recently been celebrated in conjunction with *gaṇeś caturthī* (the fourth day of the light half of *bhādon*).

Whatever the auspicious timing chosen by a particular village or neighborhood for planting the seeds, the *bhojalī* baskets are placed in a darkened space in a temple, around a temporary festival *mūrti*, or in a household shrine. They are allowed to grow for nine days, during which time they are worshipped as the goddess, Bhojali Dai (literally, "*bhojalī* mother"). One Phuljhar verse sequence identifies the goddess as Pili Bai, "Yellow Woman," the seedlings having taken on a yellow-green color from being sprouted in a dark place. The reference may also be to the goddess as a bride who, like all Chhattisgarhi brides, has been annointed with turmeric and oil prior to her wedding day, leaving a golden yellow hue to her skin.

Every evening the festival participants gather together to sing *bhojalī gīt* and serve (*sevā karnā*) the goddess by soaking her, pouring water over her sprouts. On the last of the nine days, the seedling baskets are carried in procession on the heads of the participants to the village pond or tank to be immersed. After the *bhojalī* sprouts are "cooled," and the soil washed off from their roots, they are distributed as *prasād*. Often this *prasād* is then exchanged between two participants to formalize a ritual friendship. Thereafter, the two friends will call each other "*bhojalī*" rather than by their given names or fictive kinship terms.[4]

This much of the performance "event" (or "reference" in Jakobsonian terms) is stable between the ritual as celebrated in Phuljhar and the Raipur plains. The festival context is the major frame giving definition to the verbal song genre, as indicated in its name. There are also thematic and formal features that identify the genre, elements that signal the introduction of this genre wherever it is sung in Chhattisgarh and elicit certain expectations from the participants and audiences of the performances. What we will see in the discussion that follows, however, is that the expectations these frames estab-

---

We are serving the *bhojalī dāī*.
Who will lift off the load [of the *bhojalī*]?

Daughter, you have [a brother] Hirsingh-Birsingh,
Who will lift off the load.

Mother, there is also the son of my elder,
Who will lift off the load.

The son of your elder is of another lineage.
He won't lift off your load.

[4] The friends extend the *bhojalī* terminology to the immediate kin of their friends, that is, calling the friend's mother and brother *bhojalī* mother, *bhojalī* brother, and so forth. See Jay 1973 for a fuller discussion of ritual friendships in Chhattisgarh.

lish differ considerably between performances in the central plains and on the Phuljhar boundaries of Chhattisgarh.

The most stable of the *bhojalī* frames is the melodic line (*rāg*) of the *bhojalī gīt*, one built around the repetition of a refrain after every verse. In South Asian folk song repertoires of a single community or region, the number of *rāg* is relatively limited. Specific *rāg* are associated with specific occasions, festivals, or rituals, so that, for example, the *bhojalī rāg* is rarely sung outside this ritual context or the context of its friendships. When a *rāg* is employed outside its "traditional" context, its usage is marked; it is used to develop a particular mood or to provide performative commentary by placing the two genres/*rāg* in relationship. So the fact that *bhojalī* verses are sometimes sung to the *rāg* of wedding songs (*vīhā gīt*) elicits an interpretive frame of marriage, whether or not there is direct reference to it (see Wadley 1989).

The number of verses that are or can be sung to a given *rāg* is unlimited; verses are simply joined one to another until the participants want to stop. Individual verses are not necessarily connected together as a bounded "song," although there may be sequences of internal coherence between sets of verses. The identifying refrain of the *bhojalī rāg,* introduced by the phrase "*hā̃ ho, devī gaṅgā*" ("Yes, the Goddess Ganga") at the end of the last line of the verse, is:

Devi Ganga, Devi Ganga,
A wave as your horse,
With your waves,
Soak the eight limbs of the *bhojalī*.

This is the only mention made of the Goddess Ganga in the sung verses; the sprouts themselves are worshiped as the goddess Bhojali Dai.[5]

The introductory verses with which most *bhojalī gīt* performances begin are a second framing device. Although the formulaic patterning of these verses remains stable between the two geographic/cultural areas under consideration, the specific details inserted into the formula vary in significant ways. The verses identify the principal "props" needed for the ritual celebration: the basket, the mixture of cow dung and soil that fills it, and the *bhojalī* seeds planted in the soil. A Phuljhar example is:

From where is the cow dung and soil?
From where is the basket?

[5] Recall the association between ritually planted millet sprouts and the waters of the Ganga in pilgrimage rituals described by Gold (1988); see footnote 2 above.

From where is the basket?
From where is Pili Bai?
We've planted the *bhojalī*.

The cow dung and soil are from Raigarh.
The basket is from Candarpur.
The basket is from Candarpur.
Pili Bai is from Phuljhar.
We've planted the *bhojalī*.

From the Raipur plains, the following example:

From where is the cow dung and soil?
From where is the basket?
From where is the basket?
From where is the new *bhojalī*,
Whose water drops are pearls?

The cow dung and soil are from the potter's house.
The basket from the weaver's house.
The basket from the weaver's house.
The new *bhojalī* is from the house of the king.
Whose water drops are pearls.

This Phuljhar example, like others recorded in the area, lays out a simple map, centering the festival in a specific geographic context. It first names the towns of Raigarh and Candarpur, which are inside Chhattisgarh but *outside* Phuljhar and even Raipur District, from where the cow dung and basket have been brought. But the most essential component of the ritual, the goddess herself, here called Pili Bai, is from Phuljhar. Thus the verse sequence provides a connection of Phuljhar to the rest of Chhattisgarh while at the same time maintaining its separate identity; notice that the song refers to the cultural subregion of Phuljhar as a whole rather than naming a specific town or village *within* Phuljhar.

The Raipur plains are located in the heartland of Chhattisgarh and are not part of a smaller cultural or geographic unit. Hence, the same concern for geographic identification and centering, to reinforce a separate identity, is not found in the verses sung there. In the Raipur verse sequencing, the mapping is social rather than geographic, from the potter's and weaver's houses to that of the king, from where the goddess herself comes. It is significant that in the Raipur plains, men (husbands/grooms, often called "kings" in Chhattisgarhi folklore), never the women, plant the *bhojalī* seeds into the cow dung and soil, whereas in Phuljhar, the girls themselves plant the seeds. In Raipur, the seeds are associated with male reproductive power, suggested in the line referring to the water drops/pearls (semen) from the house of the king.[6] The receptacle in which the seeds are planted, the earth/the basket, and the emerging sprouts are feminine.

Yet another formal feature characterizing the *bhojalī* genre, but not unique to it, is the high occurrence of a question-answer format between verses, which has already been seen in the introductory verse sequences, as well as in repetitions of the sequences. The interactive form itself establishes a communicative channel between speakers, both in the fictive world of the text and in the performative world of the context; the give-and-take and repetition of verses between friends reinforce the relationships being formalized through the ritual.[7] Two groups of women or girls sing back and forth to each other, one group leading out with a question verse, which is then repeated by the second group. The first group then responds with the answer, again repeated by the second group. A short example of the question-answer format, with all repetitions, follows. Elsewhere in the chapter, I have not provided the repetitions, which results, perhaps, in undue attention being paid to the semantic meaning of the text rather than its performatively constructed one (difficult to convey on the printed, silently read page, where repetition creates a totally different effect).[8]

Group 1: Instruments are sounding, *dḥimak dḥimak.*
From where are the instruments sounding?
From where are these instruments?

Group 2: Instruments are sounding, *dḥimak dḥimak.*
From where are the instruments sounding?
From where are these instruments?

Group 1: Instruments are sounding, *dḥimak dḥimak.*
From where are the instruments sounding?
From where are these instruments?

[6] Any infertility problem, however, is seen to lie with the woman; the "pearl" is rarely, if ever, faulted.

[7] See Gold (1986) for a discussion of chorally represented conversations in Rajasthani women's songs, the effect of which is quite different, given their content and context, than these *bhojalī* question-answer verses. Gold observes: "The words of Rajasthani songs often contain dramatic conversations, but the drama of these exchanges [expressing misunderstanding and conflict] is blunted or understressed or covered up by a chorused performance in which separate voices are not voiced" (17–18).

[8] See Tedlock 1983 and Fine 1984 for full-length discussions on the transformation of oral performances to the printed text.

Group 2: Instruments are sounding, *ḍhimak ḍhimak*.
From where are the instruments sounding?
From where are these instruments?

Group 1: The *telin* and *kalārin* are serving the *bhojalī dāī*.
From there the instruments are sounding.
From there the instruments.

Group 2: The *telin* and *kalārin* are serving the *bhojalī dāī*.
From there the instruments are sounding.
From there the instruments.

Group 1: The *telin* and *kalārin* are serving the *bhojalī dāī*.
From there the instruments are sounding.
From there the instruments.

Group 2: The *telin* and *kalārin* are serving the *bhojalī dāī*.
From there the instruments are sounding.
From there the instruments.

The singers of this verse sequence, performed in the Raipur plains, explained that *bhojalī* was originally celebrated by the Teli (oil presser) and Kalar (wine maker) castes and was only later adopted by other castes of the same level (*telin* and *kalārin* refer to the female members of these castes). Again, notice the importance of caste designation here on the Raipur plains, which is almost altogether absent in the verses I have recorded in Phuljhar.

Other than the *rāg*, refrain, and introductory framing verses, certain thematic concerns and images shared between the two geographic contexts also give consistency to the genre. Many verses describe the actual physical setting where the *bhojalī* seedlings are placed, the preparation of the site where they will sit, the planting and immersion of the seedlings, and descriptions of the actual worship of *bhojalī dāī* with the lighting of incense, the offering of water, and the performance of *ārtī* (flame offering at the end of *pūjā*):

Having plastered the floor and wall,[9]
Having plastered the corner,
Having plastered the corner,
We'll gaze lovingly
At our *bhojalī dāī*.

[9] These lines refer to the ritual purification of the site by plastering it with a mixture of cow dung and mud.

We went to the Acri bathing tank.
We made a bathing *ghāṭ*.[10]
We made a bathing *ghāṭ*.
Then at the side of the tank,
We immersed our *bhojalī*.

Regional Variation in Performance and Interpretation

The festival and performative contexts (in which participants serve the goddess and formalize friendships), a series of identifying framing devices, and shared images in the song texts help us to identify *bhojalī gīt* as sung in the Raipur plains and in Phuljhar as a single genre. However, these similarities also mask essential differences in how the genre is understood and received by the participants themselves and others in their communities. That the village men sitting in front of the Ganesh *mūrti* in a Phuljhar village asked the *bhojalī* participants to sing *homo* suggests to us that here the genre is categorized with other genres performed by the social group of "unmarried girls" and that this designation within the broader repertoire will affect its interpretation. It makes a difference in the reception of the genre in Raipur that the participants are both married women and unmarried girls, who do not necessarily form ritual friendships with each other, and that goddess possession is central to the festival, whereas in Phuljhar, only unmarried girls who will formalize a friendship participate.

In conversations with villagers on the Raipur plains, *bhojalī* is identified first as a goddess festival and only then is distinguished from a paired goddess festival called *javārā* as the one that is exclusive to women. It is significant that *javārā* is observed solely in the Raipur area and not in Phuljhar. *Javārā* is celebrated in villages and in urban neighborhoods during both the fall and the spring *navrātri* (the two nine-night ritual periods of the goddess that fall in the months of *caitra* [March–April] and *kuṅvar* [September–October]), although it is preeminent during the spring period. I was told that the fall celebration is optional and occurs only if a particular family has vowed to sponsor such a ritual in fulfillment of a vow, whereas it *must* be celebrated in the spring, whether sponsored by a goddess temple or an individual family.[11]

[10] *Ghāṭ*: special bathing site at the banks of a river or tank.

[11] When I observed *javārā* in the spring of 1981, it was being sponsored by a family in celebration of the birth and survival for one year of a son, after two older sons in the family had died in infancy. Although the *javārā* were kept in that family's home and the family bore the financial burden of the goat to be sacrificed, the entire village (excepting the Brahmins)

The *javārā* ritual centers around the planting and service of wheat seedlings, worshiped as the goddess; and, as in *bhojalī* celebrations, the goddess frequently possesses her devotees, particularly during the procession in which she (the *javārā* seedlings) is taken to the village tank to be immersed and cooled. The *javārā* possession of the goddess's male devotees is characterized by demonstrations of physical feats, such as piercing the tongue or cheek with a sharp metal rod.[12] Fewer women than men become possessed during *javārā*, and those that do demonstrate the presence of the goddess through somewhat less dramatic gestures than do the men. An old widow repeatedly became possessed during the procession I witnessed, each time lying down in front of the women carrying the *javārā* to the tank, so that they would have to step over her. Water was then poured over her, the goddess riding her human "vehicle" again being drenched/soaked, and the woman would get up.[13] By the time the procession of women carrying the *javārā* on their heads, preceded by musicians and male dancers who were possessed, reached the village tank, its banks were lined with men and women from a wide spectrum of village castes who had gathered to take this final *darśan* of the cooling of the goddess. *Javārā* participants include a wider social range than do those of *bhojalī*: men plant the seeds and serve the goddess with *javārā gīt* and watering, whereas women carry the *javārā* baskets to the village tank for immersion; both men and women may become possessed; and men, but not women, may form ritual friendships at the end of the festival by exchanging *javārā prasād*.

The structural similarities between *javārā* and *bhojalī* are obvious: the festivals' duration of nine nights (although *bhojalī* is not celebrated during *navrātri* itself), the planting of seedlings, *sevā* to the goddess through song, and goddess possession. The primary differences between *javārā* and *bhojalī* lie in the season of year when they are celebrated, the aspect of the goddess that is highlighted, and the primary gender identification of participants made by the community. The community-wide *javārā* festival marks the beginning of the hot season, when the goddess becomes heated and likely to become overheated and manifest herself through disease (see Babb 1975: 128). *Javārā gīt*, sung by men, describe the potentially dangerous, ambivalent form of the goddess, under numerous names. The following is the translation of a *javārā gīt* recorded by Lawrence Babb in the city of Raipur:

---

participated in the service of the goddess and the final procession to the village tank to cool her.

12 See Babb 1975:132–140 for a fuller description of the festival sequence and description of this possession.

13 This form of "de-possession" was different from that of the male devotees.

Oh Kali, killer of the demon, you carry many weapons in your hands;
your eyes are red and you wear the bloody necklace of skulls.
Sixty-four yoginis, the horrible ones, dance to the sounds of a war-band.
Oh Mother, sit on your throne and tell us how the terrible sounds will come,
As the clouds make noise at the time of the rainy season.
After hearing your voice Bakasur (a demon) and all (the demons) will run away.

(1975:135)

The heated form of the goddess is also reflected in the kinds of offerings made to her. Traditionally, the offering made to her on the last day of *javārā* is a goat sacrifice, although this practice is becoming less common, particularly in Chhattisgarh's towns. Even in the village in which I participated in *javārā* in 1981, the goat was sacrificed behind a straw screen, behind the house in which the *javārā* were being attended, with only two or three men as witnesses. I was specifically asked not to go back to try to see or photograph the sacrifice. The *prasād* of the sacrifice was then cooked by the sponsoring family and fed to the village participants.

The soaking of the goddess in the *javārā* context of the parched, barren hot season is in dramatic contrast to performing a similar *sevā* to her in the rainy season in which Bhojali Dai is already cool and the fields are filled with green rice paddy. Devi Ganga's soaking, the participants' *sevā*, brings her to fullness, splitting, fruition. The devotees sing of gazing at Bhojali Dai with love, with no mention of propitiating her anger. Although women also become possessed in the Raipur plains, no animal sacrifice occurs, and the entire festival is "cooler" than *javārā*.

Bhojalī is distinguished, then, from *javārā* by the auspicious nature of the Bhojali Dai and its identification as a *women's* festival. These two factors put the tradition into relationship with the Chhattisgarhi *gaurā* festival that celebrates the marriage of Shiva and Parvati. Although both men and women participate in the *gaurā* festival on different levels, it, too, is often characterized as a women's festival, because only women sing *gaurā gīt* and primarily women become possessed by the goddess as they are singing these songs. The intimate association of the *gaurā* and *bhojalī* genres as contexts one for the other was made explicit when during *bhojalī* possession in a plains village, the nonpossessed festival participants began to sing *gaurā gīt*, whose words and *rāg* are clearly distinguishable from *bhojalī gīt*.

In the Raipur area, both married women and unmarried girls participate in *bhojalī*. Unmarried girls bring the soil from the fields to place in the baskets, and it is they who carry the seedlings nine days later to the tank to be

Bhojalī sprouts, the goddess, being carried to the village tank for immersion, Raipur plains.

immersed. Ritual friendships may be formed between participants through the exchange of *bhojalī*, as they are in Phuljhar, but only between unmarried girls. Married women, on the other hand, are the primary participants in the singing of *bhojalī gīt* and *sevā* to the goddess; they are also the participants who are possessed by the goddess. The presence of possession limits participation in the festival to *ādivāsī* and low- to middle-level castes; high-caste women avoid situations in which there is goddess possession. As one Brahmin woman told me, "We know the goddess possesses when she's called [that is, it's not that we don't believe], and we don't want to be there in case she would come to one of us. You never know what you might do when you're possessed."

Perceived first as a goddess festival, it is this relationship with the goddess that is primary in the Raipur plains rather than the ritual friendships that are the focus of the tradition in Phuljhar. The goddess depends for her very life breath on the service given by the women during the festival through *pūjā* and *bhojalī gīt*; the yellow-green seedlings literally depend on the water poured over them by the women for their survival. The women sing:

A fish without water,
Grain without a breeze,
Grain without a breeze,
Bhojalī without service,
Longs for breath.

The service given by the women is reciprocated by the goddess granting her favor through possession of some of the participants. Several women who regularly become possessed said that when they hear the *bhojalī gīt*, they are filled with devotion toward the goddess, become so full of her emotion (*bhāv*) that they can no longer bear (*sahanā*) it; then the goddess comes to them (*devī ham par ātī hai*).[14] The presence of goddess possession reinforces the primacy of the relationship between goddess and individual participant. Interestingly, though it is the *bhojalī gīt* that incite the possession (call the goddess), none of the songs themselves make mention of possession. And when participants became possessed in the village where I witnessed the performance of *bhojalī gīt* in the Raipur plains, as mentioned above, the other women switched song genres from *bhojalī* to *gaurā gīt*. This association suggests that possession may not be inherent to the *bhojalī* tradition per se but occurs in the Raipur plains because of the influence of other goddess traditions, such as *javārā* and *gaurā*, that do involve possession.

The goddess also grants her favor by granting fertility, both to the land and to the participating women. The growth of the seedlings is associated with the fertility of the paddy fields and other crops that have been planted in the rainy season. The verbal *bhojalī* song tradition makes explicit this association of goddess, *bhojalī*, and crops:

The corn is full of starch;
The sugarcane is ready;
The sugarcane is ready;
Hurry, hurry and grow, oh *bhojalī*,
That you, too, may ripen.

The *bhojalī* is not only the goddess and seedlings but also the girls who have formed ritual friendships by the exchange of *bhojalī*. Thus the verse can also be understood as a call for the ripening of the girls and, more generally, the female participants, to fruition / fertility.

[14] Certain women are more susceptible than others to this possession. I was told that once a woman becomes possessed, she will thereafter usually become possessed whenever she hears a *devī gīt* (song to the goddess) associated with any of the goddess festivals in which possession takes place. This is why women say they are hesitant to sing these songs outside of their ritual context.

Another verse makes a similar metaphorical reference to the fertility of the fields and the female participants. The Bhojali Dai's (goddess, participant, seedling) sari and crown are likened to the ripening, golden paddy after the flood of monsoon rains.

The flood has come; the waste swept away.
The sari border of our *bhojalī dāī* is golden.
The flood has come; the small boats have floated away.
The crown of our *bhojalī dāī* is golden.

In still another verse, the participants ask directly for the blessing of fertility and, more specifically, for the blessing of a son.

We asked for milk; we asked for a son
And we asked for a blessing.
And we asked for a blessing.
Queen Kaushalya is standing there;
She gives her blessing.

In the Ramayana narrative, the queens of King Dasharath were infertile for many years. Finally, he performed a sacrifice, the *prasād* (blessings) of which his three queens partook, each then becoming pregnant. Queen Kaushalya was the oldest and gave birth to the hero Ram, an incarnation *(avatār)* of Vishnu; thus, her blessing is particularly powerful. However, the blessing of any married woman is considered to have some efficacy and it is a common custom in Chhattisgarh for such women to confer their blessings on newly married women.

It is perhaps the strong association with maternal fertility in the *bhojalī* ritual and verbal tradition in the Raipur plains that results in the association of the singing of *bhojalī gīt* with primarily married women. Unmarried girls may sing along, but they are included in the "married" category by virtue of their potential married status. Widows, no longer eligible for fertility, are excluded from direct participation, their presence considered to be inauspicious at any ritual occasion emphasizing a woman's fertility (such as certain wedding rituals). Where fertility is a dominant theme in the songs and where, through possession, the goddess-participant relationship is primary, the ritual friendship associated with *bhojalī* is downplayed, and not all unmarried participants form such friendships.[15]

[15] This follows the common pattern of formalizing friendships in Chhattisgarh, including Phuljhar. That is, the *prasād* of various rituals or festivals may be exchanged to formalize a friendship without the friendship being the focus of the ritual or mentioned in any of its verbal traditions.

The *bhojalī* tradition in Phuljhar has taken an interesting turn from what might be considered the "mainstream" Chhattisgarhi tradition. Here, *bhojalī* is always referred to in the context of ritual friendships between unmarried girls; I never heard it contextualized or associated with other goddess festivals. While the Oriya castes of Phuljhar may have little knowledge of the rituals of the festival, unless it is celebrated in their village, they all know about the friendship. They equate it with their own friendship tradition called *mahāprasād*.[16] The nature of the two kinds of friendship is, however, differentiated by the *Chhattisgarhi* castes living in Phuljhar. They specify that *bhojalī* is the friendship formed between unmarried girls; after marriage, women form *mahāprasād*. Further, adults say that *bhojalī* cannot be as serious and long-lasting as *mahāprasād*, because the girls move away from each other upon marriage and cannot fulfill the obligations of being a *mahāprasād* (these being ritual obligations similar to those of kin.)[17]

Not only is the primary emphasis of *bhojalī* on the formation of ritual friendships, but in Phuljhar, *only* unmarried, pubescent girls who are going to form a friendship participate. The girls whom I taped were between the ages of eleven and fifteen or sixteen from the Gond, Aghariya, and Saunra castes. The friends plant their *bhojalī* together in one basket, and the subsequent growth of the seedlings is associated with the strength and longevity of the friendship. The *bhojalī* seedlings are still worshiped as the goddess, but this aspect of the festival and the relationship between goddess and participant are secondary to the friendship between girls. This is confirmed by the absence of goddess possession and the association of the tradition with other girls' traditions rather than other goddess traditions. The Phuljhar villagers with whom I spoke about the *bhojalī* goddess possession I had witnessed in the Raipur plains one hundred miles away were unaware, and slightly disbelieving of, its existence.

The change in marital status of the participants and the emphasis on the relationship between the girls through friendship, rather than on a relationship with the goddess, is reflected in the thematic content of the *bhojalī gīt*. In

[16] *Mahāprasād* literally means "the great *prasād*" but generally refers to the *prasād* brought back from the Jagannath temple in Puri, Orissa. For purposes of forming *mahāprasād* friendships, however, the *prasād* of any major festival may be exchanged (rarely the *prasād* of private family rituals).

[17] Even for married women, however, the ritual and social obligations of ritual friendships are not as demanding as they are of men. For example, I was told that if a male *mahāprasād* needs help harvesting his fields, his ritual friend is under obligation to help him, even if it means neglecting his own fields; male *mahāprasād* observe death rituals for their friends, participate as kin in marriage gifting, and so on. Women in the Oriya village where I lived usually formed *mahāprasād* on the basis of the number and sex of their children; these relationships were sometimes formed by verbal assent, without the actual ritual exchange of *prasād*.

comparison with the songs of the Raipur area, there is a noticeable lack of direct reference to the fertility of either land or participants. It is natural for the songs to reflect the immediate concerns of unmarried girls, particularly when they are being sung among female peers between whom close friendships have been formed. At this point in a girl's life, she is not yet supposed to be sexually active, and her fertility is not the subject of open conversation; it is inappropriate for a girl to speak directly even about her forthcoming marriage, much less her childbearing potential, in front of her elders. Talk of her marriage is all around her, however, and is of interest to *her* as well. This concern finds expression in several verbal traditions of these pubescent girls in Phuljhar, including *bhojalī gīt*.

First, think back to the reference to the Bhojali Dai as the "yellow woman," which I suggested may be a reference to the turmeric-bathed bride. Another verse sequence explicitly identifies first the *bhojalī* and then the singer herself as a bride, homologizing the goddess, participant, and bride. The third verse of this sequence suggests the reluctance and apprehension of a young bride going to her *sasurāl* (in-laws' home) for the first time, where the wedding palanquin will carry her.

Who mounts the elephant?
Who mounts the horse?
Who mounts the horse?
Who mounts the palanquin?
Who mounts the wedding litter?

The king mounts the elephant.
The chief minister mounts the horse.
The chief minister mounts the horse.
The queen mounts the palanquin.
The *bhojalī* mounts the wedding litter.

In which village is the young girl?
In which village is the engagement?
In which village is the engagement?
Only when the instruments begin to play,
Will I mount the wedding litter.

Other verses describe the actual wedding ceremony:

The *tulsī* platform,
A crown in the courtyard,
A crown in the courtyard,

Round and round the Brahmin circumambulates,
The wedding hour is auspicious.[18]

According to the indigenous principles of genre categorization within the folklore repertoire, the fact that *bhojalī* is identified with and participation in the tradition is limited to unmarried girls places it in relationship with other genres whose performances are limited to unmarried girls. In this case, the Phuljhar girls who participate in *bhojalī* are from Chhattisgarhi-speaking castes. Oriya-speaking girls in Phuljhar have their own traditions, identified as "theirs," in which the Chhattisgarhi girls do not participate directly (although these still serve indirectly as a broader context for *bhojalī*). But one in which they *do* participate, singing in Oriya instead of their mother tongue, Chhattisgarhi, is the verbal repartee game *homo*.

In the play of *homo*, two groups of girls (rarely just two individuals) try to "outsmart" each other by responding appropriately to the verse just sung by the opposite group. The context of the game and its themes are nonreligious, sung while the girls are working (the girls in the village where I recorded these *homo* and *bhojalī* go out into the jungle to pick leaves for use in *bīṛī* making), walking to and from a bazaar, bathing in the village tank, and so forth. The girls sing of fleeting glances, flirtations, potential relationships between teenage girls and boys. And this is why the girls who were asked to sing *bhojalī* in front of the Ganesh *mūrti* on that rainy night frequently burst out in giggles, finding themselves singing of these flirtatious relationships in front of elders who would not normally be the direct audience of these songs. On one occasion, when I had asked some girls to sing *bhojalī gīt* for my tape recorder, out of context, they seemed stumped. Finally, an elderly woman began to sing out the verses, line by line, and the girls repeated. Interestingly, all these verses were descriptive of the ritual *sevā* (service) to the goddess; there were no examples of these flirtatious verses. The following *bhojalī* verse sequences are illustrative of the *homo* influence:

From where is the *dāl* [lentils] and rice?
From where the brass bowl?
From where the brass bowl?
From where the unmarried boy,
Who wanders around in the afternoon?

[18] *Tulsī* is a basil plant grown in the courtyards of most high- and middle-caste homes. The plant is a goddess and is worshiped daily by the women of the household, service that includes watering the plant. The "crown" refers to the headdress worn by both bride and groom, from which hang small strings of flowers and tinsel that veil their faces.

Narsinghpur's *dāl* and rice;
Jagdishpur's brass bowl;
Jagdishpur's brass bowl;
Jarra's unmarried boy,
Who wanders around in the afternoon.[19]

. . . .

Who dams a river, my friend?
Who obeys their mother and father?
This is the age we do this, my friend.
This is the age we do this, my friend.

I gave a brass plate to the guest, my friend.
There was no watchman at the Nikunj dam.
I plucked and took the victory flower [*jai phūl*], my friend.
I plucked and took the victory flower, my friend.

I decorated the inside of the brass plate, my friend.
Boys these days are very fashionable.
I'll take it and go to the river, my friend.
I'll take it and go to the river, my friend.

I went out to the big fields, my friend.
I kept waiting in the biggest field.
I watched the road for you, my friend.
I watched the road for you, my friend.

I sowed the field with *muṅg* lentils, my friend.
Seeing you, girl, I felt desire.
The *muṅg* crop will be good, my friend.
The *muṅg* crop will be good, my friend.

Another *bhojalī* verse suggests a sexual relationship between the singer and a male visitor through the imagery of the two of them sharing *prasād*:

Jhan, jhan sounds the *mṛdaṅg*,[20]
The cymbals also sound.
The cymbals also sound.
There's no master in our house;
Come, take some *prasād*.

[19] Narsinghpur and Jagdishpur are the two villages closest to Jarra, the village where the songs were performed, all three within easy walking distance of each other.
[20] *Mṛdaṅg* is a type of drum; *jhan, jhan*, its onomatopoetic representation.

Prasād may be any offering to a deity that is then distributed to the worshipers as a sanctified, blessed substance, but it is usually associated with food offerings. Preceded by the phrase "no master in our house," however, *prasād* takes on the sexual connotation of "feeding" when it occurs between sexes, common in South Asian folk and literary sources.

The theme and imagery of fertility are not altogether absent in the Phuljhar *bhojalī* tradition. After all, the central symbol of fertility—the planting and growth of the soaked wheat seedlings—has been retained, although on a conscious level the girls may have given it a different significance, one that mirrors the life of their friendships. The refrain to the *bhojalī rāg* is also frequently retained:

> Devi Ganga, Devi Ganga,
> A wave as your horse,
> With your waves,
> Soak the eight limbs of the *bhojalī*.

The soaking of the *bhojalī* refers not only to the soaking of the goddess but also to that of the physical seeds, which ensures quick sprouting. With this soaking, the seeds become soft and swollen, readying to split and "give birth" to the new sprout. Contextually, the image extends to the goddess, the paddy, and the friends. The horse, on the other hand, has strong associations in South Asian verbal traditions with male virility. The wave, the horse upon which Devi Ganga rides, is suggestive of the rains, essential for the fertility of the earth and the *bhojalī* and to all female fertility and productivity.

In addition to the refrain, some of the verses sung by the unmarried girls in Phuljhar retain hints of the fertility theme; however, explicit references to the crops and fertility of the land are few. One verse sequence mentions the newly harvested rice and the fragrance it emits:

> In a bamboo storage bin
> They have filled rice.
> They have filled rice.
> The breeze of the *bhojalī dāī*
> Brings sweet fragrance.
>
> In a bamboo storage bin
> A colorful braid for the *bhojalī dāī*.
> A colorful braid for the *bhojalī dāī*.
> Her forehead decorated,
> We will sow the *bhojalī dāī*.

The lines of the first verse are identical to a verse recorded in the Raipur area, except for dialect differences. However, the second verse diffuses the focus on productive fertility of the land (the harvested rice) by referring to the Bhojali Dai's colorful braid and decorated forehead, suggesting imagery of a bride rather than of a mother, with fertility being less explicitly articulated.

Another Phuljhar verse is similar to the one sung by the Raipur women in which Queen Kaushalya gives the blessing of a son. But here in Phuljhar, it is Kaushalya who is asking for a son, rather than the participants themselves asking, thus distancing the reference to fertility one step from the unmarried girls singing the song:

> In the brass plate, a little rice;
> In the brass jug, some milk.
> In the brass jug, some milk.
> Kaushalya is standing there
> Asking for a son.

I was told that childless women in Phuljhar may plant *bhojalī* in hopes of receiving the boon of fertility (and I have witnessed similar participation of married women in the *ḍālkhāī* Oriya festival tradition for unmarried girls in Phuljhar). In this case, however, their service to the goddess consists of *pūjā* (worship) only; they do not sing *bhojalī gīt* along with the unmarried girls or participate in the ritual friendships. Performatively, their limited participation places them back in a gender category in which fertility has not yet been "tested" and the possibilities are still open.

We started this chapter with the observation that though *bhojalī gīt* can be identified formally, thematically, and contextually as those songs that are sung at a particular festival in which seedlings are worshiped as the goddess, the genre is received very differently by the folklore communities in the Chhattisgarhi heartland (Raipur) and in its borderlands of Phuljhar. The shifts in perception and interpretation of the genre coincide with the differences in the social identity of the principal participants and thus, as the men in front of the Ganesh *mūrti* suggested, the other genres with which that participant identity puts *bhojalī* into play. These shifts are summarized in Table 1.

The *bhojalī* verbal tradition and the structuring of the relationships within the festival context reflect the concerns of the participants at their stage of the female life cycle. During puberty and before marriage, girls are most concerned with their relationships with their peers, as reflected in the primacy of ritual friendships in the *bhojalī* tradition in Phuljhar. Ritual friendships formed at this age are based on "liking each other" rather than on some

Table 1. Chhattisgarhi *bhojalī gīt*

	Raipur	Phuljhar
Participants	married women	unmarried girls
Primary festival relationship	with goddess: possession	with female peers: ritual friendships
Related genres	goddess festivals: *javārā, gaurā*	girls' play games: *homo*
Thematic emphasis of songs	fertility of land and participants	emerging sexuality and forthcoming marriages of participants
Life-cycle emphasis	motherhood	puberty and marriage

external circumstance such as number of children (as they often are for married women); and in Phuljhar there is a specially named friendship reserved for this age. The verbal tradition that the girls share provides an indication of their interest in relationships with their male peers, an interest that is not appropriate to voice publicly in front of anyone but their female peers. In these *bhojalī gīt* and other associated verbal genres that the girls perform, such as *homo*, they express interest in their emerging sexuality and marriage but are not directly concerned with their fertility and childbearing potential.

In contrast, the primary participants of the Chhattisgarhi heartland are married women or potentially married women (that is, unmarried girls); widows are excluded. The category of unmarried girls is distinguished only for the purpose of identifying who will carry the baskets on their heads in procession; but they sing along with the married women as members of that social group, whose central concern has become fertility and the birth of sons. Providing service to the goddess *bhojalī dāī* and strengthening their relationship with her is one way for married women to ensure this fertility; the goddess herself affirms the relationship by possessing her devotees.

Aesthetic and Social Organization

Roger Abrahams suggests in "The Complex Relations of Simple Forms" that a community's aesthetic and social organization often mirror each other (1976:196), another way of saying that indigenous genres are themselves social constructions. The significant social categories suggested by participation in the *bhojalī* tradition is, in the Raipur plains, widow-nonwidow (that is, married and potentially married), whereas in Phuljhar the nonwidow category is differentiated further into pubescent girls and married women.

The Phuljhar aesthetic organization, where unmarried girls have their "own" culturally recognized and articulated verbal and ritual traditions, suggests that this life-cycle stage is performatively acknowledged; pubescence is a marked social category in this cultural area. That this phenomenon on the Phuljhar borders of Chhattisgarh has developed under Oriya influence is suggested by the absence of such verbal, performative traditions exclusive to unmarried girls in the Chhattisgarh heartland, while the others available in Phuljhar are specifically Oriya: *homo*, *kārtik* bathing,[21] and the *ḍālkhāī* festival examined in the next chapter.[22]

Although none of these traditions is specifically a female *initiation* ritual, that pubescence is a marked category aligns Orissa (and Phuljhar) more closely with the south, where female puberty rites *are* celebrated, rather than the north, where they are not (suggesting again the usefulness of the southwest-northeast analytic cultural axis in India). In the Gangetic plains of the north and much of central India, no specific rituals mark a girl's coming-of-age. Doranne Jacobson describes a young girl's experience of first menstruation in a Madhya Pradesh village west of Chhattisgarh:

> Munni had heard older girls whispering about "*mahīnā*," something that happened to a woman every month. She had an idea what it was, but still she was not prepared for its happening to her. One day she found a spot on her clothes. She knew it was something embarrassing and tried to hide it, but her cousin's wife noticed it and took her aside. . . . *Bhābhī* also told Munni never to touch a man or even a woman during her period . . . because a menstruating woman is considered "dirty" until she takes a full bath five days after the start of her period. . . . Munni never discussed menstruation with her mother, and no men of the family learned of the event. But Munni's *bhābhī* quietly told Rambai [her mother], "Your little girl has begun to bathe." (1977:40)

Lawrence Babb reports that when he asked a Chhattisgarhi Brahmin pandit about the absence of puberty rites in the Raipur plains, the pandit replied

[21] *Kārtik* (October–November) is an especially auspicious month in the Chhattisgarhi-Phuljhar calendar, coinciding with the harvest of the rice paddy. During this month, Oriya-caste pubescent girls rise before dawn and go to the banks of the village tank or riverside to bathe ritually, bringing back to their homes brass *loṭā* (small water vessels) of water to pour over the *tulsī* plant in their courtyards. Older women accompany them to teach them the rituals and songs, and by the end of the month, younger wives may join them, again usually nonfertile women. The participation of the latter is optional, whereas that of the girls is "mandatory"; thus, it is a "girls' ritual."

[22] That unmarried girls' games and song traditions are not named as part of the folklore repertoire in the plains of Chhattisgarh does not necessarily mean that they do not have such traditions but that they are not acknowledged as culturally significant so as to be included in the repertoire articulated by the larger folklore community.

that to celebrate a girl's puberty "would be illogical because 'in old times she would no longer belong to her father's house,'" referring to the earlier custom of child marriage and still current higher-caste marriage patterns of village and clan exogamy and hypergamy (1975:80).[23]

The absence or existence of female puberty rituals and pubescence as a marked category is related to these marriage patterns. In the south, where the ideal marriage partner is one's cross cousin, a girl's fertility remains of value to her natal family because her offspring are ideal marriage partners for her brother's children; a daughter, then, can increase the prosperity of her father and brother (Wadley 1980:162). It is in this cultural area that elaborate, "public" puberty rituals are observed among many castes. Holly Baker Reynolds describes these in great detail for Tamil Hindus: "Pubescence is seen as leading teleologically to *cumaṅkali* [married woman and mother] status. . . . While it may seem "natural" for females to marry, *cumaṅkali*-s are not born, they are made, and the process begins with the rites attendant upon first menstruation" (1980:40).

In Chhattisgarh, although marriage patterns do not follow those of southern cross-cousin marriages, the lower castes do not strictly adhere to village exogamy. Further, bride-price also exists among some *ādivāsī* castes, rather than dowry, because of tribal influences as well as, perhaps, these women's participation in the agricultural work force. While it is simplistic to draw a causal relationship between marriage patterns, women's economic roles (and perhaps even women's status, more generally), and the existence of puberty rituals or pubescence as a marked social category, there does seem to be some correlation suggested in the repertoire of Chhattisgarhi folklore.

The differential performance of *bhojalī gīt* in the Chhattisgarhi heartland and on the Phuljhar periphery marks the category of pubescent girls as distinct from that of married women and gives voice to their particular interests. The final goal of the overwhelming majority of Chhattisgarhi women, however, is to be married and become mothers; and the fertility emphasis of the *bhojalī* tradition of the plains, in the very form of the *bhojalī* seedlings and their ritual watering, if not always in the verbal tradition, undergirds and informs the Phuljhar tradition of unmarried girls.

[23] The *upanayana* sacred thread ceremony for boys of the twice-born castes is the closest equivalent to a male initiation ceremony, through which the boy traditionally entered the "student stage" of religious instruction under a guru. This ritual is not observed by *ādivāsī* and low-caste males, however; and these days, even for upper-caste males, the ceremony is often an attenuated one immediately preceding marriage rituals, not one marking male puberty (Knipe 1991:24). In both Phuljhar and the Chhattisgarhi plains, the publicly articulated repertoire of "Chhattisgarhi folklore" does not include any genres that are exclusive to unmarried boys. They participate in festival and ritual traditions along with married men, much as unmarried girls do in the Raipur plains.

The *bhojalī* tradition is not an initiatory ritual of transformation per se; rather, its songs and friendships provide pubescent girls an imaginative space for expression of that stage of their lives, even while suggesting what lies ahead. The *ḍālkhāī* festival and verbal tradition of Phuljhar, analyzed in the next chapter, may traditionally have approximated more closely an initiation ritual for its pubescent participants, a transformation of girls into potential brides. A narrative told to me by an old widow as the "story of *ḍālkhāī,*" however, suggests this particular initiatory tradition challenges the dominant ideology of what it means to be a Hindu bride, that the transformation is also one of pubescent girl to adventurous, brave, and wise ruler.

CHAPTER 3

Brave Daughters, Bound Kings: A Female Tradition of Reversal

Ḍālkhāī

The festival and accompanying song tradition of *ḍālkhāī* is consistently listed, along with *bhojalī* and *homo*, in the category of traditions belonging to unmarried girls within the Phuljhar folklore repertoire. *Ḍālkhāī* is more specifically referred to as a "*holī* [festival of reversal] for unmarried girls." Celebration of the festival was quite consciously suspended in Phuljhar villages in the early 1980s, but it lives on in the memory of the folklore community, and its song tradition is still very much alive, having found new performance contexts and thus having developed new meanings. These days *ḍālkhāī gīt*, unlike *bhojalī* and *homo*, are sung outside the festival context by members from the broader folklore community: both Chhattisgarhi and Oriya speakers, married and unmarried men and women, literate and nonliterate. Sung in short fragments as work songs, as singers walk to and from the bazaar, and in joking social exchanges, *ḍālkhāī gīt* are almost always accompanied by snickers or laughter. I was frequently told that these were "bad" (*burī*, that is, obscene) songs, which implied that they were not fit for my tape recorder. I thought I would find a key to interpreting the nature of these "bad" songs by observing them in their ritual/festival context; what I learned, however, was that it was partially because they had been taken *out* of this context that they were now labeled as "bad."

I will first examine *ḍālkhāī* as a festival of reversal traditionally and ritually celebrated by pubescent girls. Much of my understanding of the festival and the significance of its reversals comes from a one-and-a-half-hour sung narrative that I call the Song of Subanbali, which was sung for me by an elderly Oriya widow to whom many villagers referred me. She was known in the village as the person who could always be counted on to know the stories behind "why we do things the way we do." Much to the dismay of several other elderly women who had joined me as an audience to the performance of the Song of Subanbali, however, the narrative never mentions the festival or its patron goddesses. When they objected at the end of the performance that, while it was a good story, the singer hadn't told me the story of *ḍālkhāī*, the performer only laughed and said, "This is the story." I decided to take seriously her own perception that this narrative would help me unravel the meanings of the festival. Further, I assumed that the festival context in which she placed the narrative was itself a commentary on that narrative. Looking at the two performance traditions in relationship also suggests ways in which ritual and narrative differ and interact.

Although the *ḍālkhāī* tradition has been trivialized on one level through the demise of its ritual context, its significance for the girls with whom it is still associated minimalized, the old widow's narrative suggests that it may have served traditionally as a festival marking a pubescent female rite of passage into the "marriageable" category. The connotations of reversal in both the festival and narrative suggest that it may also have been what Judith Okely (1991) calls a "crack of resistance" against an increasingly dominant discourse (overwhelmingly male and textual) on the "proper" action (*dharma*) for married Hindu women. That the Phuljhar village headmen have suspended celebration of the festival in recent years suggests that they, too, may understand the tradition to be one not only of reversal but also of resistance.

The Festival Tradition

As mentioned above, the most common indigenous designation of the *ḍālkhāī* tradition is that it is a "*holī* for unmarried girls." *Holī* is a north and central Indian festival celebrated in *phāgun* (February–March) that marks the end of the old year and the beginning of the new. The general mood is one of license and reversal on this day, marked most dramatically by the reversal of social hierarchies when celebrants spray indelible colored water on persons higher on the hierarchy than themselves (called "playing *holī*"). Low-caste celebrants may spray high castes, and children, their elders; women may spray the men of their households (this female *holī* play usually being limited to their own courtyards). Lawrence Babb describes the festival in Chhattisgarh as "an occasion upon which ordinary norms and conventions are temporarily overturned. If Hindu culture ordinarily puts a premium on the unassertiveness in women, on *holī* the reverse is entirely appropriate. Likewise, if Hindu culture ordinarily proscribes open displays of sexuality, on *holī* sexuality is one of the dominant and most obvious motifs of the day. There is a clear sense of reversal in the festival, which perhaps is in no way more vividly exemplified than by the feminine dress some men wear on the day of *holī* play" (1975:172). It is in this sense of performatively reversing social position and status that *ḍālkhāī* is called a young girls' *holī*: on this one day, festival participants are permitted a freedom of action and voice contradicting conventional norms and expectations of Chhattisgarhi female behavior.

This indigenous contextualization and designation of the festival, as well as knowing that it was a dying tradition still being performed in only one Phuljhar village, piqued my curiosity, and against the advice of my educated Chhattisgarhi friends, well armored with their dire warnings (which would also be given to any woman entering public space during *holī*), I attended the *ḍālkhāī* festival in the fall of 1980. Although *ḍālkhāī* used to be commonly celebrated all over the Oriya-speaking area of eastern Chhattisgarh and the western hills of Orissa, the year I attended turned out to be the last year it was ritually celebrated in Phuljhar. When I returned to India in 1985 and again in 1988 and 1993, I could locate no village in which it was still observed.

The *ḍālkhāī* festival is celebrated during the fall festival season, which marks the end of the rainy season and the harvest of the rice paddy (the tenth day of the light half of *kuṅvar* [September–October]).[1] Its primary participants are unmarried, pubescent girls from the Oriya Saunra and Sabar *ādivāsī* (tribal) castes. Other low-caste, nontribal girls sometimes accompany and celebrate with their friends, and infertile married women may participate to a limited degree (by coming out to the open performance field and making offerings to the presiding goddesses but not singing or dancing with the girls) in hopes of gaining the boon of fertility.[2]

The year I observed the festival, a group of ten or twelve *ādivāsī* girls between the ages of eight and fourteen spent most of the day dancing and singing *ḍālkhāī gīt* (songs) under a large tree on a clearing a half-mile outside their village, on the edges of what is called "jungle" (uninhabited, unsocialized space). They were accompanied on a village-style oboe (*śahnāī*) and drums by a group of three Gara, low-caste male musicians, who also play professionally for weddings. No other adults or males were present, except passersby, the infertile women who came to make special offerings and quickly left, and an elderly Christian woman who had accompanied me to the village. The majority of the consistent audience was made up of a group

[1] This is the same day as *daśharā*, a festival celebrating the victory of the hero god of the Ramayana, Ram, over the demon Ravan and Ram's return to his kingdom after fourteen years of exile. *Daśharā* is not, however, commonly observed in the Phuljhar villages in which *ḍālkhāī* was traditionally celebrated.

[2] See Chapter 2 for a similar participation level of infertile married women in the unmarried girls' *bhojalī* festival.

Ḍālkhāī dance on clearing outside village, Phuljhar.

of twenty or so younger village children, including a few boys. The two oldest dancers, ages thirteen and fourteen, led the dancing and singing, composing *ḍālkhāī gīt* spontaneously as they went. Dancing and singing alternated, with the musicians picking up the song melody while the girls danced. The younger dancers did not sing the verses at all, only joining in on the last-line refrain, "*ki ḍālkhāī re*."

The girls could not always complete verses they had started, perhaps itself an indication of the dying festival tradition; periodically, they were instructed by the male musicians to sing louder, "with a full voice," or the drummers themselves would take over the singing role. The girls seemed grateful when the Christian woman who had accompanied me, a wonderful performer in her own right who was intimately familiar with Hindu traditions, volunteered to complete a *bārahmāsā* (twelve-verse poetic form structured around the months of the year) that they were having difficulty filling. The girls completed the following *bārahmāsā* verses:

> *Ki ḍālkhāī re!*
> In the month of *māgh*, Madhav [Krishna] will come.
> I decorated the bed.

I lit a jeweled lamp and waited.
My eyes keeping vigil, my friend,
The night has passed; leave the path.
I'm addicted to the son of Nand.
I can't forget him.
Ki ḍālkhāī re!

Ki ḍālkhāī re!
In *phāgun*, color is scarce.
Radha and Madhav will throw color [the *holī* dyes].
Mixing camphor in the pool of color,
Their companions will throw color.
Jadhu and Gosai, leave the path.
Ki ḍālkhāī re!

Ki ḍālkhāī re!
In *māgh*, my beloved stayed in a foreign country.
Whom does he love, my dark one,
That he has forgotten me, forgotten me?
Ki ḍālkhāī re!

At this point the girls ran out of words, and the older woman picked up the *bārahmāsā*:

Ki ḍālkhāī re!
The month of *caitra* is cool.
Who will bring to me my Bengali lover?
On her wrists are *campā* flowers;
On her neck a *tulsī* garland.
Krishna speaks only one word to Radha
That is beautiful to the heart.
Ki ḍālkhāī re!

Then she, too, could not fill in the rest of the months of the poetic form. She told me later that when she sings this *ḍālkhāī bārahmāsā* while walking or working in the fields, she never forgets it; but she was not used to singing in the festival context with all the drumming.

Each girl, wearing a skirt and blouse, also had a long shawl-like cloth, or half-sari, draped over her shoulders and back. During the dance segments, the girls held the two ends of this cloth in front of them, bending over and shuffling backward. The cloth suggests the sari a girl begins to wear when she becomes eligible for marriage, traditionally at puberty but these days much later if she continues her formal education. (Hence, in the rural areas of Chhattisgarh, the villagers found it highly amusing when I periodically, as a married woman, wore the schoolgirl's dress of salwar-chemise [long tunic and baggy pants] rather than a sari.)

At sundown, after having danced for four to five hours, the dancers and musicians moved inside the village, where the number of both participants and audience members increased. At this time, I left to observe a local Ramayana dramatic performance (*rāmlīlā*) in a distant town that had served as the seat of power for the local maharaja before independence, the Ramayana still being the focus of my research at that time.[3] But I was told that the singing and dancing on the village main street continued throughout the night. During the course of the entire festival, in and outside the village, coconuts, milk, and flowers were offered to the presiding goddesses, Sarla Devi and Mangla Devi (also call Van Durga, or Durga of the Forest). The goddesses were represented by two *kalaś* (small brass water vessels with coconuts placed over their openings). The *kalaś* and offerings were immersed, or "cooled," in the village tank early the next morning, marking the end of the festival.

Ḍālkhāī's association with the festival of *holī*, its ethos of reversal and inversion, results from the freedom of action and voice given to the *ḍālkhāī* participants and the temporary suspension of traditional gender hierarchy in the festival context. When the girls are dancing outside the village, they may "attack" any passerby, particularly a man, by hurling dust and abuses at him, surrounding him, if they are able, until he gives them money. An unverifiable oral tradition circulates in this part of Phuljhar that in the late 1970s, during the *ḍālkhāī* celebration at a village bordering National Highway No. 6 (hardly more than a single-lane paved road out here in the "jungle"), the festival participants tried to stop truck drivers by stretching a rope across the highway, holding them up until they made payment. But the truck drivers, the story goes, were not from Chhattisgarh and were unfamiliar with *ḍālkhāī* and its traditions; they "took advantage" of the girls, and several girls were even said to have run off with them. That it was no longer safe for its female celebrants is one reason frequently cited for the suspension of the festival in recent years.

These days, the most significant reversals are perceived to be those expressed in the *ḍālkhāī gīt* that accompany the dancing, the *burī* (bad, obscene)

[3] As it turned out, although I had been continuously assured that the *rāmlīlā* was performed every year in this town, that "it *had* to be performed," I found out upon arrival that it had been canceled this year because of the year-long mourning period in observance of the death of the current maharaja's mother.

songs. Several upper-caste women told me that these songs are the reason why a large part of the festival is celebrated outside the village; once the girls return to the village, the songs are said to become less obscene, something I was unable to document. On one occasion, several months after the festival, an acquaintance began to sing some *ḍālkhāī gīt* for my tape recorder, in her own courtyard, when she was stopped by a woman running in from the village headman's house across the street. The latter told the singer, "You shouldn't be singing *burāī* (literally, badness) inside the village." The singer then went inside her house and brought out a printed pamphlet (in Oriya script) of *ḍālkhāī gīt*, presumably less obscene, but she was unable to fit the words to the *ḍālkhāī rāg* (melodic structure) that she knew.[4]

Many members of the Phuljhar folklore community attributed the declining state of the festival to the nature of these songs. Several villagers told me that "as our girls are becoming more educated, it is not proper for them to keep singing such songs." One *sarpanc* (head of a village council) who had banned celebration of *ḍālkhāī* in his village told me that the festival was *burā*, not good for "our educated girls" or for village morale. It is significant that it was the male, non-*ādivāsī* leaders of the villages with which I am acquainted who made the decision that the festival should be discontinued, not the older village women or the young, would-be festival participants, most of whom are still not educated beyond third or fourth grade.

It was difficult to make good recordings of *ḍālkhāī gīt* during the festival itself because of the loud drumming and the fact that only two girls were actually singing the words of the verses. In spontaneous nonfestival contexts, I often did not have my tape recorder with me when I heard the singing, or the singers would stop as soon as they saw a tape recorder. As a young, white, educated woman who was taking these tapes back to the United States, my interest in the tradition was not seen by educated Chhattisgarhis to be appropriate; nonliterate singers, while often pleased that I knew anything about the tradition at all, were also reluctant to sing for the tape recorder or to discuss the tradition at length when they realized that I was taking it seriously as a tradition to include in my study.

The songs I *was* able to record and hear both within and outside the festival context contained suggestive, but not explicit, sexual imagery, many of them drawing on the religious tradition of the lovers Radha and Krishna (as in the *bārahmāsā* cited earlier). I provide examples of verses sung for the tape recorder by the festival participants a week after the festival itself. Mem-

[4] When I realized several months later that I wanted to include the *ḍālkhāī* tradition in my study, I returned to this village and courtyard and asked if I could see and copy this pamphlet, but the singer said she could not find it.

bers of this social group to whom *ḍālkhāī* traditionally belongs were the only ones who sang openly for the tape recorder; but even they may have edited their songs in this situation. The first is the same *bārahmāsā* verse sung by the elderly woman at the festival.

Ki ḍālkhāī re!
The month of *caitra* is cool.
Who will bring to me my Bengali lover?
On her wrists are *campā* flowers;
On her neck a *tulsī* garland.
Krishna speaks only one word to Radha
That is beautiful to the heart.
Ki ḍālkhāī re!

Ki ḍālkhāī re!
You're only sixteen years old.
Life's purpose isn't to eat poison!
When the evening turns to night,
Speak with your eyes.
Ki ḍālkhāī re!

Ki ḍālkhāī re!
This branch is cut from the *auñlā* branch.
But your short hair isn't attractive.
Short hair needs a pair of flowers;
Short hair needs a bun to look graceful.
Keep your Oriya bun[5] tied up, my friend.
When you shake it loose, you break my heart.
Ki ḍālkhāī re!

Interestingly, the voice of these particular verses is male. He first calls out to the sixteen-year-old girl (older than any of the festival singers themselves, in this case) to realize her sexuality, not to deny it: "Life's purpose isn't to eat poison!" Separation (denial) is against the natural order, causing even the hottest month of the year, *caitra*, to be cool. In social reality, however, the girls cannot (should not) fully act on their flowering sexuality before marriage, and thus it is bittersweet, likened to the wild forest *auñla* fruit. In the third verse, the male voice calls for the girl to be a woman, to grow her hair,

[5] Oriya women wear their hair in a regionally identifiable style, with their buns pulled to the side of their head. This type of bun has a specific name, *khusā*, as distinguished from a north Indian centered bun, *jūṛā*.

but then to keep it tied up; for when it is loose (implying uncontrolled, unbounded sexuality), it breaks his heart.[6]

Other verses sung by the elderly woman during the festival itself describe the lovers Radha and Krishna waiting for each other (with another reference to hair, here binding it up in braids); the last verse describes the festival dancing:

Ki ḍālkhāī re!
Bricks, bricks, bricks,
Sitting on top of the bricks is Mahapura [Krishna].
He keeps eating his breads.
Ki ḍālkhāī re!

Ki ḍālkhāī re!
Urā, urā, urā [a grain-storage bin],
Sitting on top of the *urā* is Radha Rani.
She keeps braiding her hair.
Ki ḍālkhāī re!

Ki ḍālkhāī re!
Under the shade of the *mahuā* tree,
The shade of the *sarāgī* tree [two varieties of jungle trees],
The instruments are playing.
The young girls keep running.
Ki ḍālkhāī re!

To an outside observer, these songs do not seem any more sexually suggestive or explicit than other song traditions which are sung by the same unmarried female of this age and in this area of Chhattisgarh and which are not labeled "bad," such as the *bhojalī gīt* and *homo* repartee traditions discussed in Chapter 2. The following *homo* verse is more explicit about the sexual desire hidden in a woman's hair:

The *ḍerḥu* snake slithers,
Khasā-masā, my friend.
Her face looks old,
But there's desire hidden in her bun [*khusā*].

[6] Loosened hair in Indian society has sexual connotations unless in the context of possession or mourning. On reaching puberty, girls in north and middle India must bind their hair in braids and, upon marriage, in a single braid or a bun. In larger cities today, more and more educated women are wearing short hair, but not yet in the villages.

As important as the actual content of the songs, however, is the community's *perception* of the songs as "bad," songs that young girls were traditionally permitted to sing in this festival of reversal.

It is probable that *ḍālkhāī gīt* gained their reputation for being *burī* when they began to be sung outside the bounds of the festival, no longer restricted by ritual space and time and gender. It is difficult to document when this began to happen, but I was told that it was a recent phenomenon, perhaps coinciding with the demise of the festival. The only implicit performance restriction is that the songs be sung outside the village, although I frequently heard short phrases being sung within the village, and no specific taboo (with consequences) exists for doing so. As the context for the performance of *ḍālkhāī* songs has shifted, so have its indigenous genre designation and boundaries. In the last few years, *ḍālkhāī* has begun to be referred to less as a "*holī* festival for unmarried girls" and more as an "Oriya song," a reference that associates it with the larger Phuljhar folklore community.

The Song of Subanbali

Several days after observing the festival, I returned to the village in which it had been celebrated to make further inquiries about *ḍālkhāī*. I went first to the home of an upper-caste Kolta landowner who was an acquaintance of mine. Although the women of the household assured me that "everyone sings and dances *ḍālkhāī*," they could not give any explanation or etiological narratives for the festival; and, in fact, the girls from this caste do *not* traditionally participate in *ḍālkhāī*. The householders finally directed me to an elderly Saunra-caste *ādivāsī* widow from their village, Kaushalya Bai, who, they assured me, would be able to tell me "anything I wanted to know." They proceeded to have her called to their courtyard (so much for the fieldworker having control over how such contacts are initiated, although in retrospect, this framing of the contact gave me an indication of the authority the community had vested in the elderly storyteller).

Kaushalya Bai was a sixty-five-year-old widow who was said to have suffered many hardships in her life. She had three grown children. Her son had run away from the village, and no one knew where he lived. The village community considered both daughters to be slightly insane (*pāgal*); one had died at an early age, leaving two children for her mother to raise, and the other lived in her *sasurāl* (home of marriage). Kaushalya Bai was raising her two orphaned grandchildren and made her living by selling puffed rice and peanuts to schoolchildren in the larger neighboring village. Even though Kaushalya Bai thus occupied a somewhat marginal position in the social hierarchy of her village, she was, at the same time, highly respected for her knowledge, for being able to explain "why we do things the way we do."

Kaushalya Bai is not a professional performer in the sense that she is hired and gets paid for her performances. In fact, such professional female performers are rare in Chhattisgarh and Phuljhar.[7] Most of this singer's performances took place in front of small audiences of women; although her narratives may have religious themes, they are not usually performed as part of a larger ritual or festival but as "entertainment" (*manorañjan*). Because her repertoire of narratives and style of performance are not known to most other women of her caste and age-group, she is in this sense a specialist. Other women may be able to summarize some of the narratives she tells but not perform them. Her sister, living in another village, was similarly well known for her performance abilities and in her younger days was frequently called to sing at *ḍālkhāī* celebrations. This sister considered her own unique abilities to be a gift from the goddess, that she may serve the goddess better; she said she had no teacher or guru. Likewise, before beginning to relate segments of various etiological narratives of *ḍālkhāī*, Kaushalya Bai credited her own storytelling ability and knowledge to a vision (*darśan*) given to her by the goddess Parvati and the god Shiva.

The most complete etiological narrative Kaushalya Bai told concerned a pubescent girl who becomes determined, for unspecified reasons, to perform a sacrifice (*yagya*), an expensive ritual usually communally sponsored by upper castes and controlled by male ritual specialists. Her parents try to persuade her that she is too *young* to perform such rituals, but she is not deterred. (Note that they do not try to dissuade her because she is a *girl*.) The *yagya* she performs is called *ḍālkhāī*, during which she and her young friends sing and dance. Since that time, it is said that Oriya girls have celebrated *ḍālkhāī* once a year. The following is the narrative as reported by Kaushalya Bai:

> There was once a daughter named Raila Rani. She was the only daughter of twelve brothers who were all *ṛṣi* (sages). Her own father was Jagya Rishi, and her mother was Dalmo Bai. She was born only after her mother had completed many austerities [for the birth of a child].

[7] The year I was living in Phuljhar (1980–1981), a female professional performer in the area raised high interest and controversy in the communities in which she performed. She was a *bāhak*, a performer who sings and dances at each of the thirteen major Oriya festivals. Her two assistants were male. I heard several people say that in those villages in which a female *bāhak* performed, there would be crop failure. Nevertheless, she drew large crowds to her performances. More recently, several female *candainī* and *paṇḍvānī* professional singers have performed for radio and television, as well as making their own cassette tapes (see Chapters 6 and 7).

One day, Raila took some golden toys that her parents had given her and went to play near the temple with her friends. She made a house out of mud in which there were twelve rooms. In each room she set up a *pūjā* (worship) center for a different deity and began to worship the deities one by one.

As she was playing, Narad Muni, the ascetic of the three worlds, came by and saw Raila playing. She told him she wanted to hold a *yagya* and asked whether she would be permitted to do so. He assented. Receiving his blessings for the *yagya*, Raila returned home and asked her parents where she could perform the sacrifice.

Her parents answered her, "You are only twelve years old. How can you know what the gods and goddesses want? Don't perform a *yagya* yet." Similarly, she asked her grandparents and her brother and sister-in-law, but they, too, scolded her for wanting to perform a *yagya* at such a young age.

But Raila was not to be deterred. She went to a merchant and purchased from him some poison with which to kill herself. Then, on the shores of the Bandh Ocean, she cried out, "On which bank (*ghāṭ*) will I be liberated?" Some baby birds heard her crying and asked their mother the same question on her behalf. She answered, "If she dies on the *ghāṭ* of Lord Shiva, she will be liberated."

Hearing this, Raila ate the poison on Shiva's *ghāṭ* and died. Thereupon, a large fish swallowed her and took her to the underworld (*patāl lok*), where Barun Raja reigned. He scolded the fish for swallowing the young girl and told him to throw her up on the *ghāṭ* where he had found her.

Barun Raja removed all the poison from Raila's body and asked her why she had swallowed it. She told the king her story. He instructed her to return home where, meanwhile, her relatives and parents had become very worried. When they saw her, they celebrated her return and promised that she could perform a *yagya*. So, with her young friends, she performed this *yagya*, the one we call *ḍālkhāī*.

Kaushalya Bai provided another explanation for the festival, one in which the goddess Sarla Devi and her companions were performing a *yagya*, participating with great "joy and zeal." The young girl Raila Rani saw them while she was bathing in the tank. She returned home and told her parents that she, too, wanted to perform a *yagya*. With their consent, she proceeded. She and her young friends spent the day dancing and singing. Since then, girls perform *ḍālkhāī* once a year.

In narrating these summaries, Kaushalya Bai was distracted and seemed rushed, not completing sentences or images and frequently meandering from the subject at hand. She was assuming responsibility for transmitting knowledge about the festival, but not responsibility to an audience—in this case one composed of eight to ten girls and women who came and went from the courtyard—for an aesthetically pleasing performance. She never, in Dell Hymes's words, "broke through into performance" (1975).[8] She suggested that she come to my house in the neighboring village (the one in which she sold snacks) in a few weeks to sing for me, in a more relaxed setting, the complete story of *ḍālkhāī*. The Song of Subanbali was what she sang; we sat under a large *mahuā* tree out in the yard of my parents' bungalow; her audience members were three Christian women who worked at a girls' boarding school across the wall (one of whom was the woman who had accompanied me to the festival) and myself.

Beyond the narrative, Kaushalya Bai did not offer any further commentary on the meaning or purpose of the festival ritual. When, after the performance, one of the women complained that *ḍālkhāī* had not even been mentioned, Kaushalya Bai implied that the story in this performance mode was complete and enough, shrugging her shoulders and commenting, "That's the story!" While sharing with it a minimal narrative structure (the heroine being the only daughter of twelve brothers, a strong-willed pubescent girl who wants to perform a *yagya*, thus breaking with social expectations of a girl her age), the Song of Subanbali fully develops themes of reversal and inversion only suggested in the reported narrative. Further, unlike the etiological narratives, the fully performed narrative provides fully developed motivation for the *yagya*, which in the Song of Subanbali takes the form of a journey undertaken to defeat an evil king.

A large part of Kaushalya Bai's satisfaction with the Song of Subanbali was its performative mode. The aesthetic shaping of the narrative seemed to be, for the performer, inseparable from its content; and she was not satisfied until she had given it such shape. Two factors immediately keyed this storytelling as a semiprofessional performance: the sung recitative style (rather than the spoken prose of summarized "reports" and nonprofessional storytelling, such as folktales) and the initial frame of the invocation or salutation (*vandanā*) to the presiding deities. The *vandanā* is an indispensable frame of public professional performances in Chhattisgarh, even if the latter's primary purpose is "entertainment," whereas they are absent from privately told folktales or reported narratives such as the etiological ones mentioned above. Kaushalya Bai's *vandanā* is short, calling on the god Ram and saluting the goddesses of the festival, Sarla and Mangla Devi (note that her couplet referring

[8] Hymes makes the distinction between "knowledge *what* and knowledge *how*, or, more fully, between assumption of responsibility for knowledge of tradition and assumption of responsibility for performance" (1975:69); italics mine. He calls the latter an "authentic or authoritative performance," and the first, "illustrative, or reportive" (1975:18).

to Ram as he whose vehicle is Garuda and whose mother is Kaushalya are verbatim to those sung by the professional storyteller discussed in Chapter 5; he also calls on the goddesses Sarla and Mangla, who are associated with speech).

Kaushalya Bai sang in couplets, the second line of which either lexically repeated the first or substituted a phrase from the first with a phrase of equivalent syntactic and semantic structure; the second line expands or reinforces through exact repetition the image of the first line or completes the "sentence," seldom introducing a new image. Several of these couplets were formulas employed throughout the performance to indicate the passage of time or as transitions between the speech of one character and another, such as:

> She gave this answer, my Suban.
> She gave this reply. . . .
>
> Saying this, the barber [or other character],
> Gave this answer. . . .
>
> Hearing this, the barber,
> Hearing this, Suban. . . .

After the *vandanā*, Kaushalya Bai begins the Song of Subanbali in *medias res* with the juxtaposition of two images: the carefree young girl Suban playing with clay toys and a group of seemingly helpless kings discussing the evil Bandhiya Raja, whom she determines to defeat herself:

> At this time, Suban is speaking.
> Now, Suban is speaking.
>
> She's holding small clay dishes.
> She's holding small bamboo dishes.
>
> She went to play, oh Suban.
> She went to play.
>
> She was playing in her playhouse.
> She was playing in her playhouse.
>
> There were kings
> From the city of Bombay.

From the kingdoms of Bombay and Cuttack.
From the city of Cuttack.

. . . .

They spread out their bedding and slept,
Spread it out and slept.

Now they were talking about Bandhiya Raja,
"He is very evil.

He has defeated
Kings from all four directions.

Losing their wealth and riches,
Losing their wealth and riches,

The kings have been imprisoned.
They have been put in jail."

. . . .

Suban heard this,
And she understood.

The pubescent heroine Suban is the only daughter of king Jagya Rishi and queen Nila Rani and the only female descendant of her father's extended family of twelve brothers. Overhearing the visiting foreign kings talking about the wicked king Bandhiya Raja, who has imprisoned many other kings but whom no king has been able to defeat, Suban immediately resolves to defeat the king herself. Her parents are extremely reluctant to let her go on such a mission; they do not mention her age as a constraining factor, as do the parents of the etiological narratives, but object because she is their only daughter, too precious to risk losing. They finally give their permission, however, and help her get ready for the journey. When Suban requests permission to undertake this journey, she gives no indication as to how she proposes to defeat the evil king. But she does not take an army with her, so it is clear that she does not intend to use traditional martial means for such a defeat.

Suban's decision to set out on the journey also puts into play the reversal of traditional social roles, the central theme of both the narrative and the festival whose "story it tells." A young girl has decided to take upon herself a task rightfully belonging to kings, but one in which they have failed. For the youngest son of a king to succeed where older kings have failed is a common motif in folk narratives worldwide; in the Song of Subanbali, this role would naturally fall to Suban's older brother rather than to the adolescent girl. So, here, the reversal is carried one step further: not only does the younger succeed where elders have failed but a woman also succeeds where men have failed.

The second suggestion of reversal is the emphasis placed on the value of the female descendant. Suban's mother objects to the journey, not because she is young or female, but because she is the *only* female descendant of twelve brothers. She recounts to Suban the *tapas* (austerities) she had had to perform to receive a daughter. Such asceticism (often through the performance of a *vrat*, or "vow") is commonly performed for the birth of a first child or, if a daughter has already been born, then for the birth of a son, but rarely for a daughter specifically. Suban's father objects to the journey for the same reason, for fear of losing what he calls "his only wealth."[9]

Suban's older brother is the only person in the narrative who doubts her ability and determination to carry out her mission; and his doubts are openly based on the fact that she is female and perhaps secretly on the fact that she is usurping his role. He tries to hinder Suban by refusing his permission for her to take his wife along as a companion. He tells her:

> I won't agree to your request.
> I won't let her [Tulsa] go with you.
>
> She's from a woman's caste [*jāti*].
> Where will you take her?
>
> A woman's caste is weak.
> A woman's caste is weak.

Suban immediately proves him wrong by cursing him with the appearance of boils, burning skin, and finally an unbearable itchiness. As the symptoms begin to appear, Suban's brother not only relents but actually forces his wife on Suban. The rest of the narrative continues to disprove his position on the weakness of a woman's caste.

The gender reversal and expectations for Suban's nontraditional role are further developed in a major subplot at the beginning of the Song of Subanbali. This story is of twelve carpenter brothers who also have only "one wealth" among them, but here, it is a son. They have been commissioned to build a boat for Suban's journey, for which only a single tree in the jungle is

[9] In South Asian ritual contexts, a daughter, particularly as bride, is often called "Lakshmi," the goddess of wealth, but in north and central India, this wealth is transferred to another family upon the daughter's marriage. It is sons who provide the hope for both material wealth and continuity of the lineage. If there is only one daughter among many sons, however, she is usually highly valued in her natal family.

appropriate (identified for the carpenters by a female vulture). Their axes are dulled after numerous attempts at cutting down the tree, and the carpenters are finally convinced that they must sacrifice their only male descendant before the tree will yield to them. Ultimately, the young boy is ritually sacrificed, without protest, and the tree gives in to their axes. When Suban learns of the boy's sacrifice, she brings him back to life. The singer later told me that Suban was an *apsara* (celestial nymph) and therefore had such power; however, nowhere else in the narrative is she given this kind of supernatural power.

The subplot is not crucial to narrative progression or continuity, since the boat is not mentioned again in the rest of the song; and Suban travels to Bandhi Desh by land, "crossing and destroying fields," rather than by water. The carpenter's story is, however, integral to Kaushalya Bai's aesthetic shaping of the narrative, drawing Suban's character in a way in which straight description could not. The subplot structurally mirrors and inverts the central plot. Both the carpenters' son and Suban are the "only wealth" of twelve brothers; but the son is the sacrifice, whereas Suban, the daughter, is the sacrificer (after his captivity, Bandhiya Raja fears *he* will be literally sacrificed; instead, he is brought out to the courtyard to be figuratively sacrificed by means of his marriage to Suban). The carpenter's son is not given a name and has no individual personality; he is passive, seen and not heard, ready to be sacrificed without protest. This image of the passive male, with no "voice," dramatically frames and delineates the determination, strength of will, and active nature of the heroine Suban.

Subanbali borrows male clothing from her maternal grandfather and disguises herself as a young merchant for her adventure. The grandfather does not express hesitation over Suban's ability to undertake the task at hand but worries that, dressed in his clothes, she may act in some impure way (perhaps sexually impure) that will reflect back on him. Suban answers him confidently:

> If I do anything impure, cut off my head,
> Cut out my tongue.
>
> My eyes will burst.
> My life breath will leave me.

Suban takes her sister-in-law, Tulsa Rani, as her "wife" and travel companion. When she reaches the kingdom of Bandhiya Raja, the king's barber sees the traveling couple and returns to the king's court to report that he has just seen the most beautiful woman (Tulsa Rani), whom the king must have as his wife. The king and barber plot how they can kill the woman's "husband," Subanbali, in order to gain access to his wife. The barber first approaches Subanbali's camp with an offer to shave her, intending to slit her throat in the process (a motif identified by Stith Thompson [1946] in tale type 910C—Think Carefully Before You Begin a Task). But Suban refuses, saying she never lets a stranger shave her. Unthwarted, the barber returns to tell her that the king wants to form a ritual friendship (*mahāprasād*) with her. Suban tries to resist this suggestion, for she knows the friendship will put her under obligation to the king. But she can think of no excuse, and the friendship is solemnized through the exchange of gifts.

Mahāprasād friendships in Chhattisgarh are formed between members of the same sex but of different castes and are a favorite narrative motif and plot-building technique in the folklore of the region.[10] Rather than using the friendship simply to forward the plot, however, as a less-skilled storyteller might have done, Kaushalya Bai carefully details the preparations for the ritual, through which she further builds the character of the participants and sets up the unequal power relations between the two friends. Suban does more than is required of her in the ritual, whereas Bandhiya Raja carries out only the minimal requirements: she buys the most expensive cloth to exchange with the king (two lengths instead of one), a whole bag full of sweets, five pieces of betelnut, and five coconuts. Bandhiya Raja, on the other hand, buys only one of each required gift. The officiating Brahmin priest's warning, "If friends speak ill of each other / They will turn into tadpoles," takes on special significance given that the king has just tried to kill Suban. Although the heroine is not physically bound as a prisoner in the kingdom of Bandhi Desh, as other kings have been, she *is* temporarily bound by this *mahāprasād* friendship.

As Suban predicts, Bandhiya Raja acts quickly to force her to fulfill the obligation of doing whatever is asked by a ritual friend, in this case placing before her three tasks she must complete or be killed: to bring tiger's milk to the king, to jump over a wide pit, and to pick up two gunnysacks full of mustard seeds between evening and dawn. Suban succeeds in completing each of these, but only with the sage advice of the experienced, married Tulsa Rani. Tulsa gives her the precise words with which to speak to the tiger, addressing the tiger as "older mother," calming the hungry animal's wild nature through appeal to her sense of kinship duty and obligation (much the same as those for *mahāprasād*), and explaining that the milk is necessary for her mother's fast—who could refuse such a request? Tulsa gives

[10] See also the use of *mahāprasād* as a plot-building technique in the narrative of the *kathānī kūhā* of Chapter 5.

Suban a magic whistle to enable her to jump across the pit; and she calls on her communicative powers with the pigeon kingdom to ask the pigeon king to send five hundred thousand pigeons to help Suban pick up the mustard seeds.

When the test of the tasks fails to defeat his rival, Bandhiya Raja invites Subanbali to play dice with him. She stakes and loses all her possessions in the dicing; in the end, she is forced to put up Tulsa Rani as her stake in the game. At this point Tulsa Rani gives Suban the half-cowrie shell with which Suban's own brother had won Tulsa as bride; and with this auspicious shell, Suban begins a winning streak. She continues to defeat the king until he must put up his own person as stake, and Bandhiya Raja loses that final game as well. Subanbali ties him up like an animal and returns with him to her father's kingdom.

Once in Suban's home kingdom, Bandhiya Raja is ritually bathed and dressed in white; he fears he is being prepared for execution. Instead, when he is brought out of the horse's stable in which he had been imprisoned, he sees he has been prepared not for execution but for his marriage to Subanbali. After the wedding, Suban breaks with the norm by staying in her father's kingdom as his heir (usurping her brother's rightful position), rather than going to live in her in-laws' home (*sasurāl*).

As a young girl, Suban dons a male disguise to defeat Bandhiya Raja, but she ultimately rules the kingdom as a married *woman*. The significance of this gender reversal becomes clearer when we look more carefully at the disguise itself and how it is used in this narrative, framed by the festival of *ḍālkhāī*. Disguise—concealed identity—is an integral part of many festivals of reversal around the world, as well as literary and folk narrative traditions; it almost always implies a freedom of movement and/or action not traditionally available to the festival participants or narrative character.

Male characters in female disguise often use their new freedom of movement to gain access to women's quarters; female characters most frequently appropriate male disguise for greater mobility in the "outside"/public world. Such is the case of the *vīrāṅganā* studied by Kathryn Hansen, which are female mythical and historic figures who manifest qualities of *vīrya*, or male heroism. Historically, these women have been warrior queens, often taught the martial arts by their fathers, who rule as regents of the kingdom (such as Razia Sultana in the thirteenth century and the Rani of Jhansi in the nineteenth century). The *vīrāṅganā* is identified by male dress and an iconography that portrays her carrying a sword and riding a horse into battle. Such figures reappear in the Hindi folk drama form of *nauṭaṅkī* and again in contemporary figures such as the bandit queen Phulan Devi (Hansen 1988). The use of male disguise by our heroine fits this model only insofar as it enables mobility, but otherwise, Suban's disguise stands in distinct contrast. She finally triumphs over Bandhiya Raja and rules because of her own female qualities, not because of male, royal, or martial disguise.

Disguise not only conceals identity, thereby giving freedom of movement, but also reveals—reveals the social constraints under which the disguised persons normally live. In the case of the Afghan storytellers studied by Margaret Mills, differences in the use of the disguise motif by male and female narrators reveal differences in male and female perceptions of such social constraints and mobility.[11] Disguise may also reveal aspects of character or society that are generally not visible or openly articulated (see Don Handelman's analysis of Christmas mumming in Newfoundland, 1990:155–159). In their study of festivals of reversal in the West Indies and Nova Scotia, Roger Abrahams and Richard Bauman (1978) suggest that disguise and inversion may reveal an opposition or alternative to "ideal" norms that is continually present at some level, both in tension with and integrated into the dominant ideology of the society.

In my work with Chhattisgarhi and Oriya folk narratives, disguise is a common motif in both male- and female-narrated tales and in each case serves slightly different narrative and thematic functions. In a segment of the Chhattisgarhi oral epic *candainī* (discussed in Chapter 6) performed by a male Satnami singer of low caste, there is a wonderful scene in which the hero and heroine, on their elopement journey, are traveling through an all-female kingdom. The hero goes into a town to buy *pān* (betel leaf) and is abducted by the female *pān*-seller. She dresses him in a sari so that he will not be discovered and then proceeds to try to force him to marry her. Ultimately, the heroine comes to find him and frees him through a dicing game with the *pān*-seller. The hero's disguise conceals his male identity and thus ensures his safety in a kingdom of women only; but on another level, the disguise is humiliating and concretely reveals his own weakness, his inability to save himself through either traditional male/martial means or by means more frequently associated with women (whose disguise he has taken) and his own nonmartial caste—his wits and ingenuity. In this epic the connotations of the sari, female disguise, are multiple; a female disguise forced on the helpless hero in a narrative context in which the heroine is active, decisive, ingenious, and continually comes to the hero's rescue challenges the dominant (brah-

[11] Mills found that although male narrators tend to avoid active female characters altogether, when they *do* incorporate them into their narratives, they often cast them in masculine disguise. She speculates that male narrators may see more options for their characters if they are given a male disguise. In contrast, female narrators use the disguise motif much less; their female characters seem to be able to accomplish more as women (particularly with the availability of the veil) than disguised as men (Mills 1985:195).

minic) ideological representation of women as needing to be protected by an authoritative male.

In the Song of Subanbali, too, the heroine's male disguise both conceals and reveals. The freedom of movement and action given to her through use of male disguise makes apparent the restrictions normally placed on the movements in the public sphere of a woman in traditional Chhattisgarhi-Oriya society. Although her gender was restrictive to Suban, however, it was as a *daughter* that Suban was given reluctant permission by her parents to set forth on her adventure; the male disguise was her own decision. The action and mobility that the disguise allowed Subanbali reveal the courage and ingenuity she possessed as a woman and call into question the necessity for the initial traditional restrictions placed on women that necessitated the disguise.

Suban's disguise is not only one of gender but also a socioeconomic one. She takes the guise of a poor merchant's son, rather than that of a prince; a disguise is not arbitrarily chosen. It accentuates freedom of movement: a merchant has the freedom as well as the necessity to travel widely, even beyond the bounds of his own country. Further, as a merchant, expectations of traditional male options of *militarily* defeating Bandhiya Raja are eliminated. The disguise raises expectations that Suban's victory will be accomplished through means of trickery, wit, and wisdom, skills often attributed to both traders *and* women in Indian folktales.

Once Suban reaches the kingdom of Bandhiya Raja, because of the ritual friendship and its obligations, the prerogative for initiating action is no longer hers; this is the only time she is "bound." The king gives her a series of tasks that she must complete or risk losing her life. The traditional tale type is that of a prince who performs certain tasks to win the hand of a princess, tasks usually set forth by the princess's father. Stith Thompson identifies an inverted subtype of this tale, a type that he calls "The Tasks," in which the king covets the hero's wife and sets out tasks to destroy the hero, tasks almost identical to those in our narrative:

> (a) The king covets the wife and, on the advice of an evil counselor, usually a barber, assigns the hero tasks in which the hero succeeds through the help of his wife; (b) Quest for a wonder flower; (c) To bring tiger's milk; (d) Tasks requiring great speed: reap a field of grain in one night; build a tank or building in one night, etc., (e) other tasks (Thompson and Roberts 1960:68).

In the Song of Subanbali, the tale type is further complicated through the disguise: a princess, Suban, wins the *king*, Bandhiya Raja, in marriage through the successful completion of tasks, tasks that have been set forth by the same king in *his* effort to win the hand of Tulsa Rani, the "wife" of Suban. In this radical variation of the tale type, it is also the "wife," Tulsa Rani, who helps the "hero," Subanbali. On the level of disguise, the narrative affirms the wisdom of "wife"; Suban as husband offers few solutions to the successful completion of any of the tasks. On the level of their true identities, Suban as a pubescent daughter is receiving wise counsel from a married woman. Tulsa Rani repeatedly reprimands Suban for disobeying the word of her parents, of tradition:

> "You didn't obey the word of your mother.
> You didn't obey the word of your father.
>
> To the cities and towns, my Suban,
> They forbade you to go.
>
> The word of your grandmother, the word of your grandfather,
> The word of your brother.
>
> You didn't listen to the word of anyone.
> You didn't listen to the word of anyone.
>
> You came with one mind.
> You came with one mind, my Suban.
>
> Now you're being punished.
> Now you're being punished.[12]

But then, after saying that *she* will be blamed if anything happens to Suban,

[12] Words very close to these are spoken by the princess in the narrative told by the *kathānī kūhā* of Chapter 5, a princess who has gotten pregnant after hiding her lover in the palace for several months. The immediate context of these lines is a lamentation sung by the princess when she discovers that her husband has abandoned her in the forest and her living baby has been exchanged for a dead one:

> Why hasn't Yama [god of death] eaten me?
> I didn't obey my mother's words.
> I didn't obey my father's words.
> I didn't obey my husband's words.
> I listened only to myself, lord.
> Where did my lord go?

However, as with Subanbali, the princess is ultimately rewarded for her defiance; she is reunited with her husband after many misadventures, and they inherit the kingdoms of both sets of parents.

Tulsa reassures her that she will find a way to get Suban out of her predicament; she should not worry. Tulsa and the narrative itself both acknowledge the difficulties of and then affirm and reward Suban's defiance against traditional gender roles. The tasks and in a broader sense the journey represent a rite of passage for the young Suban, one through which she acquires new identity and wisdom. She embarks on the journey as a young girl playing with clay toys outside the foreign kings' encampment and returns ready to get married and rule her father's kingdom.

When Bandhiya Raja fails to kill Suban and win Tulsa Rani as his bride through his imposition of tasks, he makes one last effort by proposing to play the dice game with Suban. Dicing is, of course, a strong motif in both the South Asian classical and folk contexts, one that often suggests negotiation, revelation, and/or articulation of gender identities and roles. Examples include the crucial dicing scene in the Mahabharata in which the Pandavas' wife Draupadi is finally put up as stake and humiliated by Duryodhan, the god Shiva dicing with his consort Parvati,[13] and folk narrative scenes such as the *candainī* dicing described above. In the dicing scene in the Song of Subanbali, the heroine plays the traditional male role in dicing for a woman, in this case the bride her *own* brother had won through dicing. After losing everything except Tulsa Rani and with the latter's help, Suban begins a winning streak and succeeds in winning the person of Bandhiya Raja himself.

Once Suban defeats Bandhiya Raja, she binds him like an animal, putting a rope through his nose. On reaching her father's kingdom, she has her servants tie him up in the stable and give him only horse feed to eat. He is then bathed and oiled, dressed in white, and brought to the courtyard of the king, Suban's father. Bandhiya Raja fears he has been prepared for execution; however, the courtyard is decorated for a wedding—his wedding to Suban. Bandhiya Raja's fear is not unlike that of many young Chhattisgarhi brides as they leave their natal homes and move into a totally strange household and who frequently articulate their impending marriage as a kind of death.

Chhattisgarhi and Oriya marriage rituals are filled with images of female binding.[14] An Oriya village bride is brought into the marriage courtyard wearing a fancy wedding sari, but with a traditional handloomed cotton sari given by the bridegroom's family weighing heavily on her shoulders and head. She never lifts her face, nor is it visible, throughout the ceremony. She

[13] See Handelman and Shulman (in press) for a full discussion of dicing in the complex Shiva myth.

[14] See essays in *The Powers of Tamil Women* (Wadley 1980) by David, Reynolds, and Wadley for examples of female binding and control in both south and north India, particularly their discussions of the south Indian *tāli* (wedding necklace).

is literally bound to her husband when the end of her sari is tied to the end of his shoulder cloth, and she follows him in circumambulation around the sacred fire. For a woman in Chhattisgarh, marriage may be marked by five visible signs, the first three having connotations of binding: glass bangles, ankle bracelets, toe rings, vermilion powder in her part (*sindūr*), and a mark of vermilion on her forehead (*bindī*). The minimal sign of marriage is the bangles. When a woman's husband dies, she breaks her bangles; she is no longer "bound" through marriage, and her presence is considered to be inauspicious at many rituals. Among those castes that permit the remarriage of widows in Chhattisgarh, the second marriage, solemnized through a simple ritual, is often called *cuṛī pahanānā*, or "to put on bangles" (Babb 1975:82). Further, a mature woman's hair should always remain bound, except under ritually controlled contexts of mourning and possession, and her sari itself can be seen as binding.

Against these prevalent images of female binding, the reverse image of male binding, particularly of a king, is striking. Bandhiya Raja is ritually bathed, dressed, and bound like a Chhattisgarhi bride. The king's name, "Bandhiya," literally can mean either "one who binds" or "one who is bound." By the end of the narrative, Bandhiya Raja has moved from position of the binder to the bound. The narrative begins with a conversation about a king who has imprisoned other kings. It ends with that same king himself being bound—not by another king but by a young woman, his future bride. The final reversal in the Song of Subanbali occurs after the marriage ceremony, when Suban, rather than her brother, is made heir to her father's kingdom.

Ḍālkhāī as a Tradition of Initiation

Let's return now to the inter-"textual" relationship between the festival tradition of *ḍālkhāī* and the Song of Subanbali, considering the ritual and narrative as metacommentaries on each other. As Kaushalya Bai perceived when she told the Song of Subanbali as the story of *ḍālkhāī,* the narrative imaginatively develops the festival's ethos in a way in which the reported etiological narratives were unable to do. Similarly, without the festival context having been given for the Song of Subanbali, we may well have interpreted it differently.

While both *ḍālkhāī* and the Song of Subanbali identify and contribute to the identity of an independent social category of unmarried girls, unlike *homo* and *bhojalī* they are also initiatory traditions, rites of passage. The festival participants and narrative heroine begin as pubescent girls whose identities shift to brides or potential brides. The narrative itself ends in marriage; through the half-saris worn in the dance, the festival suggests the girls have now reached marriageable age (the age of the participants having increased with the increasing age of marriage for Oriya girls). Themes and images of reversal in both the festival and the narrative traditions also suggest that they serve as rites of passage (I'm thinking specifically of Arnold van Gennep's stages of such rituals: separation, liminality, and reintegration, with the liminal stage often characterized by reversal or inversion). The most complete, dramatic reversals occur when the girls are outside the geographic loci of traditional roles and expectations prescribed for them by the upper-caste, dominant discourse of eastern Chhattisgarh: outside the village (on the boundaries of the jungle) and outside the home kingdom, respectively. The narrative reversal is not circumscribed by the boundaries of the foreign kingdom, however, but is sustained after the heroine returns home. In the Song of Subanbali, although the *disguise* is limited to the journey, the freedoms and power Suban has acquired using that disguise are not restricted by liminal time and space. When she drops the male disguise, Suban returns to her father's kingdom, now a new bride *and* female ruler of the land.

Similarly, looking at the festival through the commentary of the narrative, although relaxation or reversal of norms is limited to ritually bound time and place, presumably the young participants, like Suban, are not left unchanged. They have participated in a ritual and imaginative space that has permitted them to express openly and joyfully an alternative to their traditionally prescribed female roles. These traditions transmit an important representation of women, constructed *by* women, to a new generation—of brave daughters—a representation that both reflects and continues to inform the constructions of their female world. As Teresa de Lauretis asserts, "The representation of gender *is* its construction" (1987:33).

As narrative, the Song of Subanbali is able to explore further and make more explicit the implications of the reversals only suggested in the festival ritual tradition of *ḍālkhāī*, themes of female freedom, independence, and wisdom. In *ḍālkhāī*, while the girls are permitted to step outside their traditional female roles, sing "bad songs," and mock their male superiors, the male-female hierarchy is not explicitly reversed. In the narrative, the hierarchy itself is shaken and brought down. Several male characters find themselves in what might be considered traditional female roles. And Suban is not only granted freedom of movement and action but also, first through disguise and then under her own identity, carries out actions specifically belonging to the male sphere. Unlike the *vīrāṅganā* (female warrior in male disguise) of Indian historical accounts and popular culture, ultimately Suban transforms the male role into a female one by casting off her male disguise: this is who *she* is.

As traditions of reversal and inversion, *ḍālkhāī* and the Song of Subanbali are more than what Max Gluckman (1954) has called a "steam-valve" for, in this case, the fantasies of a young, repressed female population. The festival and narrative reveal, question, and comment on an existing social order largely dominated by a brahminic, male-controlled discourse, a discourse becoming louder and more singular in Phuljhar and Chhattisgarh with increased mass media and literacy, as the region becomes less geographically and culturally isolated. But their potential appears to be more than that of revalidating those very structures; they are "cracks of resistance." As James Fernandez writes, "To point out incongruities is to suggest [the possibility of] their transcendence" (1986:291).[15] Although they may not directly challenge existing social and cultural structures, the very performance of an alternative may itself become subversive. Perhaps it is this power of performance that the village male elders recognize when they say, "Our educated girls shouldn't be doing these things," and banned celebration of the festival.[16]

As the performance of the tradition of *ḍālkhāī* is shifting, its songs being usurped by male members of the folklore community and taken outside its ritual bounds, the genre has lost its power and authority for the female community with which it was traditionally associated. It is no longer an acceptable, empowering tradition of initiation for lower- or *ādivāsī*-caste women but has shifted to reflect a male representation of women, whose sexuality must be bound; it is this representation that identifies the *ḍālkhāī git* as *burī* (bad or vulgar). At the same time, with the increase of literacy and mass media technology, fewer women are learning and transmitting oral narratives such as the Song of Subanbali, particularly when they are not "crucial" to a particular ritual (as are *vrat kathā*, stories told at rituals of fasting); Kaushalya Bai said she had taught her song to no one.[17] But folklore

[15] Reference in Raheja and Gold 1994:105.

[16] Don Handelman (1990:52–53) suggests that "the inversion of a stratified order is still a discourse about that very order of stratification that is inverted. . . . [But] the phenomenon that is inverted posits limits to which the inversion can go. Beyond this, the inversion no longer is true to its foundation-for-form: it is no longer an inversion, but becomes another phenomenon in its own right. If there is the potential for transformation through inversion, then this is likely to happen only when inversion exceeds itself and breaks its connectivity to the phenomenon it inverts—thereby creating a new phenomenon." In this case, the Song of Subanbali seems to have transcended these limits of inversion/reversal, whereas the festival itself only suggested this potential.

[17] Raheja and Gold write that in northern India, wedding music on cassettes and radio are literally silencing women's wedding songs at the ritual (1994:191).

has never been static: existing genres shift and even die (as the *ḍālkhāī* festival itself), and new contexts and forms continue to emerge (even if not always in the rather "purist" forms that some folklorists try to hang on to). The *suā nāc* tradition examined in the next chapter suggests the flexibility of folklore genres to adapt to newly emerging contexts and the creativity of their performers to find contexts in which to find voice and assert their identity.

CHAPTER 4

Land of Wealth, Land of Famine: The "Parrot Dance" in Ritual and Narrative *Suā Nāc*

The undulating circle of *suā nāc* (literally, parrot dance) female dancers on village main streets, in the courtyards of wealthy landowners, and even in town commercial districts has traditionally been as inherent to the landscape of a Chhattisgarhi harvest as are images of women, carrying hand scythes, walking to the ripened paddy fields, bullock carts piled high with cut grain, and solitary men sweeping back and forth with large winnowing baskets over the thrashed paddy. The harvest is truly transformed into ritual wealth, the goddess Lakshmi herself, only through the blessings of these *suā* dancers. When I first began asking about the tradition in the Phuljhar village in which I lived, asking where I might find dancers, I was frequently answered with some variant of, "But they *have* to come to give their blessing," or "Of course they'll come." This auspicious public context of the dance is what both Chhattisgarhi villagers and city dwellers refer to when talking about the genre. It is often called a "Chhattisgarhi" custom, a tradition whose performance involves a wide spectrum of rural Chhattisgarhi society: the landowning patrons, land-working dancers, and villagewide audiences. On several occasions, male villagers of both high and lower castes used the inclusive and plural "we" when responding to my questions about the tradition, with statements such as, "Yes, we dance the *suā nāc*," although literally, they performed neither the dance nor the accompanying song tradition. These male respondents identified with the *suā nāc*, when speaking to someone from outside the folklore community, on a level on which they never did with other female performance genres.

The dancers themselves more often claim the tradition to be specifically *ādivāsī* (tribal), since most of the dancers come from *ādivāsī* castes. When they talk about the dance, they speak less of the auspicious blessings it confers than of the vows that they have fulfilled by joining a dance troupe or the money that the dance is raising for their own *ādivāsī gaurā* festival. As *ādivāsī* castes have moved into towns and cities to work as daily-wage laborers, *bīṛī*-rolling workers, brick makers, and so forth, the dance has become somewhat distanced from the direct association with the harvested paddy. Here, *suā* troupes dance in front of shops in commercial neighborhoods, expecting shopkeepers to make some small cash donation to be used toward *gaurā* celebrations.

However, the genre is more flexible than its public performance, classification, and oral commentary suggest. The song tradition accompanying the dance is also sung outside the dance context, yet it is still called *suā nāc*. Although this performance context was never directly mentioned by inhabitants of the region in discussions of the *suā nāc* or other folklore genres, its familiar melodic introduction, "*tārī hārī nā nā mor nārī hār nā nā re suānā*" (semantically empty syllables used to introduce the melodic structure of the song), is frequently heard from women transplanting rice in the fields, walking to the local market, or gathered in a friend's courtyard on a free afternoon. In this context, the social category to whom performance of the song tradition is available, as well as its primary audience, is limited to women but extends to include non-*ādivāsī*, though still low-caste and nonliterate, women.

The emphasis and dominant imagery of the *suā nāc* shifts dramatically as it is performed in these two variant settings. As a dance tradition, the *suā nāc* establishes a communicative channel between high-status patrons and relatively low-status dancers. Emphasis is placed on the channel itself, the dance, and the nonverbal, iconographic message of the tradition, one reinforcing a public image of women as fertile, auspicious, and life-giving. In contrast, in the *suā nāc* as a song tradition sung by women to other women of their own social and economic status, between whom a communicative channel is assumed to be already present, the focus shifts to the verbal message of the text. This verbal message gives voice to the private suffering to which a woman is born, a startling contrast from the positive nonverbal images of the dance. However, just as these two facets are part of the larger, complex mosaic of being female in Chhattisgarh, so, too, their channels of communication in the *suā nāc*—the dance and the song tradition—are categorized together, both contributing to the definition and interpretive frames of the genre *suā nāc*. Images of the dance are never distant from the minds of the performers of the song tradition, and the dancers sing many of these same verbal texts while performing the *suā nāc*.[1]

The Dance

The general opinion of educated residents of the villages and towns in which I observed the *suā nāc* is that the tradition originated among Chhattisgarh's *ādivāsī* tribes, particularly the Gonds, who lived in the hills bounding the region before immigrating to the plains. In the 1930s and 1940s, Verrier Elwin and Shamrao Hivale documented the tradition among the Gonds of the Maikal Hills west of Chhattisgarh (Elwin and Hivale 1944:29–58). They report that the *suā nāc* was danced during the harvest months of November and December but may not necessarily have been associated with the harvest itself. Gond women danced the *suā nāc* for audiences of their own villages, as well as in a semicompetitive spirit in neighboring villages. When members of these tribal populations immigrated to the central plains of Chhattisgarh and became integrated into the Hindu caste system, they brought with them their oral traditions. Many of these were adapted to new contexts of performance, and the *suā nāc* was one. It became specifically associated with the harvest and moved into a hierarchical setting in which tribal-caste women dance in the courtyards or on the lanes in front of the homes of higher-caste large landowners.

Today, *suā nāc* dancers in Chhattisgarh are still drawn exclusively from these *ādivāsī* castes, and the tradition remains particularly closely associated with the Gonds. The dancers say that the primary reason for the *suā nāc* is to raise money for the nine-day *ādivāsī* festival called *gaurā*, which celebrates the wedding of the god Shiva and his consort Parvati in the Hindu lunar month of *kārtik* (October–November). The money collected by the dancers is used to make elaborate clay images of various deities for the festival, alongside of which is also placed the *suā nāc* parrot around which the women have danced.[2] The lead dancer of one *suā nāc* troupe I observed in Phuljhar was a

[1] Ironically, although the indigenous categorization of and commentary about the *suā nāc* centers primarily on the dance, with little being said about the sung words, printed collections of Chhattisgarhi folklore give us the decontextualized words alone, with no or very little contextual framing. Reading these gives us few indications of how the *suā nāc* as dance might be experienced.

[2] The Bhinjwar-caste *gaurā* celebrations I observed in Phuljhar included images of Shiva and Parvati (as bridegroom and bride), the goddess Durga riding her tiger, the Mahabharata hero Bhim carrying his club (whose inclusion in the procession of images no participant could explain to me), the village guardian deity Thakur Dev, and a group of wild animals arranged

Bhinjwar-caste woman who had made a year-long vow to serve the goddess after the birth of a son. Her vow culminated in the *gaurā* festival, during which the goddess possesses many of the participants. She and the other members of her *suā* troupe played a key role in the festival, carrying the images of the deities in procession to the site of the festival celebration and again to the river to be immersed at the end of the festivities; they were also among the first of the festival participants to become possessed. Several higher-caste women told me that this factor of *gaurā* goddess possession and the close association of *gaurā* and *suā nāc* were why high-caste women did not dance the *suā nāc*.

A *suā nāc* troupe usually consists of eight to twelve women, ranging between the ages of fourteen and forty, from a single neighborhood and of a single *jāti*. The women begin and end their dance performances in their own village, moving out in between to neighboring villages in which they have some kind of kinship, caste, or economic relationships. In their own villages, they may dance and sing in open lanes with no particular patron, as well as in the homes of landowners. In neighboring villages, however, they usually limit their performance to the homes of large landowners, where they dance in front of the entrances to their houses or in the courtyards of the homes. In the primarily Oriya-speaking Phuljhar village in which I lived during the fall of 1980, the dance troupe that came through the village consisted of twelve Chhattisgarhi Bhinjwar-caste women from a village four or five miles away. The Oriya village headman of the performance village was also the largest landowner in the village of the dancers, and he spent equal time in both villages; the dancers were laborers on his land. This link between the two villages, between headman and dancers, was concretely expressed when they both began and ended their dance sequence at his house, the first time in the courtyard and the second time on the street passing in front of his verandah. Between these two segments, the dancers performed in five other courtyards of Oriya, Kolta-caste landowners.[3]

The *suā nāc* is a circle dance that centers around one or more simple clay images of a parrot made by the dancers themselves. The parrot sits in a basket

---

on a small stool. In the Raipur plains, I observed *gaurā* in an urban Gond neighborhood, in which there were only three images: Shiva and Parvati and the Ramayana monkey devotee Hanuman, with his tail afire (a burning kerosene-soaked rag). When I told these Gond celebrants about the array of figures I had seen in Phuljhar, they informed me that in those areas where Raj Gonds (landowning Gonds) had traditionally sponsored the festival, such as Phuljhar, the festival was more "grandly" (*dhūm-dhām se*) celebrated.

[3] No Chhattisgarhi *ādivāsī* castes lived in this particular village, thus it did not have its own *suā nāc* troupe.

Suā nāc dancers, Phuljhar.

into which householder patrons place their grain and cash contributions; a less common practice today, although said to have been more standard "in the old days," is for the dancers to place the parrot image on the head of an unmarried girl and dance around her. The dance movement is a simple, deep swaying up and down from the waist and a slow side step with the feet. The dancers extend their arms to their sides at a forty-five-degree angle and bring them together in front of them, clapping their hands as they bend forward. The swaying movement is called *jhūpnā* in the local Chhattisgarhi dialect, the same word used to describe a similar, but less controlled, movement by persons possessed by the goddess in the *gaurā* festival. The terminological identification of the possession and dance movements again suggests the close relationship between the *gaurā* festival tradition and the *suā nāc.*

Each dance troupe is divided into two groups that sing antiphonally. Most verses are sung four times, introduced by the lead dancer's group, repeated by the second group, and then repeated again by both groups. Although the performance in each household is a complete unit, there is also certain continuity between performances in a given village. I shall, therefore, refer to performances in each household as "segments" and the entire village performance as a "sequence." Most individual verses are fixed (memorized), but the choice of verses within particular segments and sequences is creative, flexible, and adaptive to specific performance contexts.

The village *suā nāc* audience is multilayered. The immediate patrons of the dance are female members of the landowning household in whose home the performance is taking place, with the eldest active female householder giving grain contributions to the dancers. Often an elderly patriarch of the household is also present in the courtyard, but the dancers do not dance "for" him. When the performance takes place on the street instead of in the courtyard, other male members of the household are often sitting on the verandah and become part of the primary audience. If the village has some kind of tea stall or farmers' cooperative, the troupe may dance in front of it, and the male proprietor and customers then become the primary audience for that segment. The *suā nāc*'s secondary audience, present within audio if not visual range, consists of male and female passersby, neighbors to the primary-patron landowners, and lower-caste village women who join the ubiquitous crowds of children that follow the dancers from house to house.

As they enter each household, the dancers traditionally frame the performance segment with an introductory verse announcing their arrival, often a variation on the following: "How should we enter it, the entrance of your house, / The entrance of your house, of your house?" Only the performance segment in the Phuljhar village headman's courtyard, mentioned above, began without the familiar framing verse; here the dancers began singing only when they were already in the courtyard, with the line, "*Suānā*, oh parrot, where did you take incarnation?" The answer to the question was found in the dance itself and in the visible clay image of the parrot rather than in the song text. With this question, the women "seated," or established, the parrot in the village in a manner similar to that in which the temporary clay image of a deity is "seated," or installed for worship, during a festival. The parrot had taken incarnation in that very village and was the focal point of the dance.

Suā nāc troupes dance for five to ten minutes in each house before the female householder brings out a winnowing basket filled with grain and pours it into the basket around which the troupe has been dancing. She may also contribute a one- or two-rupee note. If an older male member of the household is present, the dancers expect and even petition a monetary contribution from him as well, one troupe going so far as to wake him from a nap to do so. The grain donations, however, are always made by a woman; male patrons give only money, a differentiation between male and female gift giving typical throughout India. Cash gifting by individuals in this kind of ritual context is a relatively new phenomenon in India and, while practically valued by the dancers, is not enough; minimally, a measure of grain must be given. The prosperity of the household, here in the form of grain, is closely associated with the fertility of the fields, the goddess of wealth (Lakshmi), and female fertility.

By deciding when she will bring out her donation to the troupe, the female householder / patron effectively determines the length of the performance segment in her own courtyard. After appropriate donations have been made, the dancers sing a benedictory verse sequence in which they confer blessings upon the household: traditional blessings for wealth, long life, and progeny. An example, with all the verse repetitions, follows (the word *suānā* in this and other examples is a term of address to the parrot):[4]

Group 1: Mother, as you receive and give,
Suānā, so will you receive blessings.
Suānā, so will you receive blessings.

Group 2: Mother, as you receive and give,
Suānā, so will you receive blessings.
Suānā, so will you receive blessings.

Group 1: Mother, as you receive and give,
Suānā, so will you receive blessings.
Suānā, so will you receive blessings.

Group 2: Mother, as you receive and give,
Suānā, so will you receive blessings.
Suānā, so will you receive blessings.

Group 1: May your house be filled with grain and wealth.
Suānā, mother may you live one *lākh* of years.
Suānā, mother may you live one *lākh* of years.

Group 2: May your house be filled with grain and wealth.
Suānā, mother may you live one *lākh* of years.
Suānā, mother may you live one *lākh* of years.

[4] Hereafter, all the repetitions of each verse will not be given in the text of the chapter; but the reader should remember that this highly repetitive style is characteristic of the dance-song performance and contributes to the performative focus being placed on the channel of the song words rather than on their semantic meaning.

Group 1: May your house be filled with grain and wealth.
Suānā, mother may you live one *lākh* of years.
Suānā, mother may you live one *lākh* of years.

Group 2: May your house be filled with grain and wealth.
Suānā, mother may you live one *lākh* of years.
Suānā, mother may you live one *lākh* of years.

Group 1: May your young son get married.
Suānā, may a grandson play in your lap.
Suānā, may a grandson play in your lap.

Group 2: May your young son get married.
Suānā, may a grandson play in your lap.
Suānā, may a grandson play in your lap.

Group 1: May your young son get married.
Suānā, may a grandson play in your lap.
Suānā, may a grandson play in your lap.

Group 2: May your young son get married.
Suānā, may a grandson play in your lap.
Suānā, may a grandson play in your lap.

The blessing completes the performance segment and the exchange between dancers and patron in each household.[5]

These exchanges do not, however, always take place this smoothly. In one courtyard, after the performers had been dancing considerably longer than usual and the householder had still not made her contribution, they expressed their frustration in song (verses that the secondary audience of women and children found highly amusing and during whose performance they laughed and giggled):

Why did we come to the big house, the big house?
Suānā, the big house which has broken hearts.
Yogi and renunciants come everyday, everyday;
Suānā, we come only once a year.

[5] *Suā nāc* dancers are not the only performers to bring such blessings to Chhattisgarhi households. Male cowherds of the Raut caste give similar blessings when they dance in front of village homes during their *mātar* festival: "As you receive and give, so will you receive blessings. / May your house be filled with grain and wealth; may you live one hundred thousand years."

The singers implied that a Chhattisgarhi householder is expected to make a donation to the *suā* dancers, who come only once a year, in the same way that she is expected to give alms to the wandering religious ascetics who come around much more often, and that she will receive similar merit for doing so. By emphasizing the wealth of the house and the ritual duty to give to those who come asking for alms, the verse sequence successfully humiliated the householder into giving a large donation.

In another courtyard, a heated discussion developed as to whether the female householder had given according to her means. The dancers, together with some village women from the secondary audience, insisted that this household should have given two, not one, rupees along with their grain, as the headman's wife had just done. This was a particularly pointed accusation, since the two families were leaders of opposing parties in a village dispute unrelated to these performances. To the amusement of the women in the secondary audience, the troupe began to dance again, singing the following verse: "Out of anger she's gone inside. / *Suānā*, she's bringing out a basket of grain." But this time, the strategy of the dancers to put pressure on their patron did not succeed. The lead dancer led the troupe out of the house in disgust, insisting that they were not, after all, beggars.

These vignettes hint at an inherent tension between the *suā* dancers and the households in which they dance. The dancers and patrons represent different levels on the social and economic hierarchy of Chhattisgarhi rural society. The dancers are land laborers, Chhattisgarhi-speaking women from *ādivāsī* castes. Their patrons are usually high-caste landowners and farmers who may be from either Chhattisgarhi or Oriya castes. The dancers also often represent geographic communities other than those of their patrons, dancing in neighborhoods or villages not their own. Finally, although the dancers are all female, the patrons and audience members are both male and female. An open avenue of direct communication, particularly folklore communication, does not normally exist between the hierarchical groups represented by the dancers and their patrons. Thus, the genre of the *suā nāc* temporarily establishes such a communicative channel through song, dance, and gifting.

The verbal song tradition accompanying the dance does not directly reflect the above-mentioned caste and economic hierarchy, possibly because of the tribal context of the origination of the *suā nāc*, characterized by relative equality rather than the hierarchy of the Hindu caste system. However, the verbal tradition of the *suā nāc* often expresses a tension between social groups of another kind: a woman's maternal home and her home of marriage (*maikā* and *sasurāl*), a new bride and her in-laws. This tension is experienced by women of all castes and economic levels in Chhattisgarh, having developed under a system of arranged marriage that ideally follows principles of hypergamy and village exogamy. The young bride thus finds herself a stranger with little status in what many folk songs call a "strange land" (*pardeś*).

The dancers may sing short selections from longer, extended *suā* narratives (sung in their entirety only outside the dance context); or their verses may be lyrical, developing a particular image or emotion from one of these narratives. One narrative, with several variants, is particularly popular in contemporary *suā nāc* performance, both within the dance and as a *suā nāc* narrative performed independently of the dance. It relates the plight of a new bride in her *sasurāl*. The three versions I recorded and other previously published variants begin with a variation on the following verses (Shukla 1969:163–168; Elwin 1946:186; Dube 1963:70–71):

> *Kahar, kahar* sings my black cuckoo.[6]
> *Suānā*, the peacock calls out at midnight.
>
> The headman of my village is not sleeping,
> *Suānā*, whose sister has gone to a foreign land.

The foreign land is the sister's *sasurāl*, called a land of famine; her brother continues to live in her *maikā*, a land of plenty. These images reflect a married woman's fond, idealized recollections of her *maikā*, where she was relatively free and pampered and which she perceives as a land of (emotional) wealth and prosperity. Although a bride is believed to bring fertility and wealth to her home of marriage, she does not directly benefit from these until the birth of a son. Her position as a new daughter-in-law (*bahū*) is at the bottom of the familial hierarchy; thus she likens her *sasurāl* to a land of famine. In the narrative, the sister sends a message to her brother to come and take her home to her *maikā* (which he would normally do several times a year in her early marriage and for certain festivals thereafter). Their mother tries to dissuade the brother from going on his mission, fearful of what the (now literally conceived) land of famine will hold for him. But he is insistent and asks her to prepare necessary supplies for the journey. When he reaches his sister's *sasurāl*, the brother asks where she lives, locates her, and carries her off on his horse, back to her *maikā*.

The following is the portion of the narrative as it was sung in the first three performance segments (for three different households) of one village

[6] In Chhattisgarh, the Indian cuckoo (*koyal*) has poetic associations with separated lovers, its cry associated with the mournful cry of a beloved separated from her lover.

sequence, beginning in the courtyard of the village headman. Intervening introductory and benedictory verses for each segment, as well as verse repetitions, have been omitted.

House 1: *Suānā*, where, oh parrot, are the members of your caste?
Where did you take incarnation?

Kahar, kahar sings my black cuckoo.
Suānā, the peacock calls out at midnight.

The headman of my village is not sleeping,
Suānā, whose sister has gone to a foreign country.

. . . .
. . . .[7]

How should I go, sister, to bring you back?
Suānā, the Jamuni River will block me halfway.

Give the boatman ten or twenty rupees.
Suānā, he'll take you to the other side, brother.

House 2: Give the boatman ten or twenty rupees.
Suānā, he'll take you to the other side, brother.

I told my mother to give me snacks and sweets.
Suānā, I'm going to see my sister.

The place you're going, my son, to see your sister,
Suānā, a great famine struck there.

For you, my mother, it is a great famine.
Suānā, for me, it is a time of plenty.

To the hungry, mother, give snacks.
Suānā, to the thirsty, give water.

Mother, give me the horse Lilihansa to ride.
Suānā, give me a sword to hold.

[7] The words of this verse were indiscernible on the tape because of a loud commotion between some children in the audience. Based on other variants of the narrative, however, one would expect this verse to tell of the message the sister has sent to her brother.

Mother, for my feet give me shoes that sound *rūcā-mūcā*.
Suānā, give me an umbrella for the sun.

Quickly, quickly, call the horsekeeper.
Suānā, he quickly readied the horse.

House 3: From lane to lane, my brother,
Narad Muni is wandering, *suānā*.

My brother, someone is playing in the lane,
A child of the street, *suānā*.

Tell, tell me, my child,
Point out the house of the fair-skinned one, *suānā*.

There it is, my brother,
The big door over there, *suānā*.

Don't go here, my brother,
Don't go there, *suānā*.

Kick it with your heel, my brother,
Push it with your arms, *suānā*.

It doesn't open, my brother,
The very big door, *suānā*.

The dancers sang only up to the narrative event in which the brother reaches his sister's village and locates her house, one of the emotional climaxes of the narrative. The householder brought out her contribution before the singers could conclude the narrative, with the brother entering the house and taking away his sister. But both the singers and audience know that once he reaches the village, the sister is assured of safe passage back to her maternal home. This narrative juncture coincides with a temporary resolution in the opposition between dancers and patron, achieved when the householder brings out her grain donation. Still, the narrative resolution is not easy; the door to the sister's house does not open readily—it will have to be broken down for the brother to gain access. The longer variant of the narrative sung outside the dance context, discussed in the next section of this chapter, also ends with a sense of uneasy resolution. The last image is one of the sister's sister-in-law washing dishes, she, too, a "sister" married into a "land of famine."

In the same performance sequence, the next three segments consisted of lyrical verses elaborating images based on another popular *suā* narrative, one that tells of a bride whose husband has gone away to a foreign land, either as a warrior or trader. In this narrative, the husband instructs his wife to water and worship daily the courtyard *tulsī* plant, a basil plant representing the goddess. He tells her that as long as the *tulsī* remains green, she will know he is safe; if it dies and withers, she will know he has died. Shakuntala Varma has published the following variant of the narrative, which takes the form of a conversation between the newlywed couple:

> Having celebrated our first marriage, I've seated you on the threshold, *suānā*.
> Now I must leave and go to battle.
>
> You are my wealth, my own, *suānā*.
> Tell me, what should I do?
>
> Eat with your mother-in-law; sleep with your sister-in-law, *suānā*.
> And please your heart with your younger brother-in-law.
>
> My mother-in-law is old; she'll die, *suānā*.
> I'll send my sister-in-law to her *sasurāl*.
>
> My younger brother-in-law is like a son, *suānā*.
> Upon whom should I fix my heart?
>
> Plant a *tulsī* in the courtyard, *suānā*.
> Fix your heart upon it.
>
> Everyday, everyday that passes, plaster its platform, *suānā*.
> Everyday, light an oil lamp.
>
> When the *tulsī* plant withers, *suānā*,
> Understand that I have died in battle.
>
> (1971:144–145; my translation of her Chhattisgarhi transcription.)

The lyrical segments sung in the Phuljhar dance sequence expand the image of the bride performing various religious rituals, filling the lonely hours until the return of her husband:

> House 4: A plate of gold filled with Ganga water.
> Having worshiped [the goddess] Durga, the queen is returning.

Tārī hārī nā nā mor nārī hārī nā nā re.
A plate of gold.

With whom will you eat; with whom will you sleep?
A plate of gold.

A plate of gold filled with Ganga water.
Having worshiped Durga, the queen is returning.

Clean the courtyard, prepare the *tulsī* platform.
A plate of gold.

A plate of gold filled with Ganga water.
Having worshiped Durga, the queen is returning.

House 5: *Tārī hārī nā nā mor nārī hārī nā nā re.*
Make a garland.

Make a garland for Shiva and the mother [Parvati].
I'm going to the Shiva temple to worship.

With whom will you eat; with whom will you sleep?
Make a garland.

Make a garland for Shiva and the mother.
I'm going to the Shiva temple to worship.

With whom will you eat; with whom will you sleep?
Make a garland.

House 6: Clean the courtyard, prepare the *tulsī* platform.
Oh Shyam, the one with many white bells.[8]

Without Ram, my eyes are longing;
Show yourself, oh lord, my brother.
Shyam, the one with many white bells.

Clean the courtyard, prepare the *tulsī* platform.
Shyam, the one with many white bells.

[8] Shyam is a reference to the dark god Krishna in his form of cowherd lover, here presumably an appellation for this husband. Ram, too, is a reference to both god and husband.

Everyday, oh daughter, pour water on the *tulsī*.
Shyam, the one with many white bells.

Without Ram, my eyes are longing.
Show yourself, oh lord, my brother.
Shyam, the one with many white bells.

Awaken the *tulsī* on the [word indiscernable] platform.
Shyam, the one with many white bells.

Without Ram, my eyes are longing.
Show yourself, oh lord, my brother.
Shyam, the one with many white bells.

Everyday, oh daughter, light incense.
Shyam, the one with many white bells.

Interspersed with the description of the ritual is the repeated but unanswered question, "With whom will you eat; with whom will you sleep?" The husband in Varma's variant suggests that she eat with her mother-in-law, sleep with her unmarried sister-in-law, and "please her heart" with her younger brother-in-law. In north and central Indian extended families, a joking relationship between a bride/sister-in-law and her younger brother-in-law is permissible (in contrast to the relationship of strict avoidance and respect with an older brother-in-law), one that suggests a potential sexual relationship. The bride of our song, however, is not satisfied with any of these suggestions: her mother-in-law will soon die, her sister-in-law will get married and move out of the house, and her younger brother-in-law is not a potential lover but like a son. The bride wants more from the conjugal relationship and suggests that no lasting companionship is possible outside of that relationship; without her husband, the bride is alone and defenseless. Tension between the bride and her in-laws is similar to that expressed in the narrative of the sister living in a land of famine, but the implied resolution differs. Rather than depending on her brother to extricate her from the "land of famine" for a temporary reprieve in her *maikā*, in this narrative the bride waits patiently for her husband's return, hoping *he* will serve as an intermediary, perhaps transforming that "land of famine" into one of wealth.[9]

[9] See Raheja and Gold 1994, chapter 4, "On the Uses of Subversion: Redefining Conjugality," for a discussion of women's folk songs in Uttar Pradesh that challenge the "ideal" subordination of the conjugal relationship to that of the patrilineal extended family and express women's longing for conjugal intimacy.

The final segment of the above-mentioned performance sequence is unique in my *suā* recordings as the only one in which the parrot is portrayed as an active participant in the sung narrative rather than as simply the addressee of the song. The parrot in Indian oral and literate traditions has numerous connotations. Visually, its vibrant green plumage suggests the lush green of fertile rice fields; its association with fertility in certain *ādivāsī* traditions is suggested by the use of parrot images in their "marriage sheds" (Crooke [1896] 1978:252). Parrots are frequently kept as pets in rural households, either caged or with their wings clipped to keep them from flying beyond the walls of the courtyard. Poetic and verbal folk traditions disregard this limitation, however, and envisage the parrot as free to fly long distances but domesticated enough to come back to its owner. Thus, with its ability to speak, the parrot becomes a perfect messenger and confidant.[10] In the *suā nāc* tradition, the parrot is the confidant of both the bride in her *sasurāl* and the dancers themselves. Every verse of the *suā nāc* is addressed to the parrot in the repeated *suānā* or *suā mor.* The parrot opens a line of communication between two distanced parties: as a messenger between the sister in the land of famine and her brother in the land of plenty; as a go-between for the bride and her husband, who has traveled to a foreign land; and, more figuratively, as the channel between landowners and land laborers.

In the last segment of the Phuljhar village performance sequence being discussed, the relationship between parrot and fertility is explicit. In these verses, the parrot brings a long-time barren woman a cluster of mangoes, with all the associations between the lush, sensual, ripened fruit and fertility.

> Go, go, my parrot, to the forest of delight, to the forest of sandalwood.
> *Suānā*, break off a bunch of mangoes.
>
> How should I walk and how should I fly?
> *Suānā*, how should I break them off?
>
> Walk on your feet; fly back with your wings.
> *Suānā*, break them off with your beak.
>
> When I return, when I return with the mangoes,
> *Suānā*, to whom shall I give them?
>
> To the twelve-year barren woman, Candanmati,
> *Suānā*, my parrot, you should give them to her.

[10] One of the most well-known parrots in Hindi literature is the parrot who serves as confidant, messenger, and matchmaker in the sixteenth-century tale of Padmavati, written by Malik Muhammad Jayasi.

Elwin and Hivale recorded two similar verse sequences in the more tribal area of the Maikal Hills on the boundaries of Chhattisgarh. In one of these, the parrot is asked by a woman to give the mangoes to a king. The primary image remains one of fertility but reflects a setting in which the sexual hierarchy is not as strong as it is in the plains of Chhattisgarh and in which the burden of infertility is not placed exclusively on the female: the mangoes are given to the king, which in folklore is often a reference to husband.

Go, go, my parrot, to the forest of delight, to the forest of sandal.
Suānā, break off a bunch of mangoes.

How should I walk and how should I fly?
Suānā, how should I break them off?

Walk on your feet; fly back with your wings.
Suānā, break them off with your beak.

When I return, when I return with the mangoes,
Suānā, to whom shall I give them?

To the twelve-year barren woman, Candanmati,
Suānā, my parrot, you should give them to her.

(Elwin and Hivale 1944:40)

These verse sequences hint at why the *suā nāc* was adaptable to performance during the harvest season and suggest a possible relationship between the dancers and the parrot. The parrot and the newly harvested grain are both symbols of fertility and auspicious blessing; they bring wealth. The harvested paddy itself is often referred to as Lakshmi, the goddess of wealth and prosperity. The *suā nāc* dancers, too, confer auspiciousness and blessings of wealth upon the households into which they enter; their dance transforms the harvest. The association of the parrot, fertility, grain, wealth, and dancers is reinforced in those performances in which the image of the parrot is placed on the head of a virgin girl around whom the other women dance. She is the virgin bride, Lakshmi herself, bringing wealth and fertility to her *sasurāl*. In the public context of the dance, it is these nonverbal, positive images of women that dominate.

Although the nonverbal images of the dance and the verbal message of the song highlight different dimensions of the female experience in Chhattisgarh, structurally the dance context and accompanying verbal tradition reinforce each other. In each case a hierarchical opposition between social groups has been defined: the *maikā* and *sasurāl* and the dancers and their patrons. The tensions are temporarily resolved with the return of the sister to her maternal home with her brother and the completion of the exchange between the dancers and householders. The hierarchical relationships are symbiotic. In north and central India, hypergamy is the common pattern of marriage; however, the families involved are mutually dependent. The bride brings ritual wealth and fertility to her *sasurāl*, and the *sasurāl* provides her with a groom. Although she may dread the leave-taking from her *maikā* and fear the fate of a bride whose husband goes to a foreign land, to remain unmarried in her maternal home is a fate often seen by a young girl to be worse than death. Similarly, the landowning patrons and *suā* dancers are both economically and ritually dependent on each other. In the *suā nāc*, the dancers rely on their patrons' contributions to support their *gaurā* festival. At the same time, the householders depend on the dancers to transform the harvest into ritual wealth through their auspicious blessings.

These parallel dimensions between text and performance context are schematically summarized in Table 2. The wealth bringers establish an avenue of communication between the disparate poles of the opposition, between the land of plenty and the land of famine; they are, in fact, the channel through which the communication takes place. This schema is visualized from the perspective of the bride and the *ādivāsī*-caste dancers, those dwelling in what they call the "land of plenty." Although, in reality, the bride and the dancers come from hierarchically and economically lower positions than those living in the land of famine, in the *suā nāc*, their symbolic wealth, in the form of fertility and auspiciousness, is paramount. In the dance, performers, rather than patrons, primarily control and manipulate the channel and its message. The establishment of this channel and the iconographic message of the dance supersedes the verbal one. The latter is often obscured or interrupted because of the peripheral noise level of the audience of children and women following the dancers, by the movement of the dancers themselves, and by the disruption between segments as the dancers move from house to house. The dance is not possible without the song, however, and its familiar words are never totally lost upon the participants.

Table 2. Parallels between song text and dance context

	Land of plenty	Auspicious wealth bringers	Land of famine
Song texts	*maikā*; forest of delight	bride; parrot	*sasurāl*; barren woman
Dance context	*ādivāsī*-caste laborers	*suā nāc* dancers	landowners; patrons

The Song Tradition as Narrative

In contrast to the dance that involves numerous castes as patrons, audience, and performers, the *suā nāc* performed *outside* the dance is sung within a single social group. Women sing with women of their own caste level and village/neighborhood; the opposition inherent between performer and audience/patron in the dance is collapsed. In this context, the genre is available to a wider social and linguistic group than it is within the dance, including non-*ādivāsī*, though still lower-caste, and Oriya- as well as Chhattisgarhi-speaking women. The channel is simplified from song and dance to simply song, although some women cannot refrain from minimal swaying dance movements in this context as well. As few as two or three women may sing together, rather than the larger troupe required by the dance. One result of the shift in audience, participants, and channel is the importance assumed by the message of the sung text. Because the channel for communication is already assumed to be present and open, the focus of the performance shifts from channel to the verbal message. Further, the nonverbal, physically concrete images of dance, parrot, and grain of the dance context are absent, and narratives are uninterrupted by introductory and benedictory verse sequences and the physical movement of the dancers themselves.

These *suā* narratives are often expanded variants of those performed in the dance context; in many, the suffering of what one singer called the female *jāti* (caste) is also made more explicit. The following is the full narrative of the brother rescuing his sister from the "land of famine," segments of which were sung in the Phuljhar dance sequence above. This variant was sung by the Christian woman, Campa Bai, who accompanied me to the *ḍālkhāī* festival (Chapter 3), while she and several other women were cleaning rice at a Christian girls' boarding school. She had heard my tapes of the Phuljhar-village performance and asked if I wanted to hear the full story, "such a sad story." Campa Bai was a woman in her late fifties, well known for her performance abilities in several song and storytelling genres, but to whom the *suā nāc* as a dance performance genre is not available. Her voice was low and the tone of the sung narrative almost that of a dirge, slow and somber. Gone were the multiple, echoing voices of the larger dance troupe, the repetition of verses, the dancers' clapping, the excited chatter of children, the general auspicious setting of the harvest. The story line was clear, direct, and uninterrupted.

> *Kahā, kahā* sings my black cuckoo,
> *Suānā*, whose sister has gone to a foreign land.

He doesn't feel sleepy; he doesn't feel even a little sleepy,
Suānā, whose sister has gone to a foreign land.

Mother, give me a snack made with butter.
Suānā, I'm going to see my sister.

The place you're going to see your sister,
Suānā, a great famine has struck there, my son.

For you, my mother, it is a great famine;
Suānā, for me, it is a time of plenty.

Mother, give me a snack made with butter.
Suānā, give me an umbrella for the sun.

Mother, for my feet give me shoes that sound *rūcā-mūcā*.
Suānā, give me a sword to hold.

Mother, give me the horse Nilhansa to ride.
Suānā, I'm going to see my sister.

His mother, hearing this much,
Suānā, quickly readied the horse.

The horse from the stable was readied.
Suānā, the sister's house drew near.

In the lane he met children, playing in the lane.
Suānā, he asked, Where, children, is my sister's house?

Has your chest broken, have your eyes burst?
Suānā, the house of your sister is over there.

Washing, washing earthen pots, his sister saw him.
Suānā, my brother has come to take me.

Wash your hands and feet, brother, sit on the stool.
Suānā, tell me, how is my mother?

Your mother is fine. Your father is fine.
Suānā, the people of your village are fine.

I'll tell my mother-in-law, my old mother-in-law,
Suānā, my brother has come to take me.

Mother-in-law, what vegetable should I cook, what rice?
Suānā, my brother has come to take me.

Cook the cheap, coarse rice,
Suānā, and kohlrabi leaves as a vegetable.

My brother eats butter; he washes his hands in milk.
Suānā, how can I serve cabbage as the vegetable?

For you, my young girl, it is cheap rice and cabbage.
Suānā, for me it is rice made with butter.

I'll tell my mother-in-law, my old mother-in-law,
Suānā, my brother has come to take me.

I don't know anything about these matters.
Suānā, your father-in-law will know.

I'll tell my father-in-law, my old father-in-law,
Suānā, my brother has come to take me.

I don't know anything about these matters.
Suānā, ask your younger brother-in-law.

I'll tell my brother-in-law, my younger brother-in-law,
Suānā, my brother has come to take me.

I don't know anything about these matters.
Suānā, oh sister-in-law, your sister-in-law will know.

I'll tell my sister-in-law, my younger sister-in-law,
Suānā, my brother has come to take me.

I don't know anything about these matters.
Suānā, the one who supports you will know.

I'll tell my husband, my husband, oh husband,
Suānā, my brother has come to take me.

Husk twelve years of my grain.
Suānā, then you can go to your mother's house.

Wash twelve years of my clothes.
Suānā, then you can go to your mother's house.

Wash twelve years of my dishes.
Suānā, then you can go to your mother's house.

Throw out twelve years of cow dung.
Suānā, then you can go to your mother's house.

My brother heard all these things.
Suānā, his heart was saddened.

Come, young girl, climb on my horse Nilhansa.
Suānā, and the far country will become near.

My horse heard all these things.
Suānā, the far country will become near.

From the fields, my light brown buffalo saw,
Suānā, the sister who had fed him chaff.

From the village square, my father saw,
Suānā, his daughter who had spilt tears.

Washing, washing earthen pots, my brother's wife saw,
Suānā, her daughter who had spilt tears.

From inside the house, my mother saw,
Suānā, her daughter who spilt tears.

It is finished; it is finished; my *suā* is finished.
Suānā, I'll go now to the tank surrounded by tamarind trees.

This narrative variant extends beyond the brother's arrival in his sister's *sasurāl*, the episode that ends the variant sung in the dance. After he reaches his sister's home, we are given a series of images that more fully illustrates the suffering of a bride in her home of marriage. First, her hierarchically lower family is abused. When the brother reaches the village and asks a child playing in the streets where the house of his sister's in-laws is, he is answered with an abuse typical of those employed in the local dialects: "Has your chest broken, have your eyes burst? / *Suānā*, the house of your sister is over there."[11]

When the brother enters the house in which his sister is living, he is not accorded the hospitality even a stranger would receive. She is forced to feed him coarse rice and cheap vegetables, not fit for company fare. What follows is a litany of kin under whose authority she lives in her *sasurāl*. She asks each of them—mother-in-law, father-in-law, younger brother-in-law, sister-in-law, and finally her husband—for permission to return to her *maikā* with her brother. Her daily duties in the household are enumerated as her husband tells her what chores she must complete before leaving. The brother is saddened by the conditions under which his sister must live and carries her off on his horse, back to the "land of plenty."

This particular performance ends with the repetition of the image of a young bride washing earthen pots, the brother's wife doing the same chore the sister herself was doing when her brother first saw her in her *sasurāl*: "Washing, washing earthen pots, my brother's wife saw, / *Suānā*, her younger sister-in-law, the tattler." With the repeated image of a daughter-in-law washing vessels, a seed is planted for a cyclic repetition of the entire narrative. A new opposition is established between yet another daughter-in-law and *her* home of marriage. This bride is also a sister, longing for her *maikā*, in which lives a brother who may come to rescue her from this "land of famine." As a narrative tradition outside of the dance, the *suā nāc* often focuses on the opposition rather than on the temporary resolution implicit in the dance itself. It describes the experience of a woman, usually a new bride, caught in that opposition, and focuses on her private experience of suffering rather than on her public image of a wealth bringer.[12] After Campa Bai had completed the narrative above, her only comment was, "There's so much sadness in the life of a woman."

A Chhattisgarhi male is never put in the situation in which he will experience this opposition between a *maikā* and *sasurāl*; his life is spatially continuous. In fact, these two words have little meaning for Chhattisgarhi husbands

[11] The term of address for a wife's brother, *sālā*, by which this brother would be addressed by most residents of his sister's *sasurāl*, is also a common term of abuse for males in both the Chhattisgarhi and Oriya languages. The term itself is not employed in this abuse, but its connotations are present and enable the young children he meets to answer his question about the location of his sister's house in this nonrespectful tone.

[12] An explicit reference to the bride as wealth bringer, the goddess of wealth herself, is found in the words of a groom's kinsman at the end of a wedding ceremony in central Madhya Pradesh: "You have given us a boundless gift, the maiden of your soul, a beautiful daughter-in-law who is called Lakshmi (the Goddess of Wealth)" (Jacobson 1976:319).

and brothers except in relation to their wives' or sisters' villages of residence. Traditionally, men rarely visit their in-laws' home; and when they do refer to that village, they refer to it as their wife's *maikā*. One *suā nāc* verse makes explicit reference to this discrimination: "To my brother they give a colorful palace. / *Suānā*, to me they give a foreign country" [my translation from Dube 1963:64]. Other published *suā nāc* verse sequences further elaborate the unique sufferings of a woman's life:

I bow to the moon and the sun, O parrot
One shouldn't be born a woman
Life of a woman is like a cow, parrot
Wherever she is wedded she has to go.

Howsoever clean I keep my husband's home and break my fingers,
Even then I am scolded by his sister.
See how unfortunate am I,
The day my husband brought me home he has to go away to earn his bread.

(Parmar 1972:167)

Moon and Sun, I fall at your feet
Give me not the birth of a girl again
From birth we wretched women are orphans
Mothers-in-law, sisters-in-law
Are always abusing us
By their continual nagging we are burnt
So I ran away to the forest . . .

(Elwin and Hivale 1944:39–40)

The analogy between a woman and a cow in the first variant of this verse sequence vividly reflects the ambiguous and shifting image of the woman/bride in the *suā nāc* tradition. A cow, like a new bride, is an auspicious symbol, a wealth bringer; her footprints are considered to be those of the goddess of wealth, Lakshmi.[13] However, a cow is also a commodity that is bought and sold. In this verse, the singer characterizes her wedding and the system of dowry or bride-price (depending on her caste) as a commercial

[13] During the month of *mārgaśirṣ* (November–December, the month following that during which the *suā nāc* is performed and *gaurā* celebrated), the goddess Lakshmi is worshiped every Thursday in the Oriya villages of Phuljhar. At the entrances to their homes, young girls draw elaborate geometric designs (*raṅgolī*) with rice flour, whose beauty attracts the goddess to the thresholds. Then, she finds her way to the inner courtyard by following the cow footprints that have been drawn from the outer *raṅgolī* to one drawn in the home's interior. The cow *is* Lakshmi.

transaction in which she, like a cow, is an object to be traded and sold regardless of her own will.

The *Suā Nāc* in Shifting Contexts

Indigenous classification of and commentary about the genre of *suā nāc* are based primarily upon its public, dance performance context, representations that both reveal and mask the meanings and flexibility of the genre. As a publicly performed genre, the *suā nāc* establishes a communicative channel between social groups. This channel and the iconographic messages it delivers are dominant over the verbal song text; it builds upon the public image of the Chhattisgarhi female as the fertile, auspicious, wealth-bringing bride. The image is coherent with the harvest context in which the dance is performed; the bride and the newly harvested grain are both equated with the goddess of wealth.

Only ethnographic observation reveals that the song tradition is also performed outside the dance, where it is still called *suā nāc*, sharing with the dance the same verbal texts, song tune (*rāg*), and physical and/or verbal imagery of the parrot. Performed as a song tradition outside the dance, the *suā nāc* serves as an expressive vehicle for women in which they verbalize a contrasting dimension of what it means to be a female in Chhattisgarhi society. The image is the privately experienced one of the new bride, or daughter-in-law, who suffers and is oppressed in her *sasurāl*, an experience women rarely articulate in a public, nonsegregated everyday discourse or performance.

The dance and nondance *suā nāc* traditions cannot, however, be totally separated from each other. They are, after all, still classified by the indigenous folklore community as the same genre. The thematic tensions of the song often parallel the social tensions of the dance context; and parts of the same or similar narratives both accompany the dance and are performed as independent narratives. Thus, the imagery of the suffering sister in a land of famine is never totally lost amid the nonverbal images of fertility and wealth of the dance context. Similarly, although the dance itself, the physical image of the parrot, and the exchange of grain and auspicious blessings are absent in *suā nāc* performances outside the dance, they continue to influence and inform that narrative song tradition because of the folklore community's familiarity with the dance. The multivalent verbal and nonverbal images of the *suā nāc* endow the genre with the flexibility that permits its performance both as a public harvest dance and as the more private, sung women's narrative tradition.

Increased literacy, changing social conditions, and mass media technology (particularly radio) have all made an impact on the *suā nāc*, the level of community with which it is identified, and the significance it has assumed for the participating dancers. In the fall of 1985, living in the town of Dhamtari across the street from a small Gond neighborhood, I kept asking my Gond neighbors when they would be going out to dance the *suā nāc*, fearful that I might miss the outings. Several men who overheard/heard my persistent questioning finally told me that, if I was so interested, why didn't I just turn on the radio on Wednesday afternoons, when All India Radio (Akashvani) played folk songs every week, including the *suā nāc*. They suggested that this would be much easier for me to tape than following the dancers from door to door and that the radio singers were "the best." On some levels, this "new" context approximated both the traditional public dance and the private narrative performance modes but was on other levels decontextualized from both. Like the dance, the radio audience is the folklore regional community, available to men and women of all castes. Without the dance, however, like the narrative mode, the focus is on the song words, poignant words traditionally voiced outside the dance context in private courtyards between female friends but now being broadcast from radios and public speakers for all to hear.

Finally, late one afternoon in that auspicious month of *kārtik*, my Gond friends called me to join them as they set out to dance the *suā nāc* on Dhamtari's main business street. The street was already decorated with banana leaves and lights, anticipating the dark night of *dīvālī*, when Lakshmi is invited into homes and businesses with lit oil lamps (these days, also candles and strings of electric "Christmas lights") lining windows, doorways, verandahs, and balconies. In urban settings, the *suā nāc* has become more and more associated with this festival and is less closely tied to the harvest per se. Urban *ādivāsī* troupes dance at the entrances of shops and receive from the shopowners only small (twenty-five to fifty paisa) monetary donations, used toward *gaurā* celebrations, rather than the ritual gifting of grain. In this setting, no permanent or traditional relationships exist between patrons and members of the dance troupe; the dancers themselves do not usually patronize these upscale shops, and the shopkeepers view their donations to the dancers as only one more of their many *dīvālī* obligations. The channel of communication between dancers and patrons is so attenuated as to be almost absent, several shopkeepers throwing out the coins as soon as they see the troupe or permitting them to dance only one or two minutes before coming out to give their donation, not waiting to receive the traditional blessings of the dancers.

The *suā nāc* troupe I accompanied that dark *kārtik* night consisted of eight dancers from the neighborhood, smaller than usual I was told, "But these days women don't want to go outside [the neighborhood]." A seventeen-year-old girl stood longingly at her doorway, watching the troupe's preparations to leave. When I asked her why she wasn't coming, she said, "I'm *matrik* [high school]-pass now; my brothers won't let me leave the house"; and one of the dancers responded, "This is what's happening these days." The troupe began by dancing in an open public space in their own small neighborhood, for no particular patron and with no gifting involved; spirits were high and there was laughing and chattering between the dancers. This mood continued as we walked the half-mile or so to the beginning of the shopping area. Here, they danced in front of six different stores before the lead dancer, after two different shopkeepers humiliated the troupe by refusing even to come out to the entrance of the store, said, "Let's go [back]! People think we'll dance, but why should we?"

Several days later, in the early morning of the last day of the *gaurā* celebrations in the same Gond neighborhood, fifteen to twenty women, including the young woman excluded from the troupe earlier, seemingly spontaneously circled around the images of Gaura-Gauri (Shiva and Parvati), which were waiting to be carried in procession to the nearest tank to be immersed, and began dancing/singing the *suā nāc*. The performance dramatically reinforced the relationship between *gaurā* possession and *suā nāc* dance movements, both called *jhūpnā*.[14] Several men in the crowd, including the neighborhood headman, laughingly joined in, singing a few repeated phrases here and there, when they were strongly reprimanded by one of the older women, "This isn't for men to sing!"

Even as Chhattisgarhi regional identification with the *suā nāc* is expanded and reinforced through Akashvani airing of its songs on its "Chhattisgarhi folk song" programming (available to all regardless of caste, gender, literacy level, or urban/rural location), the experience described above suggests that its performance as a ritual dance may become more restricted. These particular Gond women found dancing on city streets, without appropriate ritual relationships and frameworks, to be humiliating; and a growing number of their community will be excluded from such public performance as they become more highly educated, a literacy that, at least initially, restricts their movement outside their neighborhoods. The *suā nāc* performance within their own Gond neighborhood at a festival celebrated only by *ādivāsī* castes reinforces the unique identity of this *ādivāsī* community even as the wider regional community continues to claim it as its own.

[14] I had never seen or heard of a *suā nāc* performed at *gaurā* celebrations and wondered if this was an innovative context for the dance. I later asked some of the dancers whether this was something that occurred regularly in their neighborhood *gaurā*. One of the dancers answered, "No, no; we did it for *mazā* [fun] only."

CHAPTER 5

Joining Verse to Verse: Professional Storytelling and Individual Creativity
Kathānī Kūhā

In the next three chapters, we shift from consideration of genres for which a ritual context is inherent to their interpretive framing (even though the verbal tradition may also be performed outside that context) to a series of narrative genres that may be performed independently from a particular ritual or festival (although their performances may also be included as part of festival and ritual celebrations): the traditions of *kathānī kūhā*, *candainī*, and *paṇḍvānī*. All three narrative genres are performed in similar contexts, as "entertainment" events (*manorañjan*), supported by villagewide monetary collections, or at weddings and birth celebrations, when the particular households involved patronize the performers. The terms *candainī* and *paṇḍvānī* refer to a particular "story line" or plot, and the genres are limited to those particular narratives. *Kathānī kūhā*, on the other hand, is an Oriya term that literally means "teller of stories," used to identify the *performer* himself rather than the narrative he performs. His repertoire is theoretically unbounded, drawing from folktales, puranas,[1] and other religious narrative traditions. In this chapter I examine one kind of space that the folklore repertoire gives for such individual creativity within a system that identifies genres with particular communities, how such an individual establishes au-

[1] The puranas are a body of Sanskrit and regional-language religious texts that record, literally, the "old stories" of ancient days; they are a principal source of Hindu mythology. See Doniger 1993 for discussions of their flexibility and transformations in shifting contexts and the Dimmitt and Van Buitenan (1978) reader of portions of the major Sanskrit puranas in translation. The puranas are encyclopedic in nature, and thus it is fairly safe to attribute particular religious or etiological narratives to a puranic source.

thority to perform professionally (in a public context), and how the storyteller carefully creates community through performance.

Kathānī kūhā is a term used in the Phuljhar borderlands of Chhattisgarh and western Orissa for a loosely defined class of professional storytellers whose performances are not ritually prescribed and whose style and repertoire are idiosyncratic. They differ from other individual professional performers, such as the Oriya *bāhak* or Chhattisgarhi *candainī* singer, whose performances are associated in indigenous commentary with particular caste or regional communities, in that they do not claim to be part of a larger ongoing "tradition" passed on from teacher to student (*gurū* to *celā*) or to be the bearers of the "story of a particular community." In this way, the *kathānī kūhā* is similar to the individual storyteller of folktales in a domestic context who picks up his/her repertoire informally from a wide variety of sources. What is significant is the existence of a specific indigenous term that distinguishes these individual performers when they are professionals performing in a public context; it is this identification, then, that places the *kathānī kūhā* in the repertoire of public folklore in Chhattisgarh. If we understand indigenous classification and terminology to be forms of metafolklore (Ben-Amos 1976:226), then the term itself suggests that our analytic focus be on style, since this is what distinguishes the *kathānī kūhā* from others who may tell folktales from a similar repertoire—we ask what difference it makes to the shape of their performance that these stories are told by a professional.

Parmeshvara: "Singing with a Sweet Voice"

After I had lived in the Phuljhar village Patharla for several months and villagers and friends began to understand my interest in Chhattisgarhi stories and customs ("what we observe/celebrate here in our Chhattisgarh"), several people made reference to a particular individual, Parmeshvara, whose stories (*kathā*) they felt I should record. They made it clear, however, that I would have to call him to the village if I wanted to hear him, since he performed at irregular intervals. It was another case of reluctance on my part to initiate (in this case, patronize) a performance outside its "natural" context, which at that time I rather naïvely interpreted to be those performances that I just "happened upon"—another case, in retrospect, of indigenous shaping of what I have ultimately included in this study. So it was, primarily to honor the individuals who had made the suggestion and to thank the village for its hospitality, that I eventually made contact with the singer Parmeshvara and set up a performance in Patharla on a cold November night in 1980. I attended another of his performances in the village of Sirco, close to his natal village, nearly a year later; the translation of the full verbal text of this later performance is provided in the Texts, and the specific performative analyses that follow here are based on this Sirco performance.

Parmeshvara was a fifty-year-old Christian man who at that time was the only known *kathānī kūhā* performing in Phuljhar. He told me that when he first began performing as a young man, there were two other *kathānī kūhā* in the area but that both had died within the last ten years. Parmeshvara distinguished himself from these two performers by saying that they had had gurus but that he had learned his skill independently.[2] Further, he said, although there were several young boys in his village who imitated him, they were not serious about learning, and he was not teaching his skill to anyone. Neither of his sons had shown any interest in following in their father's steps: one was a high school teacher, and the other was studying in a Christian seminary. Parmeshvara was pleased that they were receiving an education and was hopeful that they would have a more secure life than he did. He did not seem concerned that he had no disciples or that the *kathānī kūhā* performance genre may be a dying art form in Phuljhar unless new performers immigrate from Orissa.[3]

Parmeshvara told me that he began telling stories in the style of a *kathānī kūhā* when he was twelve or thirteen years of age. He looks back to one particular experience as his beginning. A traveling cloth merchant from Orissa had stopped overnight in his village, and the villagers asked the merchant what he could do that would entertain them. The merchant said that he was a *kathānī kūhā* and proceeded to perform for the villagers throughout the night. The next day, as he was feeding his younger brother, Parmeshvara began to imitate the traveling merchant, telling his brother segments of the stories he could remember. His parents and neighbors overheard him and were surprised at his "sweet voice" (*priya vacan*); they encouraged him to continue learning and performing. He gradually built up a repertoire and began to perform professionally at the age of sixteen or eighteen.

Nonliterate when he began performing, Parmeshvara said he taught himself to read so that he could enlarge his repertoire by reading the Oriya puranas, the major source, according to him, of his narratives. The two

[2] Remember that the semiprofessional performer of the Song of Subanbali in Chapter 3 was just as vehement about the fact that she had not learned from anyone; in her case, she attributed her skills to the vision (*darśan*) given to her by the goddess Parvati.

[3] I did not travel widely in western Orissa and thus was unable to document any *kathānī kūhā* performances over the border from Phuljhar; hence I am unable to verify that there are, in fact, more *kathānī kūhā* in Orissa than in Phuljhar, as many of Parmeshvara's audience members asserted.

performances I recorded, however, were not "religious" in a puranic style. Parmeshvara had no puranic texts with him in his home, nor could he name specific texts that he had read. It is more likely that the singer calls on the puranas to give authority to an individualistic performance style; when he actually *does* use puranic narratives, it is more likely that he has heard these narratives in an oral context in which they were attributed to a certain purana rather than having read them himself. Parmeshvara admitted to adding "additional materials" to the puranic stories to make them more entertaining. Nevertheless, he continued, "They are not useless/superfluous [*phāltū*] songs; they're from the puranas, but I have added a lot to give them more flavor [*mazā karāne ke liye*, literally, to make them more delicious, that is, more entertaining]."

Performing as a *kathānī kūhā* has been Parmeshvara's principal source of income throughout his adult life. It is not a high-paying profession, and full performances are not sponsored frequently enough to support a family totally.[4] Between performances, Parmeshvara walks or cycles from village to village singing in front of people's houses and asking for alms. These songs are usually devotional in nature, drawing from Ramayana or other religious and mythical themes. With this supplemental income, Parmeshvara said he earned more than did a primary schoolteacher in his village.

Recently, Parmeshvara had run into a new problem. His oldest son attending seminary had asked him not to perform professionally, because it did not seem a fitting profession for a Christian. The Christians I spoke with in Phuljhar were themselves divided in their opinions on such a profession for a member of their community. Most educated Christians considered it to be a specifically Hindu tradition and, therefore, inappropriate for a Christian to perform. Most nonliterate Christians, however, saw it as only one more way to make a living, and they themselves attended and enjoyed his performances.[5] Parmeshvara said he had given in to his son's requests and had not performed professionally as a *kathānī kūhā* for three years, although I heard reports to the contrary. He had, however, continued to sing and ask for alms as an itinerant performer. Parmeshvara provides a metacommentary in one of his performances (found in the Texts) about the ambivalence with which such itinerant performers are often received, when the hero of the story takes

[4] Although Parmeshvara was never specific about his income, I was told by other villagers that he received, in 1980, approximately five kilograms of rice per performance as well as a small amount of cash and food for the day of the performance itself.

[5] I also met a Christian *bāhak*, a singer/dancer who performs at each of the "thirteen Oriya festivals." There was more criticism by members of the Christian community of his participation in a Hindu tradition because it was specifically linked to religious ritual and festival.

on the disguise of such a "beggar" in his effort to gain access to the princess and sings:

> Even reciting the name of Ram,
> People in this country abuse you.
> They insult you.
> If I sing and beg,
> Will I get any alms?
> Will I see the queen?

When I met him, Parmeshvara said he had become impatient with his son's requests, since his sons could not yet support him. After all, he continued, singing was the only skill he knew, and "no one gives rice to someone for nothing." If he could not do that, he had no income. When I asked if he would be willing to perform in Patharla, he was more than willing.

Keying Professional Performance[6]

The term *kathānī kūhā* is not used for just any storyteller but rather specifically identifies a professional (paid) storyteller. As a professional, he may draw on tales told in domestic, private contexts; but the ways these tales are received, the expectations the announcement of a *kathānī kūhā* performance raises, differ because of the singer's professional status. As I suggested above, that the folklore community has designated the teller with a unique term suggests that the focus of the communicative event will be on him and his performative style rather than on the narrative itself.[7] The audience will have higher expectations of his performative abilities than they do, for example, of a grandmother telling the same tale in her kitchen. His professional status creates a greater critical distance between the audience and performer than is present with non- or semiprofessionals, many of whom are one among equals in the settings in which they perform and whose audiences are tolerant of a broad range of abilities.

[6] I use the term "keying" as used by Erving Goffman (1974) and Richard Bauman as "the process by which frames are invoked and shifted," "explicit or implicit messages which carry instructions on how to interpret other message(s) being communicated" (Bauman 1977:15).

[7] This is not to imply that non- and semiprofessional storytellers performing in a private context are not held accountable for their style; there are certainly levels of proficiency and artistry in nonprofessional performance as well. But the level to which these performers are held is lower, and the communicative frame does not focus on the *telling* as much as on the *story*. As we saw in Chapter 3, the semiprofessional storyteller Kaushalya Bai herself distinguished between performed and reported narrative; but she was well known in the village more for her *knowledge* than for her performative style.

Parmeshvara is self-conscious of his professional status and its influence on his performances. He himself told me that his skill does not rest in the knowledge of the narratives, for many of them are well known to his audiences; rather it is his delivery style that differentiates him from nonprofessional storytellers. He feels god (*bhagvān*) has given him a special measure of strength that is not available to the general public. He gave an example of what happens when people try to tell stories without this strength: they often cannot remember what to say next, and while they are trying to think of the next word or sentence, they have to fill in with, "Ahhh. . . ." He was proud that he never had to do this, since he "knew how to tell stories."

The morning after his Patharla performance, several male villagers came to the house where Parmeshvara had spent the night and asked him if he would sing something more for them, wanting to know "what else he could do." He was reluctant and told them they surely did not understand the strength and energy it took to perform all night; he was too tired to sing so soon after a three- to four-hour performance like that. He made the analogy to a woman's difficulty in labor and childbirth, which only another woman who has given birth can understand. In the end, however, he acquiesced and sang several Ramayana-related songs of the type he sings when asking for alms.

The physical location of the performance is one of the first factors to key a professional performance in Chhattisgarh. The site for a *kathānī kūhā* performance is generally a publicly accessible location rather than a private courtyard or verandah. The Patharla performance I attended took place on a raised earthen platform built under a large tree on the main street of the village, in front of the village headman's house. This was the site of other villagewide rituals and performances, such as the *rāmlīlā* (dramatic presentation of the Ramayana) and performances of the male *bhajan maṇḍalī* (devotional singing group). Thus, even physically, the performance of the *kathānī kūhā* is in relationship with other publicly performed folklore genres of the village. Parmeshvara's audience consisted of men, women, and children from all castes of the village. The men who were the most vocal in the audience and sitting closest to the performer were from the dominant Kolta caste in whose neighborhood the performance took place. Many women sat in the audience; others watched the performance from their doorways or verandahs. This was the first time a *kathānī kūhā* had ever performed in Patharla in the memory of the audience members, and they were spellbound. There was not as much coming and going as is usually common in public performances because the audience did not know quite what to expect and was not familiar with the ways in which the *kathānī kūhā* developed his story line.

The second performance I attended was held on a clearing between two neighborhoods at the edge of a village. For this reason, the audience was smaller than that of the first performance, with many fewer women present because of the physical distance of the site from their homes. This village was only a few miles from Parmeshvara's home village, and the audience was well acquainted with him and his performance genre. They interacted with him more freely and easily than did the first audience. They were also freer in coming and going throughout the evening, many audience members remaining for only part of the performance. Parmeshvara, too, seemed more at ease with this audience than with the one to whom the genre of *kathānī kūhā* was "new." However, it is characteristic of a professional that he will, and often does, perform in front of unknown audiences whose "goodwill" he has to create and sustain.[8]

The professional status of Parmeshvara's performance is marked by the presence of the opening frame of a *vandanā*, or invocation. The presence of a *vandanā* in Kaushalya Bai's performance (Chapter 3) marked it as a semi-professional genre; the expansion and elaboration of the *vandanā* in the *kathānī kūhā*'s performance similarly sets up even higher expectations of performance than that of Kaushalya Bai. Her *vandanā* was short, almost perfunctory, and led right into narrative, using the same *rāg* (melodic structure); it simply marked the beginning of the performance and asked the blessings of the deities upon it.

The longer and more elaborate *vandanā* of the *kathānī kūhā* serves these purposes and more. Parmeshvara's *vandanā* literally "announced" the performance and called the audience to gather. Before he sang the *vandanā* of the second performance, only a few audience members were seated in the clearing. The performance had not been planned very far in advance, and many villagers were alerted to it only when they heard the *vandanā*; its length gave them time to gather. Parmeshvara's performance style incorporated both song and spoken conversation and prose; that the *vandanā* followed this style and *rāg*, accompanied by the performer's dance, gave the audience a preview of the performer's style and ability. During a break of several minutes between the *vandanā* and performance of the narrative itself, audience members and Parmeshvara talked with each other conversationally, and the performer smoked a *bīṛī*.

The content of the *vandanā* reflects Parmeshvara's awareness of his performance abilities and his willingness to take responsibility for the quality of that performance (see Bauman 1977:9–12). After praising the name of Ram and

[8] See Flueckiger 1988 for analysis of a failed performance of *candainī*, in which the singer was unable to create and sustain such goodwill and most of the audience walked away within the first hour of performance.

singing of the benefits of its recitation (finally, even protection from death), Parmeshvara sets himself up as a professional by associating his voice with the proverbial beauty and sweetness of that of the *koyal* bird (Indian cuckoo). In Indian folklore and traditional literature, the *koyal* carries associations of the season of love; its voice brings pain to separated lovers. But here, the *koyal* is also the guardian of song (the thirty-two *rāg*). Parmeshvara asks the *koyal* to endow him with the quality of its voice:

> The *koyal* bird, the *koyal* has thirty-two *rāg*.
> Give me part of your voice, oh *koyal*,
> Give me part of your voice.

In invoking the deities, Parmeshvara not only asks for their blessing but also specifically asks them to assist him in the skill of performance:

> I salute Sarasvati.
> I salute Samlai.
> Give me a verse;
> Show me the way.
>
> I salute Sarla;
> I salute Mangla.
> Play in my throat;
> Open my throat.
>
> . . . .
>
> If Sarla is here, she will play in my throat;
> She will play in my heart.
>
> . . . .
>
> Lord Narayan [Vishnu], I take refuge at your feet.
> Listen to my one request,
> That my throat may be strong.
> Lord Narayan, I take refuge at your feet.
>
> . . . .
>
> Take me across this ocean of mundane existence.[9]
> I am singing, joining verse to verse.
> Hari [Vishnu], listen to my one plea.

On the surface, these lines suggest that if, in fact, the performance is successful, it will be because of the assistance of the deities. The expression of a deity

[9] The implication of this phrase is that the performance itself may be a bridge across this ocean.

"playing" in a person is used in conversational and ritual contexts to refer to the possession of that person by a deity. To use the expression in this setting suggests the goddess herself will find voice in the throat of the performer, who has no control over the quality of that voice. Such a verbal abdication of responsibility for the success or failure of the performance is a conventional strategy in South Asian professional performances; it is, in fact, an indication that the performer submits the performance to audience evaluation.

A similar convention for accepting such responsibility is for performers to make open *disclaimers* regarding their abilities and to apologize to the audience for any mistakes they may make in the performance that is to follow.[10] Parmeshvara follows this convention in his *vandanā*:

> The black pepper tree is black.
> The black pepper tree is black.
> Look at my ignorance,
> That of a child.
>
> . . . .
>
> I have neither wisdom nor knowledge; I am foolish.
> I have neither wisdom nor knowledge; I am foolish.
> So I fall at your feet.
> I fall at your feet.

Once an audience-performer dichotomy has been established in a folklore genre, in contrast to group performances such as the *suā nāc* or *bhojalī*, the performer necessarily subjects himself or herself to some kind of evaluation by the audience. However, a continuum exists in the nature of the relationship between the audience and performer, which roughly corresponds to the status of the performer from nonprofessional to semiprofessional to professional. A child telling her friends a short folktale stands on one end of the continuum, and a professional such as Parmeshvara, at the other end, with a semiprofessional such as Kaushalya Bai situated in between. Parmeshvara's *vandanā*, as well as comments he made outside of performance, make clear that, as a professional, he has accepted responsibility for his stylistic presentation, for the quality of his voice, and for his ability to "join verse to verse."

An important stylistic feature helping to give definition to the *kathānī kūhā* as a professional genre is the combination of mediums or channels

[10] This is not a unique South Asian phenomenon; such disclaimers as framing devices that actually claim artistry and ability are common in numerous traditions cross-culturally (Bauman 1977:21–22).

employed by the performer: spoken narrative, song, and dance. Such a combination is characteristic of many professionally performed narrative genres throughout India.[11] In Chhattisgarh, it helps to differentiate the *kathānī kūhā* from nonprofessional storytellers, and even from the semi-professional and professional singers of the *candainī* epic, and the combination of mediums aligns the genre more closely with such dramatic forms as the *rāmlīlā* and the *nācā*, or "dance-drama." Semiprofessionals such as Kaushalya Bai and the traditional performers of the *candainī* epic employ only the single medium of song.

Variation between spoken narrative, song, and dance establishes the rhythm of the *kathānī kūhā*'s performance and provides an important means through which the performer can vary the texture of his narrative. Dance occurs only during the songs. His dance is a simple raising and lowering of his heels while standing in a relatively stationary position and snapping his fingers. He wears ankle bells, which serve as a percussion instrument, but utilizes no other instrument. The *kathānī kūhā*'s periodic use of song has the effect of slowing the pace of the performance, both through drawing out individual words over several notes and by increasing the amount of repetition. The song and dance unique to the performance style of the *kathānī kūhā* was key to helping to draw audience members to his performances. But in the Sirco performance, as the evening progressed and the hour became late, members of the audience seemed to become impatient with the pace, fearful that they may not hear the narrative to its end. At one point, they even asked Parmeshvara how much longer he would take before finishing the story. The performer then began to sing fewer songs and speeded up his spoken prose style by eliminating some of the repetitions.

The *kathānī kūhā*'s songs are not memorized, discrete units, nor do they occur at regular intervals. The performer may introduce a song at any time in the narrative and vary its length according to his sense of the performance's timing and rhythm. The basic *rāg* and meter of each song are similar, and the *kathānī kūhā* is skilled in fitting any part of the narrative into verse form. The songs are not purely lyrical, as they are in numerous other dramatic genres; rather, here they often present new narrative action that is not necessarily repeated again in the prose preceding or following the song.

The first song of Parmeshvara's narrative, in which the carpenter and goldsmith meet each other, is an example of the way in which song advances narrative, but at a pace slower than spoken prose. The song begins with the carpenter asking the goldsmith where he is from.

[11] Susan Wadley (1989) characterizes this use of multiple mediums as one of the distinctive features of South Asian oral epics.

"From which place have you come?
From which place have you come?
You've gotten off at the station, brother.
Where are you going?
Introduce yourself, *bābū*,
Introduce yourself."

"I've come from the east.
I'm going to the west.
I've learned a skill, brother;
I'm getting its full worth.
I'm going from place to place.
I'm using my skill.
And you, from which direction have *you* come?
Why are you asking me?
To which place will *you* go?
To which city will you go?"

"I have no mother; I have no home village.
I have no father; I have no place to go.
Where should I go, brother?
Where should I go?
I've learned a skill.
I'm going from place to place.
I'm taking contracts, brother.
I'm taking contracts."

While the songs do not occur at predictable intervals, they *do* mark most major events, a useful narrative device in a performance of this length. In the frame story, one would be able to follow the basic narrative through the songs alone; songs in the main narrative are less frequent. In the frame story, a song portrays each of the following incidents:

The introduction between the carpenter and goldsmith;
The fight that ensues between them and the goldsmith running to the king for protection;
The carpenter finding a sandalwood tree on his way home;
The goldsmith making a golden image of the king to present to him as bribe, so that he will decide in favor of the goldsmith;
The carpenter's wife attempt to allay his anxiety;
The carpenter explaining the source of his anxiety by reporting the meeting with the goldsmith and their fight;

The carpenter making the sandalwood horse for the king;
Acceptance by the king of the golden image;
The carpenter flying on the horse to the king's court and the king's acceptance of the horse
The king's son flying off on the horse;
The lament of the prince's mother over what she thinks is his certain death.

Only two of these, the song in which the carpenter's wife tries to allay his anxiety and the lament of the queen mother, are lyrical verses that do not advance the action of the narrative; both are sung by female characters.

Another performance medium available to a professional, rarely employed by nonprofessional storytellers, is the use of props. Parmeshvara uses only a kerosene lantern and a cane basket, simple but effective props. In both performances I witnessed, he requested that a lantern be brought from a home near the performance site, as well as a large basket used to carry grain. In the first village, there was some resistance on the part of the homeowner to bringing out his lantern, possibly because of the high cost of the kerosene that would be used up through the evening. But Parmeshvara refused to begin his performance without it.

The lantern was utilized in two ways. First, it was a tangible performance marker indicating that the performance had begun and was in progress. While Parmeshvara was waiting for the audience to gather, the lantern was set down on the ground. Before he began the *vandanā*, he placed it on top of the overturned basket. During the break between the *vandanā* and beginning of the narrative, while he was going around taking up a collection from the audience later in the performance, and again at the end of the performance, he placed the lantern on the ground.

The lantern was also periodically used as if it were a deity or another person on stage. During the *vandanā*, Parmeshvara sang to the lantern as the particular deity being addressed. Often in dialogues, he took the part of one character and addressed the lantern as if it were the other character, gesturing to it as one would in a conversation with another person. During the argument between the goldsmith and carpenter, Parmeshvara gesticulated angrily toward the lantern and all but kicked it over when the carpenter pushed over the goldsmith. In other dialogues, Parmeshvara addressed the dialogue directly to the audience instead of the lantern. The alternation between the two styles provided still another means of establishing performance rhythm and variation.

The mediums employed by a performer directly affect the relationship with his or her audience and the distance established between them. In a genre that is totally sung, such as that of Subanbali, the audience is distanced from the performer by the very nature of the song medium. It is difficult for audience members to participate verbally in such a genre without breaking the performance mode and rhythm. This is also true of the sung portions of the *kathānī kūhā*'s performance. The audience never verbally responded or interacted with Parmeshvara during a song. Spoken prose narrative, however, more easily enables verbal interaction between audience and performer. The high degree of such audience participation and interaction characterizes the genre of *kathānī kūhā*, differentiating it from sung or spoken nonprofessional storytelling. Parmeshvara's professional skill and confidence permitted such interaction without letting the performance be carried away or totally disrupted by the audience; Parmeshvara always remained in control. One way in which he did this was to elicit specific responses from the audience by asking questions. Questions and answers are not uniformly distributed through the performance but occur at unevenly spaced intervals. These sections of interaction alternate with relatively long sections of prose narrative and song during which the audience's response is limited to nonverbal expression or responses of assent. In this way, the question-answer sequences are still another medium available to the performer, along with song, dance, and straight spoken narrative, providing variation in the performance.

Many bardic and professional performers in India perform with the help of a *celā* (disciple) or other accompanist (in Chhattisgarh, frequently called *rāgi*, or one who keeps the *rāg*). In the traditional performance genre of the *candainī* epic, the *rāgī* repeat the last word or two of every line sung by the primary singer and add the word *mor* or *tor*. Their repetitions are constant throughout the performance as a refrain, without much variation. The Oriya *bāhak* performs with a *celā* who accompanies the singer/dancer specifically to learn the performance skill, to eventually become a *bāhak* himself. The *celā* answers questions posed by the *bāhak*, repeats certain of his or her sung lines, or responds with short exclamations. A semiprofessional Gond female storyteller brought to her performances a female friend who played the role of the audience by responding appropriately and giving the performer encouragement. This singer directed her narrative to this companion, and the rest of the audience overheard the performance. Parmeshvara had no such *celā* or companion; instead, he depended on the audience to fill this role, one that he carefully controlled.

Parmeshvara's questions to his audience were of two kinds: rhetorical questions for which he waited for an answer and questions that demanded a slightly more expanded response. To try to ensure that his audience's participation was appropriate, he usually limited his questions to those for which there could be only one answer. Generally, only members of the audience sitting closest to the performer verbalized the response, with other audience members concurring or repeating it. Parmeshvara again repeated the correct response before proceeding with the narrative. On only a few occasions did the audience give an incorrect answer, such as misidentifying a particular character, or give an answer that was not what the performer had in mind, although it may have been "correct." In these cases, Parmeshvara simply gave the answer he had been looking for before continuing, as if it were the answer given by the audience. Examples of these variations in question and response are found in the opening lines of the frame story (P. and A. are abbreviations for Parmeshvara and audience, respectively).

P. There was a bus station. . . . People get off at that station, and what else do they do?
A. They go here and there.
P. They also get on. Right? They do both. They get off and they get on. . . . And, at that station, what happened to the two buses?
A. They were standing there.
P. They were standing there. Yes, they were standing there. . . . The buses were standing there, and then the people from one bus got off and the people from the other bus also got off. Right?
A. Right.
P. Or didn't they get off?
A. They got off.
P. OK. The people from both buses got off. . . .

On a few occasions, the audience interjected an unsolicited response or question, without being prompted by Parmeshvara or having been asked a specific question; but Parmeshvara was able to integrate their responses without a break in his performance rhythm. An example is when the carpenter is talking about giving the sandalwood horse to the king as a bribe.

P. "Whatever happens, at least I've got one more chance," he said. "I remembered god and got one more chance. If I take this and put it in the king's courtyard, then in my favor, the king will—"
A. "Settle the case."
P. "The king will settle the case in my favor."

Infrequently audience members interrupted if they did not understand what was happening in the narrative or who was speaking in a particular dialogue.

When the audience became impatient near the end of the performance, its interruption was more aggressive and put pressure on the performer to hurry and complete the narrative. Even here, Parmeshvara did not lose control. He was describing the marriage of the prince and princess:

P. [The princess's father says to the prince,] "You've been given this wealth, the kingdom, and my daughter. Look, I've handed them over to you. I've given them to you." And he joined their hands there.
A. OK. Now the prince is married. What's happening to his mother and father back in their kingdom?
P. OK. What time is it?
A. It's twelve o'clock. Will he go back or not?
P. He'll go back.
A. Then tell the rest quickly.
P. I'll tell it quickly.
A. Take him back to his own kingdom.
P. OK. Then, when the king had handed over the kingdom, the prince said . . .

Eliciting verbal audience response is one way the *kathānī kūhā* incorporates the immediate performance setting into his text. When subjected to this stylistic technique, it is difficult for audience members to remain passive, uninvolved listeners. In the Patharla performance, Parmeshvara elicited their participation even further. During a scene in which wedding guests were giving the bride and groom gifts, Parmeshvara gave his audience the part of those guests. He left the center of the stage and held out a cloth to the audience members, soliciting small monetary gifts from them. Without interfering with the rhythm and continuity of the performance, for a brief period, text and context became one.

While audiences of the *kathānī kūhā* have specific expectations of his delivery style and skills, those familiar with the genre have fewer expectations of what the *content* of his narratives should or should not be. Because his performances stand as independent entertainment events, unassociated with a specific ritual or festival, the *kathānī kūhā* has a freedom not available to most other professional performers in the thematic construction of his texts. Narratives told as an integral part of a ritual or festival celebration must be "true," such as *vrat kathā* (stories told during particular religious fasts); many of these recount either the origins of the festival or ritual or the efficacies of celebrating it. Similarly, while not a *vrat kathā* per se, Kaushalya Bai believed the Song of Subanbali to be the "true" story of *ḍālkhāī*; and her etiological narratives were believed to be "historical." In such settings, narratives of fantasy that the audience does not believe to have actually happened are inappropriate.

Even those narratives performed by a professional or semiprofessional in a public context "for entertainment" are generally expected to be "true." Evidence of this expectation held by the folklore community can be found in Parmeshvara's performance in front of the Patharla audience unfamiliar with his performance genre. After the *vandanā*, the audience asked him what kind of stories he told and then requested that he perform a segment from the Ramayana or Mahabharata. Although he asserts that stories from the epics are part of his repertoire, Parmeshvara responded by saying that he would tell a story from a purana instead. That he attributed his narrative to such an authoritative, "true" source satisfied his audience. To place his own repertoire within the flexible boundaries of the puranic repertoire legitimizes them as worthy of public performance. After the Patharla performance, I asked several audience members whether they believed the story that had just been performed had actually happened. Most of them responded negatively, but they did not seem to be disappointed or to feel betrayed. It seems that once Parmeshvara had caught their imaginations in the web of his performance, their initial expectations for a "true" story were suspended.

The secular context of the *kathānī kūhā*'s performance and the fact that nothing in the definition of the genre itself limits the thematic content create at least the possibility for the performance of fantastic tales, narratives drawing images from outside everyday existence, the historical past, or the religious tradition of the audience. In Western folklore categories, narratives of this kind fall into the category of folktale or, more specifically, *märchen*, "tales moving in an unreal world without definite locality or definite characters and . . . filled with the marvelous" (Thompson 1946:8). In India, these folktales are generally told in a private setting by nonprofessionals. The *kathānī kūhā* brings such tales into the public domain. The folktale does not, however, remain unchanged in this new context. It undergoes several kinds of transformations as it moves from a privately told tale into one that is publicly performed by a professional.

The Domestic Tale in Public Performance

One of the first ways in which Parmeshvara's public performance transforms the folktale is to place it within a specific social setting and geographic locality, by framing the narrative in the geographic landscape in which the audience lives. In the second performance I recorded, in the village of Sirco, Parmeshvara begins with a scene in which two travelers, a carpenter and a goldsmith, meet at a bus stand and introduce themselves. They begin to argue and take their argument to the local king to arbitrate.[12] The king tells the two men to come back to his court in two weeks. During that time, they each make a gift with which to bribe the king. This frame story reflects the everyday world of the audience: descriptions of the bus stand, a marital argument between the carpenter and his wife, collection of wild fruit from the jungle, the wedding season during which gold ornaments are made, and the effort to bribe an official to decide in one's favor. The narrative up to this point could be a report of what had happened to one of the performer's friends. But the carpenter's gift to the king, a sandalwood horse, has the special power of flight. The king's son sits on the horse, admiring its beauty, and it flies up into the sky toward a "foreign land." With the prince, the audience is carried out of the localized frame story into a world of fantasy, away from mundane existence.

Parmeshvara situates the frame story not only within a familiar social/cultural context but, by using local place names, also within the immediate geographic setting of Phuljhar. Folktales told in a private context by non-professionals are rarely so geographically situated; if place names *are* used, generally they are of distant places such as Delhi. Most of the folktales I heard in domestic settings began with an announcement of the major characters, such as "There once was an old man and an old woman," with no geographic setting. A. K. Ramanujan has made a similar observation about the difference between what he calls "domestic tales" and publicly performed tales in Kannada oral tradition (1986:44). The folktale element is retained in the most fantastic segments of Parmeshvara's narrative, which take place in an unidentified distant land; the kingdom to which the prince flies is unnamed.

The first specific geographic reference in Parmeshvara's narrative is to the "Oriya country," from which the carpenter has come. The goldsmith says only that he is from the west (which would actually be the heartland of Chhattisgarh in this case), giving no further details. Not only does the reference to the Oriya country locate the narrative in the same geographic setting in which the performance is taking place, but it also causes the audience to identify more closely with the carpenter rather than the goldsmith, because he is from their home country (the language of performance being Oriya). Later in the performance, when the carpenter is returning from the court of King Manicandra to his village, he decides to save money by walking home instead of taking the bus. He says he will take a shortcut through the jungle rather than take the road that passes through Basna, a

[12] Great landowning *zamīndār* who had nearly total control over those who worked their lands and lived in their villages were often called "kings" (*rājā* or *mahārājā*).

town only seven miles from the village in which the performance was given. Although the carpenter's village is not named, nor is the place of King Manicandra's court, the audience knows they are located near Basna.

The third place-name reference comes near the end of the performance, within the major narrative, when the prince is returning with the princess from the foreign land to his father's kingdom. They descend from the sky on the flying horse for the princess to give birth to their son. The prince goes to a nearby village to get some help for his wife and is there seduced by a prostitute, who causes him to forget his wife and baby. Parmeshvara specifies that they descend near the village of Sirco, in which he is performing. He is carefully bringing the narrative back home, to a familiar geographic setting. Eventually, the prince, princess, and their son are reunited after many years and return to the court of King Manicandra.

It is possible to construct a rough map from the information given to us by the performer. The frame within which the narrative begins and ends is situated within the geographic and social setting in which the performance itself takes place. The village in which the prince is seduced is on the border between the known Oriya country and the unknown foreign kingdom to which he has flown. Depending on where the *kathānī kūhā* performs this narrative or a similar one, the place names and shape of the map would surely change.

As a professional storyteller, Parmeshvara incorporates (even exploits) the immediate performance context into his performance in ways that non-professional tellers of tales rarely do. His control of and creativity in the text-building process, "joining verse to verse" (tale to tale), as well as his particular performance style of alternating between song and spoken prose, permits the flexibility necessary to be able to do this. At one point in the frame story, Parmeshvara depends on a unique element of performance setting on that particular night (my presence in the audience) to support the carpenter's argument on the nature of truth and to engage the audience actively in that argument: "Trees and plants give fruit only because of truth; and because of truth, the seven oceans don't overflow their shores. If the ocean were a liar, then this American couldn't come and sit here. Could she sit here? If the ocean were a liar? How could she cross it? Right? If people came out of the ocean, how could you cross the ocean? That's why I'm saying, the trees give fruit and the seven oceans don't overflow their shores because of truth."

By deliberately setting the beginning of his narrative in a familiar geographic locality and moving into one unknown, Parmeshvara is manipulating his audience's expectations. If they have come expecting a "true" story, the opening frame story begins to prepare its members for the flight into fantasy, first by leaving some of the places unnamed, particularly King Manicandra's court. Second, Parmeshvara subtly manipulates his audience into acceptance of this fantasy by choosing artisans as the main characters for the frame story. Artisans, like storytellers, are creators of new realities out of raw products: a lump of gold is crafted into a king's image, and a sandalwood tree is carved into a magnificent flying horse. On receiving the golden image, the king calls the goldsmith "the creator of the world." Similarly, he addresses the carpenter as "god" when he sees the horse. The frame story prepares the audience for a creation of fantasy, as well as for the transposition of a folktale into public performance.

The *kathānī kūhā* further transforms the folktales he uses as building blocks for his narrative by developing the major characters beyond the stereotypes typical of the folktale. One technique that begins this transformation is Parmeshvara's use of personal names for some of the major characters. Traditional folktales, which frequently open with a formulaic phrase such as "There was once a king and queen," rarely use personal names. In contrast, a publicly performed genre, such as the epic, names its characters, even minor ones. Ramanujan points out that this usage of names in publicly performed tales but not in such private genres as the folktale parallels the absence of the usage of names in traditional households and their usage in public and formal settings outside the home (such as in school and work situations) (1986:50).[13]

The *kathānī kūhā*'s use of names in his public performance stands between these two poles. The carpenter and goldsmith are identified by their caste professionally (as such artisans often are in village everyday speech), but royal characters in the main narrative, such as King Manicandra, the prince and the princess, and the queen who raises the exchanged baby as her son, are named. The two women's names, Mohini and Mayavati, mean "she who tempts or charms" and "she who creates illusion," respectively, names that contribute both to the grounding of the characters as well as to the narrative's sense of fantasy.

More significantly, Parmeshvara develops stereotypical folktale characters by developing small action sequences that reveal their personalities. Rather than simply stating (through the words of the carpenter's wife) that the carpenter is unnecessarily argumentative, we are *shown* his nature through an argument that unfolds between the carpenter and goldsmith, as well as in the conversation between the carpenter and his wife in which she recounts other times when he has argued unreasonably. From these scenes, the audience receives a clear picture of what kind of man he is, the strength and patience of his wife, and the relationship that has developed between them.

[13] Ramanujan identifies a similar convention in ancient classical Tamil *caṅkam* poetry in which personal names are not employed in the *akam* (interior) poetry but may be used in the *puṟam* (exterior) poetry (1986:51).

Parmeshvara also takes advantage of stereotypes and builds upon them. The goldsmith fits the stereotype of one who is cunning and greedy, an artisan who cheats his customers by adding impurities to his gold. The stereotype is given life through descriptions of several interactions between the goldsmith and his customers. Common human emotions are depicted in such a way as to raise characters above stereotypes. The queen mother pampers her only son by personally feeding him his breakfast. Another queen mother reveals her emotions as she talks to herself on her way to find out if her unmarried daughter is really pregnant: "If she'd had only two or three companions, my daughter would have been ruined even more. She had twelve and twelve, twenty-four companions, and even she's been ruined. Look how bad she looks! Her hair is loose. At least she could braid her hair!"

The high level of dialogue in the *kathānī kūhā*'s performance further develops character and also differentiates his narrative style from that of the privately performed folktale. The simple folktale may include short dialogues, but they are most often attenuated; and many of the dialogues are reported rather than reproduced. Parmeshvara, on the other hand, performs most of the dialogue in a realistic style full of local idioms; it is as if the dialogues are being spoken by the characters and overheard by the audience in their own village. An example of this realism is found in the scene in which the old flowerseller is telling her friend about the princess who has refused to move from her bed since she went to the bathing tank several days before. The flowerseller makes her friend promise she will not tell anyone what she is about to hear. The friend answers: "Why would I tell anyone? Why would I tell anyone? I'm the mother of three children, living and dead. Have you ever heard, seen, or known me to tell? Why would I tell anyone?" The flowerseller tells her, speaking loudly: "Oh daughter, blooming flowers give a good smell. [In a whisper] I'm telling you; you're my daughter. For this reason, don't say anything. But, the daughter of the king went to bathe. Who knows if a water snake bit her, or a black bug bit her, or whom she saw at the *ghāṭ*. She came back from there and is sleeping. She isn't eating or getting up, or sitting up or bathing. [Normal, loud voice again] Blooming flowers surely give a good smell. Don't tell anyone."

Joining Tale to Tale

Finally, in the *kathānī kūhā* performance, discrete folktales told singly in a domestic context are interwoven with other tales or tale types into a single unified narrative. This technique, along with expanded scene descriptions, characterizations, and dialogues, enables the professional performer to fulfill the folklore community's expectation that a public performance will last several hours. The *kathānī kūhā* "joins" the tales so that the action of one provides motivation for the action in another. At least three separate folktales can be identified in the three-hour performance under consideration: (1) the story of the carpenter who makes a flying horse, which carries off a prince or king to a foreign kingdom; (2) the story of a prince who disguises himself as a woman to gain entrance to the palace to form a liaison with the princess; and (3) the tale of the exchange of a dead and a live baby, the latter falling in love with his true mother when he grows up. Although I have not heard these discrete tales in Chhattisgarhi domestic performances, two of them are available in this form in Verrier Elwin's *Folk-tales of Mahakoshal* (1944). (Mahakoshal is the eastern half of the old Central Provinces, which includes Chhattisgarh and a few districts immediately west of Chhattisgarh.) In combination, the tales undergo several transformations. I will depend on the published versions of the discrete tales to analyze the kinds of transformations made when they are put in combination with one another by the *kathānī kūhā*.

Parmeshvara begins his narrative with the story of the carpenter building a flying horse (called "The Clever Carpenters" by Elwin [1944:121–123]). His first adjustment to the tale is to make a more dramatic division between the two parts of the narrative: the section of the carpenter building the horse and that in which the flying horse carries the king or prince to a foreign land. In the published variant, both parts of the narrative take place in kingdoms far from Chhattisgarh and in the remote past. Parmeshvara separates the two sections by contemporizing and localizing the first part about the carpenter, leaving the second part in a foreign kingdom. The section in which the prince flies to the foreign kingdom thus seems more unified with the succeeding folktale segments, which also take place in that foreign kingdom.

In Elwin's variant, the carpenters sell their goods to the king, the king is pleased with them, and the carpenters do not come back into the narrative; in contrast, the carpenter/goldsmith narrative frames Parmeshvara's performance at both the beginning and the end. The king to whom the goldsmith and the carpenter present their bribes imprisons the two artisans when the prince flies off on the horse. They are to remain in prison until the prince returns or be killed if he does not return. Although the carpenter and the goldsmith are not directly mentioned again until the very end of the performance, the audience does not forget about them languishing in jail, and the knowledge of their condition provides a certain tension to the narrative. When the audience began to get restless as the hour was getting late, they reminded Parmeshvara to tell them what had happened back in the kingdom of King Manicandra. The very last sentences of the performance rather abruptly return to the initial frame and conclude it. The prince and the princess return to the prince's kingdom with their son and are united with the old king and queen. The audience then asks, "Did they let the thieves go or not?" Parmeshvara answers, "They let them go."

Parmeshvara further elaborates the story of the carpenter by providing a more interesting motivation for making the flying horse than is given in the Elwin variant. In the latter, the carpenters are young boys whose father has died; they are poor and simply making goods for the king to earn some money. Parmeshvara introduces the character of the goldsmith and the ensuing argument between the two artisans. In this variant, the horse is made as a gift for the king in order to bribe him into deciding the argument in favor of the carpenter. Parmeshvara expands the second part of the carpenter story by fitting in two more tale types and more narrative motifs. These additions further complicate and motivate the actions of "The Clever Carpenters." In the privately told tale, the meeting between the two lovers (the king of Delhi and the foreign queen) is quite simple and straightforward, without obstacles: "The Delhi king was thirsty and went to the queen and said, 'Give me water.' She said, 'Come inside.' . . . When he had drunk some water he lay down and went to sleep. The queen felt a sin in her mind and she went to the Delhi king" (Elwin 1944:121–123).

Parmeshvara's performance of this scene presents a more complicated situation in which there are two meetings between the prince and princess, the first one aborted by fear. This meeting takes place in the princess's dwelling next to her bathing tank. Parmeshvara elaborates with a "Three Bears" motif. The prince enters the dwelling without knowing to whom it belongs. He leaves signs of his presence on each of the three stories of the dwelling. The princess finally finds the prince sleeping in her bed on the fourth story. However, when she tries to wake him up with an iron rod, not wanting to touch him directly and thus seem too forward, the prince fears she is about to strike him with the rod and flees. But love between the two has been established. The subsequent separation adds tension to the publicly performed tale.

To bring about the second meeting between the prince and the princess, Parmeshvara introduces the second major tale type, which Elwin has called "The Two Friends " (1944:335–337). In the independently performed tale collected by Elwin, a prince and a princess first meet at a banyan tree outside the town in which the princess lives. The prince goes into the town with a friend to look for the princess, and the two friends take up residence with a flowerseller who makes garlands for the palace. The prince sends a garland to the princess, who recognizes that it has been made by a different hand. She asks the flowerseller who made it and is told that the old woman's daughter made it. The princess asks the flowerseller to send her daughter to the palace to live with her for a few days. Hence, the prince, in the guise of the daughter, gains access to the princess. After several days, however, he wants to return to the flowerseller's house to see his friend. The princess fears that he will not return and devises a plan to kill the friend. She sends some poisoned sweets for the prince to give to his friend, warning him not to eat them himself. But the two friends eat the sweets together, and both of them die, thus ending the tale.

In the *kathānī kūhā* variant of this tale type, the circumstances of the first meeting between the prince and princess, described above, themselves become an elaborate frame story. In both variants, the second meeting is brought about by the uniquely made garland; but here Parmeshvara again elaborates the Elwin variant by adding the uniquely Chhattisgarhi and Oriya motif of the *mahāprasād* friendship. The princess not only wants to meet the daughter but also to form *mahāprasād* with her. Parmeshvara, like Kaushalya Bai did in her narrative, relies on the audience's familiarity with this social institution and its obligations to comment on the relationship (see Chapter 3). The flowerseller verbalizes what the audience will have already noticed, that the ritual exchange is unequal. The princess washes the feet of the flowerseller's "daughter" and prostrates herself before her, but the "daughter" (the prince in disguise) does not reciprocate. The flowerseller confronts the princess with the imbalance of the ritual:

> I, too, have seated [*mahāprasād*].
> I've seen others seat it.
> There's an equal giving and taking.
> What kind of *mahāprasād* have you seated,
> In which only you have prostrated?"
> And to the prince she says,

> "I, too, have seated friendships and have seen those of others. And people feed each other, give drinks to each other, and prostrate before each other. Why is my daughter standing there like a tree? Only the princess has done the necessary ritual.

The dilemma is, of course, the disguise. In the "real" world, a man would never wash the feet of a woman and prostrate himself before her, but neither would they form *mahāprasād* friendships with each other that would require this mutual submission. The prince is using his female disguise only to gain access to his love; he himself is not transformed by that disguise and is unwilling to play the role of a woman to the point that he will prostrate before another woman.[14] Parmeshvara's performance of this scene, with its elaboration and transformation through the addition of the complications of this local *mahāprasād* tradition, greatly delighted his audience.

In Parmeshvara's variant, the prince does not have a male companion, and so he has no motivation to leave the palace. He lives there long enough for the princess to become five-months pregnant. Her pregnancy provides motivation for the third major tale type, that of the exchanged babies, to be woven to the larger narrative. It is also the pregnancy that causes the queen mother to suspect that there is a "thief" in the palace. In "The Clever Carpenters," the palace intruder is exposed by a report given by the barber's wife; in "The Two Friends," he is never exposed, for he dies first from the poisoned sweets. Parmeshvara expands the episode of the palace intruder by introducing the motif of an ingenious trap that a woman devises when the king's wise men have failed to locate him. The minister's daughter-in-law suggests a plan, one dependent on her knowledge of human nature. She gives the princess some sandal paste in which she mixes gold powder. She knows that the princess will rub the paste on her lover and that, as it dries and begins to glitter and cause him to itch, he will have to wash it off. She instructs the minister to post men at every water source in the town, and the prince is subsequently caught.

Once the prince is caught, the narrative line returns to that of "The Clever Carpenters." In both tale variants, the palace intruder—in one the king and in the other the prince—requests permission to climb up a tree to get one last breath of fresh air before he is executed. He has kept his magical horse in the tree and escapes by flying away on it. Again, the *kathānī kūhā* elaborates on the simpler folktale. The king of "The Clever Carpenters" stops to pick up the queen, and the two escape together. The executioners in Parmeshvara's variant feign the prince's execution by showing the king an animal's liver said to be that of the prince. The princess, however, does not believe her lover is dead. She insists that every man in the kingdom be called together in one place so that she can identify the prince. He does not come out of hiding on the first summons but is later found in the flowerseller's house. This motif of the search is repeated in the third tale type of the exchanged babies, when there is a similar search for the prince and he is finally found in the prostitute's home. The repeated motif provides a structural parallel between the two tales and thus a coherence to the larger composite narrative.

After the princess identifies the prince, the two of them fly off together.

[14] See Chapter 3 for a discussion of the uses of disguise in narrative and ritual.

The publicly performed tale and "The Clever Carpenters" again coincide. The final divergence comes when the prince/king stops the horse and goes to a nearby village for help: the king goes for food, and the prince goes for help for his wife and newborn baby. The king dies on the way when the horse catches fire. The prince figuratively dies when he is seduced by a prostitute in the village and forgets about his wife and child. The short folktale ends here, without answering the question of what happens to the queen who was left alone on the bank of the river waiting for the return of the king. Parmeshvara, on the other hand, answers the unspoken question in his performance by adding the tale type of the exchanged babies. With this addition, the public performance has a sense of closure and resolution not present in the variant of the independent folktale available to us.

Parmeshvara uses "The Clever Carpenters" tale type as a skeleton for his performance and dramatically expands the tale by carefully interweaving new tale types and motifs with the core tale. However, his narrative remains sufficiently loosely constructed and flexible so that it can be shortened or lengthened depending on the context in which he is performing and the response of his audience. This flexibility is noticeable especially near the end of the performance, when Parmeshvara abruptly brings the narrative to an end when the audience response dictates that he do so. In another context, he could have further expanded the story by adding more narrative knots/complications, to be resolved with another tale. Certain tale types and motifs naturally lend themselves to combination, just as other tale types are rarely found in combination. Parmeshvara is not unique in his skill to combine these separate tales into a unified narrative performance. For example, Charles Swynnerton has published a tale collected in the Punjab in which the narrator has combined the motif of the flying horse and that of the prince as the palace intruder (1963:297–300). However, the skill for building a unified narrative from shorter tales and interweaving major motifs is characteristic of the professional storyteller and less so of the nonprofessional.

Individual Creativity in a Regional Repertoire

The *kathānī kūhā* stands as an interesting case study of a genre not identified with a particular community within a repertoire whose classification and commentary centers around the identification of genre with community. Rather, it is a term associated with *individual* professional performers, and as demonstrated above, the focus becomes the individual's performance style rather than the content of the narratives. Unfortunately, Parmeshvara was the only *kathānī kūhā* performing in Phuljhar during the year that I lived there, and therefore, I am unable to make comparison-based generalizations about the kind of individual who becomes a *kathānī kūhā*. But to look more closely at Parmeshvara's identity within the social/cultural context of Phuljhar and the performative space that has been given him suggests to us another level of flexibility within the repertoire of genres and of community boundaries in the folklore region of Chhattisgarh.

Parmeshvara stands on the social margins of contemporary Phuljhar society on several levels: he is functionally nonliterate, without any occupational skills other than singing, living on the poverty line; and he is a Christian (whose parents converted from a low caste) in a predominantly Hindu culture. Perhaps more important, he is gifted in performative skills that the Christian community of Phuljhar does not (or cannot) support financially; and his Christian *jāti* precludes him from performing professionally in a genre that is identified primarily with a Hindu *jāti* or festival.[15] Yet, as a creative individual whose special gift is to "remember stories" (a quality gifted, according to him, by *bhagvān* [god]), he has found entrance into public, professional performance through the loosely defined genre of *kathānī kūhā*, associated with individual performance style rather than with a set narrative repertoire or a particular community. With his skills of engaging and captivating an audience, in a framed performative moment, Parmeshvara creates a temporarily bounded community that cuts across religious, caste, and economic boundaries, a community over which he wields performative authority and in which he is granted temporary status. As the editors of *Creativity/Anthropology* observe: "Marginality itself is a cultural category with its own institutional practices and its own space for creative innovation. Creativity often dissolves, or perhaps more precisely redraws, the boundaries of social institutions and cultural patterns" (1993:5).

In many ways, Parmeshvara and Kaushalya Bai occupy similar marginal positions, albeit for slightly different reasons, positions from which they have developed creative, idiosyncratic performance styles. Kaushalya Bai's style, however, remains unnamed as she has not entered the public, professional performance arena. I was referred to her for her *knowledge*, not her performative abilities; and when she spoke about "why we do things the way we do," she, too, temporarily stepped out of the margins into a central, authoritative position.[16]

[15] There are exceptions to this preclusion, such as the *bāhak* mentioned in footnote 5. Generally, however, first-generation converts to Christianity from professional musician castes in Phuljhar, who had previously supported themselves through professional performance, felt like they needed to "give up their instruments."

[16] There are other individuals in the folklore regional that have found space for individual creativity through slightly different modes. I think specifically of two Gond women in the

Perhaps if Parmeshvara had lived in the Chhattisgarhi plains where the epic tradition of *candainī* is common, this performance genre would have been available to him. Its narrative is nonreligious, the genre is identified with the region of Chhattisgarh rather than with any specific caste, and it is performed by a spectrum of low castes. Its performance articulates what it means to be "Chhattisgarhi" in ways very similar to Parmeshvara's narratives that draw on local culture and identity. In the next chapter I examine the ways in which the Chhattisgarhi *candainī* epic interacts with and reflects the *regional* community to which it belongs, primarily by comparing it to the epic variant that is performed as a *caste* epic in north India.

Chhattisgarhi heartland town of Dhamtari who sang for me in an idiosyncratic genre that they called both *dhārī* (literally, stream) and *bā̃s gīt* (bamboo song). They stylistically imitated with their voices the *bā̃s gīt,* a genre associated with the Raut cowherding caste and performed by males only, narrative verses sung in alternation with playing long, heavy bamboo flutes.

CHAPTER 6

"This Is *Our* Story": A Chhattisgarhi Epic *Candainī*

Candainī was the single genre most consistently mentioned in listings of what Chhattisgarhi singers and audiences from the region's heartland articulated to be the "Chhattisgarhi" folklore repertoire. As I got to know better the members of the communities in which I lived, their indigenous commentary often began to break down the nature of the social communities with which genres were identified by caste, age, and gender. However, *candainī* and the regional Mahabharata performance genre *paṇḍvānī,* with which it is often paired, almost always retained their *regional* identification; the community with which they are identified is both geographically and socially more inclusive than that of any other genre from the core repertoire. *Candainī* was repeatedly called "a Chhattisgarhi story," "*our* story." It is because of the strength of this identification between narrative and the regional community that I call *candainī* an epic tradition.

Other narratives performed in Chhattisgarh also fit the characterizations of the Western *analytic* category of epic (features of poetic/sung composition, heroic characters and themes, and length) with which there is *not* this level of self-identification.[1] For example, the Dhola-Maru epic tradition with which Susan Wadley works in western Uttar Pradesh (1989) is also performed in Chhattisgarh, and yet it is known here specifically as a *Rajasthani* (western Indian province and cultural region) story, representing a

[1] See Blackburn and Flueckiger 1989:2–7 for a discussion of the ways in which Indian epics challenge and expand the Western analytic category of "epic." Finally, we conclude, it is the scope and intensity of a community's identification with a particular narrative that is the feature that most distinguishes *epic* narratives from other narratives in a given regional or caste repertoire in India.

somewhat exoticized "other," exemplified by the hero flying away on a desert camel not native to Chhattisgarh. The north and central Indian martial epic of Alha is also performed on occasion in Chhattisgarh but is associated with specific historical kingdoms outside the region and is perceived to be someone else's history. Or, although the pan-Indian Ramayana epic tradition is arguably the most significant religious narrative in the plains of Chhattisgarh, its singers and audiences call it a "Hindi," rather than a Chhattisgarhi, story (*kathā*). The hero and heroine, Ram and Sita, are divine royalty and, in dramatic performances of the tradition, are dressed in generic north Indian royal costuming, as opposed to the Chhattisgarhi dress and jewelry that would identify them by region and caste.

Placed in the context of these long, sung heroic narratives available in Chhattisgarhi performance but not listed as part of the regional repertoire, *candainī* stands apart in the extent to which it has been appropriated by the regional folklore community as "its own."[2] To call this tradition "epic" challenges the boundaries of the analytic genre that have been defined primarily in terms of the Greek epics, particularly with regard to traditional definitions of (male, martial) "heroism."[3] This narrative is a love story, the "hero" is female, and her strategies and actions are nonmartial. I suggest that it is these very elements that both reflect and contribute to the regional ideology identified by the folklore community as "Chhattisgarhi."

Geographic and Social Boundaries of the Epic

Although *candainī* is called a "Chhattisgarhi story," its performance is not limited to the region but spreads across numerous geographic and linguistic borders from middle India to the Gangetic plains of northern India. *Candainī* differs from many Indian regional epic traditions in that its performance is *not* regionally bounded because of association with particular caste histories, regional "historical" events, or the founding of a regional religious cult.[4] Thus, it can and has been appropriated by geographically distant commu-

[2] This affirms Gregory Nagy's assertion that one can identify "epic" only by placing the tradition under consideration in *relationship* to other genres performed by a particular folklore community (April 1994).

[3] See Blackburn and Flueckiger 1989:4 for distinctions between Indian epics according to their "types of heroism": martial, sacrificial, and romantic. See also Menez 1994 and Jason 1977.

[4] The epic tradition has been reported in the Hindi dialects of Maithili, Magahi, Awadhi, Bhojpuri, and Chhattisgarhi, in the provinces of Bihar, Uttar Pradesh (U.P.), and Madhya Pradesh (M.P.). Its hero and heroine are not deified and thus the epic is not tied to a particular religious cult.

nities as "theirs" in a way in which many other epic narratives cannot be. In this chapter we will look at the different shapes and meanings that the epic tradition has taken as it has been appropriated by two such communities—the cowherding Ahir caste in Uttar Pradesh (hereafter, U.P.) and the regional folklore community in Chhattisgarh—asking what it means for *candainī* to be identified as a *regional* story.

It is important to point out that although folklorists may identify the narrative tradition in these two regions as "the same" based on common characters, constant plot elements, and shared motifs, the wide geographic mapping of *candainī* is a reality to those folklorists and not to the epic's performers and audiences. They know and understand the tradition as rooted in geographically circumscribed performance and social contexts, as being identified with, "belonging to," specific communities. None of the singers whom I met in the plains of Chhattisgarh knew that the "same" story was sung in U.P. When I mentioned this to one of the singers, he exclaimed, "Do you mean they really sing *our Chhattisgarhi candainī* way up there?"

The social boundaries of the performance communities (and note I have shifted to plural here) associated with the *candainī* epic tradition in Chhattisgarh have shifted rather dramatically in the last twenty to twenty-five years. In the conclusion of the chapter, I will look more closely at some of the changes that have influenced who the "we" is that is being represented by "our" Chhattisgarhi *candainī,* asking at what level identification is being made—textually, performatively, or both. I suggest that the increasing availability of mass media and rising literacy rates in Chhattisgarh in recent years have affected both the performances that identify *and* the identity of the "we."

The Epic Story

Epic narratives exist both as oral and as performance traditions, a distinction Laurie Sears and I made in *Boundaries of the Text* (1991:6) between a general knowledge of the "whole story" (a summary) that many in the folklore community would be able to relate and the epic as it is performed in a marked, *artistic* enactment of that oral tradition (Bauman 1977:3). The *performed* epic in India is sung in episodes (Blackburn and Flueckiger 1989:11), with the assumption that audiences themselves frame the performance within the larger oral tradition. And I would add here that *candainī* performance is framed not only by the larger *epic* story (oral tradition) but also the Chhattisgarhi folklore repertoire of which it is a part; that repertoire affects how the episodes are understood by Chhattisgarhi audiences. Thus, although scholars have spent considerable energy recording epic stories "from beginning to end," counting the number of hours and pages required to do so, this is not how the epic is received by indigenous audiences. Further, certain episodes of the epic are performed more frequently than others; and there may be episodes that exist only in the oral tradition and not in performance at all.

What follows is a narrative summary of primarily the Chhattisgarhi epic variant, drawn from the oral tradition (summaries that were told to me) and performances I attended. I have noted some of the major differences between this and the U.P. variant of the epic, and more of the substantive differences between the two variants will become apparent in the analyses that follow. In Chhattisgarh, *candainī* is the love/elopement story of the hero Lorik and heroine Candaini, both from the Raut cowherding caste. The hero and heroine are each married to other partners, but Candaini leaves her husband when she learns he has been cursed by the goddess to be impotent for twelve years. On her way back to her maternal village, Candaini is accosted in the jungle by the untouchable Bathua. She cleverly escapes his evil intentions, but he chases after her and terrorizes the inhabitants and cattle of the village. In desperation, the villagers ask the hero Lorik to rescue them; ultimately he defeats Bathua through nonmartial (and, I might add, rather dishonest) means. During this contest, Candaini first lays eyes on the hero, falls in love, and proceeds to seduce him. After some delays, primarily due to Lorik's hesitancy and cowardice in decision making, the hero leaves his wife Majari, and he and Candaini elope to Hardi Garh.

In Chhattisgarh, *candainī* performances center on and elaborate various adventures from this elopement journey (*urḥāī;* literally, flight). In fact, when I asked villagers what the story was about, most responses began with some variant of "It is the story of the elopement of Lorik and Candaini." Eventually, Lorik receives word that his brothers have all died in battle and that their wealth and cattle have been dissipated throughout the Chhattisgarhi countryside, thus leaving his mother and wife destitute. Lorik returns home with Candaini to avenge his family's honor. He succeeds in reclaiming his cattle, through battle in the U.P. variant and by wandering the countryside as a mendicant, collecting his cattle, in Chhattisgarh. When the task is completed, he takes up the position of head of the surviving extended family, including his first wife. But, it is said, Lorik did not take pride in his success. In U.P. versions, he finds that his former physical prowess and strength have dissipated, and he kills himself. In Chhattisgarh, sad and dissatisfied after his return, Lorik one day mysteriously wanders off into the countryside, never to be seen again.

In the Chhattisgarhi village of Garh Rivan (home of Lorik in the epic and

Images of "our *rāutīn,*" Candaini, Rivan village, Raipur plains. Candaini took refuge in the temple of Candi Mata, who, in anger, beheaded her and later restored the head. The two images to the left are Candaini and the one to the right the goddess.

a present-day village near the cattle bazaar town of Arang in Raipur District), one performer sang the epic's closing episode to be that of a lovers' argument. As the couple was sitting in a boat in the middle of the village tank (pond), the argument got so vehement that the boat overturned. Candaini swam to the bank and took refuge in a goddess temple. The goddess was so angered at her sudden and inauspicious intrusion that she beheaded our heroine, only to regret her action later and restore the head. In a village goddess temple on the banks of the tank of Garh Rivan, there are today two images (one beheaded and one whole) of the heroine Candaini, which keep the goddess company. The heroine is not called a goddess but simply honored as "our *rāutīn*" (cowherdress). Lorik, it is said, was never seen after this episode and is presumed to be still wandering in the Chhattisgarhi countryside.

The narrative as performed in both Chhattisgarh and further north in U.P. is not a religious epic, nor are its performances an integral part of any particular ritual or festival, although it is often performed at two festivals that themselves have been "imported" into the Chhattisgarhi ritual calendar, *gaṇés caturthī* and *durgā pūjā*, perhaps as a way of localizing them. Villagers say the epic is sung primarily for "entertainment" (*manorañjan*): nonprofessional performers may sing for small groups of friends and neighbors, and professionals may perform at annual village fairs or to provide entertainment during long winter evenings. These nonritual performance contexts do not, however, diminish the significance of the epic for the communities in which it is performed. In U.P., while the characters are not deified, they are held up as models to be emulated, of "who we would like to become." In Chhattisgarh, by contrast, they are "who we are," in larger-than-life proportions.

The U.P. Variant as Caste Epic

To understand the differences in the performatively identified communities of the Gangetic plains of U.P. and Chhattisgarh, we now take a closer look at both narrative and performative variation in these two areas. U.P. is in the Gangetic heartland of orthodox brahminic Hinduism, whereas Chhattisgarh lies on its periphery. Chhattisgarh's cultural and religious traditions are influenced by the high percentage of tribal groups that have now been integrated into the Hindu caste system. Of particular interest to us in our examination of the epic is the relatively higher status of women in Chhattisgarh compared with that of women in U.P. (see Chapter 1). My analysis of the U.P. epic variant is based on two published versions of the epic collected and transcribed by S. M. Pandey in the 1970s, one in the dialect of Awadhi and the other in Bhojpuri, as well as upon personal communication with Pandey in the early 1980s.[5] I will call this U.P. variant the *lorikī/canainī* tradition, so named in the two dialects, respectively. The Chhattisgarhi data are drawn from my own fieldwork (1980 through 1993, intermittently) and Verrier Elwin's translation of a partial version (1946:338–370).[6]

In both performance areas, the epic tradition seems to have originated with the local cowherding castes—Ahirs in U.P. and Rauts in Chhattisgarh. In U.P., where Ahir males continue to be both primary performers and audience members, however, the tradition has remained more closely identi-

[5] The Awadhi variant was recorded in Allahabad District (U.P.) and published as *The Hindi Oral Epic Loriki* (1979); the Bhojpuri variant was recorded in Benaras (U.P.) and published as *The Hindi Oral Epic Canainī*. Notice the difference in the pronunciation of the heroine's name in U.P. dialects and Chhattisgarhi—Canaini and Candaini, respectively. She is also called Canda in both regions.

[6] Episodes of Elwin's version are surprisingly similar to the episodes I heard in performance, even though they were documented forty years earlier.

fied with that caste than it has in Chhattisgarh. Pandey cites two Awadhi proverbs in U.P. that clearly identify *canainī* with the Ahir caste:

> However clever an Ahir be
> Nothing but Canaini singeth he.
>
> However many times an Ahir may read the Puranas
> He will not sing anything but Canaini.
>
> (Pandey 1979:17)

He does not provide us with the context of these proverbs, but they appear to be metafolkloric statements by members of castes higher in the hierarchy than the Ahirs, with their rather condescending tone toward both the epic and the caste that sings it. It is also possible, however, that the proverbs are used by the Ahirs themselves to extol the virtues of the epic. In either case, the association between epic and caste is clearly articulated.

Certain clans of Ahirs in U.P. identify with the epic more than just performatively: they look to the epic as the history of their caste. Gwal Ahir singers of the contemporary folk song genre called *virhā* believe the *lorikī/canainī* to be the oldest extant record of their caste group. Although most of them admit to not knowing the epic well, they claim that many of their songs and narratives are based on it and many social and religious traditions unique to the caste derived from it. For example, their worship of the three goddesses Shitala, Durga, and Vansatti is said to have been instituted by the hero Lorik and continued by the caste since that time (Coccari 1984).

The differences between caste-epic identification in U.P. and Chhattisgarh can be partially attributed to the differences in each caste's self-perception, status, organization, and ideology. The Ahirs of U.P. have traditionally viewed themselves as a local warrior caste and continue to promote that image of themselves. As certain Ahirs gained in political and economic power in the late nineteenth century, they joined forces in an effort to raise their caste status by appropriating customs (such as donning the sacred thread) and ideologies of the *kśatriya* (warrior) *varṇa* caste category (a process the Indian anthropologist S. M. Srinivas has called "sanskritization") (Mandelbaum 1972:444). Another way to confirm their warrior status was to try to associate themselves with Yadav cowherding caste of the divine cowherd Krishna, calling themselves Yadavs instead of Ahirs. Ahir intelligentsia "rewrote" certain historical documents to prove this connection,[7] forming a

[7] One such volume is V. K. Khedkar's *The Divine Heritage of the Yadavas* (1959).

national Yadav organization that continues to coordinate and promote the mobility drive of the caste.[8] Integral to this movement are retellings of caste history that reflect its martial character; and the epic is one important channel for some of these retellings.

In the *lorikī/canainī* caste epic, it is the cowherd Lorik who is the central character, rather than the heroine (as is the case in Chhattisgarh). He is portrayed as a warrior first, whose primary role is to defend the honor of the caste, often through a defense of the honor of its women.[9] One such incident is when Lorik saves the honor (*izzat*) of the caste by marrying Majari. In the Bhojpuri version, there is a certain non-Ahir king who demands to marry all the beautiful women in his kingdom. When he hears a baby girl has been born to Ahir parents, upon whom gold and silver rained down at birth, he extracts a promise from the parents that they will give her to him as a bride when she reaches maturity. Majari's mother cries over the promise they have made, knowing they will violate caste boundaries by marrying her daughter outside the caste: "How will my *dharma* be saved? How will my honor be saved? Who will end my distress?" When the time arrives, it is the hero Lorik who answers these questions by marrying their daughter and battling the king. Numerous other episodes unique to the U.P. variants specifically frame the motivation of Lorik's battles to be that of "saving the honor of the caste."

In the U.P. epic variant, female characters themselves express the need for male protection. In the Awadhi version, when Lorik's wife Majari learns that Lorik and Canda are planning to elope, she does not protest but asks Lorik to take her with them as a maidservant. She is afraid to be left behind and cries out:

> My lord, you yourself have decided to go to the East
> Under whose care have you left me?
>
> . . . .
>
> My lord, go to the east with your beloved Canva [Canda]
> But take me also as your maid-servant to that Eastern country.
>
> (Pandey 1982:74–75)

[8] As this book goes to press, the chief minister of the province of Bihar and (recently) ex-chief minister of Uttar Pradesh are both Yadavs (Mulayam Singh Yadav and Laloo Prasad Yadav, respectively), suggesting, at least on some levels, the success of the movement. In the fall of 1994, Mulayam Singh Yadav's government was embroiled in controversy over his proposal for reservations for "backward" and "scheduled" castes in educational institutions and government employment, a policy he said would "fight communal forces" in the province.

[9] What is allowed to happen to an Ahir woman directly reflects upon the ability of the Ahir male to protect her; an individual woman's honor is equated to the honor/prestige of the entire caste. See Flueckiger 1989 for other examples of this equation.

In the same version, the heroine Canda becomes pregnant before the couple elopes, and she begs Lorik not to abandon her:

> Your love has made my body heavy.
> Now that I am pregnant, from whom can I take support?
> (Pandey 1982:343; my translation)

These and other examples suggest that women in the U.P. variants are uncomfortable or afraid to act independently of male support and protection.

The dominant Hindu ideology, as expressed in both classical and folk traditions, often presents us with the apparent contradiction of the submissive and outwardly male-controlled woman who at the same time has unique spiritual or magical powers, power generated perhaps through the element of control itself.[10] Female characters in the U.P. variants have special visionary and magical powers, but the female power most frequently called on is the power of *sat,* or truthfulness. *Sat* most often refers to the specific power resulting from female chastity (truth). For a married woman, this power derives from her faithfulness to her husband and hence, in part, from his control and protection. The female character who is most dependent on this power in the U.P. epic is Lorik's wife, Majari. She remains the faithful wife (*pativratā*) during Lorik's long absence. Upon his return from Haldi, Lorik sets up a bazaar outside Gaura Garh, and Majari and her friends plan to go there to sell yogurt, not knowing it is he. On the way, there is a river they must cross, but no boatman to ferry them. At first Majari and her maidservant jointly appeal to their power of *sat* to dry up the river, but nothing happens. Majari questions her servant as to how she might have been defiled, because she knows her own chastity is intact. The servant admits that she was touched by her younger sister's husband as he awakened her from a nap. Majari then makes the appeal alone, and the river parts for them to cross.

In the context of a caste epic, Lorik, whose role is to protect caste honor and integrity, cannot afford to lose the battles in which he engages. To ensure victory, he is often granted divine protection and even intervention by the goddesses Durga and Vansatti. Further, Lorik has other means of supernatural help. His weapon is a "lightning sword" that emits flames (*bijalī kā khadg*); his horse is a celestial mount who, at the end of one variant, carries Lorik to Brahma's heaven. Although Lorik is never actually deified or considered to be an incarnation of a deity (processes common for epic heroes in

[10] See Egnor 1980 and Reynolds 1980 for discussions of this power (*śakti*) as located in specific ethnographic contexts and Beck 1982 for a similar manifestation of female power in a south Indian epic tradition.

many other Indian oral epic traditions), he comes close to deification and takes on divine and superhuman qualities in U.P.[11] In an Awadhi version, we are told of his existence in the heaven of Indrasan before his birth. The god Brahma asks him to take birth on earth to a barren woman who has been performing austerities for twelve years in hopes of obtaining a child. Lorik is reluctant and can be persuaded to do so only when he is promised that three beautiful celestial females will accompany him to become his three wives: Majari, Canda, and Jamuni (Pandey 1982:327, 577).[12] In this same version, flowers rain down from heaven upon his birth, and as a child, Lorik shows his mother extraordinary miracles. We are reminded of the precocious, naughty, and divine child Krishna, who was also raised in a cowherds' community. In fact, the Krishna biographical model continues in Lorik as lover and then warrior.

In the U.P. epic variants, however, Lorik as lover and the episode of the elopement are underplayed when compared with Lorik the warrior and the battle scenes.[13] This makes sense for a *caste* epic, since elopement and the freedom of individual choice it implies threaten caste endogamy and strict maintenance of caste boundaries. Further, the implicit freedom contradicts the social control of women articulated elsewhere in the U.P. variant; in the elopement episode, Canda is portrayed as a stronger, more willful woman than she is elsewhere in the epic. While the elopement cannot be left out totally and have the story still be the "same," the hero and the heroine in U.P. do not take full responsibility for what appears to be individual choice; they justify their elopement at some cosmic level. In the scene in which Lorik first manages to enter Canda's room for the rendezvous that begins their illicit relationship, she resists his advances as a virtuous woman should, asking if he has no shame. He answers her by reminding her of the scene in the heaven Indrapur when he is given three celestial beings to come down to earth with him to become his wives, assuring her that she is one of these women.

The northern, U.P. tradition is, in sum, a male, martial epic that has been

[11] In one Bihari version, Lorik *is* an incarnation of Krishna, sent to earth to be a companion to the goddess Durga, who has come to earth to claim her inheritance; but this version seems to be an exception to the norm for this tradition (Grierson 1929).

[12] Who Jamuni is remains unclear to me in my readings of the transcriptions and summaries provided by Pandey (1979; 1982); she is totally nonexistent in the Chhattisgarhi variant.

[13] In Pandey's published transcriptions of Awadhi and Bhojpuri versions (1979; 1982), over half the total number of lines in each version have been sung before the relationship between Lorik and Canda seriously develops and the elopement takes place. The elopement episode itself is much shorter than the episodes of any individual battle.

appropriated to promote a particular *kśatriya* image of the Ahir caste.[14] A common saying in eastern U.P. is, "If Loriki is recited for one month, there will be a battle somewhere" (Pandey, oral communication, June 1982).[15] The martial ethos of the epic is perhaps most dramatically visualized in a bazaar pamphlet titled (in Hindi) *Lorikāyan: The Battle of Hardīgarh̤* (interestingly, this episode is the only one that has been published in this popular format).[16] Its cover pictures Lorik as the classical Indian warrior, standing on a battlefield holding up a broken chariot wheel, with bodies and weapons strewn across the field and arrows flying through the air.

The Chhattisgarhi Variant as Regional Epic

Older Chhattisgarhi informants told me in 1980 that in Chhattisgarh, too, *candainī* singers used to be primarily from the cowherding Raut caste. One Raut performer sang some opening lines of *candainī,* similar to the above-cited Awadhi proverbs, that reflect this earlier association between the caste and epic:

> They eat sweet dried jaggery.
> They suck sweet sugarcane.
> The Rauts sing sweet *candainī*
> Each of the twelve months.

But its multicaste audiences and the seemingly easy adaptation of the epic to innovative performance styles available to performers from a wide spectrum of castes suggests that it was never "caste owned" in the sense that it is in U.P. The respective castes' self-image provides a possible explanation for differences in the caste-epic relationship.

[14] I add the characterization "male" because women are not part of its primary audiences and may listen to its performance only when it is held in a setting that allows them to "overhear" from behind a curtain or wall. According to S. M. Pandey (oral communication, June 1982), Ahir women may know the general outline of the narrative but have not incorporated its characters and plot into their own female performance genres.

[15] I heard a similar saying in the Phuljhar village in which I lived regarding the Mahabharata (except, instead of a battle, it was said an argument would erupt), in an explanation for why Ramayana performances were more common—a wonderful indigenous articulation for the creative power of performance.

[16] Many oral epics in India are published in these bazaar pamphlet forms; the Chhattisgarhi *candainī,* however, has not yet been so published. This particular U.P. publication and its cover illustration seem to be patterned after the popular pamphlets of another martial epic performed in U.P., the Alha Kand, which are also named according to its numerous battles.

One fifty-year-old Raut male gave the following account of the dispersion of the caste: In "former days," all the Rauts of the area used to go to Garh Rivan (the home of Lorik in the epic and the present-day village mentioned above) to celebrate the Raut festival of *mātar.*[17] Then one year, King Kadra, of a basket-weaving caste, battled against the Rauts. Many Rauts were killed, and the survivors scattered from Garh Rivan and settled "here and there." Since that time, according to the informant, Rauts have no longer gathered at Garh Rivan to celebrate *mātar* but, rather, celebrate it in their own villages. We cannot know from such an account whether the caste was, in fact, ever a power martial or administrative power. Their perception, however, is that they were once stronger and more unified than they are now.

In the more recent past, Chhattisgarhi Rauts have traditionally seen themselves as "village servants" who herd and milk the village cattle, rather than warriors who protect caste honor and boundaries.[18] Lorik, as a Chhattisgarhi Raut, is not portrayed as the U.P. martial hero brandishing a sword, riding on a horse, but mainly as a lover whose only weapon is his herding staff and who travels on foot. Further, reflecting a Chhattisgarhi ethos in which women have more mobility and arguably higher status than their sisters in the Gangetic plain, the *heroine* is the primary initiator of action in Chhattisgarhi performances; it is frequently *she* who protects and saves Lorik rather than the other way around. Thus, while the singing of the epic may have first been associated more closely with the cowherding caste of its singers, the tradition as it has been documented in the last fifteen to twenty years reflects little to suggest a strong caste identity.[19]

Part of what gives the epic tradition its regional identification in Chhattisgarh today is its performance contexts and the broad social base of its audiences and performers. Two basic performance styles of *candainī* have developed in the region. Both styles are most commonly called simply *candainī,* but when the styles *are* distinguished, the first is called *candainī gīt,* or

[17] See Babb 1975:36–37 for a description of *mātar* as celebrated in the Raipur plains.

[18] This image is changing, however. During my last trip to Chhattisgarh, in the summer of 1993, I heard many complaints from village landlords that Rauts were no longer willing to "serve" the village, that they were choosing to commute to the city for work instead. It has left many landowners desperate for "servants" (*naukar*), and many are being imported from the neighboring province of Orissa, where there is high unemployment and hence a willingness to relocate for work. It is doubtful that the Rauts will reappropriate the epic now to promote this newly emerging identity, for they had already abandoned the epic as performers, although still participating as audience members of the Chhattisgarhi regional folklore community.

[19] Rauts do have another narrative performance tradition whose musical accompaniment, bamboo flutes (*bā̃s*) five to six feet long, give the genre its name (*bā̃s gīt*). It remains specifically associated with the caste, even when listed in the core Chhattisgarhi folk repertoire. I have heard this genre performed only once, in an attenuated, midday demonstration just for me. I do not, therefore, have sufficient performative data to include the genre in this book.

song, and the second *nācā,* or dance-drama. As mentioned earlier, traditionally, *candainī gīt* singers were male members of the Raut caste who sang the epic both professionally and semiprofessionally to primarily male audiences, but with women sitting on the sidelines. Rauts sang without musical accompaniment; but essential to their performance was a companion (*rāgī* or *saṅgvārī*), who joined in the last words of every line and served as a respondent. Today, it is difficult to find Rauts who still sing in the *gīt* style without instrumental accompaniment. The only such singer I knew died in 1988, and not one of his sons was interested in learning or continuing his father's tradition. As a Brahmin overseer of a village headman's estate told me in 1993: "How can this [that is, style with no musical accompaniment] compete with video halls? There's no *mazā* [enjoyment] without instruments. Even day laborers have television now. . . . These days Rauts can't afford instruments. It was their own decision [though] not to work as village servants [to work instead in urban dairies, restaurants, and so forth]. So, with no instruments, there's no interest. Earlier, Rauts could get whatever they needed from their masters [*mālik*]. Today, what do instruments cost? Rs. 1,500. The villagers don't even ask [them to sing]."

The dates and circumstances in which members of the Satnami caste took up the *gīt* style of *candainī* performance are undocumented and vague in caste and regional memory. When I was looking for epic performances in the 1980s, however, I was frequently told that I would find *candainī* only in those areas with large numbers of Satnamis. The Satnamis are a sect to which members of the outcaste Camar (leather-working) caste converted in the 1800s; yet conversion did not raise their status from that of the lowest-caste groups. It is probable that when *they* began to sing *candainī* professionally, it began to attract more diverse audiences and to take on its current regional identification. The Satnamis added musical accompaniment to the *gīt* performance style, including, minimally, harmonium and tabla; but they have retained from the Raut performance style the combination of lead singer and one or more *rāgī* (companions), whose response lines end with *mor* or *tor.*[20]

[20] One informant told me that the difference between the *candainī* and *paṇḍvānī* traditions (and note how they are being paired in this comment) was this characteristic line ending of *mor* and *tor* of *candainī* and *bhāīya* or *bhāīge* (literally, brother) of *paṇḍvānī*. Two examples of the ways in which the *rāgī* joins in with the *gāyak* follow. The *tor* and *mor* are semantically empty, although they literally mean "yours" and "mine."

gāyak	***rāgī***
aur rājā mahar ke	*ye din tor*
ya beṭī canda ho	*ye din tor*
Of King Mahar,	on this day
She is the daughter Canda.	on this day

Because I have little comparative data to use from "purely" Raut performances, it is difficult to know exactly how the narrative may have shifted when the Satnamis began to sing the epic professionally, particularly in its portrayal of the "villain" character, the Camar Bathua, who tries to accost Candaini in the jungle. In one Satnami performance, however, Lorik meets Bathua again after their initial confrontation in the heroine's maternal village. Bathua reappears as the bodyguard of a foreign king whom Lorik has offended (by chopping off the nose of one of his subjects); so the king sends Bathua to punish him. This time their confrontation *is* martial, and Lorik is unable to defeat the untouchable physically. He is pinned to the ground, and Candaini has to beg Bathua for mercy. The Camar gives in but says Lorik must tie him up so that the king will think he has been defeated, not compassionate. Lorik eventually wins the kingdom through both battle and trickery and names it after the untouchable Bathua. When I later discussed this episode with several non-Satnami villagers, they told me that Satnamis have tended to glorify the character of Bathua and that a Raut singer would never have included such an episode, glorifying the heroism of the Camar.

The second *candainī* performance style, called *nācā* (literally, dance), includes song and dance, spoken conversations between characters, and narration in the *gīt,* responsive style.[21] According to *nācā* performers, the *nācā* developed in the early seventies in direct response to the strong influence of the increasingly popular Hindi cinema, an essential element of which is also song and dance. A *nācā* troupe consists of up to eight or ten performers, some of whom are actors, and some, musicians. An important feature of the *nācā* is the inclusion of costuming and minimal props. The hero Lorik carries a herding staff and wears traditional Raut festival dress, decorated with peacock feathers and cowrie shells; male performers put on saris and typical Chhattisgarhi jewelry to act out the female roles. The musicians sit at the side of the stage and accompany the songs of the actors or provide their own sung narration in the *candainī gīt* style. *Candainī* is only one of many narratives performed in the *nācā* style; but *nācā* troupes that specialize in *candainī* do so to the exclusion of other narratives. Although this style has grown in popularity, it is expensive to patronize; therefore, while more popular than the *gīt,* the *nācā* may be performed less frequently. When sufficient funds for the *nācā*

---

rājā ye mahar ke beṭī	*beṭī tor*
kaise gaurā ma barḥe	*barḥe tor*
The daughter of King Mahar	the daughter
Grew up in Gaura.	grew up

[21] Many *nācā* performers are able, therefore, to perform in the *gīt* style and may do so for their own entertainment.

Raut *mātar* dancers, Raipur plains. Lorik is similarly costumed in *candainī nācā,* turbaned, decorated with peacock feathers and cowrie shells, holding a herding staff.

cannot be raised, or if troupe members are singing nonprofessionally, the *gīt* style, without dance, can still be heard.[22]

The performance context of the *nācā* is important in establishing the epic's regional character. Troupes are usually multicaste, heavily represented by Satnamis but also by other middle-level castes, including Rauts; one performance troupe I met consisted of ten members from six different castes. Troupes are hired by village/neighborhood councils for annual village fairs or festivals, particularly *durgā pūjā* and *gaṇés caturthī,*[23] or as independent

[22] See Flueckiger 1988 for a description of one performer who experimented with combining elements of *gīt* and *nācā* in a public performance for which there were not sufficient funds to hire an entire *nācā* troupe.

[23] Both these festivals originated in and are specifically identified with regions outside Chhattisgarh—Bengal and Maharashra, respectively—where they are *the* major festival of the year. But they are commonly celebrated, with more or less *dhūm-dhām* (festivity, energy), in towns and cities all over north and central India. For both festivals, elaborate images of the respective deities are "seated" for a period of nine days in neighborhoods throughout the city, and various kinds of entertainment groups, including *nācā* troupes and *bhajan maṇḍalī* (devotional singing groups), are often hired to perform in front of the deity.

entertainment events. Occasionally, a family will sponsor a performance to celebrate the birth of a son or a wedding.

Nācā audiences, too, represent the caste spectrum of a particular village or urban neighborhood, male and female. *Nācā* are performed in public space such as a village or town square or main street, accessible to everyone. Persons from surrounding villages frequently walk several miles to attend *nācā* in neighboring villages. The enthusiastic and responsive participation of women in the primary audience of the *candainī nācā* stands in sharp contrast to the all-male audiences and performance contexts of the U.P. variants of the epic. In 1980 when I asked female audience members if *women* ever sang *candainī* in Chhattisgarh, they all answered negatively. I did hear segments of the epic narrative and reference to its characters in other female performance genres, which they did *not*, however, identify as "*candainī*," because of the performance context and singing style. To sing "*candainī*" means to sing in a public context and, more specifically, to incorporate at some level the responsive singing style of the *candainī rāgī*, with his end-of-line words of *tor* or *mor*. What these women were singing was identified by *context* and *rāg* (melodic structure) as a harvest-dance song (*suā nāc*) rather than by *content* as *candainī*.

In recent years, a handful of individual female performers have performed the *gīt* style of *candainī* professionally, accompanied by male *rāgī* and musicians. They are self-taught and have gained meteoric popularity because of their unusual position as professional, public *female* performers. Several audience members told me, "Who *wouldn't* go to hear a woman? There's more entertainment in that!" One such female performer is Suraj Bai, who, in 1987, was hailed in a local English-language newspaper as "the melody queen." She had represented Chhattisgarh at national and state folk festivals and had performed on nationwide television and radio; yet, the newspaper article bemoaned, she still worked as a day laborer. Over the last five years in Chhattisgarh, the epic tradition of *paṇḍvānī* is experiencing a similar rise in popularity, attributable primarily to the fact that the tradition is being performed by two professional female singers, Tijan Bai and Ritu Varma, who have gained notoriety through their performances on television and radio.

Although *candainī* female performers are still unusual, the worldview expressed by both female and *male* performers of the Chhattisgarhi epic is a female-centered one.[24] The heroine Candaini is the dominant character in the pair of lovers and the initiator of most of the epic action. In fact, in several

[24] See Velcheru Narayana Rao (unpublished ms.), "What Is Folklore in India?" for a discussion of the Sanskrit classification of members of low castes and women within a single category.

episodes *she* actually saves or protects Lorik, a reversal of the situation in the U.P. variants. Candaini and other women are not portrayed as property to be exchanged and protected; rather, they are resourceful and take initiative, relying not on the *ritual* power of their chastity as women frequently do in dominant-discourse narratives but on their own intuitive common sense.

Candaini's dominant role in the Chhattisgarhi epic first becomes evident as she makes the decision to leave her husband when their relationship is not fulfilling to her. Then, it is she, rather than Lorik, who initiates their relationship; she sees him in the competition with her assailant Bathua and sets about to seduce him. In one version, she asks her brother to build a swing for her next to the path that Lorik uses every day to get to his wrestling grounds. As Lorik passes by, Candaini asks him to swing her. When he declines, she curses him. This so angers him that he violently swings her, causing her to fall off the swing and giving him the opportunity to catch her (Elwin 1946:349).

The next time they meet, Candaini suggests a joking sexual relationship with Lorik by calling him her *devar* (younger brother-in-law), with whom such a relationship is permissible. Having grown up in the same village, they would normally call each other "brother" and "sister," precluding a sexual relationship; changing the terms of address is often one of the first indications of a change in the nature of a relationship in Chhattisgarhi rural life and oral traditions. Finally, Candaini openly invites Lorik to visit her during the night, telling him how to get past the various guards that stand at the entrance to her palace (compare this with her reluctance in the U.P. version of a similar scene, cited above).[25] As their relationship develops, it is she who suggests and pushes for the elopement to Haldi.

Candaini's resourcefulness and courage are illustrated by numerous examples from Chhattisgarhi episodes of the epic. In one performance, when the couple is eloping and their way is blocked by a flooded river, Candaini, not Lorik, figures out how to cross. She first procures a small boat from the ferryman (*kevaṭ*) stationed at the crossing. Lorik accuses her of negotiation of more than transportation with the *kevaṭ,* however, and in jealousy splits the boat and its owner in two with his sword. He then goes into the jungle and cuts down some green wood to build a raft, which, of course, immediately sinks. It is Candaini who knows it must be built with dry bamboo, tied together with lengths of a forest vine. The *kevaṭ*'s wife then comes to bring

[25] A *dhobin* (washerwoman) catches Lorik leaving the palace in haste with a woman's scarf on his head instead of his turban; thereafter, she serves as a go-between for the lovers. Compare the use of the flowerseller to gain entrance into the palace by the hero of the *kathānī kūhā*'s narrative in Chapter 5.

him his morning *bāsī* (rice left over from the evening meal that ferments overnight in the rice water and is commonly eaten as breakfast in rural Chhattisgarh). Seeing her dead husband and suspecting the eloping couple of his murder, she creates a magical (*jādū*) mouse that hides on the raft.

Halfway across the river, the mouse bites through the ropes holding together the raft. Candaini manages to reach the far shore, but Lorik does not know how to swim and starts to drown. The heroine unties her braid, jumps in, and saves him, presumably by pulling him ashore with her hair.[26] Having swallowed a lot of water, Lorik is not breathing. An old woman passing by advises Candaini to grab Lorik by one leg and drag him around in a circle to get the water out of his lungs, which successfully revives him. Her ingenuity and physical strength in this episode stand in sharp contrast to the U.P. scene in which Lorik's wife calls on the power of her chastity to cause the river waters to part.

A female worldview is again reflected in a wonderful episode of the eloping couple's journey through a kingdom of all women. Candaini sends Lorik into the town to buy them some betel leaf (*pān*). He is tricked by the *pān*-seller to follow her home, where she "keeps her best *pān*" (to feed *pān* to a member of the opposite sex in Chhattisgarhi folklore is to initiate a sexual relationship or is a metaphor for intercourse itself).[27] Once the *pān*-seller has trapped Lorik in her house, she threatens to beat him with a bamboo pole and stuff his skin with straw, poke his eyes out with a needle, and, finally, brand him with a hot crowbar unless he promises to marry her. After each threat, he gives in, only to recant a few minutes later. In the end, Candaini comes looking for her partner and meets the *pān*-seller in the bazaar. The *pān*-seller begs the epic heroine to help her with a man who refuses to marry her. Candaini discovers a sari-clad Lorik in the woman's courtyard, having been so disguised so as to hide his male identity in the all-female kingdom. Once his identity is made known, the two women agree to play a round of dice to determine who will win him as husband. Note that while this is a reversal of the gender roles in Sanskritic, male dicing games, which are played to win a woman as a marriage or sexual partner, the motif of women dicing over the fate of men is found in other Chhattisgarhi folk narratives (see Chapter 3). Candaini triumphs in her dice game with the *pān*-seller and frees Lorik from his captivity. One can hardly imagine the martial hero of the U.P. variants of the epic permitting the *pān*-seller's physical humiliations to

[26] Loose hair in Chhattisgarh has sexual connotations unless framed in ritual contexts of mourning or goddess possession.

[27] See Chapter 2 for a similar example of the use of *prasād* imagery in the friendship songs of unmarried girls.

be forced on him or to be dependent on rescue by a woman in a women's world.

Even in several episodes in which Lorik takes the primary role in a confrontation, it is still a woman who tells him how he can win, and the means are rarely traditional "heroic" ones. The first such confrontation is between Lorik and the Camar Bathua. Candaini's mother says the only man who can successfully confront Bathua is the "sporting hero Lorik" (Elwin 1946:345). Lorik's wife, Majari, however, warns him that he will not be able to defeat the Camar in a normal wrestling competition. She suggests the confrontation be one in which both men are buried up to their waists in separate pits by the other man's wife. The man who can first get out of his pit and beat the other man will be the winner. Lorik agrees to this. When the women are burying each other's husbands, Majari begins to throw gold coins on the ground. This so distracts the Camar's wife that she only loosely packs the dirt around Lorik and then runs to pick up the coins. Meanwhile, Majari has time to bury Bathua firmly. When the time comes for the men to try to get out of their pits, Bathua is stuck, and Lorik jumps right out and soundly beats the Camar.

Candaini's beauty and a male's desire for her are the source of several major conflicts in the Chhattisgarhi variant, and in these situations she is physically threatened and needs physical protection like the women in the U.P. versions. However, as we have seen above, if Lorik were left to his own strength and resources, he might or might not be able to provide Candaini with the necessary protection. Judging by her resourcefulness in other situations, one senses that if she had no male to protect her physically, Candaini would come up with alternative solutions. Furthermore, when her chastity *is* protected by Lorik, only her personal honor is at stake. The personal honor of a Chhattisgarhi Raut woman does not necessarily extend to the honor of her family and caste. One of the main episodes in the U.P. variant making this connection between the three levels of honor—the story of Lorik saving Majari from having to marry a king outside the Ahir caste—is not present at all in the reported and performed versions I have seen in Chhattisgarh. The other U.P. episode making this association explicit is Lorik's defeat of Bathua, which saves the honor of Candaini and the Ahir caste. In Chhattisgarhi versions, Candaini's mother, in asking Lorik for help, is not as concerned with honor as with physical safety: Bathua is terrorizing the entire village, so that everyone is afraid to go out of their homes, and the cattle are dying from lack of fodder and water (Elwin 1946:345).

As the role of women increases in importance in the Chhattisgarh variant, we have seen that the character of the hero also shifts. He is no longer the ideal protector and warrior. When he does engage in battle, he usually employs nonmartial, often unheroic, means to win; when the battle is honest, he battles without the aid of large armies, elephants, or other military paraphernalia that support him in U.P. versions. He is a simple cowherd whose weapons are his own physical strength and herding staff. In this epic variant that centers around elopement love, the hero's status as warrior is less important than that as lover.

An important way in which Lorik's role of lover is highlighted in Chhattisgarh is through the elaboration of the character of Bawan Bir, Candaini's impotent first husband. His impotence and passivity give emphasis to Lorik's sexual prowess and virility. One *nācā* performance portrayed Bawan as a buffoon who is always wiping his nose with his fingers and licking the snot off of them. During the twelve years of his impotence, he wanders the forest as a *sādhu* (religious ascetic) but is easily frightened by any strange noise and welcomes Candaini's company when she comes to the forest to try to persuade him to give up his asceticism. Both Satnami and Raut versions agree that Bawan Bir's impotence is the result of a curse cast on him by the goddess Parvati. A Satnami version of the curse incident recounts that Bawan used to tease the Raut girls who picked up cow dung in the jungle everyday. One day, Parvati took the form of one of these girls, and Bawan began to tease her. She revealed her true form to him and cursed him to impotence for his audacity. The Raut version says that one day Bawan Bir left a leaf cup of milk sitting on the ground, from which he had drunk. Shiva, in the form of a snake, came up to the cup and drank out of it. Subsequently, he began to acquire the rather obnoxious personality of Bawan Bir, quarreling with and scolding his wife Parvati. When Parvati realized why this personality transformation had occurred, she cursed Bawan to impotence.

Bawan Bir is also impotent in the U.P. epic variant, but the fact is given little elaboration in the performances reported by S. M. Pandey. In the Awadhi version, we learn of the impotence in a single line. The performer tells his audience that Bawan is a eunuch with no hair on his body, but he gives no reason for the condition, although (according to Pandey) the audience knows the reason is a curse from Durga. Another story circulates in Ballia, U.P., that Bawan encircled his large penis around a Shiva *liṅga* (a phallic representation of Shiva) and that the god cursed him to impotence for trying to compete with him (Pandey, oral communication, June 1982). Whatever the reason, Bawan's impotence is overshadowed in the U.P. versions by his martial nature. He, too, is a powerful warrior when he battles and defeats Lorik's older brother and confiscates all their family wealth and cattle, and again in the battle in which Lorik regains this wealth at the end of the epic.

Appropriating the Performative "Exterior" of the Tradition

In our examination of the *candainī* epic tradition as it has taken root in two very different social/cultural contexts within its broad performance range from U.P. to Chhattisgarh, we have seen how it has responded to and reinforced the identities of caste and region both textually and performatively. In U.P., the epic serves to represent the caste to itself and to other castes in the region, in the Ahirs's effort to consolidate and raise their caste status. The epic in Chhattisgarh is more self-reflexive, mirroring the region to itself, contributing to a Chhattisgarhi self-awareness of difference, particularly, for example, regarding the status of women and marriage customs.

From the information available to us, it seems safe to say that the Ahir caste in U.P. has appropriated the epic as part of a specific cause. To say the *region* has "appropriated" the epic in the Chhattisgarhi contexts described above is, perhaps, to give unwarranted self-conscious agency to a relatively loose social body.[28] In the last ten to fifteen years, however, "appropriation" *is* the word to describe the emergence of "new" performance contexts and audiences for *candainī,* both within and outside Chhattisgarh. The tradition has been self-consciously crafted and packaged for both Indian and international audiences outside Chhattisgarh as representative of the *region* (not caste, class, or gender). This appropriation coincides with increased availability of mass media technologies and communications (television and radio), as well as the academic and popularized interest in "ethnicity" that has developed in India over the last decade (as evidenced, for example, in international Festivals of India and modified "ethnic dress" as high fashion among the upper middle class of urban India).

Radio, television, and the cassette industry have provided significant new contexts for folklore performance, including the epic. Akashvani (All India Radio) has local (Chhattisgarhi) and national (Hindi) programming, with regularly scheduled folklore programs as a part of both. Such programming expands the social boundaries of groups to whom many performance genres are traditionally available; songs that women used to sing among themselves while transplanting rice or in the privacy of their courtyards are now blared over speakers from tea stalls and bus stands in urban neighborhoods and

[28] There are genres other than the epic that *have* been appropriated by folklore groups and communities within the region, however, in a self-conscious way. For example, in 1985 one village headman talked specifically about the role he thought local festivals could play in establishing a sense of village identity and improving morale. He told me he had introduced the festival of *gaurā* to his village several years ago for just such a purpose (see Chapter 8 for a description of this process).

village main streets. Although the epic was spoken of as being "Chhattisgarhi" even before its appearance on media channels, its performance on radio and television has solidified the epic's geographic regional identity, drawing its boundaries more literally than "live" epic performances, since such programming is limited to specified districts. The epic has also become uniformly available throughout these districts, even in those villages and neighborhoods where it has never been performed except over the airwaves.

In 1985 when I was trying to trace down various performance traditions (specifically the *suā nāc*) in the burgeoning town of Dhamtari, I was frequently asked why I didn't simply turn on the radio on Wednesday afternoons for Akashvani's Chhattisgarhi folklore programming, from which I could simply tape the "best singers" directly from the radio, without all the complications of live performance. Both radio and television performances are taped in rather sterile recording rooms, with specific time frames (much abbreviated from any live performance), and without a live audience with whom to interact and jointly craft the performance (try to imagine the *kathānī kūhā* performing without the live audience on whom he so depends as a "coperformer"). Further, these performances are taped under the direction of radio station personnel who often have certain aesthetic criteria that they feel "typify" the particular Chhattisgarhi genre in question, although most of them are not "native" to the region. These criteria include less repetition, more instrumentation, and a particular voice quality and stage presence of singers. When I articulated some of these differences between a half-hour radio performance of a *candainī* episode and its elaboration during a four-hour, late-night epic performance in a village square, adding that there was little *manorañjan* (literally, entertainment, but with the implication of emotional satisfaction) hearing it over the radio, the same informants who had urged me to tape from radio generally agreed wholeheartedly, although they often felt somewhat differently about television performances. In the mass media, the epic is taken out of its traditional performance contexts and recontextualized in a setting in which it "represents" on an external performative level through style and instrumentation but in which its interior is frozen, unresponsive, and generic.

Radio and television programming has affected the careers of particular singers who have been chosen and promoted by the staff. This has been the case especially for the female epic performers referred to above. Once heard repeatedly on local radio or television, they are then invited to statewide folklore singing competitions and folklore festivals in major urban centers, such as New Delhi, Bombay, Calcutta, and even London, to "represent" Chhattisgarh. As individual singers themselves become famous, the genres associated with them have become more popular as well, both within and outside the region.

Representative of the growing "academic" interest in Chhattisgarhi folklore by members of an urban, educated class, who have not traditionally participated in epic performance as singers or audience, is the playwright/director Habib Tanvir, born in Chhattisgarh's heartland (Raipur), now living in New Delhi. His troupe, Naya Theatre (New Theatre), consists of actors and actresses drawn from Chhattisgarh's villages, the majority of whom are nonliterate "traditional" dancers and performers. Along with his interest in experimental theatrical forms, an overriding concern of Tanvir's is to promote the appreciation and preservation of Chhattisgarhi folk performance traditions. To this end, he has held numerous folklore workshops in Chhattisgarh itself for performers of these traditions. The aims of these workshops are for performers to share with one another their repertoires and for Tanvir himself to document them, often then integrating their themes and forms into his "new theatre." In a 1985 interview while in Calcutta staging his play *Charan Das Chor,* Tanvir explained this task as follows: "I had to work in two ways. I had to purify their forms and themes to make them more authentic and contemporary. I found that the folk form was getting spoiled and diluted by the combined influence of urbanization, mass media, and low-grade Hindi films. The first part of my job was to weed out the falsities and purify the form. Not for the sake of purity, but because the folk form is both beautiful and a powerful medium for a message" (Bose and Bhattacharjee 1984:n.p.).

For one of his Chhattisgarhi folklore workshops, held in the late seventies, Tanvir called together the "best" *candainī* singers he had met in his tours of the region. Singers from a range of castes shared their stylistic and thematic repertoires. One of these singers was the Satnami Devlal; he was also one of several workshop participants then chosen to go to Delhi to work with Tanvir for several more weeks. According to Devlal, Tanvir stressed to the singers the importance of keeping their tradition alive and that one of the ways to do this was to keep the *entire* narrative in performance, singing it "from the beginning," when the hero and heroine were children, and so on, rather than focusing so exclusively on the elopement episode.

I attended (and was the primary patron of) one of Devlal's *candainī* performances that resulted in a "failed performance," with most of the audience of about two hundred walking away within the first hour of the performance. I have analyzed the reasons for this elsewhere (Flueckiger 1988), but one important reason cited by audience members was that he was singing "stories we don't know," ones from this reconstructed, larger repertoire of epic episodes. Devlal was also experimenting with form. He framed the performance as if it would be a *nācā,* a form influenced by the corrupting "low-grade Hindi films" to which Tanvir referred, but he did not wear the expected costume or perform the expected "song and dance." So another major complaint of the dissatisfied audience was that "he should have worn a sari."

Over the years during which I have returned to Chhattisgarh since 1980, literate and nonliterate residents of Chhattisgarh have voiced a certain unease about Tanvir's appropriation of Chhattisgarhi folklore for display outside the region. Even as he is attempting to promote an appreciation of the region and its performance genres, many inhabitants feel that the process serves no benefit to Chhattisgarh itself. Several residents of the town in which Devlal performed, who have known him since his childhood and over the years during which he developed his epic-singing skills, complained that when Tanvir chose particular singers such as him, they often forgot the Chhattisgarhi roots from which they have come, were no longer satisfied to sing in "traditional" contexts, demanded too much money, and were no longer responsive to their audiences.

Drawing on a workshop held for *candainī* performers, Tanvir later wrote a script based on the epic to be performed by his Naya Theatre troupe, called *Son Sagar,* the name of one of Lorik's beloved cattle. I was able to sit in on one of the rehearsals of this play in 1985. The actors and actresses of the troupe are Chhattisgarhi, as is the language of the play; it opens with a traditional *vandanā* (invocation to the goddess Sarasvati) and is framed and interspersed with lines sung in the traditional *gīt* style. But, performed on a modern urban stage, outside traditional performance contexts, it is not "our *Chhattisgarhi candainī*" as understood by most singers and audiences in the region. Although, according to Tanvir, there is room for improvisation, the lines are relatively fixed, memorized, and performers are unable to be verbally responsive to particular contexts and audiences.

In newly emerging performance contexts such as radio, television, and the modern stage, the epic has become decontextualized, so that it can be performed anywhere. In a sense, audiences of the epic performed through these media are not "live"; they are dispersed, unknown and unseen. Further, the Chhattisgarhi dialect of the sung "text" is itself often not understood fully, if at all, by newly emerging Hindi- or English-speaking audiences.[29] What characterizes the epic for these "new" audiences is its

[29] The Chhattisgarhi dialect itself varies widely within the region and is not *totally* mutually intelligible between speakers living even one hundred miles apart or between literate, high-caste city dwellers and nonliterate villagers.

performative *exterior,* the unique singing and instrumental styles of epic performance, which themselves become relatively frozen, or at least enough so that they *are* recognizable as "Chhattisgarhi." In these contexts, the epic tradition has become an artifact, frozen in time and space, held up for admiration and nostalgia. Thus while perhaps unresponsive to what may be perceived to be more traditional shifting performative and social contexts "on the ground," so to speak, it is responsive in a very different way to newly emerging middle-class audiences.

The *candainī* living epic tradition has shown a tenacious ability to adapt to shifting and emergent performance contexts: to take up the cause of a caste trying to raise its status in U.P., and in Chhattisgarh, to integrate non-Raut singers into the circle of its performers and instrumentation and the *nācā* song and dance into its performance style as it competes with Hindi cinema and video halls. Over the last decade, however, at the same time as performers continue to be drawn from low-caste groups, the performance contexts of the Chhattisgarhi epic have bifurcated. The first are those live performances in traditional, late-night, open-air village squares in which primarily lower-class-caste audiences continue to interact with and help to shape the interior "text" of the tradition. It remains to be seen how flexible this interior can be in its interaction with a rapidly changing social world, how long or in what ways its performances can compete with video halls and movie theaters, and who the singers and performers will be in the next generation as literacy rates rise. The second context is physically distanced from its audiences, on stage or over the airwaves, audiences that now include an increasingly educated middle class. For these audiences, the epic's narrative interior no longer reflects "who we are," but its performative exterior may nostalgically remind them of "who we were."

CHAPTER 7

Paṇḍvānī Heroines, Chhattisgarhi Daughters

Paṇḍvānī

The Sanskrit, pan-Indian epics of the Ramayana and Mahabharata are often paired in Western scholarship of South Asian texts, even as that pairing reveals significant differences between the two (see, for example, Shulman 1991 and Smith 1980).[1] More recent field-based scholarship suggests that in folk performance, however, the two traditions are rarely paired and, in terms framing this study, do not fall within the same performative repertoire and intertextual system of genres (Hiltebeitel 1988; Lutgendorf 1991; Sax 1991; Smith 1990). In Chhattisgarh, the Mahabharata folk genre of *paṇḍvānī* (the name taken from the five Pandava brothers/heroes of epic) is called a *Chhattisgarhi* genre, whereas the much more commonly performed Ramayana tradition, available in a wide variety of performance styles, is not. In this chapter, I consider what difference it makes to indigenous understandings of *paṇḍvānī* performance that the genre is situated within the *regional* repertoire, or system of genres, in which it is continually paired with the regional *candainī* epic. Focusing specifically on performance of the *paṇḍvānī* narrative episode of Nal and Damayanti,[2] what kind of commentary—sometimes only

[1] The Sanskrit analytic terms for the two epics distinguish them as separate genres: *itihāsa* (history) for the Mahabharata and *kāvya* (poetry) or *caritra* (biography) for the Ramayana. The distinction is a literary one, however; one of the *paṇḍvānī* singers to whom I spoke used *caritra* for the Mahabharata narrative in the general sense of "story."

[2] Note that I use the Hindi transliteration Nal instead of the Sanskrit transliteration Nala. I specifically elicited the Nal and Damayanti episode from the *paṇḍvānī* singers I met in the summer of 1993 in anticipation of a paper I presented in November 1993 at the Wisconsin Annual Conference on South Asia on a panel titled "Nala and Damayanti: Varying Visions of Love and Self."

hints thereof—does this intertextuality provide us for how the narrative may be received and interpreted in situated performance?

"According to Our Hearts": A Chhattisgarhi Genre

In search of *paṇḍvānī* performers in the summer of 1993, I set out during an evening hot-season dust storm, on the back of the scooter of an anthropologist from Ravishankar University, for the village of Darba, about an hour east of the city of Raipur. Over ten years earlier in this village, I had recorded a *paṇḍvānī* performance, which happened to be of the Nal and Damayanti episode, from a middle-aged blind singer of the Marar (vegetable-seller) caste. I hoped that he would still be living, would be willing to perform this narrative segment again, and that he and others would be able to provide some insight on *paṇḍvānī* as a *Chhattisgarhi* genre.

During the year and a half I had spent in Chhattisgarh from 1980 to 1981 and on several return visits since then, *paṇḍvānī* was consistently mentioned as a central genre of the repertoire of genres identified as Chhattisgarhi. There had been, however, no *paṇḍvānī* performances during this time in any of the villages or urban neighborhoods in which I had lived or visited, except for that of the above-mentioned blind singer. At that time, although the *memory* of *paṇḍvānī* performance still helped to identify and characterize the Chhattisgarhi folklore region through frequent reference, few living performers still regularly sang *paṇḍvānī* in public, professional contexts.

In contrast, the *candainī* epic tradition was continually in the public eye (and "ear") through local performances, in government-sponsored competitions, in the news media, and on the radio. In the late 1970s and early 1980s, exposure of this epic tradition outside Chhattisgarh was promoted by the playwright and director Habib Tanvir (mentioned in Chapter 6), who wrote a contemporary dramatic work based on *candainī*. Using Chhattisgarhi actors and traditional performers, he staged this work in New Delhi and other urban centers, even as far away as London.

Over the last five to seven years, *paṇḍvānī* performance has experienced a dramatic performance revival and popularity comparable with that of *candainī* in the 1980s, particularly as representative of "things Chhattisgarhi." Like *candainī*, it has come to represent the region among folklore and intellectual circles outside Chhattisgarh, in various government-sponsored performance competitions, as well as on radio and television. This has largely been due to the influence of one particular female *paṇḍvānī* singer, Tijan Bai, in whom, according to many Chhattisgarhi residents, the government (and subsequent audiences and singing competition judges) showed particular interest because of her uniqueness as a woman in public, professional performance.[3] Her grandfather was a performer and she says she informally learned from him at an early age, never having been discouraged from doing so for being a girl. Even after she began to perform publicly, she continued working as a laborer in one of the Bhilai steel mills and, at the same time, earned her high school equivalency degree. A few other girls have followed in her lead in *paṇḍvānī* public performance, and the female performer of choice in the media in 1993 was the sixteen-year-old Ritu Varma. I heard several comments that year by residents in Raipur and Dhamtari that Tijan Bai was losing her popularity to Ritu Varma because of her age (the former was about thirty-five years old at the time).

Tijan Bai has appeared frequently on Doordarshan (the government-sponsored television channel), sings in various folk festivals in Delhi and other urban centers, has received various national-level performance and artistic awards, and participated in the Festival of India in Paris during the summer of 1993. She dresses the part of a "typical" Chhattisgarhi villager, wearing easily identifiable Chhattisgarhi jewelry, although some pieces are actually seen only rarely in the gullies and streets of Chhattisgarh today (because of both the expense of gold and the attitude held by educated women that this jewelry is "backward"). Tijan Bai accompanies herself on a colorfully decorated and painted *tambūrā* (single-stringed instrument), which has come to be identified specifically with *paṇḍvānī* performance. Her success and popularity has revived *paṇḍvānī* performance all over Chhattisgarh in a variety of contexts. Hence, I anticipated an increased awareness of the genre in the village in which we found ourselves on that hot, dusty evening in May.

The Brahmin village headman with whom I had stayed in Darba village and in whose courtyard I had taped *paṇḍvānī* those many years earlier had since moved to Raipur to live with one of his sons. His large, double-storied house in the middle of the village was now empty except for a few servants and his Brahmin *darogā* (overseer of the estate). After cups of tea and general discussion with the *darogā* and several other men who had gathered in the courtyard about shifting caste dynamics caused by industrialization in nearby Raipur and an associated demise of many Chhattisgarhi folk performance genres, the *darogā* assured us that the blind *paṇḍvānī* singer, Mani Ram, was

[3] I have made efforts to meet Tijan Bai over the last few years, but she has always been "out of station" whenever I have visited Chhattisgarh. In the summer of 1993, when she was constantly referred to as *the paṇḍvānī* singer whom I should meet and record, my standard answer became that I would need to go to Delhi or France to hear her—an answer that delighted and amused her referees. Most of them had themselves heard her only over the radio or on cassette tapes, never in live performance.

still living and sent someone to call him. Meanwhile, he asked if we would like to watch a tape of the televised Mahabharata on the VCR while we were waiting. I hesitated, feeling somehow that this would "corrupt" the setting for what I hoped would be the forthcoming *paṇḍvānī* performance as soon as the singer arrived. However, the question was rhetorical; and soon, seated in the courtyard under a dark, moonless sky, a group of twenty or so children, women, and the male servants of the estate were gathered with rapt attention in front of a tiny black-and-white screen on which stiffly acted characters spoke Sanskritic Hindi that few of the audience could fully understand.

To my dismay, the drone of the Mahabharata on the VCR continued as a backdrop to our conversation when Mani Ram finally did arrive at 11:00 P.M. or so. It was now too late to start a performance; but, he assured me he would return in the morning to sing (albeit then without the naturally congregated audience that was present late that night). The TV performance, however, provided an important opening in my conversation with the singer. When I asked him what difference there was between this "TV Mahabharata" and *paṇḍvānī,* his answer was immediate and decisive: "The Mahabharata of the TV is according to the *śāstra* [authoritative, religious texts]; *paṇḍvānī* is according to our hearts. *Paṇḍvānī* is *Chhattisgarhi.*" In a neighboring village, another singer gave me a similar response: "The TV is for everyone; there are many written Mahabharatas. This [*paṇḍvānī*] stands alone. Those who read from paper, they know the TV Mahabharata."[4]

A third singer, Pancam, who makes his living as an electrical appliance (radios, televisions, fans) repairman was puzzled when I expressed to him my specific interest in the Nal and Damayanti narrative and asked him if this episode was in the repertoire of his performance troupe. He assured me it was, but asked:

> [Pancam:] Can't you do this research by reading? Whatever you want to know, you'll find in writing.
>
> [Indian anthropologist who accompanied me to this village]: No, there's some difference between the books and what you sing. The things you enjoy [*majedār bāt*], like the weddings of Sahadev and Nakula [the twin Pandava brothers], you won't find those there.
>
> [Pancam:] If you printed everything we sing and put it in the bazaar [that is, in books to sell], it would take up from here to there [extending his arms out wide]. But, that's stopping now. At first, those who sang *paṇḍvānī* sang *every*

[4] "*tv sabhoṅ ke hai; bahut likhe mahābhārat hai. yah ekton ke hai. jo khāgaz se paṛte, unko tv mahābhārat malūm hai.*"

> detail: they came by this road, they passed this village—they sang about every well, river, and *talāb* [tank]. Nowadays, what do they do? They come from there 'direct'[5] to here.

What does it mean for a performance genre to be "Chhattisgarhi," to be sung according to the heart rather than the *śāstra?* Note that in the following discussion, I will use the word *śāstra*/shastric with the connotations implied in this statement by Mani Ram—as a textual or textually based performance tradition shared across regional boundaries, to be distinguished from what are perceived to be uniquely Chhattisgarhi (regional) oral traditions.[6]

I must admit that I first looked for the answer to this question in the verbal, transcribed *texts* of the three full performances of the Nal and Damayanti narrative that I recorded in the summer of 1993, suspecting that the Chhattisgarhi variants of the narrative would reflect a particularly *regional,* rather than what our singer calls "shastric" (and I gloss as Sanskritic/brahminic), vision of women, fate, and divine intervention (such as I had found in comparing the *candainī* regional epic with the caste tradition of U.P.). While many of these can be found, the *paṇḍvānī* performance styles themselves and the genre's place within a distinct repertoire are just as crucial in its definition as a Chhattisgarhi genre.

The Nal and Damayanti Narrative

These Chhattisgarhi performances reflect numerous regional variations and localizations, but on the level of plot, the performances follow the general contours of the Sanskrit narrative amazingly closely.[7] Perhaps this should not be surprising, since the shastric narrative of Nal and Damayanti already shares certain features that seem to characterize the alternative regional vision expressed in genres such as *candainī.* As J. A. B. van Buitenen elaborates in the introduction to his translation of Book 3 of the Sanskrit

[5] Words in single quotations indicate English words that were used in otherwise Chhattisgarhi or Hindi conversations.

[6] The shastric/Chhattisgarhi distinction in this context is equivalent to the *mārga/deśī* distinction referred to by Blackburn and Ramanujan as "[the] contrast often cited by scholars (but rarely used by the *folk* themselves) as an indigenous Indian expression of a folk/classical contrast. In fact, these terms represent only different (the local and pan-Indian) expressions of the same tradition, not different traditions" (1986:14).

[7] The skeleton of the narrative is quite readily available in the performance Mani Ram sang the morning after the video showing. The performance was only an hour long and disappointingly perfunctory, for he remembered having sung it for me over ten years before and could not understand why I had asked for this particular narrative again. I rather lamely explained that the tape had gotten old.

Mahabharata, *The Book of the Forest* (1975:182–185), Nal and Damayanti is already a female-centered tale, with an active heroine, and a narrative with a folktale-like, domestic quality.

This story of the heroine Damayanti and hero Nal is told to the Pandava eldest brother Yudhishthira (in forest exile, mourning the loss of his kingdom through dicing) by the *ṛṣi* Brihadashva, as the story of a prince who had suffered even more greatly than he. Nal, king of Nishadha, was the most beautiful of men and Damayanti the beautiful princess of Vidarbha. A pair of geese serves as matchmaker between the two, sparking the love between them through descriptions of their respective beauty. Damayanti's lovesickness is reported to her father, who decides it is time to call for her *swayamvar* (the ritual in which a princess publicly chooses a husband from among her suitors by garlanding him). Kings and princes from all over the world arrive in hopes of being chosen by the exquisite princess (the *swayamvar* characterized, in one Chhattisgarhi performance, as a 'beauty competition,' to which "kings from 'America,' 'England,' 'Australia,' everywhere" arrived). Nal adorns himself and joins in the migration toward Vidarbha.

The gods, too, hear of the *swayamvar;* and four of them decide to attend. In the Sanskrit version, they truly hope that one of them will be chosen as the bridegroom, whereas in the Chhattisgarhi version, they attend the *swayamvar* to test the love of Nal and Damayanti. On the way, they meet Raja Nal and ask that he serve as their messenger to the princess, informing her of their intentions. Nal miraculously finds entry into the palace and delivers the message, to which Damayanti replies that because this is a ritual of true self-choice, she will marry only Raja Nal. When the gods hear her reply, they arrive at the *swayamvar* as (what the Chhattisgarhi singer calls) 'duplicates' of Nal. In the Sanskrit version, the princess beseeches the gods, by the power of her truthfulness, to reveal their divinity; only then is she able to discern who among the five is the human Nal because only the gods do not sweat, blink, or touch their feet to the ground. The kings and gods return to their respective realms, rejoicing in what they know to be an auspicious match.

One god, Kali, however, was late to the *swayamvar.* Angered, he vows to make the princess pay for her choice of a human over the gods by unseating Nal from his kingdom. For twelve years, however, the nearly perfect Nal commits no transgression through which Kali can initiate his plan. Then, one morning, Nal fails to perform the appropriate ablutions before worshiping; this is Kali's opportunity to enter his body and take advantage of his defects (*durguṇ*). As the Chhattisgarhi Kali says, "Every man has his defect, and Nal's is dicing." Kali sends his brother Dvarpa to persuade Nal's brother Pushkar (who had already lost everything he owned through dicing) to challenge Nal to an all-out dicing competition. Protesting that he has nothing to stake, in the Chhattisgarhi version, Kali gives Pushkar two oxen. The dices are loaded, and beginning with the oxen, Nal loses all his possessions until he and Damayanti are left with only a single garment each; and they are banished to the forest.

Upon Pushkar's threat of hanging anyone who helps the couple, no subject offers them even a drop of water. After three days, Nal sees a pair of birds and throws his only garment over them in an effort to capture them for food; but they fly off, leaving the prince naked. Now the couple wanders the forest sharing Damayanti's single sari. Nal tries to persuade his wife to return to her mother's place without him, but she is a true *pativratā* (faithful wife) and refuses. One night, as the couple has lain down to rest and Damayanti has fallen fast asleep, Nal carefully cuts the shared sari in two and abandons his love at the crossroads.

Damayanti awakens to find herself alone and desperately calls out for her husband before realizing her dreadful fate. She has numerous adventures in the forest and kingdom of Cedi before finally finding her way back to her father's kingdom of Vidarbha. Nal, meanwhile, has his own forest adventures. He saves a snake from a fire and is repaid with only a snakebite, which leaves him cruelly deformed. But the snake assures him that because of this deformity, no one will recognize him in his exile. He promises the prince that the poison that has entered his body will afflict only Kali and will cause him no pain; further, he will always be victorious in battle. He advises Nal to offer his services as a charioteer to the king of Ayodhya.

Meanwhile, Damayanti has sent scouts throughout the land to look for her husband. She instructs them to ask of all they meet a riddle that only Nal will be able to answer.[8] One such scout enters the city of Ayodhya with the riddle, and the king's charioteer gives the answer. When Damayanti hears his answer, she knows Nal is alive and holds a second *swayamvar,* hoping to lure him back from his exile. The king of Ayodhya instructs his charioteer, the disguised Nal, to deliver him to the *swayamvar* in a single day. On the way, they pass a *vibhītaka* tree, and the king, wishing to display his skill in counting, tells Nal the difference in the number of leaves and nuts on the tree and those on the ground. Nal insists on stopping to verify the count; it is exactly as the king has said. Nal then asks for the knowledge of this magic, offering in return the secret of his charioteering skills. As soon as Nal receives the secret of counting (the secret of dice), Kali is vomited out of his mouth.

At Vidarbha, Damayanti sends her servant to ask the identity of the deformed charioteer who makes the chariot fly as only Nal can do. She poses a series of tests through which she knows that he can be, in fact, only her

[8] See Shulman 1994 for a discussion of the riddle in the Nal and Damayanti narrative.

love. Finally, Nal admits who he is; and after a three-year separation, the couple is reunited. Nal returns to his own kingdom to challenge his brother Pushkar to one final dicing, through which he successfully reclaims his throne. And so, the narrator asks the Pandava Yudhishthira, "Hearing of the misery and grief of Raja Nal, what is the basis of *your* complaint?"

Candainī and *Paṇḍvānī:* A Dialogic Relationship

What most differentiates *paṇḍvānī* performance from *shastric* performance genres available in Chhattisgarh, most notably Tulsidas's *Rāmcaritmānas,* are the identifiable regional styles and contexts in which it is performed: the instruments used in accompaniment, the use of a *rāgī* (echo voice and companion to the lead singer), the *rāg* (melodic structure) itself, as well as the identities of both performers and audience and the traditional and newly emerging contexts in which *paṇḍvānī* is sung. Further, its performance is episodic (characteristic of Indian oral epics such as *candainī*), rather than approximating the recitation style of devotional texts such as the *Rāmcaritmānas,* which are often cited "from beginning to end" (either over the period of seven, nine, or thirty days or on a weekly basis) until they are completed. One young apprentice singer exclaimed, "Who knows the beginning; who knows the end!" A nonprofessional female performer said, "There are eighteen nights of *paṇḍvānī,* but I know only bits and pieces."[9] These performance elements situate *paṇḍvānī* in a regional, Chhattisgarhi system of genres and poetics quite distinct from the coexisting shastric repertoire. It is *these* genres with which *paṇḍvānī* interacts dialogically—these intertextual relationships that provide the primary lens through which *paṇḍvānī* performance, including that of the narrative of Nal and Damayanti, is interpreted by the Chhattisgarhi folklore community. M. M. Bakhtin characterizes this process of intertextuality as follows: "Utterances are not indifferent to each other, and are not self-sufficient; they are aware of and mutually reflect one another. . . . Each utterance is filled with echoes and reverberations of other utterances to which it is related by the community of the sphere of speech" (1986:91).

[9] There are a limited number of episodes of the "unending" Mahabharata narrative current in *paṇḍvānī* performance, although many more episodes of the narrative may be part of the oral tradition, that is, known to the audience members through other performance genres as well as the televised serialization of the Mahabharata (see footnote 15 below for those available on cassette tape in Raipur in the summer of 1993). I have not attempted to contextualize the Nal and Damayanti narrative within this unbounded Mahabharata oral tradition/repertoire of episodes except as the performers themselves have done so, for it would be conjecture on my part as to what episodes are known or unknown to Chhattisgarhi audiences.

As mentioned earlier, the genre with which *paṇḍvānī* is most closely associated in Chhattisgarh is the epic *candainī*. In fact, the Brahmin overseer of the rural estate in Darba village, as someone who does not participate directly in the tradition as performer or audience member but who is quite conversant with the folk repertoire performed in his village, frequently confused the two genres in our conversation. When I asked him the contexts in which *paṇḍvānī* is performed these days in his village, he began describing a performance group in a neighboring village that was hired for particular festivals. I recognized that this was the same *candainī* troupe that I had recorded twelve years earlier and asked, "Do you mean *candainī?*" He quickly caught himself, "Yes, yes. *Candainī*. Well—*paṇḍvānī;* they do it all." The electrical-repairman singer mentioned above, the leader of a six- to eight-member performance troupe, characterized contemporary *paṇḍvānī* performance:

> These days, anyone can sing *paṇḍvānī* [that is, it is possible that a group that had sung *candainī* exclusively twelve years ago *would* have begun to sing *paṇḍvānī* in the interim]. Harijans, whom we call Satnamis, used to sing *paṇḍvānī*. Rauts sang *candainī* and the songs of the flute [*bā̃s gīt*]. And we [Sahus] sang *rāmsaptah* [term used for particular style of Ramayana performance in Chhattisgarh]. In the old days, a few people knew *paṇḍvānī*. *Tambūrāwālā* [literally, belonging to the stringed instrument *tambūrā*]—that's what people called *paṇḍvānī*—and *mañjīrā* [a kind of cymbal]; there used to be just two [instruments]. Now there are lots of instruments. [To add the phrase] "Listen, son; listen, brother"—that's Mahabharata *caritra* [literally, biography, but here, more generally "story"].[10] You can tell the story [*kathā*] in two minutes or two days; that's what it's like.

Paṇḍvānī and *candainī* have followed a remarkably similar course of stylistic development over the last fifteen years. Initially, both were sung a cappella, with a lead singer and a single companion (*rāgī*). The Darba singer Mani Ram, who still sings in this style, said the only difference between *candainī* and *paṇḍvānī* is that singers of the former add *tor* or *mor* to the end of every line and *paṇḍvānī* singers add *bhāīya* or *bhāīge* (literally, brother). The style is composed of short, almost staccato couplets of nearly repetitious lines. Each couplet advances the story line, and little room exists for elaboration of scene or emotion or for commentary on motivation. Mani Ram added rather sadly that this traditional singing style is extremely rare these days in Chhattisgarh: "People have no interest without instruments."

[10] Notice the characterization of *paṇḍvānī* by its "tag phrase," *bhāīya mor,* a characterization repeated below by the singer Mani Ram.

Of these two traditions, *candainī* performers were the first to experiment with shifting styles, adding instrumentation (minimally a harmonium and *ḍholak* [a kind of drum]) and more singers. Songs are interspersed with the narrative line of the lead singer, elaborating a *bhāv* (emotion) or indicating passage of time or the transversing of space. These days, the most popular *candainī* style is that of the dance-drama with costumed actors (*nācā*). The chief identity of the singers shifted in this period from that of the Rauts to primarily Satnamis. It was during this period that urban elites began to show interest in the regional epic.

The *paṇḍvānī* tradition followed a similar development about a decade later: the performance style of the "old days" with the single singer and a companion; and more recently, the addition of instrumentation (specifically the brightly decorated *tambūrā*) and a large performance troupe, which have become crucial to reviving *paṇḍvānī* as a popular style. It has not yet been adapted, however, to the *nācā*. Like *candainī*, the identity of *paṇḍvānī* singers has expanded beyond the boundaries of its traditional performance group, Satnamis, to include a wide spectrum of castes. Finally, the "exterior of the text," to borrow a phrase from Wendy Doniger (1991:32), has come to represent the region to intellectual and cultural performance communities outside Chhattisgarh with particular interests in "things ethnic."

Paṇḍvānī and *candainī* "new style" singers employ almost identical formulas to indicate breaks between episodes or the passage of time: "And so, they began to say, began to speak, ohhh" or "began to go, began to move, ohhh."[11] Contemporary *paṇḍvānī* and *candainī* performance styles also share the presence of a *rāgī* (respondent), who interacts with the lead performer in spoken narrative. The *rāgī*'s comments are often the occasion for local humor; they differ from the humorous interludes in *rāmlīlā* dramatic performances because they are not performatively distinct episodes or interludes but punctuate and are integrated into the primary narrative. "Listen" to the following excerpt taken from the first few minutes of the performance, when the lead singer, Manmohan (whose performance we will look at more carefully later in the chapter) is describing Damayanti's fragile state of *viraha* (separation from her love, Nal):

> Singer: The *rājkumārī*'s [unmarried princess] condition deteriorated. Damayanti burned in the fire of separation, in the separation from the love of Raja Nal.
>
> *Ragi*: Oh, with the fever of *ṭimbu* [local vegetable]?

[11] "*kathāvan lāge, bolan lāge, ooo*" or "*calan lāge, jāvan lāge, ooo.*"

Singer: No, in the fever of love. The *rājkumārī* worried twenty-four hours a day; she was struck with worry; she was immersed in thought.

Ragi: Oh, she worried about the tap [play on words between word for tap / *nal* and name of the hero / Nal]!

Singer: No, no! This is about Raja Nal, not about 'boring' [the term in Chhattisgarh for tube wells]!

Beyond the emergence of similar performative styles, performers of the two genres of *candainī* and *paṇḍvānī* employ several narrative motifs and formulaic descriptions that resonate with each other in performance. The heroines Candaini and Damayanti are both Chhattisgarhi daughters, identified by the formulaic sixteen *śṛngār* (adornments),[12] several of which are unique to Chhattisgarh and worn by female professional *paṇḍvānī* singers such as Tijan Bai (for example, the *bandūriya* necklace and *kaṇkaṇī* armband). In contrast, the Ramayana heroine Sita is described and visually portrayed in lithographs and *rāmlīlā* as wearing vaguely generic north Indian royal clothes and jewelry. The two heroines are also accompanied by the formulaic "fourteen companions, seven in front and seven behind"; they live in similar seven-storied palaces, in quarters tightly guarded, into which the heroes of their tales must try to enter.

Because of the generic association and performative relationship between *candainī* and *paṇḍvānī,* audience members who hear of the daughter Damayanti stranded in the middle of the jungle, threatened by a hunter, are more likely to make an association with the heroine Candaini in the jungle (described in Chapter 6), where she relies on her own ingenuity to get out of a similar situation, than with Sita in her forest dwelling, from which she is kidnapped. Damayanti is not, of course, the eloping Candaini. She is a *pativratā* (faithful wife) and finally depends on the power of her *sat* (truth, that is, chastity) to escape the hunter who attempts to accost her in the jungle after she has been deserted by Nal; but the power is humanized. In Mani Ram's performance of this episode, Damayanti successfully curses the hunter but then wanders the forest as a crazy woman whose sanity is restored only when she tells her story to those who take her in as a daughter (an indigenous commentary on the power of story and performance). In these lines, Mani Ram specifically uses the term *nonī,* the affectionate term for daughter in several dialect variants of Chhattisgarhi. In the performance by the Sahu-

[12] These include ankle bracelets, a silver waist belt, bracelets, a chain in the part of her hair, a beautiful sari and blouse, red dye (*mahur*) on her feet, and henna on her hands.

caste singer, Damayanti also finally resorts to her power as a *pativratā* to curse the hunter to die, but not before trying a strategy available to all Chhattisgarhi women, that is, appealing to the stranger as a daughter, a sister.[13] His own inhumane self is underscored by the fact that he cannot be shamed into responding appropriately to this strategy.

The dicing motif shared between the two traditions, and yet distinctively different, is of particular interest to us here, given the centrality of dicing to the Nal and Damayanti narrative. Recall from our discussion of *candainī* that as Lorik and Candaini are passing through an all-female kingdom, Lorik, disguised in a sari, is sent into the city by Candaini to buy some *pān*. He is enticed into the home of the *pān*-seller, who threatens him with a series of physical abuses unless he promises to marry her. When Candaini finally comes looking for him, she secures his release by winning him back in a dicing duel with the *pān*-seller. The motif of women, rather than men, winning and losing partners through dicing is common in several other Chhattisgarhi folk narratives as well (for example, in the Song of Subanbali discussed in Chapter 3), a motif that presents us with an alternative to the more shastric pattern of male dicing for a woman (or a man putting up a woman as stake in that dice game).[14] The latter is, of course, central to the main story of the Mahabharata in which Yudhishthira dices against Duryodhan (whose uncle Shakuni throws the dice on his behalf). The Pandava king stakes his wealth, his brothers, himself, and finally his wife Draupadi. Dicing in the Nal and Damayanti narrative follows this same pattern, and Chhattisgarhi audiences surely make the association between the two narratives of dicing and loss, as it is explicitly stated by the narrator of the story-within-a-story.

However, because *paṇḍvānī* is itself situated with a "Chhattisgarhi" repertoire, alternative dicing images and gender ideologies from this repertoire also come into play and frame the reception of Nal's dicing. It makes a difference to this reception that Damayanti is characterized as a Chhattisgarhi daughter (interestingly, Nal remains more distant, always addressed

[13] Damayanti uses this same strategy to persuade the gods who appear at her *swayamvar* in the form of Nal to reveal their true forms.

[14] Alf Hiltebeitel reports an episode of female dicing from a Telugu folk Mahabharata tradition in which Draupadi (wife of the five Pandava brothers) plays a game of dice to recover her husbands' lost kingdom, even after she herself has been humiliated in the dice game between Yudhishthira and Duryodhan. She is triumphant in her efforts (dicing directly against Duryodhan this time, not Shakuni); but the Pandavas refuse to take back their kingdom under these conditions, "preferring to win it back in battle and on their own" (1988:238). Hence, the suggested alternative ideology of gender and power is not totally "played out," as it is, for example, in the Song of Subanbali.

as Raja, "king"). In one performance, the singer directly localizes or resituates the dicing between the brothers Nal and Pushkar when he characterizes it to be like the custom of male friends and relatives gambling through the night as they celebrate the Chhattisgarhi festival of *gaurā*. The performer rhetorically asks his audience, "After all, don't all brothers play dice at the festival?" In this variant, there is no mention made of the influence on the dicing scene of Kali or any other outside force.

Finally, both *candainī* and the *paṇḍvānī* narrative of Nal and Damayanti are love stories in which the love is first characterized by the heroine's self-choice and then her determination to hold onto that choice against overwhelming odds. The heroes of both stories are seemingly less committed to their love when obstacles are placed in their way. Lorik gets cold feet and tries to back out of the elopement several times before he is almost literally dragged by a washerwoman to the tree where he is to meet Candaini; Nal carries the message of the gods to Damayanti with the suggestion that since they are gods, whose anger can destroy the world, she should *really* choose one of them as her bridegroom.

The heroines, however, are undeterred in their choice. Damayanti asserts that the choice she has made in her heart, long before the *swayamvar,* is equivalent to marriage itself: "I've already accepted you as my husband; I'll marry no one else." Furthermore, she orders Nal to take this message back to the gods, with the following instruction about the nature of true "self-choice" in the *swayamvar:* "The meaning of a *swayamvar* is that one chooses according to her heart. In this *darbār* [court], there is no fear; there is no force. Whomever the girl garlands, that is her husband. Whomever I desire, that is whom I will garland. There's no sin in this, no reproach; it's nothing like that. Go and tell them this!"

Kali, the god who is angered over having missed the first *swayamvar* and instigates Nal's downfall in the dicing match of the Sanskrit variant of the narrative, in the Chhattisgarhi version later criticizes the heroine for this very independence, which she had declared to be above reproach at a *swayamvar:* "This ordinary [*sādhāraṇ*] girl is too proud [*ghamaṇḍ;* thinking she can choose a human over the gods]. I'm going to tear apart this union," which he succeeds in doing only temporarily.

The traditions of *candainī* and Nal and Damayanti characterize an ideal love as one of not only erotic passion but also companionship. The forest scenes give literal space for this companionship to be externalized. Candaini and Lorik face obstacle after obstacle together, alone against the world they encounter in foreign countries and the jungle. They cook together, make rafts together, plot against and trick enemies together. Of course, the story of Nal and Damayanti dwells on the betrayal of just such companionship.

In summarizing the story for me outside of performance, one singer started with the frame story of the Mahabharata hero Yudhishthira:

> The story begins here: there was Arjun; Arjun leaves them all, the four [other Pandava] brothers and Draupadi; . . . and over here, there's Bhim; Bhim also goes by himself to wander; Dharm Raj is left all by himself, Yudhishthira. . . .
>
> [A *ṛṣi* finds the weeping king, who complains,] "What's the use of having so many brothers and such a big family? There's no one in the world with greater grief than I have. . . . Having left behind such a large kingdom, leaving the entire family, I have come into the jungle . . . but . . . now there's no one here to give me companionship."
>
> The *ṛṣi,* standing in front of him, says, "Son, do you think that you're disconsolate? You're most fortunate; you won't find anyone so fortunate, even if you look. . . . I know everything: that your kingdom has been lost, your brothers defeated. You came to do *tapasyā* [austerities] in the jungle, and now in the jungle, you have no company. . . . Son, if you think you're disconsolate, you haven't even seen sorrow. What you think of as sorrow is actually your flower. What is sorrow like? Let me tell you about Raja Nal."
>
> [The singer continues,] Whoever tells the story in our caste [Sahu] has to start the story with this question, "What is sorrow; what is happiness?"

Yudhishthira's sad state is attributed by the *ṛṣi* as one resulting from lack of companionship; by so framing the story that follows, he characterizes the sorrowful separation of the lovers Nal and Damayanti as the loss of companionship. Yet the tale of sorrow that follows is actually more that of Damayanti's sorrow than Nal's.

Another singer elaborates on what true companionship means in the uniquely Chhattisgarhi terms of ritual friendship (ritually solemnized friendships between same-sex, cross-caste friends). This test of true friendship/companionship, rather than that of erotic love alone, is the test that the hero Nal fails. In this performance, Damayanti responds to Nal when he tries to persuade her to leave him in the forest and return to her mother's place:

> [She first calls on shastric authority and then switches to "Chhattisgarhi" authority when she recalls the mode of ritual friendship (*mahāprasād*).]
>
> The *śāstra* say, "Whatever patience, whatever stamina a man has, it will be tested [*parīkśa*]. Whatever dharma he follows, the test of that dharma is the test of friendship: that is, [the test of] *mahāprasād, phūlphūlvārī* [names of specific kinds Chhattisgarhi ritual friendships]—these are tested.
>
> One could say a woman's test is calamity. Yes, it's good to have a *mahāprasād* friend and for this friendship to survive calamity. Whoever stays with another

in sorrow and happiness, that is the friendship of *mahāprasād*. . . . You're experiencing such suffering, such trouble; I won't leave you, my master.

The king then understood that she was no ordinary woman who would leave him.

A Performative Crossroads of Two Poetics

In contrast to the *candainī* tradition, *paṇḍvānī* has been picked up by many "shastric," Ramayana performance troupes. The consecutive, year-long television serializations of the Ramayana and Mahabharata that riveted India in the late 1980s have placed these two traditions in a performative/generic relationship with each other that did not traditionally exist in Chhattisgarh; the Ramayana tradition is dharmic/shastric, whereas *paṇḍvānī* is regional, local, not normative in the sense that the shastric devotional text of the Hindi *Rāmcaritmānas* is. It is difficult to say whether the television phenomenon "permitted" Ramayana performance troupes to add *paṇḍvānī* to their repertoire by legitimizing the Mahabharata in some way, or if this innovation has been in response to the increasing popularity of *paṇḍvānī* in Chhattisgarh itself.

Let's look more closely now at a performance by such a troupe, whose repertoire includes *rāmsaptah, paṇḍvānī,* and periodically even *candainī* (although Ramayana performances are most common). As its lead singer says, "Whatever people call us for, that's what we'll sing." The newly emerging performance configuration between *paṇḍvānī* and Ramayana has influenced the *paṇḍvānī* performance style of this troupe dramatically. In the performance under consideration, the performer negotiated between a regional poetics and a more shastric and devotional poetics, a Ramayana-like performance style, incorporating elements of each. This particular audience, however, still understood *paṇḍvānī* to be firmly situated within the regional repertoire. This variance in the intertextual context the audience and singer brought to the performance resulted in audience-performer negotiations at some point and, finally, for the audience, a disappointing ending.

In my search for Damayanti in the Chhattisgarhi countryside, I had initiated this performance, although it played itself out before a "traditional" audience in a Gond neighborhood on the outskirts of the town of Dhamtari. I had learned of the lead singer, Manmohan Sinha, from a man who periodically had performed with his troupe and who was a neighbor of the Gond friends I was visiting. The performance took place in the front courtyard of their house, next to the major thoroughfare of the villagelike neighborhood.

Manmohan is a forty-five-year-old high school graduate who makes his

Paṇḍvānī singer Manmohan Sinha, holding the characteristic *tambūrā,* Dhamtari, Raipur plains.

living as a day laborer (and was, at the time of this performance, hired as a construction worker). He said his grandfather had also been a professional performer; and it was from him that he had learned "whatever it is that I know." After what I, as a nontraditional *paṇḍvānī* patron, felt to be some rather awkward negotiations of an appropriate performance fee, Manmohan agreed to come the next night to perform for three hours. He contemplated whether he would be able to sing the entire Nal and Damayanti *kathā* in that time but concluded it would, with some effort, be possible. He was rather emphatic that, after working all day in 115-degree heat, he would not be able to perform longer than this. The initially scheduled performance was canceled because of an unexpected, dramatic hot-season downpour. My Gond hosts assured me, however, that the troupe would show up the next night, since I had given Manmohan a "good faith" down payment; and they did.

Arriving at 9:30 from a village five to seven kilometers away, the performers were served tea and *bīṛī* before Manmohan carefully unwrapped his brightly painted and decorated *tambūrā,* creating a key performance frame for *paṇḍvānī* as a Chhattisgarhi, rather than "Hindi," performance. He set up a large lithograph of the divine baby Krishna on a folding chair at one end of the courtyard, performed *ārtī* (lamp offering to the deity), and lit incense. By this time, word of the troupe's arrival had spread through the neighborhood, and an audience of approximately fifty had gathered, two-thirds of whose members were middle-aged or older women. As Manmohan was setting up, I asked several of the women whether they knew this *kathā* of Nal and Damayanti that was about to be sung. They assured me that it was common knowledge, but one woman said she (and probably most of the others) had not heard it performed for ten or fifteen years. "Still," she said, "we should know it, shouldn't we?"[15]

Manmohan's opening scene is that of the geese (*haṅs*) who, through their descriptions of the beauty of our hero and heroine, "awakened the *bhāv* (emotion) of love in the hearts of Nal and Damayanti.[16] Love was born on both sides." The *kathā* is set up, then, as a love story, one whose full ripening is assured when the performer then calls upon the authority of Swami Tulsidas, author of the authoritative *Rāmcaritmānas* (which came as a complete surprise to me, based on my experience of more traditional *paṇḍvānī* performances), whom he quotes as having said:

> If love remains true,
> If love one for another remains steadfast,
> Then the two will surely meet each other.
> One will receive the other.

In this variant, the gods come to Damayanti's *swayamvar* not as serious contestants but to test the unusual love about which they have heard. The gods say, "We'll go to the *swayamvar.* If their love is that great, we'll go to test it. If

[15] Nal and Damayanti is not part of the recorded repertoire on radio or television of either Ritu Varma or Tijan Bai (as of summer 1993). In the cassette tape stores of Raipur's bazaars, I was able to locate two cassette tape recordings of Tijan Bai and one of Ritu Varma, titled, respectively, *subhadrā haraṇ* (The Seizure of Subhadra), *abhimanyu vadh* (The Slaying of Abhimanyu), and *kuntī aur gandhārī dvārā śiv pūjā* (Kunti's and Gandhari's Worship of Shiva).

[16] He did not provide the Yudhishthira frame story, which the singer mentioned earlier had told me was crucial to its performance.

the love is true, from the heart, then, we'll have to find out about it; we'll have to test it."

When the four gods come to the ceremony, all in the guise of Nal, Damayanti calls on the goddesses Sharada Mai and Sarasvati Dai; but then "an idea comes to her" to appeal to the gods as a daughter (the same strategy used with the hunter in the jungle):

> Prostrating at their feet, joining her hands, Damayanti said, "You're the father; I'm your offspring, like a daughter. With my heart, words, acts, and soul, I've [already] accepted Raja Nal as my husband. Protect me, help me, so that I can identify Nal, so that I can garland Nal.
>
> I'm like your daughter; I'm dependent on you. . . . And if you test me in this, if you challenge me, and I can't identify Nal, I'll commit 'suicide'! All my faults and sins will be on your heads."
>
> [*Rāgī* responds,] 'Murder' will be committed.
>
> "All my faults and sins will be on your heads." In this way, Damayanti spoke to the gods; and the gods understood that her love was genuine. "Her love is absolutely true; it's a love from the heart. She has 'passed' the test of love. She's succeeded. We'll give her our true *darśan.*" And the four gods took their true forms and went away.

Of course, the rest of the narrative continues to test that love; it is guaranteed fruition not only because of Tulsidas's reassurance that true love is rewarded (particularly in the context of devotional texts) but also because of the intertextuality with genres such as *candainī,* in which the heroine is resourceful and clever and finally succeeds in achieving her goals.

But now, to return to Tulsidas's voice of authority—it suggests a shastric performance frame for the Ramayanization, if you will, of *paṇḍvānī*. We will see that this process is not complete, however, and finally causes the audience some consternation. The narrative recitation of the lead singer is interspersed with sung portions by the *maṇḍalī* (performance troupe) of men accompanying him. Some of these songs simply repeat or elaborate what the lead singer has sung; but many others end with lines that approximate those of Ram *bhajan* (devotional hymns), unrelated to the narrative story line. For example, Manmohan sings of the gods' meeting with Nal on his way to the *swayamvar:*

> [Spoken] The gods arrived in front of Raja Nal and said:
> [Sung, with accompanying musicians joining in]
> Oh Siya Ram, Lakhan, Siya, Ram; oh Ram, oh Siya Ram.

The gods spoke, oh Ram, Siya Ram; they joined their hands and spoke, oh Ram, Siya Ram.[17]

These *bhajan*-styled songs, usually ending with the line, "*Bolo bṛndāvan bihārī lāl kī jai*" ("Recite/speak the praises of Brindavan's Biharilal [the god Krishna]"), are the most obvious indication that the lead singer has situated his *paṇḍvānī* performance in a shastric *bhakti* (devotional) repertoire and intertextual sphere. He also uses periodic *bhakti* idioms in the narrative line itself, such as that voiced by Damayanti when she expresses her commitment to Nal as her husband when he brings the message from the gods that they will be coming to her *swayamvar:* "Ever since I heard your praises from the geese, I've worshiped [*pūjā*] you like a god. If I marry anyone, it will be you. Maharaj, whatever happens, I don't want the happiness of heaven. I want only the happiness of your feet [*caraṇ*]. I'll be content only in your service [*sevā*]. I won't marry anyone else." The word used for worship (*pūjā*) carries specific connotations of worshiping a deity, as does the word *sevā* when associated with *pūjā*. So, too, the word *caraṇ* is used in devotional contexts, rather than the more colloquial Chhattisgarhi word for feet, *pair.*

Echoes of the shastric and Chhattisgarhi repertoires with which Manmohan's performance of Nal and Damayanti is in dialogue continue to play off of each other throughout his performance. Even as he is citing Tulsidas or singing Ram-type *bhajan,* a consistent relationship with the Chhattisgarhi performance repertoire is maintained through the instrumentation and especially through the active dialogue with the *rāgī* (companion), whose *hā̃, ho,* or humorous one-line responses (often misinterpretations of particular words used by the lead singer) literally punctuate the performance, line by line, even phrase by phrase.

Two and a half hours into the three-hour performance, Manmohan had carried the narrative only as far as the *swayamvar.* He told his audience, "Time is precious; I'm going to have to shorten this a bit," to which the *rāgī* responded, "Yes, hurry it up!" This created a dramatic break in the performance rhythm. The singer intended to skip over the wedding with the cryptic line, "And so, according to our Hindu 'customs,' the wedding was fulfilled and wedding songs were sung." But the women of the audience insisted on more—that the Chhattisgarhi bride Damayanti be sent off to her *sasurāl* (in-laws' place) with the appropriate wedding songs, Chhattisgarhi *vīhā gīt* (one of the genres regularly mentioned as part of the Chhattisgarhi performance repertoire). Manmohan resisted their pleas and tried to con-

[17] "Siya Ram, Lakhan" is a variant of "Sita Ram, Lakshman," which are the names of the hero, the heroine, and Ram's brother, of the Ramayana.

tinue; after all, *vīhā gīt* are an exclusively female genre. But, the women prevailed, and reluctantly, the entire *maṇḍalī* launched into the wedding songs in a *dehātī* (village) Chhattisgarhi. The initial song brought on a much longer description of the wedding itself, followed by more *vīhā gīt,* this time sung with full enthusiasm. (The traditional *paṇḍvānī* style of "former days" with its short sung lines would not have allowed for this kind of innovative localization and response to the audience.) These songs, then, firmly established Damayanti as a Chhattisgarhi bride and the women of the audience as key participants in the shaping of the performance, women who became noticeably more verbal and interactive after this incident.[18]

The expectations of the shastric/*bhakti* performance style and that of Chhattisgarhi *paṇḍvānī* came into *direct* conflict only at the very end of the performance. By 1:30 in the morning, Nal and Damayanti had only reached the crossroads in the jungle, where, exhausted, Damayanti fell asleep. Like the Sanskrit hero, Nal experiences great inner conflict about whether to leave Damayanti; but he finally turns from her:

> He was of two minds, arguing back and forth.
> Half said, "Yes, yes"; but he came back.
> He saw in front of him the body of Damayanti.
> He cried . . . tears filled his eyes.
> There, a king's daughter, sleeping without being bid farewell.
> . . . .
> He went and came several times; but Raja Nal finally left Damayanti.
>
> [Song]: My queen was left all alone, *bhāīya mor* [the *paṇḍvānī* performative end phrase].
> He left her all alone in the jungle.

The singer then describes the nature of the "vehicle" of a household, one needing both man and woman, that has now been broken: Nal leaves the union, alone; Damayanti awakens and calls out for her partner but realizes she has been left, alone. Manmohan ends the narrative performance with the line: "The woman was left alone in the jungle"—Damayanti abandoned at the crossroads. And the audience is left with the closing frame: "*Bolo bṛṇdāvan bīhārī lāl kī jal.*" Turning to me, Manmohan asked that I turn off the tape recorder, then said, "It's late. I'm finished."

[18] In Chhattisgarhi women's Ramayana *maṇḍalī* performances of the episode of Sita's wedding, the narrative is feminized by the elaboration of the wedding scene, the bride taking leave of her maternal home, and the singing of wedding songs; but the songs are not drawn from the Chhattisgarhi repertoire, for Sita is not a *Chhattisgarhi* bride, not "one of us."

The women in the audience were aghast, "But you can't leave our daughter in the middle of the jungle!" Manmohan answered simply, "Well, you know the story." Perhaps the performer was capable of suspending the performance in the middle of an episode because of the influence of the traditional shastric style of the *Rāmcaritmānas* performance, where the goal is to create and elaborate the various *bhāv* of *bhakti* rather than to sustain a narrative. V. Narayana Rao has articulated this difference as one between performances whose purpose is "communion" and those whose purpose is "communication" (oral communication, May 1992). In the recitation of a devotional text, an episode or scene may be suspended midway, to be picked up again the next day or the next week. But this is a *bhakti* aesthetics. Here, in a Chhattisgarhi performance, for an audience of Chhattisgarhi daughters, it was not acceptable to leave Damayanti at the crossroads over night, and the women were still complaining at the community tap (*nal*) the next morning as they filled their water vessels. Perhaps this image, more than any other, articulates what it means for the Chhattisgarhi *paṇḍvānī* to be sung "according to our hearts."

CHAPTER 8

Conclusion: Shifting Boundaries of Genre and Community

The focus of this book has been to identify key principles of indigenous genre identification and organization within what is identified as a "Chhattisgarhi" repertoire. A complete ethnography-of-speaking analysis of the performance repertoire of Chhattisgarh would go beyond this marked repertoire to include pan-Indian traditions, privately performed and conversational genres such as folktale, proverb, and jokes. My purpose has not been such an exhaustive analysis of the performance repertoire and rules of usage but to ask what difference the frame of *indigenous* genres and the principles of organization within the marked repertoire make to the reception and interpretation of performance.

In this conclusion, we shift to a consideration of the *levels* of identification of genre and community and the significance and fluidity of those boundaries within the Chhattisgarhi repertoire. Using the indigenous principle of the social organization of genre and repertoire, three *analytic* levels of folklore community in Chhattisgarh can be identified, through which some of this fluidity can be accounted. The first level I identify as the *folklore group;* and it is this level that is most frequently associated with specific genres by Chhattisgarhi informants. The folklore group identifies the performers themselves; they are the singers, players, or dancers, and, for some genres, also the audience. The folklore group may be identified by combination of social variables: caste, age, gender, and marital status. While membership in some groups is relatively stable (such as those dependent on caste and gender), membership in others (dependent on marital status or age) is temporary. The stability of some folklore groups may be even more fleeting, such as the folklore group (a multicaste audience whose members may come from several villages) created through the performance of a professional performer for the duration of a single night's performance. These performers, like the *kathānī kūhā* storyteller and the Oriya *bāhak* singer/dancer have the skill to manipulate an audience into a cohesive body, which afterward dissipates again into diverse groups based on gender, caste, and village.

While primary folklore groups can usually be identified through indigenous oral commentary and metafolklore, such commentary does not always articulate "nontraditional" or newly emerging performance settings and participants; close ethnographic observation reveals unarticulated "rules of usage," the *flexibility* of the system of genres and identities of the folklore group. Local commentary consistently identifies *ḍālkhāī,* for example, with unmarried girls, but in contemporary performance, men and married women have begun singing the songs of the festival outside of that ritual context. The fact that the songs are identified as "bad" (*burī*), as well as belonging to unmarried girls, provided a clue toward the existence of their nonfestival performance context.

The second analytic level of community identified through performance is what I have called the *folklore community,* a term and definition adapted from Dell Hymes's "speech community" (1974a:51). For analytic purposes, identification of this community is the most interesting of the three, although it is one rarely verbally distinguished from that of "region" by members of the community itself. The folklore community is one that shares both the knowledge of a particular folklore repertoire *and* the rules by which its members communicate through those genres. Members of a given folklore community know and agree upon who is traditionally permitted to perform particular genres and under what circumstances. I include the word "traditionally" here because with the spread of mass media communication and modern literacy, some of these rules are changing and their regulation is not always clear.

A third level of community identified through performance is that of the *folklore region,* the largest social and geographic grouping and, as mentioned above, one that is self-consciously expressed by inhabitants of Chhattisgarh. The folklore region is characterized by a shared repertoire of performance genres but not necessarily by identical rules of usage for those genres. A single region may be composed of numerous folklore communities whose repertoire of genres is similar but whose performance contexts and "rules" may differ. In many ways, a folklore region is "imagined" in the same way that, according to Benedict Anderson, the nation is an "imagined community," because the members of the community "will never know most of their fellow-members, meet them, or even hear of them, yet in the minds of each lives the image of their communion" (1983:15).

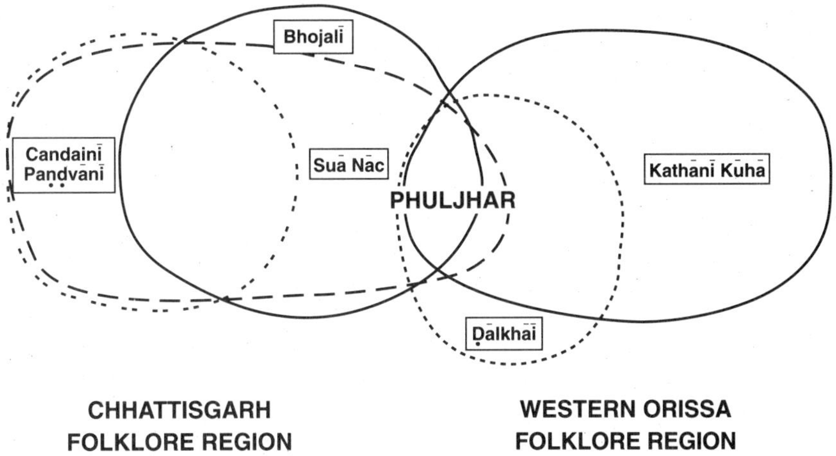

Map 2. Isogenres indicating the Chhattisgarhi and western Orissa folklore regions

The regional repertoire of "Chhattisgarhi" folklore, many of whose genres are said to be of tribal (particularly Gond) origin, was not difficult to determine. Pan-Indian traditions, such as *rāmlīlā* performances of the Ramayana epic or *bhajan* devotional songs, were rarely, if ever, mentioned as part of this repertoire. Although members of the folklore region have a sense of a bounded region, to determine its geographic borders is more difficult. One can conceptualize, however, "isogenres" (equivalent to the isogloss of linguistic studies) for each genre of the regional repertoire, showing the relative geographic spread of its performance. The repeated overlap of such isogenres begins to build up the rough outlines of the folklore region (see Map 2 for a geographic conceptualization of the genres analyzed in this study). The process of delineating a folklore region is particularly revealing on the border areas between two regions, where selected isogenres of each region overlap. In Phuljhar it is exactly this overlap between Chhattisgarhi and Oriya language and folklore genres that contributes to the definition to the subregion.

While performers and audience members of individual folklore communities in Chhattisgarh have a strong sense of the folklore region, they rarely differentiate between "region" and "community" as I have defined them. They assume that the folklore repertoire of their local community is spread throughout the region and that its genres are regulated by similar rules of usage. Performers and audience members alike were surprised and sometimes disbelieving when I reported to them the degree of variation in rules of usage between various folklore communities I had visited in the course of my fieldwork.[1] The extent of variation between Chhattisgarhi folklore communities became apparent to me only as I lived in and traveled between villages and towns in both the border area of Phuljhar and the central plains around the city of Raipur. The greatest degree of variation between rules of usage for the genres considered in this study is that of the *bhojalī* festival and song tradition examined in Chapter 2. The song tradition can be identified as a single genre through its terminology, its festival context, and repeated formal and thematic features of its songs. However, the social identification of the genre, the folklore group with which it is identified in each area (unmarried girls in Phuljhar and married women in the Raipur plains), and coexisting rules of usage create unique interpretive frames and intertextual relationships for the genre as it is performed in the two distinct geographic areas and folklore communities.

Levels of Inclusivity in the Social Organization of Genre

Although a genre can often be identified through performance with a single folklore group, rarely does an exclusive one-to-one correspondence exist between a genre and a specific folklore group in local commentary and conversations about that genre. The nature and inclusivity of the folklore group and/or community with which a particular genre is identified shifts depending on the identity of the speaker and listener and the social or performative context in which the statement is being made.

In the Chhattisgarhi dialect, the pronouns "we" or "our" (*ham, hamārā*) are used for both the singular and the plural;[2] the words' inclusivity varies according to the context in which a statement is made. As suggested in my introduction, it took some time for me to catch the nuances of these levels of inclusivity. Anthony Cohen (1982) identifies similar variation of inclusivity in place-related identity in British rural communities as "ascending and descending 'levels.'" He finds that each ascending level simplifies and thereby increasingly "misrepresents" the identity of the speaker/s; each descending level presents an increasingly complex "picture" of identity (10). Ellen Badone applies Cohen's concept of ascending and descending levels to her data on geographic social groupings in Brittany and argues that "identity

[1] Fredrik Barths (1969) found that this lack of awareness of cultural variation between similar communities is typical of most ethnic groups, including the Pathans with whom he worked.

[2] In fact, first-person singular is used only very rarely in everyday Chhattisgarhi conversation. Its use has the implications of drawing attention to oneself as distinct from one's family and/or community, which is rarely appropriate.

needs to be conceptualized in terms of a series of nested local, regional and national levels" (1987:186).

There is a distinct difference in the levels of inclusivity assumed in male and female speech/commentary about Chhattisgarhi folklore genres. Male informants tend to associate themselves with a broader spectrum of genres in which they do not directly participate as performers than do women; they characteristically identify genres with the wider communities of which they are a part, such as village or region, rather than with the more limited folklore group of performers only. When I was asking general questions about repertoire, Chhattisgarh men often told me that "we sing the *suā nāc,*" a genre performed exclusively by women. The "we" was used to refer to a social group based upon decisive factors other than the gender of the performers. Women rarely identify themselves in this inclusive sense with male genres, and they spoke "on behalf of" the Chhattisgarh region less frequently than did their male relatives. This phenomenon may be partially attributed to the fact that women have less physical mobility than men and thus identify with more limited communities. It may also be due in part to the secondary position that women occupy in the social hierarchy; those higher in the hierarchy (caste, age, as well as gender hierarchies) more easily co-opt the traditions of those below them in such discussions than vice versa.

Performative Identification of Social Categories

We have seen in the discussion of *bhojalī* that the social organization of genre—the folklore groups identified through performance—suggest indigenously perceived significant social categories within the larger community; the social and aesthetic organizations reinforce each other (Abrahams 1976:194). The identification in Phuljhar of *bhojalī* as an unmarried girls' genre suggests that the social category of pubescent girls is a marked one in this subregion; the absence of genres so identified on the Raipur plains suggests that unmarried girls are "counted" in the category of married women. This principle is further exemplified in the comparison of social distinctions marked in the performance of *bhojalī* and a related male goddess tradition called *javārā* on the Raipur plains (see Figure 1). In both festivals, wheat or barley seedlings are planted, allowed to grow for nine days, and worshiped as the goddess; the presence of the goddess is affirmed through her possession of her devotees. The primary difference between the two festivals is that women sing the songs associated with the worship of the goddess in *bhojalī* and men sing *javārā* songs.

By placing these two traditions in relationship, we observe that gender is

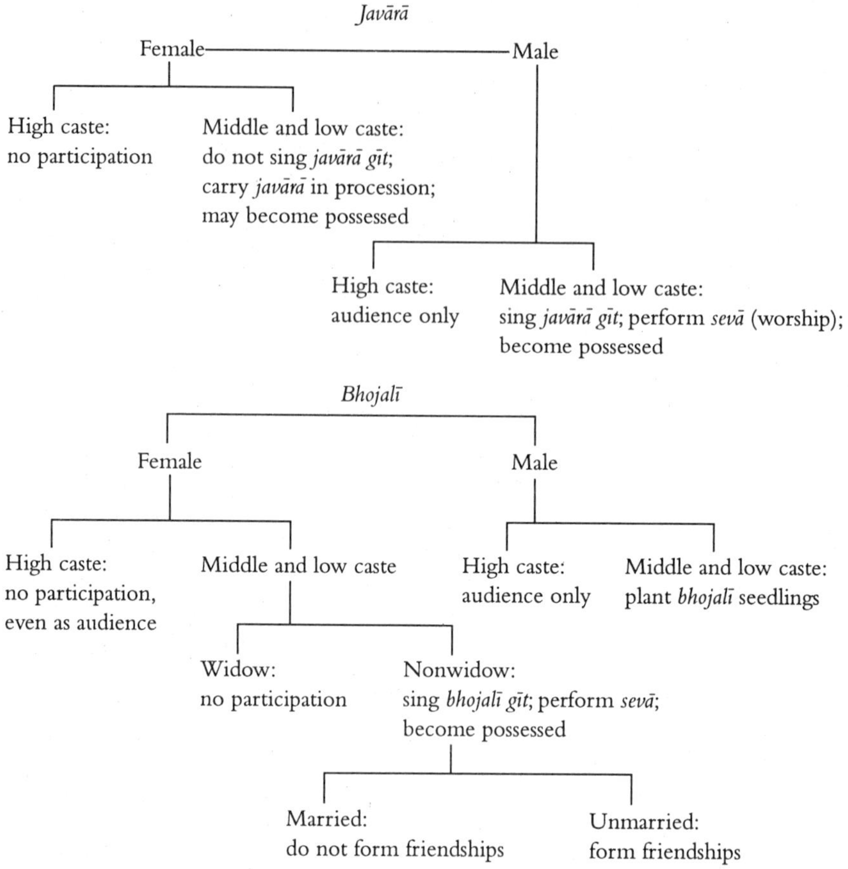

Figure 1. Social organization of *bhojalī* and *javārā* performance on the Raipur plains

the primary social division in the folklore community. Gender distinction is characteristic of the Chhattisgarhi regional folklore system as a whole; although audiences may be mixed, no traditions exist (at least in the Hindu community) in which men and women perform together. In dramatic genres with female characters, such as the *nācā* dance-drama, female parts are played by males in female dress.

Next, a caste distinction among both *javārā* and *bhojalī* participants is indicated, although it is less accentuated in the male *javārā* tradition than in the female *bhojalī*. Among female performers of *bhojalī*, there are no high- or even middle-caste women represented; they say they are afraid of becoming possessed by the goddess if they participate in the festival at any level, even as observers. As one woman articulated, "You never know what will happen."

Women who become possessed at festivals such as *bhojalī* and *gaurā* often have with them a female companion who adjusts the devotee's sari and physically keeps her from falling down so that she remains modest. Whether or not possession is present, however, women of different caste levels rarely perform together in genres belonging to the Chhattisgarhi repertoire.[3] In the *javārā* tradition, men of all caste levels may participate in some way, as audience, singers, and/or devotees of the goddess. Caste distinction as it is observed through the organization of the folklore system is typically less pronounced among men than women;[4] men also perform together in other folklore genres, such as *candainī nācā* dance-dramas and *bhajan* (devotional) singing groups.

The social groups identified by *bhojalī-javārā* performance further suggest that the marital status of a male is less significant as that of a female. Males are rarely segregated by their marital status for participation in most genres, widowers are not excluded from participation, and unmarried boys have no unique public-performance genres, participating with the married men in such performances. The female *bhojalī* tradition, on the other hand, differentiates between categories of widow and nonwidow as well as married and unmarried: widows may not participate, and while unmarried girls sing the *bhojalī* songs in the company of married women, *only* unmarried girls ritualize a *bhojalī* friendship at the conclusion of the festival.

Shifting Boundaries of Genre and Community

Increasing literacy, the spread and popularity of mass media communication, and shifting social institutions and economic and social relationships between patrons, performers, and audiences are affecting and changing traditional associations between many folklore genres and their communities. Songs that used to be sung and heard primarily by women may now be heard blasting loudly over All India Radio's folklore programming in public contexts. In many villages, professional dance-drama troupes, epic singers, and storytellers are having to compete with "video halls" (any kind of structure

[3] I specify genres within the Chhattisgarhi repertoire because of the relatively recent emergence of the temple-based, multicaste Ramayana *maṇḍalī* (singing groups); when such *maṇḍalī* meet in private homes, however, they are still restricted to a shared caste level, if not specific *jāti*.

[4] Edward Henry does not find this caste distinction in female performance in the Bhojpuri-speaking region of north India, where, he writes, "Women's songs move easily between castes" (1988:107). However, he does not indicate if he means that they perform together or perform the same genre separately or if he is speaking of specific *jāti* or caste levels.

to which admittance is charged to view a Hindi film shown with a video machine), and more recently with the increasingly available and affordable television. In 1993 when I asked the leader of a men's singing troupe that performs primarily *rāmsaptah,* and less frequently *paṇḍvānī,* which was more popular in Chhattisgarh, Ramayana or *paṇḍvānī,* he sighed, "*Paṇḍvānī,* Ramayana, *candainī.* But yes, whatever there is, *lok sāhitya, lok saṅskṛti* [folklore and folk customs], it's all finished now with TV. You'll get very little of it. Whatever it is—*nācā-wācā*—now there's [only] video."[5]

Formal school education of more and more audience members has resulted in a decreased interest in certain performance genres and a reemergence or realignment of other genres. Accompanying increased literacy has been the development of a perception of what it means to "act literate," action that may preclude participation in certain performances and festivals. For example, the primary reason given by male village elders for the demise of *ḍālkhāī* as a festival tradition is that "our educated girls shouldn't be singing these songs." As we have seen, though, while increasing literacy seems to have had an indirect detrimental effect for the *festival* setting for the songs, the *song* tradition itself is alive and well outside the ritual setting. As the performance context has shifted, so, too, has the identity of the community with which the genre is associated; the genre is now identified more frequently with the Phuljhar folklore community of eastern Chhattisgarh, male and female, rather than with the folklore group of unmarried Oriya girls. It is called a "Phuljhar song," or an "Oriya song," more often than it is a "*holī* song for unmarried girls."

In the *suā nāc* we saw a second example of shifting boundaries and identification of social groups with a particular folklore genre. The tradition has undergone numerous changes in performance context during the years in which I have done fieldwork in Chhattisgarh and is an example of the ascending and descending levels of identification with a single genre. Although the dancers (that is, the folklore group) are *ādivāsī* women, crucial to the definition of the genre in its dance context is its non-*ādivāsī* "audience" and the channel established between performers and patrons for the exchange of auspicious blessings and the gifting of grain and cash.

Because of the many levels of participation in the tradition, as well as its wide geographic spread throughout the region, the *suā nāc* is an important genre in helping to define the Chhattisgarh folklore region. And it is on this

[5] The use of an "echo word" (in this case, *wācā*) in Hindi and its dialects indicates the general category into which the first word of the pair fits. So *nācā-wācā* implies *nācā* and other similar performance genres, or *pān-wān* indicates those things that are consumed along with *pān.*

level that the genre is often identified by male informants, first as a Chhattisgarhi genre and only later as a female or *ādivāsī* tradition. Upper-caste women, on the other hand, most often identify it as an *ādivāsī* dance. Meanwhile, *ādivāsī* women themselves are frequently more specific as to the nature of the social group to whom the dance belongs—according to the *jāti* of the participants (beyond the general category of *ādivāsī*), their village or neighborhood, or the nature of their vow to the goddess the previous year, for whose fulfillment a particular woman may be participating as a dancer.

Increased literacy, changing social conditions, and mass media technology (particularly radio) have all made an impact on the genre of *suā nāc* and the communities with which it is identified. In Dhamtari young high school graduate Gond women (or perhaps it is their families) did not feel it appropriate to dance in public as do the *suā nāc* troupes. Further, because there is not a traditional, ritual relationship between dancers and shopkeepers in the urban areas, many other women, particularly the older ones, no longer want to dance in that context. As I mentioned earlier, several Gond women in the town of Dhamtari asserted, "People think we'll dance, but why should we?" The women dancing the *suā nāc* in urban neighborhoods are aware at some level that the genre gives identity to their caste, as well as reflecting and giving voice to their interests as women. Thus, as traditional settings for the dance are eroding in the towns and cities, its performers have discovered innovative contexts in which to maintain the tradition in order also to maintain their community, specifically the *gaurā* festival for whose images the *suā nāc* traditionally raised funds.

Because of its popularity throughout Chhattisgarh and its various levels of performative identification, the *suā nāc* is one of the genres frequently performed and recorded for the folklore programming of All India Radio. So while "live" performances, particularly in the urban areas, may be becoming more private or limited, recorded performances that are broadcast are available to all as audience, regardless of caste, gender, or education level. Similarly, two performance settings have also emerged for the *candainī* and *paṇḍvānī* epic genres: one in village courtyards and squares, and the other on public airwaves or on the proscenium stage in front of upper-middle class, educated audiences.

Although the relationship between genre and community is a strong indigenous organizing principle of the Chhattisgarhi folklore system, we have seen that it is not a static one. An indigenous awareness of the power of performance to identify and sustain community is found on numerous levels throughout Chhattisgarh. In a discussion with a rather young village headman (age forty-five) who had come to his position through the recent acquisition of land rather than hereditarily, he talked specifically about the role he thought folklore could play in establishing a sense of village identity and in improving village morale. He told me he had introduced the *gaurā* festival to his village only seven to eight years earlier. Many of the daughters-in-law marrying into his village come from villages in which *gaurā* is a vibrant tradition, but for some reason it had not been celebrated in this village. So the headman asked the women if they would be willing to introduce *gaurā* to their village of marriage. He thought this festival, specifically, would increase village cohesion because of the numerous folklore groups it could involve and the large public procession to the village tank that ends the festival. After several years of *gaurā* celebration in the village, the headman was satisfied with the results it had brought and was thinking of other new villagewide traditions that he could sponsor and "cause to be introduced."

Modern education and an effort by Chhattisgarhi literati to place Chhattisgarhi folklore within the broader schema of pan-Indian folklore have introduced another organizing principle to the Chhattisgarhi folklore system, alongside that of performative communities. This is one based on *formal* distinctions; its categories are *gīt, kahānī/kathā,* and *nāṭak/nācā* (song, story, drama). All India Radio's folklore programming also relies on these distinctions. Although the terms *gīt* and *kahānī* are currently used by members of Chhattisgarh's folklore communities, they are not distinguishing categories of genre. It remains to be seen whether this system of formal genres will be adapted more fully by Chhattisgarhi performers and audiences in their oral commentary and metafolklore, together with or replacing that of genre and community.

Recognizing indigenous genres and categories, their stability and flexibility, suggests frames through which a scholar from outside a particular folklore system can begin to explore the interior of performance texts in ways that are consistent with indigenous perceptions and understandings. In the folklore region of Chhattisgarh, a central principle characterizing its repertoire has been the social organization of genres. The changes that are restructuring traditional associations between gender, genre, and community have begun, however, to redefine and alter the interpretive frames of indigenous genres, and to affect the meanings of their performance.

PERFORMANCE TEXTS

The Song of Subanbali

Performer: Kaushalya Bai of Sitapur Village,
Raipur District, M.P.
December 20, 1980

Ram, Ram, Shri Hari Ram.
Ram, Ram, Shri Hari Ram.

Ram, whose vehicle is Garuda,
Who is the son of Kaushalya.

I salute you, Sarla Devi.
I salute you, Mangla Devi.

Be pleased, Sarla,
Be pleased.

First, I bring food from far away.
I bring it from the heaven of Kapil.

Shivshankar is her vehicle, Sarla.
Shivshankar is her vehicle.

At this time, Suban is speaking.
Now, Suban is speaking.

She's holding small clay dishes.
She's holding small bamboo dishes.

She went to play, oh Suban.
She went to play.

She was playing in her playhouse.
She was playing in her playhouse.

[She overhears some kings talking; they have camped nearby.]

There were kings
From the city of Bombay,

From the kingdoms of Bombay and Cuttack,
From the city of Cuttack.

The kings were resting.
They had set up their tents.

They cooked their food.
They ate and drank.

They made comfortable beds,
The kings and their sons.

They spread out their bedding and slept,
Spread it out and slept.

Now they were talking about Bandhiya Raja.
"He is very evil.

He has defeated
Kings from all the four directions.

Losing their wealth and riches,
Losing their wealth and riches,

The kings have been imprisoned.
They have been put in jail."

They spoke like this.
Such were the answers spoken.

The daughter, Suban,
The daughter, Suban,

Suban heard this,
And she understood.

"Listen to the foreigners.
Listen to the kings.

Listen to their answers," she said.
"Listen to their words."

"I'm going to my mother.
I'm going to my father.

I'll take my wealth [dishes] and go.
I'll take my wealth."

Suban was disturbed.
Suban was disturbed.

Her mother is Nila Rani.
Her mother is Nila Rani.

She was watching for her on the path.
She was looking for her daughter.

The daughter was disturbed as she went.
She was upset as she went.

Now, my Suban,
Hearing them, my Suban,

Suban went running.
She went running.

She jumped into her mother's lap.
She jumped into her father's lap.

"Listen, my mother,
Listen to my answer.

Give me a boat of sixteen lengths.
Give me a boat of nine lengths.

I'm going to the country of Bandhi," she said,
"I'm going to the country of Bandhi."

Her mother, Nila Rani,
Her mother, Nila Rani,

Gave this response.
Nila gave this answer.

"Out of twelve *ghāṭ*, I chose one.
I prostrated myself at the *ghāṭ* of Shiva.

As a result, I received you, my daughter.
I received you.

Where is this country of Bandhi and its king?
Where is this country of Bandhi and its king?

Your mother doesn't know," she said.
"Your father doesn't know."

"Give me a boat of sixteen lengths.
Give me a boat of nine lengths.

I'm the daughter of Shivshankar.
I'm the daughter of Vishtankar.

I won't stay in your house one minute.
I won't stay a moment."

Her father is Jagya Rishi.
Her father is Jagya Rishi.

She's the only daughter of twelve brothers.
She's the only daughter of thirteen brothers.

Suban gave this answer.
She gave this reply.

"I have only one daughter.
I have only one wealth.

She says she won't stay a minute.
She won't stay a moment.

Go, go, my servants.
Go, go, my attendants.

Quickly call them," he said.
"Quickly call them,

The carpenter Kunja," he said,
"The twelve carpenters."

At this time, the servants
And the ministers heard him.

They went in a minute.
They went in a moment.

They went to the home of the carpenter Kunja.
They went to the dwelling of the carpenters.

The servants entered.
They entered.

"Come, come, Kunja carpenter.
Come, come, carpenter brothers.

Listen to the answer.
Listen to the reply.

Be quick!
Be fast!

Kunja the carpenter
And the twelve others,

Go to Jagya Rishi.
Go to Anna Rishi.

He'll give you the answer.
He'll give you the word."

At this time the twelve brothers,
The carpenters,

Went on their way,
Went on their way.

Kunja the carpenter and the rest
Entered

And greeted him [Jagya Rishi].
They greeted him.

The carpenters stood there.
They stood there.

"Why have we been called?
For what reason have we been called?"

He [Jagya Rishi] spoke in this way.
He spoke in this way.

"At this time, Kunja carpenter,
Listen, Kunja carpenter.

A boat of sixteen lengths,
A boat of nine lengths,

"Build it," he said.
"Build it

For Suban," he said,
"For Suban."

Hearing him, Kunja the carpenter
And the twelve carpenters

Went on their way,
Went on their way.

They entered their home.
They met at their dwelling.

At that time, the carpenters
Sharpened their axes.

They pealed the bark off.
They sharpened all of them.

They sharpened the other tools,
Everything of theirs.

The carpenters got everything ready,
The rice and lentils.

They tied them in a bundle.
It was midnight.

The night was dark.
The night was dark.

The carpenters were sleepy,
But sleep didn't come.

The roosters crowed.
The roosters crowed.

At this time, Kunja the carpenter
And the twelve brothers,

The carpenters went on their way.
They went on their way.

The carpenters, outside their home,
Outside their dwelling,

At that moment, with all their hearts,
At that moment, they entreated god.

They went to Mayalgiri mountain.
They went to Citrakuti mountain.

The carpenters went to Hansgiri.
The carpenters went to Hansgiri.

The carpenters went to Candangiri.
The carpenters went to Candangiri.

They went to Hilgiri.
They went to Nilgiri.

The carpenters went to all six mountains,
But they didn't find a tree.

The carpenters became despondent
And sat down.

"If we don't bring back a boat,
If we don't bring back a boat,

The king will cut us in two.
Jagya Rishi will cut us down.

He'll chase us from the kingdom.
He won't let us stay in the country."

At that time, the carpenters,
The carpenters, saying this much,

Went to the mountains,
Mayalgiri and Kailashgiri.

There were *śīśu*-wood trees there.
There were *śīśu*-wood trees.

They left these trees
And went under some other trees.

The carpenters spread out a cloth
And lay down.

They lay down and slept.
They were despondent.

The carpenters,
Yes, the carpenters.

At this time, from Kailashgiri,
From Mount Kailash,

An old snake was coming,
Feeling restless [with hunger].

The mother vulture in the *śīśu* tree
Had left her children.

She had gone to bring food
For the children.

The snake climbed up the tree
To eat a mouse.

At this time, the children
Began to cry.

Seeing him, the children
Became worried.

At this time, the carpenters
Turned over and saw him [the snake].

"If, as we're watching,
He swallows

The children;
If he swallows them,

We'll be faulted.
We'll have committed a sin."

Turning over, the carpenters got up
And grabbed their swords.

They cut him in nine parts.
They cut him in nine parts.

The snake fell to the earth.
He fell to the earth.

At this time, as his life was leaving,
He spoke this word:

"Oh carpenters, having killed me,
Oh carpenters, having killed me,"

He said, "The boat, as it's leaving,
The boat, as it's leaving. . . ."

Saying this, the snake's breath left him.
Saying this, the snake's breath left him.

At this time, the mother vulture,
The poor mother vulture,

The mother vulture, for her children,
For her children,

Was bringing them food,
Was bringing them their meal.

At that time, she was forcefully feeding
The children.

"Your eyes are closed, children.
Your mouths are closed.

Listen, my children,
It's for you.

I went the distance of twelve *kos* [twenty-four miles];
I went to bring food.

For what reason," she said,
"Are your eyes closed?

What sorrow has struck you
So that your mouths are closed?

I'm forcefully feeding you, children,
But you aren't eating."

"Listen, mother,
Listen to the answer.

Listen to our words, mother.
Listen to our words.

If we had died,
If we had died,

Who would have eaten the food?" they said.
"Who would have eaten the food?

Look below, mother.
Look under the tree."

At this time, the mother vulture
Looked on the ground.

She looked below.
She looked below.

At this time, the mother vulture,
The vulture heard this.

Her breath flew away.
Her breath flew away.

"What if my two sons had died?
What if the snake had eaten them?"

The vulture spoke like this.
She flew down.

"Listen mother,
Listen to our answer.

What has happened to them,
To the sons from a foreign country?

They haven't touched anything.
They haven't cooked.

They're just lying there.
They're just lying there."

The children spoke like this.
They gave this answer.

At this time, the mother vulture
Flew down.

The vulture went to the carpenters.
She went to the carpenters.

She met them.
She went to them.

"Listen, my sons,
Listen to my answer.

What has happened to you?
What misfortune has fallen on you?

You aren't bathing, my sons,
You aren't shaving.

You aren't cooking.
You're still hungry."

At this time, the carpenters,
Hearing her, the carpenters,

Getting up, the carpenters sat up
And entreated her.

"We've come, having wandered over
Seven mountains, mother.

Over seven mountains, mother,
We've come, and are very tired.

We haven't found a tree," they said.
"We haven't found a tree.

If we don't bring back,
If we don't bring back,

A nine-length boat,
A sixteen-length boat,

Jagya Rishi, Anna Rishi,
Will cut us in two.

He'll cut off our heads.
He'll chase us from our homes.

He won't let us stay in our homes.
He won't let us stay inside.

He won't let us stay," they said.
"He won't let us stay."

Hearing them, the mother vulture
Gave this answer.

"Go, my sons,
Go to bathe,

Shave your beards," she said.
"Shave your beards.

Cook some food,
And eat the food without worry.

I'll check and give it to you, my sons,
I'll measure and give

A sixteen-length boat,
A nine-length boat."

They heard the words of the mother vulture,
The mother vulture.

They heard her answer.
They heard her words.

Hearing her, the carpenters
Went to bathe.

At this time, the carpenters,
At this time, the carpenters bathed.

Sitting cross-legged, the carpenters
Took out their food and ate without worry.

They were happy.
They ate without worry.

Evening fell.
Evening fell.

The vulture brought,
The vulture brought,

The children from the *sebhilī* [cotton tree]
To the *titulī* tree.

"Listen, sons,
Cut the tree, carpenters," she said.

At this time, the carpenters,
Hearing this, the carpenters

Began to cut the tree, oh look,
Began to cut the tree.

The bark of the tree didn't give in.
The axe didn't cut.

"Our carpentry is useless.
Why doesn't Yama [god of death] eat us?

Of twelve brothers,
There's only one wealth [descendant; usually reference to son].

What should we do?" they said.
Kunja the carpenter asked,

"What should we do?
We have no plan."

Saying this, the carpenters
Thought to themselves.

The carpenters thought in their hearts,
Thought in their hearts.

"Go, go, youngest brother.
At this time, youngest brother,

Go to our house," they said.
"Go to our house," they said.

"Enter inside.
From inside the house take these things:

Take some white rice.

Take the sweetened milk of the *dhanu* cow [cow of wealth].

Take the wide-mouthed oil lamp.

Go without hesitation.
Go to the house with joy.

Find your son and your sister-in-law.
She'll be holding him on her lap.

Take him in your arms,
Brother, go with joy.

If your sister-in-law asks,
If your sister-in-law asks,

Say you're going to the jungle, to the forest.
Say you're going to the jungle, to the forest.

'Where are you taking our son?' she'll ask.
'Where are you taking our son?' she'll ask.

Your sister-in-law will speak like this.
She'll give this answer.

'Of twelve brothers, there's only one son.
Of twelve brothers, there's only one son.

He'll go to the jungle, the forest,
To learn the skill of carpentry.'

Saying this much, brother,
Bring the son."

He said this much,
Kunja the carpenter.

Hearing this, the youngest brother went home
At this time, the youngest brother went home.

He walked very slowly.
He reached his home.

He took some white grain.

He took the sweetened milk of the *dhanu* cow.

He took the wide-mouthed oil lamp.

The carpenter arrived outside his home.
He arrived outside his home.

At this time, Kunja carpenter's wife
Was holding their son.

She embraced him.
She gave him a kiss.

At that time, the carpenter took the son.
At that time, the carpenter took the son.

Seeing him, the sister-in-law asked,
The wife of Kunja the carpenter,

"You went to the jungle, the forest.
You went to the jungle, the forest.

Where will you take our son?
Where will you take our wealth?"

"Listen, my sister-in-law,
Listen to my answer.

Of twelve brothers, there's only one son.
Of twelve brothers, there's only one wealth.

He'll see the jungle, the forest.
He'll learn the skill of a carpenter."

The youngest brother
Said this much.

Taking his son,
He went on his way.

The other carpenters, ahead,
Met him there.

At this time, the carpenters,
Seeing their son,

Seeing him, they cried.
Seeing him, they cried,

"Our innocent, innocent son!
Our innocent, innocent son!

Suban caused this to happen;
She's given this punishment.

Look at him, Suban,
Look at him.

The innocent, innocent one!
Jagya Rishi, look at him."

Crying out like this, the carpenters
Became despondent.

Hearing this, the eldest
Carpenter, Pandu,

Went to the ocean,
Went to the Ganga.

He bathed his son.
He bathed his dear son.

Having bathed him,
He stood him up.

He went to the *ghāṭ* and finished.
He finished bathing him.

At sunrise, at the time of sunrise,
He came to the tree.

He brought white rice.
He brought sweetened milk from the *dhanu* cow.

The carpenter lit the lamp.
He lit the lamp.

He stood their son there.
He stood their son there.

The carpenter drew out his sword.
He cut off the head of their son.

They offered the child to the tree.
They offered the child to the tree.

At this time, to the *śīśu* tree,
At this time, to the *śīśu* tree,

They gave one stroke, oh look,
They gave two strokes.

The tree was nine lengths.
It was sixteen lengths.

In one moment, the carpenters,
In the time of one second,

A sixteen-length boat,
A nine-length boat,

The carpenters made it immediately.
They made it in a second.

Quickly, quickly, the carpenters
Joined the boat together.

They joined the boat.
They joined the boat.

The current of the three-river confluence,
The current was fast.

It was the current of the Jamuna.
It was the current of the Sarasvati.

It was the river Ganga.
It was the river Ganga.

They put the boat in there.
They put the boat in there.

The boat went peacefully.
It went for sixteen days.

The boat went on the Mahanadi River.
It went on sixteen rivers.

At this time, the carpenters,
Hearing this, the twelve brothers said,

"The action was worthless.
The action was worthless.

How can we go home?
How can we go back?"

Saying this, the carpenters
Thought to themselves.

They came to the house after walking sixteen *kos*.
They came to Suban's house,

The home of Nila Rani,
The house of Jagya Rishi.

The twelve brothers, the carpenters
Entered that place.

"Oh mother, my Nila Rani,
Oh father, my Jagya Rishi."

At this time, Suban,
At this time the stubborn Suban,

My Suban heard this.
She found out.

My Suban came running.
She came running.

"How far is my boat?
How far is the boat?"

She asked, my Suban.
She asked, my Suban.

My Suban came running.
She saw the boat.

"Your son is sitting in the boat.
He's coming peacefully; he's coming happily.

Listen, carpenters.
Listen, fathers.

You twelve brothers ran off," she said.
"You twelve brothers ran off," she said.

"You offered your son to the boat.
You offered your wealth to the boat.

The water is very deep, carpenters.
The water is very deep, carpenters.

The high waves of the river are striking.
The high waves are striking.

You left your son, carpenters,
And came back.

The water is very deep,
Of the river Ganga.

The waves are high, carpenters,
And you left your son."

Hearing this, Kunja, the carpenter
Thought to himself,

"We cut off his head.
We cut off his head.

Where will we find our son?
Where will we find him?"

"Go, go, carpenters,
Go bring your son

From the boat which I told you to make.
From the boat which I told you to make.

Go to your son.
Go to your wealth."

[The singer later explained that Suban was an *apsara* (celestial nymph) and thus had power to bring the son back to life.]

The carpenters went to bring him.
The carpenters went to bring him.

They took white rice.
They took the sweetened milk of the *dhanu* cow.

"Take a golden stool," she said,
"Take a golden stool," she said,

"And wash his feet and my boat.
Wash the boat."

They greeted and supplicated him [their son].
They greeted and supplicated him.

They brought the boat home.
They brought it to the house.

They brought back her boat.
They brought back her boat.

As much wealth and as many riches,
As much money [as she had],

She put in the boat, my Suban.
She put in the boat, my Suban.

Cows went in; calves went in.
Goats went in; elephants went in.

Elephants went in; horses went in.
Elephants went in; horses went in.

She was taking all of this, my Suban.
She was taking all of this, my Suban.

She went to her brother.
She went to her brother.

At this time, Lalit Raja [Suban's brother],
Lalit Raja heard her.

"Give me my *bahū* [daughter-in-law] as a companion," she said.
"Give me my *bahū* as a companion," she said.

I'm going to Bandhi Desh, my brother.
I'm going to Bandhi Desh, my brother."

In this way he spoke, my Suban.
In this way he spoke, my Suban.

"I won't agree to your request.
I won't let her [Tulsa] go with you.

She's from a woman's caste [*jāti*].
Where will you take her?

A woman's caste is weak.
A woman's caste is weak.

Father hasn't seen it [Bandhi Desh]," he said.
"Mother hasn't seen it.

Where is this country, the kingdom of Bandhi?
Where is this country, the kingdom of Bandhi?

You're making up the name, my Suban.
You're making up the name, my Suban.

I won't let your *bahū* go with you.
I won't let your *bahū* go with you."

At this time, Suban spoke.
She gave the answer.

"If you don't let *bahū* go with me,
If you don't let *bahū* go with me,

You'll have burning;
You'll have itching.

You'll have boils;
You'll have burning."

It began; it started to happen.
The boils appeared.

Lalit Raja
Gave the *bahū* forcefully!

At this time, Lalit Raja
Let the *bahū* go with her.

He let her go with Suban.
He let her go.

She called the villagers of the kingdom.
She called the ministers.

"Look after my mother; look after my father.
Look after my brother; look after the kingdom."

In this way, she spoke
To the ministers.

The daughter Suban,
The daughter Suban

Sounded the bell and conch
And took the *ṭipkī* drum and *nagāṛā* [reed instrument].

She went out from the house.
She went out from her dwelling.

She went to Khairapur.
She went to Khairapur.

The king of Khairapur,
Of Khairapur, was her maternal grandfather.

"Give me your clothes, my grandfather [for a male disguise]
And take my clothes."

"Your life is very young.
Your love is very young.

Taking my clothes you'll do something wrong [impure], Suban.
You'll do something wrong."

"If I do anything impure, cut off my head.
Cut out my tongue.

My eyes will burst.
My life will leave me."

In this way, Suban spoke.
She gave the answer.

Suban took her grandfather's clothes,
Took her grandfather's clothes, my Suban,

And went on her way.

She went peacefully, my Suban.
She went happily.

She crossed kingdom after kingdom,
With the goats and sheep, elephants and horses.

Suban took all of them with her.
Suban took all of them with her.

They crossed the highland where the *muṅg* pulse grows.
They crossed the wheat fields.

They went through grain fields, through rice fields,
And destroyed them.

They [owners of fields] couldn't say anything to Suban.
They couldn't say anything to Suban.

They asked, "From which country is this king?
From which country is this merchant?"

Seeing her, they were surprised.
Seeing her, they were surprised.

All the cows and calves went.
All the cows and calves went.

All the goats and sheep,
Grain and wealth, they all went with her.

At this time, my Suban,
At this time, my Suban,

My Suban went on her way.
She went on her way with ease,

To the kingdom of Bandhi Desh,
The kingdom of Bandhiya.

She entered the kingdom, my Suban.
She entered the kingdom, my Suban.

She set up tents, my Suban.
She set up tents.

Tents between the fields,
Tents on the high ground,

She made a protective wall around them.
She made a protective wall around them.

The cows and calves, goats and sheep,
She put them all there.

She was satisfied, my Suban.
She was satisfied, my Suban.

The barber from the kingdom of Udigarh,
The barber from the kingdom of Udigarh

Came to take his bath.
Came to take his bath.

He saw the *bahū*, my Suban.
He saw the *bahū*, my Suban.

Her beauty was like the sun,
The beauty that he saw.

"Of the kingdom of Bandhiya,
Of the country of Bandhiya,

She will be made queen.
[Words indistinguishable]," he said.

The barber, saying this,
Went on his way.

He came in front of the king of Bandhi Desh,
The kingdom of Bandhiya.

The barber spoke this word.
He gave this answer.

"Listen, oh king,
Listen, my *bābū*.

From which country are the foreigners,
From which country are the foreigners,

Who have come here?
Who have come here?

They have set up tents.
They are cooking and eating.

She is brilliant like the sun.
She is beautiful.

She will be queen of this country.
She will be queen of this country.

. . . . [words indistinguishable]"

Saying this, the barber
Gave the answer.

Hearing him, the king said,
"Take a knife and go.

Cut off the king's head.
Cut his throat.

Bring the queen
Bring the queen.

I'll give you five villages
And let you leave your barber's work."

The king spoke in this way.
He gave this answer.

Hearing this, the barber
Went back.

"Oh king [to Suban], I'll shave
Your face and head."

In this way, the barber spoke.
He gave the answer.

Hearing this, the barber spoke.
Hearing this, Suban spoke.

"I'm serving my country.
I'm serving my country.

I'm not the son of a king.
I'm not the son of a *bābū*.

I'm the son of a moneylender.
I'm the son of a moneylender.

I'm trading marijuana.
I'm trading turmeric.

I've brought on loan
All the cows and calves of the village.

[She's selling them for the village.]

I've brought on loan
All the cows and calves of the kingdom.

I'm the son
Of a poor moneylender.

I have no wealth and riches.
I'm poor,"

Suban said.
Suban spoke.

My Suban declared happily,
My Suban declared happily,

"I won't be shaved
By any barber,

Outside my home," she said,
"Outside my dwelling."

Hearing this, the barber
Was disappointed.

"You're greedy for money.
You're greedy for money.

You're asking for only one rupee.
You're asking for only one rupee.

Take five rupees, barber,
And go away from here."

At this time, the barber
Went to Bandhiya Raja.

He went to the place of the king.
His heart was unhappy.

His heart was saddened, the barber's.
His heart was saddened, the barber's.

He was disappointed, the barber.
He was disappointed, the barber.

He entered the place of the king,
The place of Bandhiya.

"Listen, oh king,
Listen, my *bābū*.

[He reports what Suban has said.]

'In my kingdom, I'm the son of a moneylender.
I'm not the son of a king.'

This is what he [Suban] said.
This is what he said.

'From the cities of the kingdom,
From all the landed gentry,

I've brought elephants,' he [Suban] said.
'On loan,' he said.

'The cows and calves, goats and sheep,
I've brought on loan.

I'm the son of a moneylender.
I'm going to Banij.

I won't be shaved
By another barber.

I've brought with me
The barber of my city,

The one who serves me
In my city.'

This is what he [Suban] said, oh king.
This is what he said, oh king.

'To receive one rupee,
You've come here.'

This is what he said, oh king.
He gave five rupees."

So the barber spoke.
His heart was not content.

Again and again, three times,
He went [to Suban].

"I'll become his [Suban's] *mahāprasād*," he [the king] said.
"This would be good."

Bandhiya Raja said,
"I'll seat *mahāprasād* with him."

This is what he [Suban] said,
This is the answer he gave,

"A king as great
As Bandhiya Raja,

This Bandhiya Raja says
That he will seat *mahāprasād* with me.

I'm the son of a moneylender.
I'm the son of a poor man.

How can I seat *mahāprasād*?" he [Suban] said.
"How can I seat *mahāprasād*

With a king?" he said,
"With a king?

Listen, barber,
Listen to my answer.

I am poor," he said,
"I am poor."

The barber tried to entice him [Suban].
The barber said,

"He has wealth in his house.
He has wealth in his house.

What does poverty matter?" he said.
"What does poverty matter?" he said.

"People go on paths and roads,
From towns and cities," he said.

"And they form friendships.
They form friendships.

They become relatives," he said
"They become relatives," he said.

[People who meet each other while traveling become *mahāprasād*.]

"Such a great king,
Such a great *bābū*,

Won't he give his wealth
To you?

You are poor.
Don't go begging.

If you seat *mahāprasād*,
You'll get respect."

Saying this much, the barber
Tried to entice him [Suban].

Suban heard this.
She had the four *guṇ* [attributes/qualities].

[Because of her *guṇ*, she understands what he is trying to do.]

"Go, go, barber.
You're saying I must.

I'll seat [a friendship]," she said.
"I'll seat [a friendship]," she said.

At this time, the barber,
Hearing this, the barber

Went on his way
To Bandhiya Raja.

He went to the place of the king,
To Bandhi Desh.

Going to the place of the king, the barber,
The barber was happy.

He laughed aloud [at Suban].
He laughed aloud.

" 'I'll seat *mahāprasād*,' " he said,
He said happily.

"He [Suban] said, 'No, no,'
He said, 'No, no,'

But in the end,
He [Suban] agreed.

'I will seat it [the friendship],' he [Suban] said.
'I will seat it,' he [Suban] said."

At this time, Suban
Went to Mathura bazaar.

She brought expensive cloth [with gold thread].
She brought expensive cloth.

For Bandhiya
Suban brought expensive cloth.

She brought two pieces
Of expensive cloth, my Suban.

She brought two pieces.
She brought two pieces.

Expensive cloth, oh Suban,
For her friend, Bandhiya.

She brought it for him.
She brought it for him.

Jalebī and *peṛā* [two kinds of sweets],
Jalebī and *peṛā*,

She brought a sack full of them.
She brought a sack full of them.

One coconut is necessary;
She brought five.

One betel nut is necessary;
She brought five.

She brought five pieces of *pān* [betel leaf].
She brought five pieces of musk.

My Suban brought these.
My Suban brought these.

Look, Bandhiya brought cotton cloth.
Look, Bandhiya brought cotton cloth.

A single coconut, Bandhiya,
A single coconut, Bandhiya,

Bandhiya brought
A single coconut.

Two pieces of *pān*.
Two pieces of *pān*.

Having decorated it [the brass plate on which the gifts are placed],
Having decorated it, [he said]

"Go, go my servants,
Go, go, my servants.

Servants of the Bandhiya king,
Come to me.

Take these gifts," he said,
"Take these gifts.

I'm going to seat *mahāprasād*.
I'm going to seat *mahāprasād*."

At this time, the barber
Called out loudly,

"Go, go, Bandhiya Raja,
To the moneylender's son.

Go, go to seat it [formalize the friendship].
Go, go to seat it.

I'll send the servants," he said.
"I'll send the servants," he said.

"I'll go with her [Suban said],
With my wife.

Servants take these gifts,
Take them to that place.

To the city of Bandhiya,
To the house of Bandhiya.

We will enter it," she said,
"We will enter it."

At this time, the barber
Went on his way,

When Bandhiya
Said, "Call my servants."

With four or five servants,
With four or five servants,

She [Suban] went on her way.
She slowly went on her way.

To the country of Bandhiya,
To the city of Bandhiya,

Suban came near.
Suban came near.

She entered it.
She entered it.

At this time, my Suban,
Bearing those gifts,

She took them out
And entered.

With five or six servants,
She prostrated [before the king].

Hearing this, the servants said,
"Tulsa Rani,

He [Suban] brought her with him.
He brought her with him.

She is like the sun.
She is brilliant, like the daughter of fire.

Suban," they said, "is the son of a king.
Suban," they said, "is the son of a king.

Look at the queen.
Look at her beauty.

Seeing her, in city and town,
People are in wonder.

From which country has the king come?
From which country has the queen come?

We have never seen
Such beauty."

City and townspeople came,
And children, too.

Women came,
And men, too.

They looked at her with pleasure.
They looked at her.

The servants put down
The gifts.

They put them down
In the courtyard of the king,

Where there was
A Brindavati [Tulsi] platform.

A *kalaś* [ritual water pot] was installed,
One holding an oil lamp.

A Brahmin was reading the Vedas.
He was reading the Vedas.

At this time, the Brahmin
Gave this answer,

"If ritual friends speak ill of each other,
They will become tadpoles."

Saying this, the Brahmin,
To the daughter, Suban,

And to Bandhiya Raja,
He gave this answer.

They took the coconuts seven times,
The coconuts seven times,

And passed them back and forth.
They supplicated each other [for friendship and protection].

They greeted each other.
They supplicated each other.

They put cloth pieces on each other's shoulder.
They put cloth pieces on each other's shoulder.

They supplicated each other.
They appealed to each other.

At this time, the coconut,
The *jalebī* and small *khājur* fruit,

They ate them, sitting cross-legged,
In the city, in the town.

They were content.
They were satisfied.

At this time, Bandhiya Raja,
Hearing this, Bandhiya Raja,

Fed him [Suban] *pān*.
Fed him *pān*.

They fed each other *pān*
And went away happily.

To their own houses,
They went on their way.

"They are cooking
Today in that dwelling, my friend.

Let's go celebrate," she [Suban] said.
"Let's go celebrate,"

Suban said,
The daughter said.

"Today I won't eat [in my house]," she said.
"Today I won't eat," she said.

"Where they're cooking,
Where they're cooking food,

That's where I'll eat," she said.
"Where they are cooking,

I'll eat there.
I'll eat there."

"Greetings, my *mahāprasād*,
Greetings, greetings," she said.

At this time, Suban
Went on her way.

Her *bahū*, Tulsa Rani,
Went ahead,

Repeating the name of god, "Hari-Hari,"
She went to the jungle of Brinda.

The tent was set up.
The tent was set up.

Suban went on her way
In a chariot.

To her own house, oh Suban,
To her own dwelling,

She entered, my Suban.
She entered, my Suban.

She was happy, my Suban.
She was happy.

Morning dawned, Suban.
Morning dawned.

Bandhiya was calling.
Bandhiya was calling.

"Go, go, barber,
Call my *mahāprasād*," he said.

At this time, the barber
Came there [to Suban].

"Listen, my king.
Listen, my *bābū*.

[Your] *mahāprasād* is calling you.
[Your] *mahāprasād* is calling you."

Suban went on her way.
She walked there.

She went on her way.
She went on her way.

Oh daughter, my Suban,
Suban *devatā* [literally, goddess].

She went slowly.
She went there,

To the kingdom of Bandhiya.
To the kingdom of Bandhiya.

Suban entered.
Suban entered.

She greeted and met him.
She greeted and met him.

At this time, my Suban,
Hearing him, my Suban,

Sat down with content, Suban,
Sat down on a chair.

He gave *bīṛī* and matches,
Bandhiya Raja.

"I'm the son of a foreigner.
I'm the son of a moneylender.

I don't smoke *bīṛī*, *mahāprasād*.
I don't smoke *bīṛī*, *mahāprasād*."

Speaking in this way, oh Suban,
She gave the answer.

Now, now, Suban.
Now, now, Suban.

"Listen, *mahāprasād*,
Listen to the answer.

A *mahāprasād* like you
Must surely observe fasts [if you don't smoke].

You must surely observe fasts.
You must surely observe fasts.

Go bring some tiger milk,
Some tiger milk [for a fast].

You must surely fast," he said.
"You must surely fast."

At this time, my Suban
Hearing this answer,

She came to her *bahū*.
She came to her wealth.

Lowering her face,
With a despondent heart,

She met her *bahū*, oh Suban.
She met her *bahū*.

Her *bahū*, Tulsa Rani,
Had cooked a meal.

She had cooked a vegetable dish,
Not one, but fourteen.

She had cooked all kinds, Tulsa.
She had cooked all kinds, Tulsa.

"Now, now, Suban,
Listen to the answer.

You went to your *mahāprasād*.
You went to your *mahāprasād*.

What happened that, with a sad heart,
You're coming to me?

You're coming to me," she said,
"With a despondent heart."

"Listen, my *bahū*
He's doing a *kūṭur kūṇī* [*kūṭ*, literally a plot, scheme] fast.

He told me to bring tiger milk,
To bring tiger milk.

If I go near a tiger,
If I go near a tiger,

I won't be able to return
To my mother and father's home.

I'll be in the tiger's stomach," she said.
"I'll be in the tiger's stomach," she said.

At this time, Tulsa Rani,
Hearing this, Tulsa Rani [said],

"You didn't obey the word of your mother.
You didn't obey the word of your father.

To the cities and towns, my Suban,
They forbade you to go.

The word of your grandmother, the word of your grandfather,
The word of your brother.

You didn't listen to the word of anyone.
You didn't listen to the word of anyone.

You came with one mind.
You came with one mind, my Suban.

Now you're being punished.
Now you're being punished.

. . . . [couplet indiscernible]

'You've killed her with hunger.
You didn't serve her.

Suban has become dried out [thin], my Suban.
Suban has become dried out, my Suban.'

This is what your mother will say.
This is what your mother will say.

Eat this good meal," she said.
"Eat and be content.

Be content and eat the meal.
Be happy and eat the meal.

Don't be worried about anything, my Suban.
Don't be worried about anything.

Now, now, my Suban, don't worry.
Now, now, my Suban, don't worry."

At this time, my Suban,
Her heart was going *ḍhak-ḍhak* [sound of heart beat].

She ate some food,
And she left some food.

"Comb your hair, my Suban.
Eat a piece of *pān*."

At this time, her *bahū*,
Mother Tulsa Rani,

Counseled her, oh Suban.
She counseled her.

Her heart didn't obey, oh Suban.
Her heart didn't obey, oh Suban.

It went *ḍhak-ḍhak*, oh Suban.
She went to sleep that night.

The cock crowed.
Morning dawned.

The cock crowed, my Suban.
She took the brass vessel [to bring the tiger's milk].

"Listen, my Suban,
Listen to the answer.

When you meet the tiger, say this:
When you meet the tiger, say this:

'Listen, mother, my uncle's wife,
Listen to the answer.

My mother is fasting.
She's fasting.

She has sent me
To bring milk.'

Saying this, my Suban,
Saying this, my Suban,

Giving this answer,
Giving this response,

She'll give milk in your hand.
She'll give milk in your hand.

Go happily, my Suban,
Go happily."

Hearing the word of her *bahū*,
At this time, the word of her *bahū*,

Obeying the word of Tulsa,
Obeying her, Suban

Went happily, my Suban.
She went happily.

She went to Candangiri, my Suban.
She went to Kailash [names of two mountains].

Slowly, slowly, the sun rose.
She came to the tiger.

The tiger saw her.
She saw her.

"My next meal is coming.
My food is coming,

That which I'll swallow today.
That which I'll swallow today."

At this time, Suban,
Hearing her, Suban [said],

"Listen, my aunt,
Listen, my aunt,

My mother is fasting.
She's fasting.

She has sent me
To you for some milk.

I've come for some milk, mother.
I've come for some milk, mother."

Saying this, my Suban,
She gave the answer.

Hearing this, the tiger,
At this time, the tiger [said],

"Listen, my son [Suban in disguise],
Listen, my son.

Stay far away.
Stay far away.

I have a tiger's head,
A head that seizes.

I'll swallow up
Such a beautiful son.

Don't come in front of me.
Stay far away.

Go far away, my son.
Go far away, my son."

At this time, Suban,
Hearing this, my Suban,

Put down the brass vessel.
Put down the brass vessel.

She went far away.
She stayed behind cover.

Hearing this, the tiger,
Hearing this, the tiger

Put her milk
In the brass vessel

And called out,
And called out,

"Listen, my son.
Listen, my wealth.

Take the milk, my son.
Take the milk, my son.

I'm going away, my son.
I'm going away.

Don't fear, my son.
Don't be afraid.

Take it with pleasure, my son.
Go happily," she said.

At this time, my Suban,
Hearing her, my Suban,

Brought it with pleasure.
Brought the milk with pleasure.

She brought
The milk in front of Bandhiya.

When she brought
The milk, at this time,

Bandhiya was surprised,
As was the barber.

"The tiger didn't eat him.
The snake didn't bite him."

In this way, Bandhiya spoke.
He gave the answer.

Hearing this, he gave the answer.
Hearing this, he gave the reply.

"Listen to your *mahāprasād*.
Listen to the answer.

We'll go to the wrestling grounds.
We'll go to the wrestling grounds.

There will be a hole of fourteen *kos*.
There will be a hole of fourteen *kos*.

It will be long,
Fifty feet long.

Having spread a net below,
We'll cross the hole."

At this time, it was sunrise.
It was sunrise when she heard him.

After this, she went.
After this, she went.

Her heart wasn't happy, oh Suban.
Her heart wasn't happy, oh Suban.

Deep, deep, fifty deep,
Such was the hole.

Twelve *kos*, twenty-four *kos*,
What plan should she make?

At this time, Tulsa Rani,
Hearing her, Tulsa Rani

Gave the answer, oh daughter,
Gave the reply.

"Listen, my Suban,
Listen to the answer.

You didn't obey the word of your mother.
You didn't listen to the word of your brother.

You came without worry, Suban.
You came without worry, Suban.

You're receiving the fruit of that, Suban.
You're receiving the fruit of that, Suban.

Don't be even a little afraid.
Don't be even a little fearful.

Don't worry, my Suban,
Don't worry.

Live happily, Suban.
Live happily, Suban.

Salute your *dharm* [social/religious obligations].
Salute the earth, your mother.

Stand here, my Suban.
Stand here, my Suban.

You'll fly over the hole, Suban.
You'll be standing over there.

Take this whistle
And clap.

Stand there happily.
Stand happily.

Happily, my Suban, happily.
Happily, my Suban, happily.

Upon coming to one side, my Suban,
. . . . [line indiscernible]

Bandhiya's face will be dark.
His face will be dark.

The *mahāprasād* you have seated
Is making you sad again and again.

Bandhiya is coming with evil intent.
Bandhiya is coming with evil intent.

At this time, the gods and *dharm*
Are my witness.

Be happy, my Suban.
Be happy, my Suban.

Returning to the country of your mother and father,
Returning to the country of your father,

Returning to the country of your brother, my Suban,
May you be victorious."

At this time, my Suban,
Hearing this, my Suban,

Bandhiya said, "Look,
On the *muṅg* highland

A large measure of mustard seed,
Spread it out and return."

"A measure of mustard seed,
A measure of mustard seed

Is spread out, oh Bandhiya.
Is spread out, oh Bandhiya."

The barber went there.
At that time, the barber,

In the evening, went to tell him [Suban].
In the evening, went to tell him.

"Listen, oh foreigner.
Listen to the answer.

Your *mahāprasād*, one measure
Of mustard seeds has spread out.

[You must] pick them up.
Pick them up."

At this time, my Suban,
She [Tulsa] called her.

"Come, Suban, eat your food.
Come," she called.

Her face was downcast.
Her face was downcast.

She [Tulsa] went up to her ear.
She went up to her ear.

At this time, my Suban,
She didn't hear anything.

"What happened, my Suban?
What happened, my Suban?"

She didn't hear her, Suban.
She didn't hear her, Suban.

"Listen, my *bahū*.
Listen to the answer.

On the *muṅg* highland,
On the *urad* highland,

He has spread out
A big measure of mustard seed.

He has told me, 'Pick up
One measure of mustard seed, [or]

I'll cut you in two.
I'll cut off your head.'

How can I pick it up, *bahū*?
How can I pick it up, *bahū*?

I have no wisdom.
I have no wisdom."

"Listen, my Suban.
Listen, Suban.

You didn't obey the word of your mother.
You didn't listen to the word of your father.

You came without worry, Suban.
You came without worry.

You're receiving the fruits of this, Suban.
You're receiving the fruits of this.

At this time, my Suban,
Eat your food in peace.

Be happy, Suban.
Be happy, Suban."

Hearing this, Suban,
Hearing this, Suban

Ate some food.
Ate some food.

She slept a little, Suban.
She slept a little.

Then she couldn't sleep, not at all.
She turned from side to side.

Hearing her, Tulsa Rani,
Mother Tulsa Rani

Wrote a letter,
Wrote a letter

To the kingdom of pigeons, my daughter.
To the kingdom of pigeons.

"Listen, father.
Listen, father.

I'm in Bandhi Desh, father.
I'm in distress in this kingdom.

Take pity on my distress.
Be prepared.

Send to me
One *lākh* [100,000], five *lākh* pigeons.

Bandhiya Raja
Has spread out mustard seeds.

Send pigeons
To pick them all up, father."

At this time, she wrote
The letter.

In the pigeon kingdom, at midnight,
They received the letter.

"The daughter is in distress.
The daughter is in distress.

The letter came in the night.
The letter came in the night.

To which country has she gone?
In which place is she staying?

Our daughter is distressed.
Our wealth is distressed."

Hearing this, Tulsa,
Tulsa sent the letter.

"Go, go, pigeons.
Go, go, pigeons.

Don't eat them, pigeons.
Don't eat them.

Fill the measure,
A large measure of mustard seeds.

Put them over there,
Next to the measure,

Two winnowing baskets of mustard seeds.
Two winnowing baskets of mustard seeds.

Hearing this, Bandhiya will see.
At this time, the barber will see.

Coming to the highland in the morning,
They'll see with their eyes.

In the morning,
They'll see with surprise

What has happened, Bandhiya.
What has happened, Bandhiya."

"Our daughter is distressed.
Our daughter is distressed.

Quickly, pick them up.
In a moment, pick them up."

In an instant,
In an instant,

The pigeons came and filled it,
A measure of mustard seeds.

Lākh upon *lākh* of pigeons,
Five *lākh* came.

They picked them all up
In a moment, all the mustard seeds.

They filled
The measure in an instant.

They filled
The measure in an instant.

Taking two winnowing baskets,
They put them on the ground.

They created a whir with their wings.
The pigeons flew away.

The pigeons flew away.
The pigeons flew away.

At this time, it was sunrise.
The sunrise appeared.

Dawn broke.
The sunrise appeared.

At this time, Bandhiya,
At this time, Bandhiya [and]

Everyone from town and city went to see.
Everyone from town and city went to see.

The measure of mustard seeds
Was filled.

Two baskets of mustard seeds
Had been put on the ground.

"Well done! Well done, Suban!
Well done, moneylender!

You picked up
This many mustard seeds.

Our playful son,
. . . . [line indiscernible]"

At this time, Bandhiya Raja
Looked with astonishment.

"Listen, barber,
Go now on your way.

Tonight, barber,
I will play dice.

Tonight, barber,
I will play dice,

With my *mahāprasād*.
With my *mahāprasād*."

At this time, the barber
Went to tell her [Suban].

"Listen, foreigner,
Listen to the answer.

Your *mahāprasād*
Will play dice with you.

He'll play dice," he said.
"He'll play dice."

"Listen, barber,
Listen to the answer.

At what time will we play?" she said.
"At what time will we play?" she said.

"Tonight is the time.
Tonight is the time,

We'll play dice," he said.
"We'll play dice," he said.

At this time, my Suban,
Night fell.

She ate some food, Suban.
Her mind was at peace.

Taking a thousand, a thousand,
Five thousand rupees,

She entered the company of Bandhiyar [literally, friend Bandhiya], Suban.
She entered the company of Bandhiyar, Suban.

She threw down
Sixteen cowrie shells, cowrie shells.

At this time, my daughter,
She threw down the gamble.

He threw down the gamble, Bandhiya.
He threw down the gamble, Bandhiya.

Hearing this, my Suban
Was playing.

She lost everything, oh Suban.
She lost everything, oh Suban.

The cows went; the calves went.
The horses went; [words indiscernible].

The elephants went; the donkeys went.
She lost everything.

Suban lost.
She lost everything.

To her *bahū* Tulsa Rani,
To her *bahū* Tulsa Rani,

She went to her platform, Suban.
She went to her platform, Suban.

"I've lost everything,
All my riches and wealth, my *bahū*.

Come, *bahū*, I'll stake you in the dicing.
Come, *bahū*, I'll stake you in the dicing."

At this time, Tulsa Rani,
Hearing this, Tulsa Rani

Gave the answer, Tulsa,
Gave the word.

"Your brother is lame.
Who will serve him?

If you gamble with me,
You'll leave me in Bandhi Desh.

Only one of us will return, Suban.
Only one of us will return, Suban.

What will you tell your brother?
What will you tell your mother and father?

What will you tell the people of your kingdom,
If you stake me in the dicing, Suban?"

She didn't heed her, Suban.
She didn't heed her, Suban.

"Come, come, *bahū*, I'll stake you in the dicing.
Come, come, *bahū*, I'll stake you in the dicing.

I have lost everything,
Wealth, riches, everything."

At this time, my Suban
Came, bringing her *bahū*.

She came, bringing her [and said],
"I'm ready."

"I have a half-cowrie shell.
I have a half-cowrie shell.

Listen, Suban,
Listen to the answer.

When your brother got married,
When your brother got married,

He won me
With this half-cowrie shell.

Take it,
This half-cowrie shell, Suban.

Stake me in the dicing, Suban.
Stake me in the dicing, Suban."

Hearing this, Suban
Took her.

She took her *bahū*, Suban.
She took her *bahū*, Suban.

She seated her in the dicing, her *bahū*.
She seated her in the dicing, her *bahū*.

Bandhiya won her.
Bandhiya won her.

He was overjoyed, Bandhiya.
He was content.

"I've won her," he said.
"I've won her," he said.

"It was my destiny [*karm*]," he said.
"It was my destiny," he said.

He was delighted, Bandhiya.
He was delighted, Bandhiya.

The barber was delighted.
The barber was delighted.

Bandhiya was lovesick.
She was beautiful in every aspect, Tulsa Rani.

He took her to his storehouse.
He took her to his storehouse.

Happily, he put her there.
Happily, he put her there.

She [Suban] got up from the gambling, the *mahāprasād*.
She got up and threw.

With the half-cowrie,
She was ready, my Suban.

She was ready, my Suban,
With the half-cowrie.

It was thrown and sounded *phaṭ*.
It was thrown and sounded *phaṭ*.

"Listen, *mahāprasād*.
Listen to the answer.

Throwing and picking it up, it is one turn.
It is one turn.

I have one half-cowrie.
I have one half-cowrie.

Throw once, *mahāprasād*.
Throw once, *mahāprasād*."

"Why should I throw a turn
For a half-cowrie?"

Bandhiya Raja
Asked the question.

The city dwellers,
The kings from the city [said],

"You have won
Lākh upon *lākh* of rupees.

You have won
All the cows and calves.

You have won
All the elephants and horses.

The *bahū*, too,
You have won.

Throw once more.
You seated a *mahāprasād*.

It [the friendship] was entrusted to you.
It was entrusted to you."

He threw his turn, Bandhiya.
He threw his turn, Bandhiya.

At this time, Bandhiya
Threw his turn.

Suban, with a cowrie in her hand
Came quickly.

She came with a cowrie
In her hand, my Suban.

At this time, my Suban
Had sixteen cowries.

She held them in her hand.
She held them in her hand.

[She had won sixteen cowries with the throw of her half-cowrie.]

She entreated Dharma.
She appealed to Mother Earth.

She threw
Sixteen cowries, her cowries.

She had nine turns.
She had nine turns.

She won everything back from Bandhiya.
She won everything back.

She won the watch from Bandhiya,
His wealth and riches.

Cows went; calves went.
She won everything.

All that was in Bandhiya's kingdom,
All his riches.

She won everything, my Suban.
She won everything.

He brought his wife
From the storehouse.

He staked her in the dicing, Bandhiya.
He staked her in the dicing, Bandhiya.

He coveted
The *bahū*, Tulsa Rani.

At this time, the barber
Brought the wives.

Then she [Suban] won.
Then she won.

He brought and staked
His seven wives.

"You'll win in the dicing, Bandhiya.
You'll win in the dicing, Bandhiya."

Hearing this,
He staked Tulsa Rani.

He staked
The *bahū*, Tulsa Rani.

She won, Suban.
She won, Suban.

At this time, Bandhiya Raja
Staked himself in the dicing.

Hearing this, Bandhiya Raja
Staked himself in the dicing.

She won him, my Suban,
She won him.

When she won Bandhiya,
When she won Bandhiya,

She put a rope in his nose.
She put a rope in his nose.

She put it in his nose.
She put it in his nose.

She tied him to a tree, Bandhiya.
She tied him to a tree, Bandhiya.

Everyone went to the storehouse,
Everyone went to the storehouse,

In the kingdom of Bandhiyar,
In the house of Bandhiyar.

There were many, many kings,
From the city of Bombay.

From the city of Cuttack.
From the city of Bombay.

Having won the kings [having won their freedom]
Who had been put in jail,

They were happy, oh Bandhiya.
They were happy, oh Bandhiya.

She brought them out.
She brought them out.

Suban, my daughter,
Oh Suban.

"Listen, all you kings.
Listen, all you kings.

How much money did you bring,
Riches and wealth?

Tell the truth, *bābū*.
Tell the truth, *bābū*."

Some said,
"I brought a thousand rupees."

Some said, "Ten thousand
I brought."

Some said, "I brought five."
Some said, "I brought ten."

Saying this,
They went in front of Suban.

Hearing this, the daughter Suban
Made everyone happy.

"All your wealth and riches,
All your wealth,

Take it and go, oh kings.
Take it and go.

Your mothers and fathers will be waiting [for you].
Daughters and relatives will be waiting.

Go happily, oh kings.
Go happily, oh kings."

Hearing this, Suban,
At this time, Suban,

The people of Bandhi Desh [said],
The people of Bandhi Desh,

"We'll make you king.
We'll fasten the crown [on your head]."

Hearing this, Suban,
At this time, Suban [said],

"I won't be king.
I won't be king.

I won't stay in the city of Bandhi.
I won't stay in the city of Bandhi.

I'll go to my own country,
To the people of my kingdom.

The brother of Bandhiya
Is in the kingdom of Bandhi.

Go bring him.
Go bring him.

I'll give the throne to him.
I'll give the throne to him.

I'll hand over to him,
To his brother, all the wealth.

I'll go to my own country.
I'll go to my own country.

My mother and father will be waiting [for me].
My grandmother and grandfather will be searching.

I'll go without worry, Suban,
I'll go happily."

At this time, Bandhiya Raja's
Brother, they brought him.

She gave him red [royal] clothes, Suban.
She gave him red clothes, Suban.

His brother
Took the king's throne.

His brother
Took the king's throne.

She readied a lame horse.
She readied a lame horse.

She bound Bandhiya to it.
She bound Bandhiya to it.

She made it run on the *muṅg* highland.
She made it run on the *muṅg* highland.

She took back four times
The wealth she brought.

She took back four times
The number of cows and calves.

There was a single *bahū*;
Now there were three *bahū*.

She took these with her, Suban.
She took these with her, Suban.

She went happily, Suban,
She went back to her country.

She went to her father's country.
She went to her mother's kingdom,

With a content heart, Suban,
[Went] to her kingdom.

She arrived
At her house, Suban.

She arrived, filled with joy.
She arrived, filled with joy.

"Tell my mother and father,
Tell my mother and father,

Tell them I have come;
Their daughter has come.

Tell them Suban has come;
Their *bahū* has come.

In this way, tell them,
The people of the city and town.

Tell them and come.
Tell them and come.

Go, go, young goatherds,
In front of my mother.

Give the news.
Tell what has happened."

At this time, the goatherds
Went running.

[They came] in front of the queen mother,
In front of her father, the king.

"Your daughter Suban
Is coming."

Calling the sons and citizens [of the kingdom],
They went to the ministers.

"Go to welcome her," they said.
"Go to bring her back."

"Listen, goatherds,
Listen, goatherds,

Tell the truth,
Not lies."

"I'm telling the truth, mother,
Not lies."

Hearing this answer,
Hearing this answer,

Jagya Rishi,
Anna Rishi

Sent his servants to the city and town.
He sent his peons.

He called and sent them.
He called and sent them.

Quickly they brought them,
The sons and citizens.

With cymbals and drums,
With cymbals and drums,

They went to welcome her.
They went to bring her.

At this time in her house,
They were all delighted.

She touched their feet,
The feet of her mother and father.

She touched her feet, Suban's mother's.
She touched her feet.

Her *bahū*
Touched their feet.

She greeted them
And stood in front of them.

They stood and then sat down.
They stood and then sat down.

She had taken her grandfather's clothes.
She had gone to Khairapur.

At this time, Suban
Stood in front of her grandfather.

"Listen, grandfather,
Listen to the answer.

Take your clothes, grandfather.
Take your clothes, grandfather.

Give me my clothes, grandfather.
Give me my clothes, grandfather."

She was a young girl, my Suban.
She was a young girl, my Suban.

She gave back her grandfather's clothes.
She took her own clothes.

With joy, the *bahū*
Met her.

"Where did my brother go, *bahū*?
Where did my brother go, *bahū*?"

"Your brother went home,
Your brother went home,"

Tulsa replied.
Tulsa replied.

At this time, Suban
Went to her mother's house.

"Go, go, servants,
To where the lame horse is.

Tie Bandhiya in the horse stall.
Tie Bandhiya in the horse stall.

Kulūd, *muṅg* and *urad,*
Boil and give them to him.

Give him horse feed.
Give him horse feed."

They boiled and gave [to him],
Muṅg and *urad.*

They treated the barber like a dog.
Everyone hit him.

Everyone in the city and town,
Everyone hit him.

They treated him like a dog.
The barber was treated like a dog.

At this time, her mother Nila Rani
Gave the answer.

"Listen, daughter,
Listen to the answer.

There's been a birth in the horse stall.
There's been a birth in the horse stall.

A man has been born.
A man has been born, daughter.

You've taken this action.
You've taken this action.

You went to play in other lands and kingdoms.
With joy you came back.

In the horse stable, you put
Someone, a man,

And fed him horse feed, Suban.
And fed him horse feed, Suban."

"I'll tell you the story.
You haven't heard it.

Where horse feed is eaten, he'll eat horse feed.
He'll stay tied up in the horse stable.

Then he'll come to his senses, Bandhiya.
Then he'll come to his senses, Bandhiya."

"At this time, my Suban,
It is the will of Bedhiri [learned Brahmin, *bedī*],"

Her mother said,
"That Suban get married.

We'll call
All the people of the kingdom.

From which country and kingdom
Will you marry?"

At this time, Suban [said],
At this time, Suban,

"Have leaf plates and bowls sewn,
With twigs and leaves [for the wedding banquet].

Buy grain and rice [and]
Fancy clothes.

Buy and bring all these things;
Bring all these for me.

Then I'll tell you [whom I'll marry],
Then I'll tell you,"

Suban said.
Suban said.

All the fancy clothes,
The wealth and riches,

Everything was prepared.
Everything was prepared.

Jagya Rishi,
At this time, Anna Rishi

Gathered everything together.
Gathered everything together.

He quickly brought everything
To the earthen Tulsi platform.

Dḥīrī, dḥīrī sounded the *mṛdaṅg* drum.
The cymbals also sounded.

"A marriage will be performed soon," they said.
"A marriage will be performed soon," they said.

"Go, go, my servants.
Go, go, my servants.

Go, and bring him,
The one tied in the horse stable.

Take sweet-smelling soap.
Take warm water.

Untie and bring him,
The one tied in the horse stable.

Bathe him.
Bathe him with joy."

They heard this, my Suban,
They heard the word.

The servants and attendants,
The servants and attendants

Went running
And untied him.

They untied and brought him
To the steps of the well.

With warm water
They completed his bath.

They massaged him with oil.
They bathed him.

They brought him to the platform, Suban,
And seated him.

They dressed him in
New white clothes.

At this time, Bandhiya,
Hearing this, Bandhiya [thought],

"I'm in a king's house.
I'm in a king's house.

They'll offer me in *pūjā* [as a sacrifice].
They'll offer me in *pūjā*.

I won't survive today," he said.
"I won't survive today," he said.

"Go, go, servants.
Go, go, attendants.

Lift him up and bring him
To the leaf-canopied [wedding] courtyard."

At this time, Bandhiya
Was brought to the platform.

They lifted him up and brought him.
They entered the leaf-canopied courtyard.

"My father is Jagya Rishi.
My father is Anna Rishi.

My grandmother is Ranna Khairani.
My grandfather is Ranna Khairaja.

He is Barun Raja.
She is Barun Rani.

They are my father's [parents],
Ranna Khairani.

The king of Khaira
Is my father's [father].

My mother's [parents] are Barun Rani,
Barun Raja."

Their invitations arrived.
Their invitations arrived.

People and riches arrived
At the house of marriage.

From the city and town they arrived.
From the city and town they arrived.

At this time, the marriage
Was performed.

Their hands were tied together,
Were tied together [in marriage].

From city and town,
The riches of the storehouse.

"These are all yours, Suban,
These are all yours.

This wealth, these riches,
The paper money and coins,

The dry fields and wet fields,
The house and courtyard,

These are all yours, Suban.
These are all yours, Suban."

They gave their blessing.
They gave their blessing.

They were married with joy.
They were married with joy.

The food was cooked.
The vegetables were cooked.

Potato curry, banana curry,
Everything was cooked.

Going to city and town,
Everyone was called and fed.

They went with joy.
They were happy.

At this time, Tulsa Rani,
She with a patient heart,

Joyfully she gave her,
To her sister Suban,

A cot, to Suban,
A palanquin, to Suban.

"Here is your house, sister.
Here is your dwelling."

Tulsa Rani
Spoke in this way.

With joy in their hearts, all the people,
The wedding guests,

Whoever had come,
Went back to their homes.

They [Suban and Bandhiya] entered
Their home.

The wedding was over.
They lived happily.

Kathānī Kūhā: Of Friendship, Love, and Memory[1]

Parmeshvara *Kathānī Kūhā*, Sirco Village,
Raipur District, Madhya Pradesh
October 12, 1981

P = Parmeshvara
A = Audience members
LAUGH = laughter of audience

[Performer places a lit kerosene lantern on a basket in the middle of the performance clearing.]

[Sung *vandanā*]

A—h, A——h, A——h
Ram, Ram, Shri Hari Ram.
If you repeat Ram's name,
All your pain will be destroyed.
He who is the first cause of the yogis.
He who takes away pain from the saints.

Mother Kunti held to Ram's name.
Her five sons became famous.

Yudhishthira held to Ram's name.
His body was taken to heaven.

[1] The indented lines are songs. The breaks within the songs are conceptual breaks to aid the reader of the printed text, not performative ones, that is, the *rāg* (melodic structure) indicates line breaks, but no discrete verse breaks.

Arjun held to Ram's name.
With his bow, he supported the earth.

Bhim held to Ram's name.
With his club, he destroyed the army of the Kauravas.

Nakula held to Ram's name.
With the heart of Kunti, he made the earth one.

Sahadev held to Ram's name.
He knew politics and the impossible.

Draupadi held to Ram's name.
She was saved in the court of the Kauravas.

The pigeon held to Ram's name.
He was saved from the mouth of the crocodile.

The Baula cow held to Ram's name.
She was saved from the mouth of the tiger.

Prahlad held to Ram's name.
He killed Hikhya and was given Indra's heaven.

Sugriv held to Ram's name.
He was made the king of Kishkinda.

Vibhishan held to Ram's name.
He was given the kingdom of Lanka.

Hanuman held to Ram's name.
He was saved in the womb of the demoness.

Vibhishan held to Ram's name.
He was given the kingdom of Lanka.

Ahalya held to Ram's name.
She received salvation at the touch of his feet.

Ram, Ram, Shri Hari Ram
Ram, Ram Shri Hari Ram,
Whose vehicle is Garud,
Who is the son of Kaushalya.

By holding to Ram's name,
By reciting the lord's name,
The god of death will not touch you.
He will not touch you.

The *koyal* bird, the *koyal* has thirty-two *rāg*.
Give me your voice, oh *koyal*,
Give me part of your voice.

I salute Sarasvati;
I salute Samlai.
Give me a verse;
Show me the way.

I salute Sarla;
I salute Mangla.
Play in my throat;
Open my throat.

The black pepper tree is black.
The black pepper tree is black.
Look at my ignorance,
That of a child.

I salute my mother and father.
I salute the village gods.
I salute the east and the west.
I salute the north and the south.
I salute those gathered here.

I take refuge.
I sing a song.
I take refuge.

If Sarla is there, she will play in my throat;
She will play in my heart.

I fall at your feet, Mother Sarasvati.
Listen to my one request.
Victory to Mother India, I fall at your feet.
Listen to my plea of sorrow.
Lord, listen to my plea of sorrow.

I have neither wisdom nor knowledge; I am foolish.
I have neither wisdom nor knowledge; I am foolish.
So I fall at your feet.
I fall at your feet.

Lord Narayan, I take refuge at your feet.
Listen to my one request,
That my throat may be strong.
Lord Narayan, I take refuge at your feet.

Hari, listen to my one plea.
You went and stayed in the queen's palace.
You killed the demon Kamsa.
You made Ugrasena king.
Asking for sweetened milk, you annihilated Putna.
The greatest sinner was gone,
Taking refuge in your name.

Hari, listen to my one plea.
I am foolish and unknowing.
I take refuge in you.
I am singing,
Taking refuge in your name.

Take me across this ocean of mundane existence.
I am singing, joining verse to verse.
Hari, listen to my one plea.

[Lengthy break in performance, during which the lantern is removed from the basket and turned off; the audience members and performer converse.]

P. There was a bus station. There was a bus station. And what happens to the buses at that station? They gather there and go out in all directions. People get off at that station, and what do they do?

A. [Give indiscernible answer, so performer asks again.]

P. People get off at that station, and what else do they do?

A. They go here and there.

P. They also get on. Right? They do both. They get off and they get on. At that station, they get on and off. At the station, there's no other food, only fried snacks.

So, what happens?

A bus came from the east and a bus came from the west. And, at that station, what happened to the two buses?

A. They were standing there.

P. They were standing there. Yes, they were standing there. There was the station. The buses were standing. The buses were standing there, and then the people from one bus got off and the people from the other bus also got off. Right?

A. Right.

P. Or didn't they get off?

A. They got off.

P. OK. The people from both buses got off. One man got off one bus and another man got off the other, and what did they do? One sat under the shade of a tree. Both sat under the shade of the same tree. Sitting in the shade, one man said, "Brother, I've come a long distance. I had matches, but they're all gone. I have only *bīṛī* [leaf cigarettes].

"Brother, I bought new matches, but my *bīṛī* are all gone. I have only matches," he said.

Both of them took out their matches and *bīṛī*. They smoked them there, and there they introduced themselves to each other. Both of them smoked their *bīṛī*, and then what did they do? They introduced themselves to each other. What does "introduction" mean?

A. To get to know each other, to know.

P. Where are you from? Where are you going? This is the way an introduction is made. There, they both introduced themselves to each other.

[Song]
Tāre tāre tāre tāre re tāre tā tāre re re nāre nāre re.
[These semantically empty syllables introduce the melodic structure of the song.]

"From which place have you come?
From which place have you come?
You've gotten off at the station, brother.
Where are you going?
Introduce yourself, *bābū*,
Introduce yourself."

"I've come from the east.
I'm going to the west.
I've learned a skill, brother;
I'm getting its worth.
I'm going from place to place.
I'm using my skill.
And you, from which direction have *you* come?
Why are you asking me?
To which place will *you* go?
To which city will you go?"

"I have no mother; I have no home village.
I have no father; I have no place to go.
Where should I go, brother?
Where should I go?

I've learned a skill.
I'm going from place to place.

I'm taking contracts, brother.
I'm taking contracts."

P. Yes. —LAUGH— "What kinds of work can you do? You said you are from the east, from the Oriya region. What kinds of skills have you learned?"

"Count them. I make gold and silver half-moon earrings, round earrings, earrings for the inner ear, necklaces, and nose rings. Are you counting? I have that many skills. That's why I've come from the east to the west. Whatever work I find, I'll do it and collect my wages. That's what I do. Will you take contracts from *anyone*?" he said.

"I know how to do woodworking," he said. "Do you know what I'm called? I'm called a carpenter. I know how to do woodworking, brother. What do I do with big buildings? I make them. I make big buildings; and I also collect my wages. I'm like you; but you're a little—just this much—of a liar."

"What! What have I done to you that you're calling me a liar?"

P. "Say yes. Say yes; say yes. You're a bit of a liar; say yes. Don't lift your ass and shake it in front of me [that is, don't insult and challenge me]. This world is greedy and sinful. What *don't* people covet? Even if there's only one beautiful leaf left, they pick it and take it home. And you're greedy for gold, aren't you? You'll weigh it. There's sand inside, isn't there [to make it heavier]. If you said yes, it wouldn't be right. Then why are you shaking it in front of me?"

"*You're* a nice person!"

"How's that?"

"Trees and plants give fruit only because of truth; and because of truth, the seven oceans don't overflow their shores. If the ocean were a liar, then this American couldn't come and sit here. Could she sit here? If the ocean were a liar? How could she cross it? Right? If people came out of the ocean, how could you cross the ocean? That's why I'm saying, the trees give fruit and the seven oceans don't overflow their shores because of truth. What wrong has the tree done? It's just there, and its mind is on god; and god is merciful to it. Then that tree bears fruit in bunches."

Tāre tāre tā tāre tāre tā nā tāre tā tāre nā tā nā.

The carpenter was strong.
Slowly, slowly, the argument grew.
He took hold of his wooden hammer,
Took his wooden hammer.
He struck [the goldsmith] twice.
He struck three times.
He went behind the *bābū*.
He went in front of him.

Then he left him.
Then he left him.

The son [goldsmith] fled.
Look, he fled.

King Manicandra was seated.
King Manicandra was seated.
King Manicandra was seated.
He was dispensing justice.
He was seated in the assembly.
Manicandra of Madhukatak.
Manicandra of Madhukatak.
He is the king.
He cares for his subjects.
He is a virtuous king.
He cares for his subjects.

He went to that assembly.
He fled to that assembly.
Behind him was the carpenter,
Was the carpenter.
Manicandra saw them.
Manicandra saw them, brother.
"Wait! Stop!" the king said.
He forbid them [from coming forward].

P. Of the two, who was the stronger? Who was fighting?

A. The carpenter and the goldsmith.

P. The carpenter and goldsmith were fighting; so of the two, who was the stronger?

A. The carpenter.

P. OK. He was a woodworker, right? The carpenter was stronger than the goldsmith. OK. So who was beaten?

A. The goldsmith.

P. The goldsmith was beaten. Having been beaten, where did he flee in fear?

A. To the king.

P. He reached the place where King Manicandra was dispensing justice to his subjects. The goldsmith went there and said, "I'll be saved here," he said. "If not, I have no chance," he said. He had been beaten badly. That's why he went to the court, to the place of justice.

There, the king saw him and said, "Look, one man is following behind; one man is fleeing without looking where he is going. [to the two men] Stop! Watch out!" He forbid them. He stood up and finished the case over which he was presiding. He finished it and said, "Come, come, come," and he called them. "Come, come, come," he said; and he put one of them on each side of him. And he said, "One person was ahead, and one person was behind. Why were you ahead? Tell me that. Then I'll ask the one who was behind. Why were you in front? Tell me that. If you don't tell me, it won't work."

[Crying] "Oh king, I got off the bus and he, also, got off, and both of us sat down in the same place. We smoked *bīṛī* and introduced ourselves to each other. I said I was a goldsmith from the east. He said he was a carpenter from the west. That's what we said. I'm telling the truth, oh king. He gestured with his fingers like this and said, 'You're this much of a liar.' I hadn't done anything wrong to him. I said, "How can you talk like that?' and, as I sat down, I lifted my ass a little. Then he said, 'Say yes; don't lift your ass toward me.' And he said, 'This world is greedy and sinful. Whoever is not greedy in this world, his eyes are not pure [that is, he's a liar].' And, oh king, he said, 'You weigh it, and there's sand inside, isn't there?' "

"Then I said, '*You're* a nice person!' And he asked, 'How's that?' And, sitting down, I said, 'The trees and plants give fruit because of truth. Because of truth, the seven oceans don't overflow their shores. And that tree, right where it is, bears fruit in bunches. What wrong has it done that you are cutting it, breaking it into pieces, and piercing it, just to feed your stomach?' "

"I was sitting there and I started to get up. He got angry and gestured like this, and what did I think? I thought he would say, 'Go, go away,' but, oh king, that didn't happen! He struck me here [pointing to his ass] twice. I've never been beaten like that in my life. Oh king, I bow to you. Decide justly on this, or I won't be saved."

The king was amazed. —LAUGH— Of the two, who was the liar? I ask you, who?

A. The goldsmith was the liar.

P. You'll explain that, won't you? —LAUGH— If he's a liar, then what happens? This is hardly a lie. Then, did he lie? You'll explain that, won't you? Did he? —LAUGH— Of the two, both men were liars, and neither was a liar.

The king didn't see the difference between the two. He thought, "Whom should I make small, and whom should I make big? What the carpenter has said is true; and what the goldsmith has said, that, too, is true. How will I decide justly? And between them, whom will I make small? Now their blood is hot. I'll tell the carpenter, 'You're a liar,' and saying that, I'll say, 'The goldsmith has been beaten. My decision is that you'll live like a louse [that is, as a parasite].' No, it will be very difficult. I'll have to make that decision again."

No, what did the king do? He said, "Go, both of you be present at the hearing on the fifteenth." He said, "Go, be present at the hearing on the fifteenth day of this month," and gave this order. Because of this order, the two who had been going out to work didn't go to work. Each returned to his own place.

Each returned to his own country. The goldsmith had money. He bought a ticket and reached home quickly. The unlucky carpenter had no money. He was only a woodworker. It was all gone. What did he do? "No," he said, "If I go by way of Basna, it will take me a long time. I'll take the shortcut through the jungle." Right?

A. Right.

P. He wasn't afraid. The jungle was his playground. Because of that, he avoided the road on which he would have to spend money. He thought, "If I go by bus, I'll reach home by evening; and if I go this way, I'll reach home quickly and won't have to eat anything." Right?

Tāre tāre tāre tāre re tāre tā tāre re nāre nā re.

The son was going on the jungle road.
He was going on the forest road.
The son was looking at the trees.
He was looking at the plants.
The son was approaching them.
He was looking at the trees.

"I could use these.
I could use these,"
The son said to himself.

He entered the jungle.
The *bābū* entered the forest.
He was walking in the jungle.
He was going on and on in the jungle.

The son looked at one tree.
He looked at the wood.
It was a sandalwood tree.
It was a sandalwood tree.
Carrying it, the son brought it [and]
He put it in his house.

P. He reached home. What did he find in the jungle?

A. Sandalwood, sandalwood.

P. He looked at many trees while he was returning, right? Seeing this tree, what did he say? "You're a beautiful tree; I could use you. What can I say?" he said. Right? He was praising the tree. What was he looking at?

A. The sandalwood.

P. He looked at the sandalwood tree. He looked at the sandalwood tree. He admired it. He looked at it and kicked it with his foot. It moved, and he said, "Now I can pick it up." That's the way it was; that was his custom. Yes. He went to pick up the tree. "If I can kick it and it moves," he said, "then I'll be able to pick it up easily. If not, it will have to stay there. —LAUGH— I know I would get too tired [carrying it]."

What did he do first? He kicked it. Right? He kicked it and the tree moved. Yes. It moved and he picked it up. He had one wish—to be able to pick it up. Do you understand? He had one wish; and he brought the tree and put it in his house. He put it there. When was his court hearing?

A. The fifteenth.

P. He had to be present on the fifteenth. He had to be present on the fifteenth.

Then what happened? It was the season for weddings in that country. It was the season for weddings in that country, but there was no good goldsmith. He was returning home.

[A customer arrives at the goldsmith's house.]

"Oh, daughter of Haldipali!" [the goldsmith's wife].

"What is it?"

"Where has your *bābū* gone?"

"Oh God! He went out yesterday. For the whole night I didn't blow out the lamp. Welcome, sir. He hasn't been home since yesterday. He went away."

"Where did he go?"

"He went over there. He told me, 'If I get work, if I get work over there, then I'll send for you,' he said. And he went yesterday. I've been sitting here waiting. What should I do? I've never left the house. Oh, why do I have such bad luck!"

[Performing the following lines, P. goes around collecting money from members of the audience.]

"If you've received old rice," she said, "then give old rice. If you've received new rice," she said, "then give new rice. If you've received a rupee," she said, "then give a rupee. If you only like change," she said, "then give it."

"We two old people, husband and wife, decided that we'll have ornaments made for both our son and daughter. We didn't even wait a day. We came right away."

"If you'd told me *then*, he wouldn't have gone away. Today he's gone, and now you've come. What should I do! [sobbing] I'm about to give birth, and he's gone so far away. What should I do, oh lord! If I stay here, there will soon be two children. I can't imagine how much work there will be! What should I do! These chicks, how can I support these two chicks? They come one after another," she said.

Then, who came holding a bag? —LAUGH— Then, who came? The goldsmith, right? The goldsmith came right up to the door. He came.

"What's happened?"

"May you have a great fortune! I was just talking about you. Take the water jug and wash," she said, and filled the jug with water and gave it to him. Right? The one who had been crying now filled the jug with water and gave it to him and was happy. She was happy and washed his feet with the water and sat down.

The old couple came quickly and brought this much. What did they bring?

A. Gold.

P. Gold and silver. They came bringing both. His wife washed the goldsmith's hands and feet and sat down. Then he went outside and said, "Your daughter is my daughter. Brindavati is your daughter, isn't she?"

"Yes, yes, she's my daughter. Make this for Brindavati and this for the man you abused by saying, 'Where have you come from, you with the pimpled ass.' Make this for that pimpled-ass one. Will you do it for forty or fifty rupees?"

"Don't talk about money now, brother. When it goes on her hand, then send a basket of rice. [to himself] It'll be enough for many days."

A. A basket full.

P. Yes.

P. He gave the gold and silver [to the goldsmith] and had gone a little ways down the road. [He meets a friend.] "Greetings, *mahāprasād*."

The friend answered, "Greetings, *mahāprasād*. Where are you going?"

"I've been to the goldsmith's. I'm going to bring a wife for my son and give my daughter as a bride. It's the season for weddings. That's why I've taken gold and silver to him."

"My family was wrong!"

"Really?"

"Yes. They said he'd gone away. I felt bad. I'll tell him to make some for me, too," he said. He said, "I'll give him the gold ahead of time. How much should I give?"

When he was returning, after leaving the gold, he met another person and greeted him.

"Where have you been, *mahāprasād*?"

"I've taken gold to the goldsmith's."

"What happened? They said he'd gone away."

"No, he's in his house. He's returned. He's returned. Yes, he's returned."

"Then I'm going to take him the broken heavy silver necklace. When I tell my daughter-in-law to wear it, she won't." Saying this, he, too, took the silver and went to the goldsmith's.

All the people of the city liked his work. They brought all their silver and gold and gave it to him.

There was a trunk at the goldsmith's. The trunk was filled, overloaded with gold and silver. Then he told the people to stop, saying, "Now, don't bring any more. I'll make all these first. Then bring more. Don't bring any more now." One trunk was filled with gold and silver. It was filled and the days passed. The days passed and the time came closer [for the hearing]. What happened?

E tāre tāre tā tāre nāre re nāre nāre nā nāre nā nā.
Bābū tā nā nā nā nā nā.

He was worried.
"If I give something,
If I fall at the feet of the king,
The king will give me the decree.
He'll speak on my behalf,"
The son thought to himself,
In his heart.

All the silver in the city,
All the gold in the city,
The goldsmith had collected it.
He had gathered it.
A silver chair,
A silver chair,
A golden image, oh look.

He had seen Manicandra.
He had seen Manicandra.
The goldsmith made his form,
Made his form.
He sat it in the chair.
He made a golden parrot.
The goldsmith put it there.
He put it there.

The son looked at it from a distance.
The son looked at it from a distance.
"The king will take it," the *bābū* said.
He was pleased.

"I'll go one day early.
I'll meet the king.
I'll go to the hearing later.
I'll be present."

P. He was happy. "Whatever happens," he said, "I'll give the king many things; then I'll beat the bastard." Who?

A. The carpenter.

P. The carpenter. "I'll beat the bastard. I'll give the king so much that he'll surely take my side," he said. He made the things and got them all ready. He got everything ready, and there were still two days left. "I'll go three days early," he said. "I'll go now," he said.

Meanwhile, the carpenter couldn't sleep, he couldn't sleep. Why couldn't he sleep? [He was thinking,] "He's a goldsmith. He must have some valuable things. He'll make them and give them to the king, and the king won't take my side. He'll take his side. I don't have any money. I don't have any silver or gold either. What should I do?" That's why the carpenter was worried. He had one worry. There is no medicine for the fever of worry. If you worry, will you be able to sleep?

A. No.

P. What?

A. No.

P. If you worry, will sleep come?

A. No.

P. It won't come. So, sleep didn't come. When sleep didn't come, the poor thing, having slept only three hours, got up. Who?

A. The carpenter's wife.

P. Yes. What do you call something you comb your hair with? What is its name? *Paniyā* [a comb], right? Yes, the carpenter's *kaniyā* [low-caste word for wife]. —LAUGH— She woke up after sleeping three hours. She got up, and what did she see? He was sitting there. Sitting and worrying.

"What shall I do? In the king's court, I beat the bastard twice. He shit and pissed [out of fear]. But now what should I do? Oh lord, tell me. What do I have that I can take as a gift to the king? This is hard for me." This is how he worried. The poor thing wasn't sleeping. So, she got up from her peaceful sleep.

A. The queen?

P. No.

A. The *kaniyā* [his wife].

P. She slept for three hours and then got up; and what did she see? And what did she do? He was sitting and worrying. She saw him and said, "So wise, so wise. —LAUGH— You are so wise. —LAUGH— You are so wise, so wise. You were sitting. I saw you like that and got up." —LAUGH—

"To whom are you faithful?
Oh lord, listen to my request.
Accept my respect.
You are a bee.
You are a bee.
You can sit on a flower.
Oh lord, you can sit on a flower.

Don't get drunk on the juice.
Don't get drunk on the juice.
Come to my house,
Oh lord, listen to my request.
You'll go away.
Oh lord, you'll go away."

P. She's really winning him over, right?
A. Yes.
P. She's winning him over with *rasa* [sweet words], right?
A. She's winning him over.
P. Has she won him over?
A. No.
P. What?
A. No.
P. That won't do it. What she's saying to win him over, that won't do it. Will it?
A. What will happen?
P.

Tāre tāre tāre tāre re tāre tā tāre re tāre.

"I went to a foreign country.
I went to a foreign country.
I met, look,
I met
A goldsmith, look,
A goldsmith.
I asked for an introduction.
I asked for an introduction.

When he spoke to me,
He lied.
He lied.
He jumped on me.
He jumped on me.
And the bastard stood up.
He was ready to fight.

I couldn't bear it.
I couldn't bear it.
I beat him twice.
I beat him three times.
He was afraid for his life.
He went to the king.

Now there's a hearing,

A hearing.
I'll go tomorrow; there's a hearing.
I'll go tomorrow; there's a hearing.
Worry is eating me up, oh queen.
Worry is eating me."

P. "Oh lord, one receives the fruits of one's actions. Can well water be compared to the Ganga?"

"What did you say?"

"One receives the fruits of one's actions; and, can well water be compared to the Ganga? Do you understand? One receives the fruits of one's actions. You're very quarrelsome."

"How's that?"

"You went to plow and I went to transplant rice. Do you remember the pouring rain that day? You came home shivering with cold, and I, too, came home shivering. There were leftovers to eat, one and a half bowls. [I said,] 'Brother-in-law of my sister with the runny nose, let's eat it with salt and hot peppers.' —LAUGH— Then, you beat me with the plowing stick. Why? Had I done something wrong? —LAUGH— Had I? Had I? Had I wronged you? Had I abused you or fought with you?

"You'd come home because of your empty stomach, and I'd come home because of *my* empty stomach. We came home together, and I said, 'Let's divide it into two servings and eat it with salt and hot peppers.' So what had I done wrong? Then you began to beat my back with the plowing stick, harder than the rain falls in the month of *śrāvaṇ*. What a noise it made! Your mother came to intervene, and she got a cut as wide as a finger. Do you remember? What had I done wrong?

" 'What happened?' your mother said. 'What's happened after only three days?' she asked. 'My husband took my hand and we got married. Even knowing, he didn't know; and not knowing, he didn't know. He beat me only when he saw that I'd done something wrong.'

" 'Where will I go from here. Maybe there I'll get beaten too. Oh my god!' I said. Then I thought, 'I have a husband.' So I cooked the food again and said, 'Come, eat.' And didn't you eat till you were full?

"Do you remember what happened one day later? An aunt who loved me very much died. I'd cooked delicious food for you that day, and you'd said, 'It is good.' My aunt was no longer living. My uncle must have been in a bad way. My aunt was young. She wasn't old at all. When I heard the news, I couldn't cook. You said, 'Your aunt has died, but what happens to me? Your aunt has died, but what happens to me?' And, jumping up, jumping up, you beat me. Do you remember that incident? Since the birth of my oldest son, your hand hasn't beaten me. So now what's happened? What? That's why I said, 'One receives the fruits of one's actions.' I'm your wife. That's why I've endured all this; that's why I've cooked and given you food. But could he [the goldsmith] bear it? He did the right thing. He couldn't bear it. That's why he went to the king. Now go. You're the one who fights a lot. You're the one who lifts your hand. He did the right thing. Would you like it? No, you wouldn't. The pain lasts for many days, do you know that?" —LAUGH—

P. She's speaking like this, but her heart is sad, isn't it?

A. It is.

P. Saying, "I've made a mistake," her heart was sad, wasn't it? But, she's speaking for the sake of the next time.

Then what happened? Before morning broke and the cock had crowed, he bathed and returned. He bathed and returned; and having returned, he collected all his carpenter's tools, right?

A. Yes.

P. Right?

A. Yes.

P. The ones he trained with. All his tools, he took all his tools outside and put them in his carpenter's workshop.

A. Yes.

P. What?

A. He put them in his carpenter's workshop.

P. And what kind of wood had he brought back?

A. Sandalwood.

P. What kind?

A. Sandalwood.

P. Sandalwood. He'd picked it up and brought it from the jungle, right? He brought the wood and now was working on it. The carpenter was working. He climbed up on the sandalwood he had brought and began to work. He was using all the tools he had, one by one.

Tāre nāre nāre nāre re nāre nā nāre re nāre nāre.

He recited the name of Narayan.
He recited the name of god.
The son [carpenter] was busy with the wood.
He was busy with the wood.
He made a horse.
He made a horse.
He put a bridle on it.
He put a bridle on it.

He held the bridle with his left hand.
He held the bridle with his left hand.
The horse flew into the sky,
Flew into the sky.

He held it with his right hand.
He held it with his right hand.
The horse came back to earth,
Came back to earth.
The son was pleased,
And he gave thanks.

P. "Whatever happens, at least I've got one more chance," he said. "I remembered god and got one more chance. If I take this and put it in the king's courtyard, then in my favor, the king will—"

A. "Settle the case."

P. "The king will settle the case in my favor. He'll certainly settle the case," he said. And he got ready. He got ready, and a day and a night passed. Then it was the morning of the hearing. The day the carpenter had gotten the horse ready, the goldsmith had arrived at the king's palace.

Manicandra was seated.
Manicandra was seated.
The son [goldsmith] went to meet him.
He joined his hands in respect.
"I'm a poor son.
I'm an orphan.
I fall at your feet, oh king,
And join my hands.
Grant my entreaty, oh king.
Accept my respectful bow.
Have pity on me, oh king.
Fifteen days have passed,
But the pain of my body has not gone away. —LAUGH—
I fear for my life."

"May you be blessed, goldsmith.
May you be blessed.
You are the creator of the world,
The creator of the world.
You have made my image.
You have made my image.
Look how much gold you have used,
How much wealth you have used.
You're giving me a bribe,
Giving me a bribe.
As long as I live,
I will worship you."

The king took it
And put it away.

P. Was he greedy? Was he? Or wasn't he?

A. He was.

P. Yes, he was. Then he took it inside, didn't he? He was greedy and took it inside.

"Hey you who loves to fight, shouldn't your wife go too? Your wife. If not, what will you do?"

"I've thought about my wife and made a plan. You should stay at home and pray like this, 'Oh god, oh eternal lord, oh powerful lord of the world, feed my husband *pān* and bring him from that place,' and he'll give me the decree."

She answered, "*Āā-īī-go*! Who do you think I am? A big basket's worth of *mahuā* [kind of wild jungle fruit] has fallen. Why should I stay sitting at home? Won't I lose a basket of *mahuā*? I'm going to pick up *mahuā*."

"So, has your *mahuā* collecting become so important?"

"Yes."

"Is he there when you pick up *mahuā*?"

"Who?"

"God."

"Yes, of course he is, isn't he?"

"Show me that he's there."

"I'll pick up one *mahuā* and say, 'Oh god,' and do it again the next time."—LAUGH— "I'll gather my *mahuā*, and do something for you at the same time. Why should I lose a big basket of *mahuā*? *Āā-īī-go*! I'm going to pick up *mahuā*." Right?

A. She did the right thing.

P. Did she go?

A. Yes.

P. She went to collect *mahuā*. When she went to collect *mahuā*, he went to bathe. "It will take me only a minute to get there," he said. "It will only take me a second," he said. "I'll pull the reins and I'll be there." He said this, didn't he?

He leisurely bathed and came back. He ate a bowl of *bāsī* and *pasiyā* [leftovers] and went to the horse and said, "Look, I'm bowing to you and asking you, don't stop anywhere else until you stand in the king's courtyard. Then I'll try to lead you to the side, but stay in the middle. Look, I'm bowing to you and asking you to do this."

Tāre tāre tāre tāre tāre tāre tāre tāre tāre tāre
Tāre tāre tā tā tāre tā nā tāre nā nāre nā.

He sat on the horse.
He sat on the horse.
The son [carpenter] pulled the reins.
He pulled the reins.
He pulled to the left.
He pulled to the left.
The horse flew up into the sky,
Flew into the sky.
The king [carpenter] was moving through the sky.
He was flying.
The harder he pulled,
The faster he flew.
The king was flying through the sky.
He was flying.

When he arrived at the king's court,
When he arrived at the king's court,
He stopped the horse.
He got off the horse.
He put the reins on his shoulder.
The son went to the king.
He joined his hands in respect.

"May you be blessed, carpenter.
May you be blessed, carpenter.
May you be strong, carpenter.
May you be strong.
You've come on your horse, carpenter.
You are a god."
The king praised him.
He said, "Aha!"
He went to the court. —LAUGH—
He placed them on each side of him. —LAUGH—

"Decide in my favor, oh king.
Decide in my favor."

The king had one son.
Manicandra had one son.
The prince's name was Malya Basant,
Malya Basant.
The son was eighteen.
The son was eighteen.
He was sitting inside.

He was eating.
The son had been born as the result of [austerities].
The queen didn't give him leftovers.
She fed him herself.
She sat down and fed him.
The son finished eating.
He came out of the palace.

The prince went to the courtyard.
He went to the courtyard.
The prince saw the horse.
He saw the horse and was drawn to it.
He saw the horse and was drawn to it.
The prince walked all around the horse.
First he looked at the horse's tail.
Then he looked at the ears.
He looked at the feet.
He looked at the head.

"You're not a living thing!
You're not a living thing! [If you were,]
I would race you.
I would make you fly into the sky.
I would race you.
I would make you fly into the sky."
He was thinking and thinking this.
He was thinking and thinking this.

The prince could no longer bear it.
"I'll just sit on it and then get off.
I'll just sit on it and then get off,"
The prince thought to himself.
He walked around it
And sat down on it.
The reins were on the shoulder.
He picked up the left rein.
The prince pulled it.
He pulled it.
The prince flew up into the sky,
Flew into the sky.
"If I hurt him, he'll come down," he thought.
But the horse flew into the sky,
Flew into the sky.

P. "He's alive!" he said. Right?

A. Right, he is.

P. "He's alive! How will I get off?" he thought.

A. He pulled.

P. Yes. He pulled with all his strength. "If I hurt him, he'll come down," he said. Will he come down?

A. He won't come down; he'll climb higher.

P. He'll climb higher; he won't come down. And he pulled harder, and the horse was—

A. Flying faster.

P. He was flying. *Sar sar sar, SAR SAR SAR,* ***SAR SAR SAR*** was the sound of his flight.

P. "Oh my god! My son was eating just now and now is outside. So what happened? There's the sound of *sar, sar, sar, sar*. Maybe my son's urinating outside," she said.
—LAUGH— And she went outside. —LAUGH— Who?

A. His mother.

P. She went outside. She went outside, but she didn't see anything. She lifted her head, and what was there?

A. He was flying on the horse.

P.

"May my black karma be burned away!
May my birth into this caste burn!
Why haven't I died, lord?
Why hasn't the god of death eaten me?
I practiced so many austerities.
I recited the name of god.
I received a son, oh lord.
I received a son, oh lord.
Oh son, I'm already dead.
I'm already dead.

You'll fall on some mountain.
You'll drown in some ocean.
You won't return, my son.
You won't return.
You've done me wrong, my son.
You've done me wrong.
The damn carpenter fought.
The damn carpenter fought,
And he's ruined my lineage.
He's ruined my name."

P. She was crying. Why was she crying?

A. For her son.

P. What was she doing for her son?

A. She was crying.

P. She was crying. At that time, the neighbors asked, "Oh king, what are you looking at?"

"What happened?"

"What did these damn people bring for your son, that has taken him and flown off? You only had one son, and you're looking at him," they said. "How is it that your son is flying off like an airplane, like an airplane? Look, what did they bring? Who brought it? We don't know them; and you've placed them on each side of you and are flattering them. Your lineage is ruined; your son has died. Your wife over there isn't going to survive either; and what are *you* looking at?"

This is what they said, and what did the king do to the two men? He grabbed them immediately; he grabbed both of them. He grabbed them, and then what did he do? He tied them up. He tied them up and judged them. He judged them, and then what did the king say? He said, "But among all of us, I am the liar." Who was the liar among all of them?

A. The king.

P. "I am," he said. "Between these two, the carpenter and the goldsmith, I am the liar." He said, "Why should I hang them on the gallows?" he said. "I won't hang them on the gallows. But all this has happened because of them; so, as long as there is breath in their bodies, what will they do? They'll remain in captivity." The meaning of "captivity" is to be punished in jail. "As long as they live, what will they do? They'll remain in this jail."

"Go," he said. He gave the order; and giving the order, he said, "My queen, why do you exhaust yourself [by lamenting]? Worship at the feet of god. There is no god greater than Karma [fate].

She understood, but said, "The reward for truth is [indiscernible on tape]."

"If this is a reward for truth, then he'll come back one day; and if this is a reward for falsehood, he'll keep going over there. Don't cry and wail uselessly. If you think he has died, then give the grain to be husked. After tomorrow, the next day, I'll perform his third-day death ceremony. Do you understand? What use is your crying and wailing?" What? Did he say the right thing? Did he?

A. He said the right thing.

P. He said the right thing. Now, all the people from the city began to lament, and the king and queen began to cry. He was their only son. As much as he [the king] explained to them [the futility of their wailing], how could they obey him?

A. They couldn't obey him.

P. They couldn't obey. They're like we are. Even after he explained, could they obey?
A. They couldn't obey.
P. What?
A. They couldn't obey.
P. Their mourning was beyond description.
So, with one hand . . . What kind of rider was he [the prince]? A rider who guided with one hand.

Three days and three nights [passed].
Three days and three nights.
He couldn't bear it,
Couldn't bear it.
The son changed hands.
He changed hands.
He held on with his right hand.
He held on with his right hand.
The horse came down,
Came down.

The prince was pleased.
He was pleased.
"Be blessed, carpenter.
Be blessed, carpenter.
Carpenter, I'll go back to my country.
I'll go to the city.
Carpenter, I'll give you a village.
I'll give you a village.
Carpenter, enjoy yourself.
You've learned your trade."

P. What was he saying? Whom was he praising?
A. The carpenter.
P. The carpenter. "Very good, carpenter," he said. Right?
A. Yes, yes.
P. "You've learned your trade very well," he said. Right?
A. Yes, yes.
P. "Very well. I'm going back to my country, so what should I give you?" he said. Right?
A. "I'll give a village."
P. "I'll give you a village. I'll give a village," he said. Right? "I'll give you a village, and you'll be made the owner and you'll enjoy it. Well done, carpenter. You're a skilled carpenter," he said. Right?
A. Yes, yes.

P. "Look how far he took me and is bringing me back," he said. He was praising the carpenter. It wasn't the horse that he was praising. Whom was he praising?
A. The carpenter.
P. He was praising the carpenter. "Well done, carpenter," he said. "I'll certainly give you a village," he said. And the horse slowly, slowly, slowly, slowly, slowly . . . Where was he when he was praising him?
A. He was coming down.
P. He was coming down, that's where he was praising him. On the ground?
A. No, he was still above.
P. He was above, and he was praising the carpenter. He hadn't come down. Now he was coming down.

Tāre tāre tāre tāre tāre tāre tāre tāre tāre
Tāre tāre tāre tā tā tāre tā nā tāre nā nāre nā.

Slowly, slowly, the son came down.
The son stood on the ground.
He stood on the ground,
In the king's garden.
In the king's garden.
The horse came down.

In that flower garden,
There was a Shiva temple.
They were worshipping Shiva there,
Doing penance.
That's where he got down.
He looked in the Shiva temple.
He went to the bathing *ghāṭ*.
He bathed.
He bathed and paid respects to his ancestors.
He looked in the Shiva temple.
He admired the Shiva temple.
He admired it.

"I don't have a water jug in my hand.
I don't have a water jug in my hand.
What shall I do, Lord Shiva,
To give you water?"
He thought about it.

P. From a distance, he sprinkled water with the palm of his hand.
A. He gave water to Shiva.
P. How?
A. He sprinkled it with the palm of his hand.

P. Right. He didn't have anything with him. How could he dip it [the water] out? Could he take it out and pour it? That's why he sprinkled continuously. —LAUGH— It flowed. Didn't the water flow?

A. It [the god] became soaked.

P. It became soaked. There were flowers. He picked them and offered them to both of them [Shiva and Parvati]. He offered them to both of them. He offered them and went out of the temple. Then he went up again. He went up and what happened then?

There was a four-storied building there. A building of four stories had been built there. How long had it been since he'd eaten?

A. Three days.

P. Three days, right? He'd last eaten the day he left.

A. Yes, yes.

P. So, his stomach was growling. Wasn't it looking for something to eat?

A. Yes.

P. So, he thought to himself, "A house has been made here. Where there's a house, there are fields," he said. "Wherever there's a house, there must be fields. There must be something here," he said. "I'll go inside," he said, and he went to the door. There was a lock on it. —LAUGH— Wasn't there?

Tāre tāre tāre tāre tā nā tāre tāre tāre tāre tā nā
Tāre tāre tā tāre tāre nānā tāre nā nāre nā.

He grabbed it with his left hand.
He grabbed it with his left hand.
He shook it back and forth. —LAUGH—
The prince shook it off and threw it away.
He entered the building.
He saw the *pītāmbar* [yellow silk] cloth.
The *bābū* pulled at it and took it.
He put it on.
The prince climbed to the second floor,
Climbed to the second floor.
There, he saw some oil.
There, he saw some oil.
The son became pleased.
He was happy.
There was oil in a white bottle.
He turned the bottle upside down.
The *bābū* patted it on his head.
He patted it.
The bottle was dry, empty of oil.
He put it on a shelf.

He rubbed the oil from his feet up.
The *bābū* —LAUGH— rubbed it in.

P. There was a comb. There was a mirror. He combed his hair. His wet hair left oil on the comb. It sprayed the mirror like a shower. He combed his hair. He combed his hair and climbed up to the third floor. There, beautifully laid out . . . in all four directions, —LAUGH— in all four directions, . . . What had been spread out? Only sweets. Just sweet things [to eat]: *laḍḍū, peṛā, jalebī,* candy, and things like *bundī, sev,* and what all do they call those things? I don't know. I'm just an Oriya man. So, everything was there: *rasgullā, gulāb jāmun,* and all kinds of things. Everything had been put there.

"What should I eat? What should I eat? What should I eat?" he said. He went round and round, round and round, round and round, round and round, round and round, round and round, round and round, round and round, round and round, round and round, round and round, round and round, taking one of everything. He took one of everything and became full to the brim. He became full to the brim and said, "I enjoyed that. Whatever happens now, at least I'm satisfied. I'm the son of a king; I've eaten the food of a king," he said.

He was content. Content, he climbed to the fourth floor, and what happened? There were four beds on which four comforters had been spread. There were four ivory beds, and there were pillows and cushions about this high. They were spread out and he was full to the brim. Now what did he need?

A. He needed to rest.

P. He needed to rest, right? That's what he needed. "I need to see what this is like. It looks so thick; how strong is it?" he said. And he gave it a push. It moved this much. —LAUGH— It was cotton, right?

A. Yes.

P.

Tāre tāre . . .[2]

The son lay down on the bed.
The boy lay down on the bed.
He hadn't slept for three nights.
The *bābū* fell asleep.
He fell asleep.
The time was seven *ghaṛī* [unit of twenty-four minutes].
The time was seven *ghaṛī*.

[2] Here and in the songs that follow, I have not provided the full lines of semantically empty syllables that introduce the melodic structure of the song, since their variation is meaningless in printed transliteration. The melodic introduction will henceforth be indicated by *Tāre tāre . . .*

The *bābū* was sleeping.
He was sleeping.

There were twelve ahead and twelve behind.
There were twelve ahead and twelve behind.
The daughter was going very slowly.
The daughter of a king,
Of a king.
Her name was Mohini [literally, enchanting one].
Her name was Mohini.
Twelve and twelve, twenty-four companions.
The daughter was coming and bringing them with her.
They were meeting there.

P. Where? At the *ghāṭ*. Why were they going to the building? Twelve ahead and twelve behind, and where was she?

A. In the middle.

P. In the middle. What had been built there? A gardener's tower had been built. The twelve ahead and twelve behind, they were all on an outing.

A. On an outing.

P. Did they own the building, or did they give money and rent it?

A. They owned it.

P. That's how it was. Then what happened? They were taking her there to bathe. At that time, they went there; they went to the *ghāṭ*. Wouldn't they go there?

A. They would.

P. They went to the *ghāṭ* and said, "What! Why is it wet at this time of day? It must still be from yesterday," they said. "The water is still rippling." They bathed her and then she said, "Now all of you go. When it's time for me to go back, come and get me. Now go," she said. "Go home," she said.

They used to accompany her there and then go back; then at four o'clock, they used to come and bring her back with them. She used to stay in the building and rest there. She used to bathe there and not go right home. That's why the building had been built there.

The four necessities were there, in the building. It was made that way. What does the "four necessities" mean? The *pītāmbar* cloth—that's the first necessity. Something to rub oneself with [oil] is the second necessity. Something to eat is the third necessity. And something to sleep on is the fourth necessity. So the four necessities were put there. So she went, and where did she go after bathing? She went to the Shiva temple. She went to the Shiva temple. Someone had just poured water there. Would it be dry then? "What! A horse must have kicked it!" Right? —LAUGH—

Tāre tāre . . .

"Yesterday I poured water here.
Yesterday I poured water here.
Lord Shiva, you got so wet.
You got so wet.
You didn't get any heat from the sun.
No gusts of wind blew on you.
Lord Shiva, your body didn't dry.
Your limbs didn't dry.
That's what I did," the daughter said.
She had brought water and poured it.

P. When did she say it was from?

A. Yesterday.

P. "Yesterday I poured water here. Who would have come here? I poured it yesterday, so it's wet. Yesterday the sun didn't hit it, and the breeze didn't blow here. That's why it isn't dry," she said. And she brought water again and poured it. She brought flowers and offered them and prostrated herself. Wouldn't she prostrate?

A. She would prostrate.

P.

"I've done penance for twelve years.
I've fasted for thirteen full moons.
Lord Shiva, I've worshiped you.
I've served you.
Lord Shiva, I've been chaste.
I've been chaste.
Lord Shiva, give me a husband.
Listen to my entreaty.
Fulfill my desires and give me a husband.
Fulfill my desires and give me a husband.
Lord Shiva, listen to my entreaty.
Accept my worship to you."

P. She went. She saw that the lock on the door had been broken open. "What!" she said. "This is so strong; how did this happen? Oh well, it's OK," she said and then went in. She entered and saw the cloth, and wouldn't it look different?

A. It would.

P. He had stood there and pulled it. She hadn't done that. He had stood and pulled it. —LAUGH— She looked at it and said, "What! OK. I might have done that yesterday." She took it down. Right? OK.

Then she climbed the last step and saw that all the sweets were half-eaten. Nothing was left untouched. Everything was in pieces. Where he had taken a handful, the plate was clean. —LAUGH— Right? —LAUGH— He had taken a handful so there was nothing left in that place. That's how he picked them up, squeezed them, and filled his mouth. Then he went to the next plate and took a handful from the edge and swallowed it. This way, everything was half-eaten. Wherever she looked, it was half-eaten. She looked and said, "How did this happen? How? These are taken from the side. I eat from the middle, and everything in sight is half-eaten. —LAUGH— What should I do? Perhaps Mahadev [Shiva] has given me a husband, and that's why my mind is spinning. Maybe I did eat a little of everything. No, it must have been me. I'm going crazy uselessly," she said, and she, too, began to eat. —LAUGH—

Tāre tāre . . .

She finished the food in the building.
She finished the food in the dwelling.
She climbed to the next floor.
The daughter saw the bed,
The bed.
It was an ivory bed,
Filled like the one at home.

The son was sleeping.
He was fast asleep.
The daughter looked at him from a distance.
The daughter looked at him from a distance.
"He went to sleep.
He fell asleep."
That's what she thought to herself.
That's what she thought in her heart.

Sundari [the beautiful one] ran up to him,
Ran up to him.
Sundari looked at his feet.
She looked at his hands.
Sundari looked at his teeth.
She looked at his teeth.
She looked at these three things.
She looked at these three things.

"He's from a good family," Sundari said.
"He's from a good family.
I won't abuse him.
I won't insult him.
I'll call to him lovingly.
I'll call to him lovingly.

I'll get to know him,
Get to know him."

P. She got to know him. Where all did she look? —LAUGH— She looked at his feet; she looked at his hands. What else did she look at? She looked at his teeth. She looked at these three things and said, "He's from a good house. I won't abuse him without a reason. He's from a good house, and that's why he entered so courageously. Right? He's from a good house and that's why he entered so courageously. He came and then what happened?"

"He was hungry and thirsty; he was sleepy. That's why he came. What's wrong with that? Even if I'd been here and he'd come, I would have given him the bed. No, even if I'd been here and he'd come, I would have been hospitable and given him the bed. He slept and then what happened? No," she said, "I'll call him. If I didn't say something, then it would be a different matter."

"Listen, foreigner.
Listen, stranger.
Listen to my call.
Listen to my voice.
Pay attention.
Remember what happened.

Tell me who you are, brother.
Tell me who you are.
Listen to my call.
Listen to my voice.
Pay attention.
Remember what happened.
Listen to my call.
Listen to my voice."

Calling and calling, she got tired.
Calling and calling, she got tired.
He didn't pay attention.
He didn't remember.
He hadn't slept for three days.
He hadn't slept for three days.
The *bābū* was sleeping.
He was asleep.

Calling and calling, she got tired.
Calling and calling, she got tired.
Sundari began to abuse him.
She insulted him.

"You were wise.
You had a good plan.
Look how you're keeping quiet.
Look how you're keeping quiet,
When I call out and say, 'Get up!'
When my hand touches you,
You'll say, 'You're mine.'
Then you'll sit up."

P. "You're quiet," she said. Right? "You're asleep, and what have you done?"

A. "You're keeping quiet."

P. " 'Until she takes my hand to wake me, I won't get up.' That's what you've planned and so are keeping quiet. OK. You're wise, but what? If I would extend my hand, you'd say, 'You're mine.' That's your plan. —LAUGH— I won't touch you. I won't touch you. I won't touch you. I won't touch you. I won't touch you. I won't touch you. What are you thinking? 'She'll touch me,' you're saying. —LAUGH— I won't touch you. I won't touch you."

As much as she tried,
As much as she planned,
When she called him, her nose began to run. —LAUGH—
The son didn't pay attention.
He didn't remember.
There was an iron rod in the building.
There was an iron rod in the building.
The daughter picked it up and brought it.
She lifted it up and brought it.
She put it on his rib.
She poked it a little.
Startled, the son woke up.
Startled, he woke up.
His sleep had been broken.

He saw the girl.
He saw Sundari.
The son fell in love with her,
Fell in love.
He saw the rod in her hand.
He saw the rod in her hand.
The son thought, "Maybe she'll hit me again."

He quickly ran away.
He went outside.
His horse was in the garden.

His horse was in the garden.
The son climbed on it
And flew away.

P. He looked from above. Wouldn't she see him from the window?
A. Yes.
P. What happened?

"May my black karma be burned away!
May my birth into this caste burn!
Why didn't I die, lord?
Why hasn't death eaten me?

"The son of Indra, Citrasen,
The son of Indra, Citrasen,
Came from heaven,
Came from heaven.
He didn't receive my service.
He didn't receive my welcome.
He fled, lord.
He fled.

"I didn't get a husband in this world.
The creator sent him from heaven.
He didn't receive my service, lord.
He didn't receive my respect."
—LAUGH—

P. "I've been made into a stick; I've been made into stone. That's why I picked up the iron rod. If I hadn't picked it up, but had held out my hand and touched him with my middle finger, then everything would have been alright. What should I do? I've kicked a priceless jewel with my feet. Oh creator, I didn't get a husband in this world. That's why you sent him from heaven. My karma is broken. I'm cursed. I didn't touch him with my hand, but picked up the iron rod. Oh my god!"

She didn't put on the lock. She didn't close the door, didn't close the door. She got up and ran out. —LAUGH— Where?

A. To her house.
P. To which house?
A. To her father's house.
P. Right? To her father's house. She ran there. Had her companions come to get her? In one breath, she came running, and inside the seven-storied palace, she pulled down her bed and, without putting on any bedding, laid down.

"I did this stupid thing without any reason," she thought to herself. "I won't get another husband in this world. I hadn't gotten one in this world. That's why the elephant Airavat brought Indra's son, Citrasen. Then, cursed that I am, I picked up the iron rod. My karma is broken!" she said.

Her tears kept falling. —LAUGH— She gave up food; she gave up water. She quit getting up and sitting up. Everything.

He [the prince] went and went and went, and after going a long ways, he said, "I lost my chance. She's a fox and I'm a tiger, but I was afraid of her and ran away. Even if she did have a weapon in her hand, I have no equal. But, seeing the weapon, I became afraid and ran away in my sleep. Why does she live like that, next to the *ghāṭ*? If I'd stayed and asked her at least that much, . . . I left for no reason." Saying this, he turned the horse around.

A. That horse.

P.

Tāre tāre . . .

Slowly, slowly, the son went.
He went and came back.
The son entered the building.
He entered the dwelling.
He left the horse in the flower garden,
Under a *semar* [*semal*, silk-cotton] tree,[3]
Under a *semar* tree.
The *semar* was laden with flowers and leaves.
He put him there.
The son entered the building.
Entered the building.

"I'll sleep here tonight.
I'll sleep here tonight.
I'll get up when the cock crows.
I'll get up when the cock crows.
I'll be awake when she comes.
I'll close both eyes.
If she picks up the iron rod,
Picks up the rod,
I'll be ready.
I'll brace myself and pull.
She'll fall with force.
She'll fall with force."

P. Right? Did he say the right thing? He, too, was a prince, right?

[3] The *semal* tree is "proverbial in poetry as a disappointment to birds attracted by the tree's large, red flowers" (McGregor 1993:1038).

A. Yes, yes.

P. "At that time, I'll say, 'You didn't touch me, so how did it happen? How did it happen that you fell on top of me?' " Saying this, he got ready. What? Did he get ready or not?

A. He got ready.

P. If that had happened, would he have run away? He got ready. "'Why did you fall?' I'll say." Saying this, he got ready. He chose his food and ate until he was full to the brim and then slept well. Thinking, "I'll get up in the morning," he slept well.

How could *she* sleep? How could *she* sleep? Her eyes were wide open.

"Get up, young girl," they said when it was time to bathe.

"Go away. My nose is running and—SNEEZE! —LAUGH— How can I go to bathe?" she said. "I went to bathe and that's why I'm in this condition. Why should I go bathe?" And she didn't go to bathe. So, she passed the night somehow.

His sleep broke, and he woke up. He had slept soundly. At seven o'clock, the poor thing got ready and combed his hair. "That other day, I wasn't ready, and she woke me up with a rod. Today, I'll be ready." Saying this, he combed his hair. He combed his hair and lay down. And when she was supposed to come he closed his eyes. He closed his eyes. He squeezed his eyelids shut and when they hurt, peeked out. He squeezed his eyelids shut and when they hurt, peeked out. But, there was no one there.

"Young girl, get up! The village wives have already bathed and come back and are ready to cook. And what's happened to you? You don't want to bathe. Come on, at least let us bathe you with lukewarm water. Why aren't you getting up? Get up!"

"Go away! My nose has been running since yesterday. I won't bathe. —LAUGH— I won't bathe." Her nose had been running for three days.

Half the day had passed. He was still squeezing his eyelids shut. —LAUGH— What time had he met her?

A. Seven in the morning.

P. It was afternoon. He was still closing his eyes. But there was no one there.

"She must not come every day. She must come once every three days," he said. Today has passed. For sure she'll come tomorrow," he said. He stayed overnight again.

A. Everything was there: food, water, everything.

P. What else did he need? He stayed again. Again, he closed his eyes.

They were trying to get her up, but did she get up? When it was afternoon again, he said, "She won't come. Three days have passed. If she comes every three days, then after one day, she would have come, on the third day. She must come every seven days. If I stay seven days, then what will happen to the food in this building?"

A. "It will be finished."

P. "It will be finished, and she'll scold me. 'A hungry, thirsty person has come from somewhere, and look, he's eaten all the food.' "

A. That's what she'll say.

P. " 'He's licked the plates clean,' she'll say. And what will she think of me? She'll think I'm hungry and a glutton. I won't stay that many days. Surely, somewhere, she must be sitting on a stool, braiding her hair," he said. "I'll go and look for her." Eating *pān*, he went and looked for her all around, all around, all around, all around. But, she didn't come outside, so how could he see her?

He saw one *lākh* [100,000] of women.
He saw one *lākh* of women.
"It's not her," the son said.
His time was up,
But, he didn't see the princess.
With a sad heart, he returned.
With a sad heart, he returned.

The prince entered the building,
And he ate.
He thought of a plan.
He thought of a plan.
"What can I do to meet her?"
He thought of a plan.
He thought of a plan.

"I'll dress like a *yogī* [ascetic].
I'll dress like a *saṅyāsī* [renunciant].
I'll enter every house.
I'll ask for alms.
I'll sing verses and beg.

I'll sing verses and beg.
They'll have mercy on me.
They'll hear my verses and give alms.
They'll come outside,
Come outside."

A. He went to beg.

P. He ate until he was full to the brim. He ate until he was full to the brim. He ate until he was full to the brim. Then he tore off a loincloth with his teeth and wrapped it around his waist. Isn't that what he would do?

A. Yes, yes.

P. It was long. He wrapped it around his waist and put on a sacred thread. He put on the sacred thread, and then what did he do? He rubbed dust and ashes all over his body. He became dirty.

A. Yes.

P. Wouldn't he become dirty?

A. Yes, yes.

P. He became dirty, and then what did he do? There was a copper vessel. What does a "copper vessel" mean? It was a small bucket. Where?

A. In the building.

P. What kind of bucket was in the building?

A. A brass one.

P. Copper. There was a copper bucket. So he took that bucket and went. He took the bucket and tied his hair up. And, carrying the bucket, he entered the city. When he reached the city, he went to one house and said, "Sita Ram, Sita Ram."

"Go away! Get out! I'll first throw out the dog shit and then come. What kind of 'Sita Ram' is this!"

Wouldn't he die? Would she [first householder] give anything to him or come out? Then he went to a second house.

"My child has been crying since early this morning. Now I'm nursing him and putting him to sleep. Go over there. Who are you?"

Was his spirit broken? —LAUGH— Did he get anything from her [second householder]?

Tāre tāre . . .

"Even reciting the name of Ram,
People in this country abuse you.
They insult you.
If I sing and beg,
Will I get any alms?
Will I see the queen?"

He thought this way to himself.
He thought this way to himself.
The son began to beg for alms,
Began to beg for alms.

P. "Hari [Krishna] goes ahead and Arjun follows behind. Playing the *sāraṅgī* [kind of violin], they charm people's hearts. There's a famine in our kingdom. Mother, that's why I'm wandering from house to house, asking for alms. Mother, if you can give, give; if not, don't. I'll ask for alms at ten doors. My father's name is Suresan; my mother's name is Sushila. My aunt's name is Campavati, the one who caused so much trouble. She ground me with a grinding stone and tried to cut me in pieces under the thresher. When I didn't die, she tried to poison me. The moon is rising; Raja Danddhar [Yama, the god of death].

The son was wandering from house to house,
Was wandering from house to house.
The son was begging.
The son had become a beggar.
The son was begging.
The son had become a beggar.
The son, singing and singing, was begging,
Was a beggar.

P. "Hari goes ahead and Arjun follows behind. Playing the *sāraṅgī*. They charm people's hearts. There's a famine in our kingdom. Mother, that's why I'm wandering from house to house, asking for alms. Mother, if you can give, give; if not, don't. I'll ask for alms at ten doors. My father's name is Suresan; my mother's name is Sushila. My aunt's name is Campavati, the one who caused so much trouble. She ground me with a grinding stone and tried to cut me in pieces under the thresher. When I didn't die, she tried to poison me. The moon is rising; Raja Danddhar.

He wandered from house to house.
He wandered from door to door.
The old flowerseller had made a garland.
She delivered it and was coming back.
The old woman met a trusted friend.
She met a friend,
On the same road the son was walking on.
The flowerseller was on that road.
The old woman stopped her [her friend].
"Don't tell anyone," she said.
The prince was listening.
The boy was listening.

P. "Why would I tell anyone? Why would I tell anyone? I'm the mother of three children, living and dead. Have you ever heard, seen or known me to tell? —LAUGH— Why would I tell anyone?"

"Oh daughter, blooming flowers give a good smell. [In a whisper] I'm telling you; you're my daughter. For this reason, don't say anything. But, the daughter of the king went to bathe. Who knows if a water snake bit her, or a black bug bit her, or whom she saw at the *ghāṭ*. She came back from there and is sleeping. She isn't eating or getting up, or sitting up or bathing. [Normal, loud voice] Blooming flowers surely give a good smell. Don't tell anyone."

He heard this conversation.
He wandered around and then came to her.
He fell at her feet.
He joined his hands together.

"Listen to my entreaty.
Accept my greetings.
Mother, teach me,
Teach me.
Mother, listen to my entreaty.
Accept my greetings.
I've taken the initiation of a *bhramacārī* [religious student, the first of four stages of life].
I've wandered from country to country.
I've stayed in village after village.
Mother, I don't know anything.
I don't know anything.
Mother, teach me,
Tell me what you know."

P. "This isn't right! You've taken the initiation of a *bhramacārī* and what is it that you're asking me? What are you asking me to give? If I kick you, you'll fly far, don't you know that? You're asking me about my ancestors, whom you don't know, my ancestors, whom you don't know. Is this some kind of magic that I should teach you? You bastard! Look how you've fallen at my feet, saying, 'Teach me.' Is this some kind of magic?"

"I bow to you, Mother. What I want to know, you can teach me. That's why I fell at your feet. You're saying, 'No.' Then, why did I fall at your feet? What were you whispering and saying, 'Don't tell anyone.' What was that? I thought you could teach me that."

"You bastard! Was that some kind of magical incantation?"

"Then, what was it?"

"You bastard! Three days ago, the king's daughter, Mohini, —LAUGH— went to bathe and after coming back from that *ghāṭ*, she's been sleeping in the seven-storied palace. She isn't getting up, isn't sitting, isn't eating, isn't bathing. You bastard! That's what I was saying. Was I teaching a magical incantation? So, have I taught you something?"

Did she teach something, —LAUGH— or didn't she teach anything?

A. She taught very cleverly.

P. And wasn't she telling?

A. Who was telling?

P. The old flowerseller. —LAUGH— But she taught him. She said, "No," and then taught him.

A. Yes. She first said, "No," and later she taught him.

P. Yes. "Old flowerseller, on which street do you live?"

"Go away! —LAUGH— Why are you asking my neighborhood? You've taken the initiation of a *bhramacārī*. So, why are you asking my neighborhood?"

"Yes, yes. You're like my mother. What harm is there in telling me?"

"That's it over there, that small alley. Do you see it? They call it 'the hut.' That's it."

A. "That's the one."

P. "That one is mine."

He came back from that place.
He came back from there.
The son went to that building,
To that building.
He threw off his *yogī* dress.
He had gold in his hand.
The son went to the store.
He sold it.
It was worth nine thousand rupees.
The son sold it.

For his head, he bought some [fake] hair,
For his feet, shoes.
For his hands, he bought bangles,
For his forehead, a gold ornament.
For his nose, he bought a nose ring,
To decorate his feet, some colored powder,
He was like a bride for whom austerities had been done [to find a husband].
That boy looked like that.
He looked like that.

He wore a *pītāmbarī* [yellow silk] sari.
He bought flowers.
The son put them in his hair.
He braided his hair.

P. Was he ready?

A. Yes, he was ready.

P. Yes, he was ready. He found these things and got ready in that building. Where was he? At the old flowerseller's place, right?

A. Yes.

P. She was there [on the road]; that's why all this happened. If she hadn't been, then what would have happened? Could that much have happened when he was begging? It couldn't have happened. But he was nearby, and that's why so much happened so quickly. He was ready.

Tāre tāre . . .

It was seven o'clock.
It was seven o'clock.
The boy was holding a bag,
Holding a bag.
He walked very, very slowly.
He bowed his head.
He saw the house of the old flowerseller.
The prince met her there.
He met her there.
The old woman had picked flowers and brought them.
She was sitting on a broken cot.
She was breaking off a thread.
She was making a flower garland.
She had made only two or three garlands.
When he reached there,
She looked at the feet of the boy.
She looked at his feet.
She quit making the garland.
The old woman looked closely.
—LAUGH—

P. She looked closely. "You husband-eating daughter! Who are you, daughter? I don't recognize you. Who are you? I don't recognize you."

"Weren't you calling to Phenki? I'm that Phenki, or do you think I'm someone else?"

"May I die, daughter! Daughter, I thought you would be short. You're taller than I am! What! May I die, daughter! Daughter, you went to Bhilai [an industrial city near Raipur], so I thought you must be working as a day laborer. Daughter, look how beautiful you look."

"Go on! What do we do for rich Marwaris, Punjabis, or Bengalis? We make garlands. Yes, we make garlands. Do you understand? We don't work like common people. I sent two or three letters. Didn't they arrive? —LAUGH— Did they arrive?"

"Daughter, I couldn't go to Bhilai. May I die, daughter! You're so robust, so tall. What! May I die! Daughter, you're a city dweller. I'm going to get sugar and jaggery. Make some good strong tea and drink it. I'll make the garlands and take them to the king's house. I'll bring some rice and *dāl* from there. Both of us, mother and daughter, will cook and eat it. Make a little city food, and I'll eat it." —LAUGH— What did she go to buy?

A. Jaggery and tea leaves.

P. She went to buy them. There were two or three garlands on that thread already made. He took them off and threw them away. And he made a garland without a thread and put it aside.

A. He made a garland.

P. He made it, and making two more, put them aside. He put them in a basket. Of course, he had paper. He took out a little. He took out a little and wrote the letter *s* on it and above it put the vowel *e*. So what was it?

A. *E*? *E*?

P. What do you have when the vowel *e* is put above *s*?

A. *Se*.

P. That's all. That's all he wrote, nothing else. He wrote *s* and put the vowel *e* above it and put the piece of paper in the flower garland and sat there quietly.

A. Yes, yes. —LAUGH—

P. So, she brought back the jaggery and tea. "My daughter, make some tea. My daughter, make some tea." She was pleased. "My daughter, make some tea," she said. "I'll make the garlands." She put down the tea and jaggery and went to the flowers. What had happened to the flowers?

A. They'd already been made into garlands.

P. They'd already been made into garlands. "What!" she said. "Daughter, you didn't use a single thread. May I die! Daughter, you didn't even use a single thread. Daughter, teach me how and *then* go back." She said this and the girl was pleased.

When she took the basket of flower garlands and was ready to go, [he asked], "What will you tell them?"

"I'll tell them, 'Look, my daughter made these.' "

"That's OK. Go."

A. "Tell them that."

P. What?

A. He said, "Tell them that."

P. "Go, if you'll say that, then go."

"Yes, I'm going right now. I'll bring back some rice and *dāl*." She went quickly, quickly, quickly, quickly, quickly, quickly, quickly, quickly, quickly, quickly, quickly, quickly, quickly, quickly, quickly, quickly, quickly. —LAUGH—

A. She arrived there.

P. She arrived there.

She arrived at the king's courtyard.
She arrived at the king's courtyard.
The old woman gave the flower garlands,
Gave the flower garlands.

The girl saw the flowers.
She was startled.

The daughter got up and stood up.
She stood up.
The daughter took a garland.
She put it on.
The daughter took a garland.
She put it on.
The daughter took another garland.
She saw the letter.
She took the letter out.
She took it out and looked at it.
No name was visible.
No work was visible.

P. "Old woman, what have you brought with the flowers? Is this a letter or what? Don't you think the person should write his name and village? What it this? Old flowerseller, what is this, mother?"
A. She was startled.
P. "Who made this garland and has written *se* on the left side?" Would she ask this, or not? —LAUGH—
A. She'd ask.
P. He could hardly write, "I was asleep, was asleep. You brought an iron rod and poked my ribs. It was me. I've come and I'm here."
A. How could he write that?
P. How could he write that much? "Old flowerseller?"
"Yes."
"Who made the garlands today? You've never made ones like these before and written *se* on the left side."
A. It's become difficult. —LAUGH—
P. What? —LAUGH— It was good. He had enticed her.
A. He had enticed her.
P. Why did he need to write all the details?
A. Yes.
P. He sent the right thing. He knew she would ask. She would ask. That's why he made *s* into *se*. She would know and understand the *se*.
"Why are you asking? Whoever it is, give the rice and *dāl*. Then I'll tell you."
"Tell me the name. Only then can you take the rice and *dāl*. Who is it? Tell me."
"Who? She was born here; she grew up here. These days, she's gone and

lives in the city. My sister and oldest daughter. My oldest daughter has come from Bhilai. She made this flower garland." —LAUGH—

"Yes. What does she look like?"

"What can I say? Your lips aren't equal to her heel. —LAUGH— Yes. That's what she looks like. Yes."

"So, she's your oldest daughter? Go, call her here."

"Why?"

"I want to form *mahāprasād* with her. I want to form *mahāprasād*. Go."

"First, give me some rice and *dāl*. We're dying of hunger and thirst. We'll eat first and then come. Then you can form *mahāprasād* or talk together. Give me my rice and *dāl*."

"No, it'll be too late. I'll give you your rice and *dāl*, you cook it, and in that much time, we'll form the *mahāprasād*. Then, both the *mahāprasād* will be finished and the cooking of your food will be finished. Both tasks will be finished. Go, call her here. I won't give it now."

A. She won't give it. She won't give it.

P. "Daughter?"

"Yes?"

"You've broken our karma!"

"What happened?"

"If we hadn't made garlands today, then there wouldn't have been any trouble. —LAUGH— If we hadn't made garlands today, then there wouldn't have been any trouble. You've broken our karma!"

"What happened?"

"I told her my oldest daughter made these garlands. Then she sent me to call you. She said, 'If you don't go, I won't give you your rice and *dāl*.' I'm going to die of hunger because of you, and you, too, will die of hunger. Daughter, what will we do?"

"We'll go. We've worked, so why shouldn't we collect our pay? We'll go."

Didn't she say the right thing?

A. She said the right thing.

P. She didn't say the wrong thing?

A. She said the right thing.

P. She said the right thing. They'd made the garlands, and she'd worn them, right? Why should they remain in debt?

"We'll go."

"OK. Then, let's go. Have you seen the palace? Then, follow behind me."

Quickly, quickly, quickly, quickly, quickly, quickly, quickly, quickly. They went quickly. —LAUGH—

The minister's son and the barber's son
Were seated on their stools on the verandah.
They saw the old flowerseller.

They said, "Old woman, come here."
They called her.

"I'll beat you bastards! I'll beat you!"
The old woman abused them.
She insulted them.
The boy was following behind her.
He was coming behind.

Cow dung was brought.
It was plastered in front of the doorway.
There, a ritual design was drawn.
The daughter [princess] placed a low stool there.
She put down a brass plate.
The daughter put milk and water there
And stood, waiting.

The girl [prince] was walking.
The daughter was walking.
The flowerseller brought her.
She stood in front of the courtyard.
The girl took hold of her hand.
She pulled and brought her toward her.
The daughter stood her there,
Stood her there.

The flowerseller was watching,
Thinking, "What will she do with my daughter?" —LAUGH—

The king [prince] was standing there,
Was standing there.
She washed his feet with water.
She washed his feet with water.
She patted it on her head.
The daughter washed them with milk.
She threw it on her womb.
The daughter prostrated at his feet.
She joined her hands together.
The daughter stood up and
She took his hand.
The daughter took him with her,
Took him with her.

The flowerseller was watching.
The flowerseller was watching.

The old woman went around her.
She stopped her. —LAUGH—

"I, too, have formed [*mahāprasād*].
I've seen others seat it.
There's an equal giving and taking.
What kind of *mahāprasād* have you seated,
In which only you have prostrated?
Young girl, tell me this,
Then take us inside."

A. The prostration wasn't equal, right? Why did only she prostrate?

P. He stood there like an old tree. The girl had done everything. The old flowerseller was watching him. "What! I, too, have seated friendships and seen those of others. And people feed each other, give drinks to each other, and prostrate before each other. Why is my daughter standing there like a tree? Only the princess has done the necessary ritual." This is what the old woman was thinking. How could she know about the difference inside? —LAUGH—

A. About the *se* inside.

P. How could she know what *se* was? When the old woman asked about the inequality, then everything became confused, right?

A. Yes, yes.

P. It became difficult. The princess would die if she told and die if she didn't. If she didn't tell, they couldn't go inside. If she told, everything would be spoiled. What did she say?

"Flowerseller, listen. I'm a princess. Your daughter has come to my house, and that's why I'm serving her. When I come to your house, *I'll* stand up and what will you do?"

A. "You, too, will serve me like this."

P. "You, too, will serve me like this. Haven't we seated a beautiful *mahāprasād*? One day, I'll certainly come to your place. I won't come everyday, but one day, I'll certainly come, and you'll serve me. Now, don't block my way. Let me take my *mahāprasād*," she said. She took him into the seven-storied palace and left him there. And, in a grain basket, she brought a basket of rice and gave it to the old woman.

A. Yes. She said, "Go and cook this."

P. The old woman picked it up quickly but couldn't put it on her head. The old woman was weak. The old woman couldn't put it right on her head. First she put it on her shoulder, then, with difficulty, she put it on her head. When it was on her head, the old woman was so pleased that I can't describe it.

"If my daughter stays eight days,
If my daughter stays fifteen days,
There won't be room at my place [for all the rice].

There won't be room.
If there's this feeling everyday,
She'll keep giving this much everyday.
Where will I put it?"

P. Where?

A. She was looking for a place to put it.

P. "She's giving this much at the beginning," she said. "If my daughter stays eight or ten days, then she'll give this much everyday. Where will I put it?"
She was worrying and saying—

A. "She'll give this much everyday."

P. She was worrying and saying, "She'll give this much everyday."

A. Yes. "Where to put it?"

P. She was looking for a place to put it. The old woman went away. Then she [the princess] said, "Oh no! You must be hungry." She cooked him all kinds of foods and vegetables. She showed him where to sit. She showed him where to sit and said, "Come and eat." The boy sat down quickly.

A. Yes, yes.

P. Didn't he sit down?

A. If he was being served food, of course he'd sit down. He was hungry. What happened?

P. "Come and eat," she said, and he sat down quickly. Then she went behind him and didn't give him any [food].
"Come on! You haven't brought any!"

"You gave hope and then took it away.
You gave hope and then took it away.
You're standing behind me,
Standing behind me.
Queen, I'm dying of hunger.
I'm thirsty."

"You wrote something with the flowers.
You sent it to me.
Where did you put *se*?
Where did you put it?
Until I see that form,
Until I see that dress,
Master, I won't give you the meal.
I won't give the food.
If I give the meal,
I won't see that form.
Then, we'll eat together.
Then, we'll eat together."

P. Did she feed him? —LAUGH— Did she feed him?

A. Why would she feed him? She didn't feed him.

P. "If you stay in this disguise," she said, "what will we do?"
"We'll eat," he said. "We'll form *mahāprasād*."
Did she feed him?

A. Why would she feed him?

P. She didn't feed him. That's natural. By not showing himself, he would feel badly, too, wouldn't he?

A. He would.

P. He would. What did he write and give to her? —LAUGH— "Look," he said, "to save my life, to see you, to meet you, I made this plan. I spent a lot of money. Don't take away my life," he said. "I, too, am a prince. I'm Malya Basant, the son of King Manicandra of Madhukatak. Do you understand?" he said. "Now don't kill me. Save me. I'm the son of a king's family. I made this plan to save my life."
"When your life ends, mine will end," she said. "Why should I stay alive?"

A. "Saying this, I'm going now."

P. "Saying this, I'm going. When yours ends, by that time, mine will have already ended. If you show some finger . . ." she said.
What did he think? Why was he so afraid?
"Show it. I'm hungry." —LAUGH—

Tāre tāre . . .

He threw his clothes right there.
He threw his clothes right there.
The *bābū* showed his true form,
Showed his true form.
The daughter's heart was satisfied.
She brought a brass plate and served him.
The daughter brought another plate.
He ate with his hand.

"I'll eat his leftovers," she thought.
"I've given him too much." —LAUGH—
The daughter was serving the meal,
Was serving the meal.

The prince's heart was satisfied.
The *bābū*'s heart was satisfied.
The *bābū* ate all the food.
He ate it all.
If it had been scrubbed, it wouldn't have been cleaner.
If it had been washed, it wouldn't have been cleaner.

The boy ate like that.
He ate like that.

A. OK.
P. He finished eating.
A. He made it absolutely clean.
P. He made it absolutely clean. How many doors were there?
A. Seven.
P. Seven doors. He stayed behind the doors. He stayed with her all night, and during the day, he stayed with her companions. She gave him a key and locked her room. No one knew about this. Someone had come, broken in and entered, and no one knew about it. —LAUGH—

Four months passed.
Six months passed.
She was five months pregnant.
The daughter began to look different,
Began to look different.
Twelve and twelve, twenty-four girls,
Twelve and twelve, twenty-four girls,
Stayed with the daughter,
Stayed with her.
But the girls didn't know.
No one knew.

P. Wasn't there anyone? There wasn't. Everyone was the same. But, one girl was clever.
A. Yes.
P. "Look! The princess is becoming very fat," she said. "How fat she looks!" She had a suspicion, and the suspicion was right. She was right. She said, "This is the right time. I won't get this chance again. If there's no conflict now, I'll be insulted later," she said. "Saying, 'Our daughter shouldn't get into trouble or be distressed,' her mother and father are giving us one hundred, sixty, eighty, ninety rupees and have hired us, and now this has happened. They'll surely say, 'Why didn't you tell us?' and will scold us. I'm going."
P. Did she go?
A. She went.
P. "Oh queen!"
"Yes."
"If you want me to, I'll take whatever oath you ask, whatever oath. I don't know, but I think your daughter is four or five months pregnant. Doesn't she look pregnant?"
"What!"

A. What did she say?

P. What did she say? —LAUGH— "I've told you this, but go and see what you think, if it's true or not. Then tell me. No one knows about this, only you and me."

"Oh god! May I die! May both my eyes burst! —LAUGH— Where is she?"

"She's on the cot. Where else would she be? She's sitting on the cot."

When she [her mother] went, her [the daughter's] hair was loosened. What hair? The hair on her head. She went up from behind her.

"If she'd had only two or three companions, my daughter would have been ruined even more. She had twelve and twelve, twenty-four companions, and even so she's been ruined. Look how bad she looks! Her hair is loose. At least she could braid her hair!" —LAUGH—

A. She was looking at her.

P. What?

A. She was looking at her.

P. Yes.

A. She was pretending to look at her hair, right?

P. What?

A. She was pretending to look at her hair.

P. She was combing her hair, and what was her mother doing?

A. She was looking at her.

P. She was looking at her, right? She saw her and believed it. She combed her hair and braided it. At last she said, "Daughter, look, listen to my words. Whose union is with the best, she knows the best thing to do. This is a fact in this world, daughter," she said. "This isn't only true for you and me, daughter, but also for the big, big households. Whose union is with the best, she knows the best thing to do. Do you understand? If he's from the best house, then we'll make the best plan, and if he's from a bad house, we'll make a bad plan. But, tell me truthfully if he is or isn't."

What did she say? What did she say? What did she say?

"I'll tell you truthfully. What is the situation, toothless woman? What is the situation, toothless one? Why are you coming and asking me, having taken out your teeth? Get up and go away!"

"Daughter, I'm your mother. I won't trick you. Daughter, when a cow becomes pregnant and can't bear it, she sleeps. When a woman becomes pregnant, it stays in the middle, and she sticks out in front. Why are you being so obstinate? —LAUGH— Today it's small, so no one knows. But when it grows, it can't be hidden; it sticks out in front. Why are you hiding it from me? Do you think there aren't any bricks here to throw? —LAUGH— People would say, 'She fell, broke her teeth, began to bleed, and was taken to the hospital.' There we would tell the doctor, 'If you give her a shot, she'll die.'

What do you think? You've brought a bad name on my house! You've brought shame on me!"

"Oh king!"

"Yes."

"Something very shameful has happened."

"Who did it?"

"Our daughter."

"How did she do it?"

"She's five-months pregnant."

"*Thū—rre*! —LAUGH— Why has the bitch come here? *Thū—rre*! Is it true?"

"It's true."

"Go now, go."

He called the minister. He called the minister. He called the minister, Birupakhya, and said, "Minister, someone has stolen and eaten a priceless treasure from my seven-storied palace. Catch him within three days and bring him in front of me. If you don't catch him, what will happen to you? I'll have you hung from the gallows by your backside," he said. "Go now."

But the minister shit and peed [out of fear]. Now what did the minister do? He divided the city into neighborhoods. Is that what he did?

A. He did.

P. He divided it into neighborhoods and said, "Brothers, there's priceless gold in the king's seven-storied palace. Someone has stolen and eaten it. Catch him for me." Would people obey his order or not?

A. They would.

P. What?

A. They would.

P. They surrounded the palace walls for the entire night. What did they surround?

A. The wall and its shadow.

P. And whom did they surround?

A. Whom did they surround?

P. That poor thing couldn't get out. Everything they needed was inside: a place to go to the bathroom, things to eat, to drink, to wear, everything. Right?

A. Yes.

P. In the seven-storied palace. It was all surrounded, so where could he go? —LAUGH—

A. Where were they looking for him?

P. They were looking. Morning broke; morning broke. They each went back to their own houses.

"Brother-in-law of the nose-blower, tell the truth. You surrounded it, so what did you see?"

"I saw only the shadow and that wall."

"What did you see?"

"I surrounded it all night, but I saw only the shadow and the wall."

"Why didn't you look inside the house? You should have looked there. That was the king's order."

"*Chī*! Who knows since when and from where he's come and since when he's been staying in the house, surrounded?" That day passed.

A. Yes, yes.

P. The next day, it was the turn of the next neighborhood. "Go, brothers." They went. They did the same thing. What?

A. They surrounded the shadow and the wall.

P. It became morning.

A. Two nights passed.

P. They went again. Two nights passed.

A. Yes.

P. The last neighborhood, on the edge, was left.

A. Yes.

P. He brought them. For the third night, they circled the shadow and the wall. It became morning. When it was morning, the minister said, "Citizens, greetings to your mothers and fathers and greetings to you, too. I brought you here for the entire night and put you to a lot of trouble. It was useless. We didn't catch anything. So, I'm leaving, sons. Whomever I've helped, say 'He was good'; whomever I've harmed, say 'He's gone.' Fathers, go now, go back to your own work. Today I'll go. Now go."

A. The minister was talking.

P. "You're telling us to go and saying 'I'm going today.' What? Won't you stay here? Won't you go home?"

"I won't go to my mud house."

"Where will you go?"

"I'm going to my house in heaven."

"Is your life over today, father?"

"Yes, it's over." —LAUGH—

"You see and know death. That's why you were made minister," they said, and they went away. They went away, and then what did he do? He didn't go on the open road. "Ohhhh, ohhhh, ohhhh, ohhhh," he groaned. He snuck out through the garden path. —LAUGH— Yes. He snuck out through the garden path. There was a broken cot lying there. He put the broken cot upright and laid down, groaning, "Ohhhh, ohhhh, ohhhh, ohhhh." He knew when the king found out—

A. He'd hang him on the gallows. That's why he got a fever, from his worry.

P. [The minister's daughter-in-law said to his son,] "Hey, cardplayer! Hey, cardplayer! Hey, cardplayer! The old man hasn't eaten since yesterday. He went out at night, and now it's noon, one o'clock. The two children are calling, 'Grandpa, grandpa, grandpa, grandpa,' and who knows where the old man has gone?"

"People are so stupid. If they don't see someone for a minute, they go crazy. And the old man has only been gone since yesterday. If I don't go to play cards today, the least I'll get is a beating. Wait and see. —LAUGH— Go, go. He must be at the king's house."

"Because the old man isn't here today, I haven't cleaned the brass [vessel] yet. Usually, by now I would have washed it three times. Look how dirty it is, lying over there," she said and went behind the house and began to wash it. She scrubbed it vigorously with ashes. Because of that noise, she couldn't hear anything else. When she quit scrubbing with the ashes and began washing with water, she heard the moaning, "Ohhhh, ohhhh, ohhhh." —LAUGH— She heard that noise. Whose?

A. The minister's.

P. The minister's. She left the brass pot and said, "Where has that son-eating bitch given birth this time?" And she peered out. Whom did she see?

A. The minister.

P. How was he related to her?

A. He was her father-in-law.

P. Her father-in-law. "Who's there?"

"Oh, mother, it's me."

"Why are you sleeping here?"

"This is the last time we're going to meet."

"Are you going away today?"

"Yes."

"Then be sure to write the office of the minister in your son's name." —LAUGH—

"That'll happen of its own accord. I don't have ten sons! It'll be written of its own accord. I'm going away today."

"Is that why you have this fever?"

"Yes."

"Then come. Don't spend money on the road unnecessarily. Take some food with you. And why do you have a fever, tell me? Tell me why you've got a fever."

"There was an order that I had to obey within three days. For three days, I made an encirclement. I couldn't catch the fox. So today, as soon as I reach the palace, the king will hang me from the gallows by the seat of my pants. —LAUGH— It'll be good for you. It'll be good for you."

"Why would the king hang you from the gallows by your seat?"

"His daughter has met a man, and he'll hang me from the gallows from my seat. —LAUGH— It's good for you."

"Why is it good?"

"I was just going to tell you that, when I thought of something. My son is always with five people [playing cards]. It'll be morning; he always stays out until sunrise. My eyes are getting bigger and bigger, and I'm going to swear."

"What happened today? What happened today? What happened today? What happened today?"

"Who was it, mother? Who else could it be! The minister can go to the king's house, and the king to the minister's. No one else can come and go like that. Why wouldn't I get a fever? —LAUGH— Thinking, 'It's your son' has brought on a little more fever."

"Get up, go and eat some food." Would he eat?

A. Where else would he eat?

P. What?

A. Where else would he eat?

P. He would have eaten if it concerned himself, but whom were they talking about?

A. They were talking about his son.

P. They were talking about his son. So, she didn't feed him. He ate this much [indicating a handful].

"Did you eat?"

"You didn't feed me, daughter, so what should I do? Should I take it to my son?"

"Where?"

"At the king's house."

"What bastard has asked you to take it? He went without even telling his daughter, or did he just go? Go, tell him that. Even if you are old. What? Should *I* go? Let him come here."

"Whatever you're planning, you're going to destroy the entire lineage because of it. —LAUGH— You're going to destroy the entire lineage."

"Father-in-law?"

"Yes."

"A king has eight qualities [*guṇ*], and a minister has sixteen qualities. That's what people say. So, why are you a minister?"

"What do you mean?"

"A fever has gripped you over such a little thing, and you're asking death to come get you. What will you do when something more important happens?"

"What?"

"Go tell the king this. If you give me two and a half measures of gold and one measure of silver, I'll catch him within seven days."

[The king to the minister.] "Minister!"

"Yes."

"What happened?"

"He slipped away. If you give me a measure of gold and a measure of silver, I'll catch the thief within seven days."

"Go, weigh it and take it. Go, weigh it and take it."

He weighed it and brought it home. "Mother, here's what you asked for," he said. He gave it to his *bahū*. When he gave it to his *bahū*, what happened?

"Call all the servants and give each one his share, and give them each a rock. Tell them to scrub their share of the silver and gold."

So, the silver and gold were given to the servants of the household. They made gold paste and they also made silver paste, and on the sixth day, they mixed them together. They mixed them both and made a sandalwood paste. Both of them. They made both of them into a sandal paste. They put both on a plate, and what did they do then? She wrote on a sheet of paper, "Oh daughter of the king, ever since I got married and came here, I haven't met you. But, I'm coming to your place to meet you."

A. "Come."

P. "Come today at four." She was happy. "Today the minister's *bahū* is coming to meet me," she said, and she was happy. "She's the mother of two children," and she was happy.

She [the *bahū*] put the children to sleep. She put them down, having fed them until they were full. She took the plate of sandal paste and went at four o'clock. The king's daughter was ready. "She'll come," she said.

As soon as she arrived, [the princess] took the plate of sandal paste and took it inside. She had the *bahū*'s hands and feet washed. She greeted and welcomed her. She made tea and breads. They ate and drank, then sat together for an hour.

"Queen, I only came for this much time. Now, I must go."

She got up quickly and went away. She went away quickly and said, "Father-in-law, call everyone in the city today, and what should you do? Put a watchman wherever there's water. Grab and bring whoever comes at night to bathe. Do this until morning."

A. "Until the cock crows."

P. "Only after it's morning should the watchmen leave and stop bringing anyone who's come to bathe at night."

The minister heard her order and put a watchman at every bathing place. What had they kept watch over for three days? They'd kept watch over the house and wall.

A. The wall.

P. Today they kept watch over the bathing places. Inside the seven-storied palace, when the meal was over and everyone was asleep in their beds, she [the princess] got a chance to serve him. "Listen," she said. "The minister's *bahū* came to meet me today. If she'd brought something to eat, it would have come out already. If it had been something to eat, I couldn't bring it to you now. But it wasn't something to eat. I've saved it. Come, I'll rub some sandal paste on your body, then a little on mine, too."

A. "I'll rub some paste."

P. "I'll rub it on." She took off his clothes and made him lie down, and began to rub on the paste.

A. The sandal paste.

P. She began to rub the sandal paste on his whole body. She rubbed it on, and what was left, she put on her own body.

A. She rubbed it on.

P. She rubbed on the paste.

When it dried,
When it dried,
How did the boy look?
He began to sparkle.
The son himself knew,
"I won't survive.
My death has come.
My death has come."

P. "They'll see. They'll see this form. Today my death will come."

"How?"

"What is this? Look! How will I survive? Again and again I told you, 'Save me. Don't take my life.' Look at this! You made this plan to kill me. Now look!" he said. "Yours will go away. What will happen to mine? Now look! They've caught me. That thief. You thought no one knew. That's why, in order to catch me—"

A. "You made this plan."

P. "Go, go to the pond with the small pebbles. Bathe there and clean yourself; then come back," she said. There, too, there were watchmen. Weren't they watching?

A. There were watchmen.

P. They were also at that bathing place. He went and saw them. So, at the edge, what did he do at the edge? "I'll immerse myself," he said. And he entered the water and went all the way in. He went in, and when he came out he shone and sparkled, shone and sparkled, shone and sparkled, shone and sparkled, shone and sparkled, shone and sparkled, shone and sparkled, shone and sparkled, shone and sparkled, and they saw him. Wouldn't he shine?

A. He would.

P. "Snake, snake! Snake, snake!" Those who were watching the bathing place called out, "Snake, snake! Snake, snake! —LAUGH— It's a cobra snake!" they called out.

He sat by the edge of the water. It was the pond with small pebbles. He took a handful of pebbles and scrubbed himself. He scrubbed himself so hard that one layer of skin came off. What did he do after scrubbing himself? He washed himself with water, so that he made a noise. Wouldn't there be a noise?

A. There would.

P. When he was washing, they looked two or three times and said, "What! What is that? If it were some kind of cat drinking water, it would have made the noise *chakal, chakal.* Why is it making the noise *ghablak*? —LAUGH— Let's go around and see," they said, and they went around. So that poor thing had scrubbed himself and was bathing.

A. He was sitting down.

P. He was sitting down.

They surrounded him on all four sides.
They caught the prince.
They tied him and brought him,
Tied him and brought him.
They tied him up for the night.
They tied him up for the night.
"This is the thief," they said.
"This is the thief."

It was seven o'clock.
The sun rose.
The minister's *bahū* knew it was him.
"Take him," she said.
The *bahū* said, "This is the thief;
Take him."

P. "Is *this* the one?"

"It is. Yes. Take him."

"Oh king!"

"Yes."

"This is the thief. This is he. Yes."

"Are you the thief? From whom did you steal?"

"From who else? I stole from the king."

"OK. So you're giving me an answer. You're giving me an answer about my things. How strange!" he said. "Oh Kam, Ram, Sam, and Dam [king's henchmen, later identified as grasscutters], take him and finish off his life on the crossroads, where the road divides."

A. The daughter had sent the prince, and if he didn't come back by sunrise—

P. She would think that he must be cleaning himself. And she was cleaning herself inside, but it wasn't coming off. —LAUGH— She would think that he was still cleaning himself. The paste stuck like cement sticks to bricks. She'd given it to him. It dried and then it wouldn't come off. She thought he was still scrubbing himself, and that's why the sun had already risen.

"Go and grab the bastard! If you've got anything with you, now's your chance. We're going to take you to the crossroads and will kill you with a sword. If you've got anything with you, give it to us. Now's your chance to keep your name alive."

"I have nothing. Look. I'm ruined! I have nothing."

"You must have something. The king's daughter is very clever." They pulled and pulled on everything. "You must have something. You're a naked *bābā*."

"When I left my country,
When I left my country,
The mother who gave me birth thought,
My mother deliberated in her heart.
And she went to her storeroom.
She gave me this much.
My mother gave me this much.

I brought that gold.
I brought that gold.
I've hidden it far away, brothers,
Hidden it far away.
If you believe me,
Come with me and see.
I'll give it to you and die,
Give it to you and die.
You'll remember me for seven generations.
You'll remember me for seven generations.
My name will live on.
My name will live on."

P. "The water pot [*kumbh*] is this big, isn't it, father? The water pot is this big, isn't it, father?"

"Yes. It's like a *baiṭhī* bowl [type of Oriya vessel]."

"Is it pure gold?"

"Yes, pure gold."

A. "It's gold."

P. "It's pure gold."

"Then where did you put it? Then where did you put it? Then where did you put it?"

"I put it at the top of a tree. I didn't put it on the ground. I thought maybe white ants would eat it, so I put it up high."

"Let's go. Hey, Kam?"

"Yes."

"You'll be the one to climb the tree. Go quickly, take it out and bring it down. Go and climb up there. The prince will show you where it is," he said.

"Where is it?"

"It's here."

"Climb up."

Kam climbed up quickly, quickly.

"Oh, stop, stop, stop, stop!" he said.

"Why?"

"There's a magical amulet around it. If you know how to take it off, it's OK; otherwise, if you don't know how to take off the amulet, both your eyes will burst, *bābū*, they'll burst."

"Kam, come down, come down, come down! Don't climb up there!" Would he come down?

A. Of course, he'd come down.

P. He came down.

"Yes. Surround me on all sides of the tree, you four people. Surround me, and I'll climb up, take it out and bring it. If you surround me, how can I escape?"

He said the right thing, the prince. —LAUGH—

"Surround me, Kam; Ram, surround me; Dam, surround me," he said. They surrounded him. He climbed slowly, slowly. He climbed slowly, slowly. He reached the place.

A. Near the horse.

P. Near the horse. He put one leg on one side and one leg on the other, and what did he do? He sat himself in the middle, sat himself in the middle. Two fingerwidths, three fingerwidths, four fingerwidths.

"Are you looking, bastard? Is he taking it down? —LAUGH— How's he taking it down? —LAUGH— How's he taking it down?" —LAUGH—

Tāre nāre . . .

He pulled hard.
He clung to its [the horse's] body.
The son flew up into the sky,
Flew into the sky.

The *ghāsiyā* [grasscutters] were watching.
They threw up their hands;
They beat themselves.
"Bastard! What have you done to us?
How did you trick us?
You said, 'There's lots of gold,' and tricked us.

You said, 'There's lots of gold,' and tricked us.
Bastard, you flew into the sky,
Flew into the sky."

P. "Kam, what should we do?"

A. "What should we do?"

P. "What should we do? Go, bring a lamb. Bring it and come back. We'll cut it up and send it." He went. He brought back a young lamb, one that was in the house. They killed it, and there was lots of blood, and they went back.

"Oh king!"

"Yes."

"We obeyed your order."

"OK. Go, you're free to go now. Go."

"Look, don't any of you bastards say anything. —LAUGH— Remember then, if anyone tells, then . . ." Didn't they do it well?

A. They did it well.

P. "You're very clever. You're very clever."

"How so?"

"The poor boy, what a beautiful boy he was. You hid and kept him. You got pregnant by him. Today, the *ghāsiyā* cut the poor boy into three or four pieces. The *ghāsiyā* Kam, Ram, Dam, and Sam have come back. Do you understand?"

"Where?"

"At the crossroads."

A. Is the minister saying this?

P. No, the king. "You had such a great plan. Today, you knowingly had someone else's son killed. Did you act properly? He was living with you, and we didn't know it. Do you understand?"

"I had him killed? Whom did I have killed?"

"You had your lover killed, whom else would you have had killed? We caught the poor boy. Will you ever get such a beautiful boy again?"

"Did I have him killed?"

"Yes. You had him killed."

"Oh father, listen to me.
Oh father, listen to me.
Accept my entreaty, father,
I beg of you.
Bring back my lord.
Bring back my master.
Accept my entreaty,
I beg of you.
If you don't bring him back,

If you don't bring him back,
And I'm nine months pregnant,
I'm eight months pregnant,
To whom will you give me,
And cause your name to be written?"

P. Wasn't she mocking him?

A. She was.

P. Hadn't he already died? "Daughter, I myself entreat you a thousand times; I beg of you. Don't say this to me. They've already killed him; they've already killed him. I'll call kings from all directions, and whomever you want, what will I do? I'll marry you to him. Whatever you say, and nothing else."

"If my lord had died,
If my master had died,
My heart would have throbbed;
Tears would have streamed from my eyes.
My gold bracelets would have turned black;
I wouldn't have been able to sleep.
My lord is alive."
She made her plan.

P. "Queen, oh queen!"

"Yes."

"Call someone who knows how to blow [a healer], and have him blow on your daughter. She's gone crazy. She's gone crazy. She says the boy who was killed is alive. She's gone crazy. She's gone out of her mind."

A. "She's gone out of her mind." Will the *ghāsiyā* be spared?

P. Will they be spared, or won't they be spared?

"Who do you think is crazy? What are you planning to do? Why do you think I've gone crazy? My husband is still living; he hasn't died."

"Where is he?"

"He's in this country."

"Even if he's in this country, I won't be able to recognize him."

"*You* may not be able to recognize him, but I'll recognize him. You may not be able to, but I'll recognize him. Make every man in this country come, turn by turn. Look, the king's daughter will know her husband. Make them stand in line."

[Conversation between two men called for the lineup.]

"Hey, *mahāprasād*!"

"Yes."

"You know that necklace your grandfather used to wear? Wear it and come sit by the side of the road."

"Why? What's happening?"

They were standing in lines: the old men and young boys, mature men and middle-aged men, line after line. Who was going to look at them?

"Make a platform over there," she said. "Make a platform over there," she said. They made a platform. "No," she said, "he's alive." She said, "Go now." She insisted, "Go, go and call them, the *ghāsiyā*."

"The king has ordered you to come."

"Oh, my house is ruined! Someone told! —LAUGH— Oh woman from Haldipali!"

"Yes."

"Give me your hand; I'm going to spit in your palm." —LAUGH—

"Where are you going that you want to spit in my hand first?"

"I'm going away today and won't come back. I'll stay at the king's house. Do you understand? Find the children. You used to always say, 'I'm going to my mother's place,' and you couldn't go. Take the children now. I'm going away."

"Where?"

"The king is calling me."

"So, what will happen?"

"He'll have us hung by our seats from the gallows."

"Who?"

"He'll have us four brothers hung by our seats from the gallows."

[The king asks,] "Have they come?"

"Yes."

"Sit down." As they [the *ghāsiyā*] sat down, they shit in their pants; that's how afraid they were.

"Why are you afraid? Tell the truth. Did you kill him or let him go; tell the truth. Did you kill him or let him go; tell the truth. If you killed him, nothing will happen, and if you let him go, nothing will happen. But tell the truth. You're thinking, 'We'll flatter him and tell him. We'll flatter and appease him.' What will you save through flattery? Tell me the truth," he said.

"Oh king, he escaped. He flew away and escaped."

"How?"

"We don't know. He said he'd put a lot of gold at the top of a tree, and he flew away and escaped. We didn't kill him. He got away."

"OK, OK, OK, it's OK. It's OK," he said. "It's OK. Go now, go. Bathe and wash; cook your food and eat," he said and called them.

A. Who?

P. The village watchmen. He gave the order, "Bring out all the men of the city," he said. They brought everyone out, including the one sitting on the edge of the road wearing the necklace. They set up a platform facing north. And she looked, but was he there? What? Was he?

A. No. Why would he be there? He'd escaped; he'd flown away. Would he have stayed there?

P. He wasn't there. He'd flown away. So what did he do? He flew away but turned around, changed his clothes, and went to the old flowerseller's place.

A. Poor thing.

P. "Mother, greetings."

A. He went back again. —LAUGH—

P. The old flowerseller's eyes popped out. "Who are you?" He was wearing long pants, a long-sleeved shirt, underwear, and an undershirt. "Who are you?"

"You bastard of an old woman! You said you were my mother, so I got married. Didn't you send me three letters? We got married. Where did she go? Today I came myself, and your eyes popped out. Where did she go?"

"Who?"

"Your oldest daughter. Hasn't she come back?"

"Yes, she came, my son."

"Then quickly show her to me, or else I'll lose my job."

A. "Show her quickly."

P. "My house is ruined! That child-eater left such a beautiful son and went with her *mahāprasād*. Sit down, my son," she said. "I'm going to bring jaggery and tea leaves. I'll make tea, you drink it and stay seated here. I'll go bring her. She's somewhere else, at the house of her *mahāprasād*.

"I won't drink any tea. My eyes won't be satisfied until I see her. Bring her quickly!"

A. "Go, go quickly!" She went quickly. The boy had come.

P. "Princess!"

"Yes."

"Her husband has come!"

"Who's come?"

"Her husband! Her husband! Her husband!"

"Mother, it he the wirelike man?" —LAUGH—

"What kind of wire?"

"Are you saying the wire husband, that tall one?"

"Yes, I'm saying that wire, your *mahāprasād*'s husband, has come."

"So, what should I do?"

"Bring her out. He wants to see her."

"Who?"

"Your *mahāprasād*."

"Where is she? Isn't she with you? Aren't you ashamed of yourself?"

"What answer am I supposed to give?" —LAUGH—

"She left a long time ago. Before your vegetables had even cooked, we'd formed our *mahāprasād*, and she left."

"Ohh, my dharma is broken! The minister's son had called out to her [as we were coming here]. Maybe he ran off with her somewhere." —LAUGH—

"Where is she?"

"Son, she's a loose woman. She ran away somewhere. She's not here," she said.

"Oh dear! I've lost my job and my wife, too! What should I do?" he said.

"As long as you're going to stay here, stay at my house and eat my rice and *dāl*, if you've lost your job. Are you going to be a day laborer now?"

Whose was he?

A. He was her's.

P. He was her's. Right? He had stayed. Over here, people were standing in line after line.

"All those standing here are crows and herons. All those standing here are crows and herons. There's not one swan among them, father. There's not one swan among them."

"Are there any others in any other house? Maybe there are some visitors, so go and look." —LAUGH—

"Yesterday, in our neighborhood, at the old flowerseller's house, [I heard], 'I'll give, and you eat. Here, take a little more.' She was saying, 'Here.' But I can't say who it is."

"Go to the old flowerseller's and ask if there's a man there, or what."

"Old flowerseller!"

"Yes."

"Is there someone in your house?"

"Yes."

"Who is it?"

"My own son-in-law." —LAUGH— Wasn't she giving the right answer?

A. She was giving the right one.

P. "Is he your son-in-law?"

"Yes."

"Well, here's an order from the king. Bring him outside."

"Why? Why should he go?"

"The king's daughter is identifying her husband. She said, 'He's the one in the old flowerseller's house.' "

"No, he's not."

"Then why should he go?"

"He just came yesterday, and she [the princess] is about to deliver her baby. So why should *he* go? And if she says so, then tell her this."

"You're right."

"Then go back."

"What should we do? The old woman's logic is right. What did she say? 'He came yesterday, and she's about to deliver. So why should *he* go?' she said.

—LAUGH— She's right. Let's go." They went back. She didn't let him go.

"Let's go, *mahāprasād*. Let's find out what happened, why the flowerseller won't let him come. I'm going to see."

A. Who's saying this?

P. Some other people. All the people of the city had gathered there, right?

"Let's go. 'Old flowerseller!' "

"Yes."

"Take a small bowl of thick castor oil and apply it around your waist."

"Who's talking?"

"It's the king's order. He told us to tell the old flowerseller this. He said you should leave everything else, get some oil, and apply it around your waist."

"That will be very difficult to do. It's thick oil, castor oil, —LAUGH— *bābū*!"

"Yes."

"Whose order is it? The king's? What did he say?"

"He said, 'Tell the old flowerseller to get some thick oil and apply it around her waist. I'm coming to see if she obeyed.' His whip is new. It's very hard, not at all soft. That's why he sent this order."

"What will he do with the whip?"

"He'll beat you, of course." —LAUGH—

"Why would he beat me?"

"Because you're not bringing me out," [the prince said].

"Then get up and get out! You're going to get me whipped! Get out! Hey, come get him! Come get him!" she said.

They were going back after having said that much, right? They said that she should bring him outside. What an ingenious plan they had, so that he would come out of his own accord. They got him to come out; they got him to come out and called him over. When they called him over, the princess came and grabbed his hand. This is him," she said. Isn't that what she would say?

A. It is.

P. "This is him," she said. "This is my husband," she said. "Now all of you go and bathe," she said.

A. She sent everyone to bathe.

P. "This is my husband," she said and grabbed his hand. And everyone believed her. Everyone believed her, and the king said, "Daughter, you did this of your own will, not my will. People are gathered here now, so I'm going to end this public shame," he said. And what did he do? He joined their hands and gave his daughter's hand to the boy and also put the kingdom in his name. He said, "You've been given this wealth, the kingdom, and my daughter. Look, I've handed them over to you. I've given them to you." And he joined their hands there.

A. OK. Now the prince is married. What's happening to his mother and father back in their kingdom?

P. OK. What time is it? [With this question, the performer shifts out of the narrative world into the village performance setting.]

A. It's twelve o'clock. Will he go back or not?

P. He'll go back.

A. Then tell the rest quickly.

P. I'll tell it quickly.

A. Take him back to his own kingdom.

P. OK. Then, when the king had handed over the kingdom, the prince said, "As they say, 'A dog eating his own rice is greedy for the rice of others.' There's a big problem. If my relatives lived here, then I'd say it's good. But who's here to enjoy it? And why should I enjoy the belongings of others here when they're still worried over there?" He was worried, and what did the prince say?

"Mohini, listen. I'm the son of a king. I'm an only child. My mother and father must be worrying about me. They don't know if I'm dead or alive. You stay here; I'll go for a little while."

A. "I'll come right back."

P. "I'm only going for a little while. You stay here. I'll come back in two or three days. I won't leave you," he said.

"Oh no!" she said. "Don't talk like that. Don't talk like that," she said. "Why should I stay here in someone else's house and leave my own house [that is, now identifying with her husband's house as her own]. I'll give birth there [in his parent's house]. If I give birth in my mother's house, will my name live on?" she said. "I'll go, too. I won't stay in a house that's not my own."

A. She spoke the truth.

P. What?

A. She spoke the truth.

P. Would he say no?

A. Why would he?

P. He sat her down. On what?

A. On the horse.

P. On the wooden horse, right? He seated her and told the people of the city, "Take care of the old man and woman [the king and queen]. I'm going. I promise to come back one day," he said. Then both of them sat down, and he pulled the reins of the horse. As they were going, would the horse be able to fly like he used to, quickly, quickly, quickly, quickly?

A. He wouldn't be able to.

P. Slowly, slowly, slowly, slowly, slowly, slowly, they arrived after three days and three nights.

A. Then it was the same [as the time it took the prince to come there].

P. Yes.

A. It was the same.

P. What was the same?

A. His journey.

P. It was the same: three days and three nights. It was the same. Morning broke, and he [the horse] came down. After three days and three nights, he came down. In what kind of place did he come down? In Sirco [the village of the performance]. He came down this far from that dam. He came down, and why did he come down? Her labor pains had begun as they were flying in the sky. Her labor pains had begun, and that's why he came down in that grove. After they came down, what happened?

She gave birth right away. She gave birth to a boy. Yes. She gave birth to a boy. It was a boy, and he thought, "Oh no! After this, her body must be cold. I have to warm her; then she'll be all right," he said. And what did he do?

You could see it [the village] from there. He climbed on the horse right away and flew away. "I'm coming right back. Take care of the child," he said. He went quickly. There was a prostitute's house there. There was a prostitute's house, and when he reached there, she saw that he was handsome, right?

A. Yes.

P. The prostitute saw he was a handsome man. She said, "Of all the men that I've enjoyed, I've never seen a man like this; I haven't seen one," she said. And what did she do? She quickly made some *pān* and gave it to him to eat. He forgot everything. He forgot everything. He stayed in the prostitute's house and didn't go back.

The princess saw that it was becoming evening. She thought to herself, "He said he was bringing *suṇṭhī* and *pīpal* [postpartum village medicines] and went to his country. I wonder what he's doing there. He must be bringing a car for me to go back in."

Where was the car?

A. He'd forgotten her.

P. Then what did she do? Night fell. Night fell, and she put the child to sleep with her and went to sleep herself. There where she'd gone to sleep, Mayabati Rani of the country of Mayab, who was several months pregnant, miscarried. It was a boy, and he died. Her companions were going to bury him at the graveyard. As they were going to bury him, the [other] baby cried, and what was the mother doing?

A. She was sleeping.

P. She was sleeping. As they were going, holding the dead baby, they thought they'd heard a witch. What kind of witch? They went to look, and what did they see? She was sleeping, and the baby was crying. So what did they do there? They left the dead baby and took the living baby and returned. They brought it and gave it to Mayabati Rani. They gave it to Mayabati Rani. Wouldn't the princess begin to look for him?

A. What else? Wouldn't she begin to look for him? And did she [Mayabati Rani] have to look for anything?

P. Right. She didn't need anything. She didn't need to worry about feeding, looking after, or putting the baby to sleep. She was happy. "My son had become quiet; now there's life again. That's why they've brought him back. They've done the right thing," she said. She was happy. "So, where's he from?" she said.

"The mother was dead, and the baby was crying, so that's why we put the dead one in the arms of the dead and brought this one for you. Take care of him," they said.

She was happy, and she took care of him. As she was taking care of him, the other woman woke up.

A. The queen, Mohini Rani.

P. Mohini woke up. She woke up, and what happened? It was a dead baby. The baby had died.

"Oh no!" she said. "Mine was living. Mine was living. Where did this dead one come from?" she said. "Mine was living. Where did this dead one come from? Something terrible has happened!" she said. "This isn't him," she said. Wouldn't she recognize him?

A. Of course she would. Why wouldn't she recognize her own son?

P.

"May my black karma burn!
May my birth into this caste burn.
Why haven't I died, lord?
Why hasn't Yama [god of death] eaten me?
I didn't obey my mother's words.
I didn't obey my father's words.
I didn't obey my husband's words.
I listened only to myself, lord.
Where did my lord go?
Where is my master?
Where did my son go?
Who took him?"

P. "My husband went away and didn't come back. I had a son; where is he?"

A. "He went away."

P. "He went away, and a dead one has replaced him. A terrible thing has happened! How can I keep living? I'm going to enter the jungle, and surely a tiger or snake—"

A. "Will eat me."

P. "Will eat me," she said, and she entered the jungle. But not even a fox showed itself.

The old Brahmin of that country, whose name was Haridas, had gone out to ask for alms. After spending the night in a village, he was returning. She was sitting there crying in the jungle. A beautiful woman was sitting there crying.

She was Mohini Rani. The Brahmin came and saw her and said, "You're such a beautiful daughter. Why are you sitting and crying in this dense jungle? Tell me why," he said.

"I have no mother or father, no place to stay. That's why I'm crying," she said.

"And I have no fruit or flower [descendant]. Come with me. I'll make you my daughter and take care of you," he said.

"OK," she said.

The people of that country saw her coming with the Brahmin Haridas and said, "Old Brahmin woman! There's your man. Your forehead has split open!" ["You poor thing!"]

Wiping her forehead, [she asked], "Where is the blood?"

"No, not literally! He's bringing someone else."

"What is she like?"

"Mayabati Rani doesn't even compare to her; that's what she's like."

"He has no skin on his seat and no hair on his head. What does she see in him?"

A. "She's coming."

P. "She's coming. Maybe she's coming for innocent reasons. Why am I listening to all the talk of these people?" she said. And she stayed there. She saw he was bringing her behind him. As he came closer to her, he said, "Old woman, this is our daughter."

"If I'd listened to the gossip of the other women, I would have been partner to sin today," she said. And what did she do? She took her into her lap right away, took her inside the house and loved her very much. She [the princess] forgot her husband and son and stayed in the Brahmin's house. She stayed in the Brahmin's house.

And he [the prince] was in the prostitute's house.

A. And she stayed in the Brahmin's house.

P. She stayed in the Brahmin's house. He stayed in the prostitute's house. In the king's house—

A. Their son was living.

P. Their son was living. Their son grew day by day, day by day, day by day. As he grew, he also studied. After he'd finished his education, what did he begin to wonder? "How far is the city? How many streets are there? How many alleys are there? I don't know. Until now, I've been kept busy with my education. I'm going out today, and what will I do in this country? I'll walk all around it." Saying this, what did he do?

He put on royal dress. He ate breakfast. And as he was going from street to street, street to street, alley to alley, what happened?

Having bathed, [the Brahmin's daughter] had loosened her hair and was combing it. At that time he entered their street. A woman saw him and said,

"Hey, the king's son is coming! Tie up your hair. It isn't good to have loose hair. Tie it up! Tie it up!" she said.

"OK," she said. And with her left hand, she tied it up, and the king's son came and stood there. At that time, he stood there. He stood there and saw her and said, "I've seen all the women in the city, but such a woman I've—"

A. "I've never seen."

P. "I've never seen. I've never seen a woman like this," he said and quickly went back to his house. He returned quickly and inside his house, he laid down on his cot and went to sleep. He laid down on his cot and went to sleep. While he was sleeping, his mother and father saw him.

"My son went to wander around in the city, so why is he lying down on his cot now and sleeping?" Calling and calling to him, they got tired.

Upon his return, he'd gotten obstinate. They tried to feed him, but he wouldn't eat. Finally, they called an old matchmaker. They called the old woman and said, "Why won't our son eat? Make him happy," they said.

The old matchmaker, the old grandmother made many preparations. She made many plans. "Hey, old woman," he said, "why are you making so many plans here and there. Why are you looking here and there, here and there?" he said. "Go and tell them that only if I marry that Brahmin's daughter will my life be saved. Otherwise, I'll die," he said.

"How sad! Here you are, a great king, and following the desire of your own heart, you fell in love with the daughter of a mendicant," she said. "Call Haridas," she said.

"Oh Haridas!"

"Yes."

"My son loves your daughter. Will you give her to him or not?"

"I can't say. I'll go and ask my daughter."

"Why did the king call you?"

"The king's son has fallen in love with you and says he'll marry you. What answer should I give to them?" he said.

"Tell them 'No.' "

"If I say 'No,' they'll drag you there."

"What do you mean, they'll drag me there."

A. "What do you mean?"

P. "They'll drag you there," he said. "What kind of father am I that I can protect you?" Didn't he say the right thing?

A. He did.

P. "OK. Tell them to give a calf and a cow of the same color. This evening the king's son should come to my house, and I'll give an answer," she said.

And he said, "King, my daughter will get married, but she wants to give the answer to your son. He should come to our house at sunset and bring with him a cow and a calf of the same color."

"OK," [the king] said.

"And bring two hundred rupees."

Instead of two hundred, he gave four hundred. And he gave a calf and a cow of the same color. When evening fell, he put on royal clothes and shoes.

"You called me," he said. And as he knocked, knocked, knocked, knocked, what did she do? She lit four lamps in the four corners and made up a bed and prepared all kinds of food. What was the king's son going to do?

A. He was going to sit inside.

P. Thinking, "He'll come to my house," she got ready. She got ready. When he came, they were tied in front of the door. Who were tied?

A. The horse, cow, and calf.

P. He jumped down on one foot, and it landed on the calf's tail. He was standing on it. On the tail. He was about to put down the other foot when the calf said, "Mother, he's crushing me with his foot! Mother, he's crushing me with his foot!"

"He's crushing you, but what can I do? Can a mother seize her son?"

Hearing this, would he step down with his other foot? He turned around and went back. He turned around and went back. He went home and said, "There's something strange. The cow talks. Why did she say this?" he said. As he wondered about this, the night passed; he didn't sleep at all. Morning broke.

Mayabati Rani saw him. She said, "My son has gone to the Brahmin's house," and she made all kinds of food and said, "Get up, son, and brush your teeth."

"Mother, I won't eat and I won't stay here. If you tell me the truth, I'll stay; otherwise, I won't stay."

"Tell me what happened. Tell me. Why would I lie to you?"

"Was I born through your womb, or did you find me somewhere else and raise me? Tell me this."

A. "Tell the truth."

P. "Tell the truth."

"Son, I didn't give birth to you and raise you," she said. "I found you and raised you. What happened to the one born through my womb?"

A. "He died."

P. "He died. My companions went to bury him. Your mother had died there. So they brought you and gave you to me and put the dead one there."

"Then the cow spoke the truth, didn't she?"

A. Yes, yes.

P. "The cow is my mother. That's why the cow couldn't act, and that's why she spoke the truth. This isn't my mother," he said.

"Who is she?"

A. "She's my mother."

P. "She's my mother. Call the old Brahmin."

"Brahmin!"

"Yes."

"Tell the truth. Is this really your daughter?"

"I had gone begging, and she was sitting in the jungle crying. So, I brought her back with me."

"Call her here."

"Where are you from? Tell me who you are. The old Brahmin said you're not his. Where are you from?"

"The son of King Manicandra of Madhukatak, Malya Basant. The son of King Manicandra of Madhukatak, Malya Basant. I'm a king's daughter, of the lineage of the sun, Surya. My name is Mohini. I was going with my husband on a flying wooden horse. I had labor pains and gave birth to a son in the jungle. My husband brought us to this country. If he went to his own country or stayed in this country, I can't say. I went to sleep, holding my son, in the jungle that night. Who brought a dead son and put him there, and who took my living son?"

A. "Took him."

P. "Who took him," right?

A. Yes.

P. "I'm that son." Isn't that what he'd say? "I'm that son, but who are you? You're my mother. You're my mother, and I'm that son. So how will the people of this country believe this?"

The proverb says, "Have faith in the truth, and you'll receive hidden wealth."

"If you're my mother, and I'm the son born of your womb, then if I say, 'Mother!' and open my mouth, milk will flow from your breast into my mouth."

Her breasts had been dry for eighteen years, but when he opened his mouth, a stream of milk began to flow. Calling on god, the mother and son stood there, and everyone knew—

A. They were mother and son.

P. They knew they were mother and son. They knew for sure that they were mother and son. They met each other. After they met, the boy asked, "Mother, where did my father go?"

She said, "Son, your father came to this country, to this city, to get some medicine. After getting the medicine, he went somewhere, but where, I can't say."

"Mother," he said, "my father must be in this country. I won't be able to recognize him, but you'll recognize him."

"Yes," she said.

They called all the men of the city. They called all the men of the city.

They called them all, and did she recognize him? Did she?

A. Who knew where he was?

P. Was he there?

A. He was at the prostitute's house; he must have been at the prostitute's house.

P. "Look, are there any other men somewhere else?"

Then what did someone say? "There's someone in the prostitute's house. There's someone in the prostitute's house."

"Go and tell the prostitute to bring him outside."

"Oh Hirabati!"

"Yes."

"It's the king's order that you bring out whoever is in your house."

"Who's talking? I'll shit on his face!"

What did she say?

Tāre nāre . . .

Slowly, slowly, they all went there.
Slowly, slowly, they all went there.
The daughter [prostitute] swore at them;
She insulted them.
The king couldn't bear it.

He asked for a new whip.
The king went there himself.
He went there himself.
He called Hirabati.
He called Hirabati.
He hit her with the whip.
He hit her twice.
He hit her three times.
The prostitute's navel burst.
With pain, she sat up.
The prostitute crawled, crawled over to him.

She wiped it [the spell] off.
The prince began to remember.
He began to remember.

P. The horse was in the courtyard.

A. Yes.

P. He came, sat down on it, and flew off. Where did he go?

A. To the jungle.

P. To that jungle where the child had been born, that's where he flew to. When he arrived there, he began to roll around on the ground and cry. —LAUGH—

A. Why would he find them there?

P. "Why did I leave you and go away? A tiger must have come and swallowed both mother and son!" he said. He was rolling around on the ground and crying. They ran after him. "That's him!" they said, and they ran after him. They ran and—

A. Grabbed him.

P. They grabbed him and brought him. She said, "Look, this is your son, and here I am and here you are. The three of us have met. Don't be out of your mind."

"Yes," he said, "the three of us have met. Yes, this is my son. But, look how big he is! Look how big he is!"

"That's natural. We're talking in the present, so that's why he's so big. You're talking as if he were *born* today." —LAUGH—

A. "Fourteen years have passed."

P. He's a boy of eighteen.

A. "Eighteen years have passed."

P. "All right, then let's go back to our country."

But the king, joining his hands together, begged them to stay. "This country is all yours," he said.

"Yes, this country, too, will be mine," he said. When he left them, he said, "I promise to come back one day and be your king."

The three of them climbed on the horse. They climbed on the horse and went to their own country. Here, the old man and old woman [king and queen] had been very worried. The old man and old woman were very worried. They were worried, and when they heard the news, they were relieved. And in a beautiful way—

A. The five of them met.

P. The five of them met. The king was happy, the queen was happy, and they all ate together, content and happy.

A. They stayed there and lived. Did they let the thieves [carpenter and goldsmith] go, or not?

P. They let them go.

[Performer removes the lantern from the basket and turns it off.]

Sample Transcriptions of Performance Texts

(Page numbers are those on which verses appear in text)

Chapter 2: *Bhojalī*

Page 30:

devī gaṅgā devī gaṅgā
lahar turaṅgā ho
tumhar lahar bhojalī
bhīje āṭḥo aṅgā

Page 31:

kahā̃ ke to khātu māṭī
kahā̃ ke to caṅghoriyā
kahā̃ ke to caṅghoriyā
bhojalī jamoiyā
hā̃ ho devī gaṅgā . . .

raygaṛh ke to khātu māṭī
candarpur caṅghoriyā
candarpur caṅghoriyā
phuljhar ke to pīlī bāī
bhojalī jamoiyā
hā̃ ho devī gaṅgā . . .

kahā̃ ke khātu māṭī
kahā̃ ke ṭuknī
kahā̃ ke ṭuknī
cūhaya motī pānī
hā̃ ho devī gaṅgā . . .

kumhār ghar ke khātu māṭī
karrā ghar ke ṭuknī
karrā ghar ke ṭuknī

rājā ghar ke javā bhojalī
cūhaya motī pānī
hā̃ ho devī gaṅgā . . .

Page 32: (without all the repetitions provided in the translation)
dḥimika dḥimi mor bājan bajāī o dḥimika dḥimi
mor bājan bajāī o kahā̃ ke bājan
āy rāhilā o kahā̃ ke bājan
. . .
telin kalārin dāī bhojalī ujhānay o telin kalārin
dāī bhojalī ujhānay o jihā̃ ke bājan
āy rāhilā o jihā̃ ke bājan

Page 33: līpī dāren potī dāren
chāṛī paren konhā ho
chāṛī paren konhā ho
hamre bhojalī dāī ke dekhat rabo conhā
hā̃ ho devī gaṅgā . . .

Page 34: acarī tariyā gayen
pacharī piṭāyen ho
pacharī piṭāyen ho
ajab gajab tariyā ke pār bhojalī paloyen
hā̃ ho devī gaṅgā. . .

Page 38: jal binā machlī
pavan binā dhān
pavan binā dhān
sevā binā bhojalī
ke tarasthay parān
hā̃ ho devī gaṅgā . . .

Page 38: mā̃ḍī bhar jondharī
poris kuśiyare
poris kuśiyare
jaldī jaldī baṛhā
bhojalī huśiyāre
hā̃ ho devī gaṅgā . . .

Page 39: āī gaīs pūrā bohāī gaīs kacrā
hamro bhojalī dāī ke sone sone añcarā
āī gaīs pūrā bohāī gaīs malgī
hamro bhojalī dāī ke sone sone kalgī

Page 39: dūdh maṅgen pūt maṅgen

au maṅgen āśīś
au maṅgen āśīś
tḥāre hai kosilyā
devathay āśīś
hā̃ ho devī gaṅgā . . .

Page 41: kaunav ceghe hāthiyā
kaunav ceghe ghoṛvā
kaunav ceghe ghoṛvā
kaunav ceghe pālukī
kaunav ceghe ḍolvā
hā̃ ho devī gaṅgā . . .

rājā ceghe hāthiyā
devānā ceghe ghoṛvā
devānā ceghe ghoṛvā
rānī ceghe pālukī
bhojalī ceghe ḍolvā
hā̃ ho devī gaṅgā . . .

kaun gā̃ ke kārī tūrī
kaun gā̃ ke sagāvā ho
kaun gā̃ ke sagāvā ho
jabhe ānbe nādhik nādhī
tabhe ceghav ḍolvā
hā̃ ho devī gaṅgā . . .

Page 41: tulsī ke caũrā
mukut bhaige āṅganā
mukut bhaige āṅganā
phire phire bāmhan devtā
bharī ha lagānā
hā̃ ho devī gaṅgā . . .

Page 42: ghīr ghīr motar āye
bhītar lage tālā
bhītar lage tālā
jarrā gā̃ ke tūrāman lā
lege pulīs wālā
hā̃ ho devī gaṅgā . . .

kahā̃ ke to dār cāur
kahā̃ ke to baṅganiyā
kahā̃ ke to baṅganiyā
kahā̃ ke to dīṛva chokrā

bulthe maṅjhiniyā
hā̃ ho devī gaṅgā . . .

narsiṅgpur ke dār cāur
jagdīśpur ke baṅganiyā
jagdīśpur ke baṅganiyā
jarrā ke dīṛva chokrā
bulthe maṅjhiniyā
hā̃ ho devī gaṅgā . . .

Page 43: jhan jhan murdaṅg bājā
bāje bāje kartāle
bāje bāje kartāle
hamar ghar ke mālik nāithe
lebo parsāde
hā̃ ho devī gaṅgā . . .

Page 44: bā̃se ke ṭhoṛā me
bharī daren cāur
bharī daren cāur
kahar mahar karte
bhojalī dāī ke rāhū
hā̃ ho devī gaṅgā . . .

bā̃se ke ṭhoṛā me
raṅga coṭī dāī ke
raṅga coṭī dāī ke
māthe he raṅgoiyā
bhojalī bonā dāī ke
hā̃ ho devī gaṅgā . . .

Page 45: thārī nā ākā cāur
gārḥulā me dūdh
gārḥulā me dūdh
ṭhāre hai kauśalya bāī
māṅgthe putra
hā̃ ho devī gaṅgā . . .

Chapter 3: *Ḍālkhāī*

Page 53: ki ḍālkhāī re
māgh re mādhav āsibe balī
sej sajāṛī hī pākhuṛā malī

mānikyar dīp jālī basīchī
cakśu ujāgare dūtī lo
pāhī galā nītī chāṛī de bāṭh
nandar cāṭ rāhī kesarī nāī pāre bhūlī
ki ḍālkhāī re

ki ḍālkhāī re
phāgun mās re phāgu durlabh
phāgu khelu thībe rādhā mādhabh
phāgu kuṇḍare karpur mesāī
phāgu khelu thībe ilī lo
jādhu gosāī chāṛī de bāṭh
ki ḍālkhāī re

Chapter 4: *Suā Nāc*

Page 82: tore ghar ke muhutī kaise samāū nīe
tore ghar ke ho re tore ghar ke muhutī

Page 83: [without verse repetitions]
jaise o maiyā tum liho aur diho
re suānā ho jaise mẽ liho re āśīś

anne aur dhanne tor ghar bharīa
re suānā jiho maiyā lākho vārīś

bālak beṭā bīhā karī lāne
re suānā ho korā me nātī khelā

Page 84: baṛe ghar baṛe ghar kahā̃ te āe
e suānā baṛe o ghar die man ṭare

jogī bairāgī sabo din sabo din
e suānā hamu diā bachar din

Page 85: rise ke mare bhītar paśī jāe
e suānā herio āno sūpā bharī dhān

Page 86: kahar kahar kare mor kārī koilī re
e suānā ho mirīgā bole re ādhī rāt

e nind soiche mor gāõ ke gauṇṭiyā
e suānā jekar bahinī gae pardeś . . .

Page 92: jao jao suā andanban candanban
re suānā ṭorī āno āmā ghāū

kāhe reṅgī jāiho āū kāhe uṛiho
re suānā ho kāhe me lānī ho ho ṭor

pavo reṅgī jāibe pakurī uṛī āibe
re suānā ho cõce mẽ ānī ho ho ṭor

āne bar ānihõ māi āmā ghaūlā
re suānā ho kone lā dihõ re dharāy

bārah bachar ke candanmatī tḥaṛgī
re suānā johī lā suā debe re dharāy

Page 99: chāṭī tor phāṭige re ā̃khī tor phūṭige
re suānā wahī de tor bahinī ke ghar

Page 99: hā̃ṛī dhovat dhovat bhaujī dekhat he
re suānā līgirrā lagāy ke nandan har

Page 100: bhāī lā dehẽ raṅg mahalā dumhalā
re suānā ham lā tai dehẽ videś

Initial Verses of "The Song of Subanbali"

ramo ramo śri horī rāmo je
ramo ramo śri horī rāmo

garūrḥ la bāhan gu rāmo
kauśalyā nandan

banu acche sarlā debī me
banu acche maṅglā moro

prasanna hoibe sarlā
prasanna hoibe

ādī kandar gurī ānī mūī
kapīl sarg ānī

śibankar bāhunī re sarla
śibankar bāhunī

ete bele suban baile
ete bele suban baile

kurḥī kā̃cī dharī karī
hāthe ṭupulī dhārī

khel ghar gale re suban
khel ghar gale

e khel gharẽ khel khelile
khel gharẽ khel khelile

rājestī je māne re
mor bambāī śahar

kaṭak rāj ra bambāī
mor kaṭak śahar

kāl paṛī thīle rājestī
tumba gāṛī thīle

rūndha moro re randhāī karī
mor khāī karī mor pī karī

sej ka palaṅg karī re moro
rājestī je pua

dasāī suile go se māne
dasāī suile

ete bele bandhiyā rājā re
eṛe duṣṭḥ māno

Kathānī Kūhā: Initial Lines after the *Vandanā*

P. guṭe steśan te thīlā. guṭe steśan te thīlā. āū seī sṭeśan thī̃ moṭor sena kā̃r haū̃che? ki ā . . . senu jamā haū̃che ār senu pher dūsar dūsar dig ke moṭar cālū hoū̃che. je sṭeśan thī lok utī̃rsan aur kā̃r karasan?

A. ipāk sepāk jāisan.

P. je sṭeśan thī̃ lok utī̃rsan aur kā̃r karasan?

A. caghsan ghale.

P. neī? duhī ṭa hesī, hẽ? utī̃rsan aur caghsan ghale. je sena caghā utrā hesī sṭeśan thī̃ āū kichī neīna agbār bhajiyā̃ ai.

je sena kā̃r haū̃che? purub digū̃ ghale gāṛī ailā ār paścim digū̃ ghale gāṛī āilā. āū se sṭeśan thī̃ duhẽkar gāṛī kā̃r helā?

A. ṭḥāṛ helā.

P. ṭḥāṛ helā, hā̃, sena ṭḥāṛ helā. se sṭeśan thī̃ gāṛī ṭḥāṛ helā. ṭḥāṛ helā sehī samay thī̃ je se gāṛī lok ghale utīrle ārī gāṛī lok ghale utīrle. neī?

A. hā̃.

P. ki neī utrī̃?

A. utīrle.

P. utīrle. acchā, duhī gāṛī lok utīrle. je senu se duhī gāṛī jane jane duī lok jāikarī̃ kā̃r kale je? guṭe chāī tale basle. duhī lūka guṭe chāī tale basle, āū se chāī tale basbā mātar ke jane bailā, "bhāī, muī̃ bahut dhurīyathū̃ āsuchẽ lekin mor na kāṛī thīlā sarī galā bīṛī ṭā ache," bailā.

"je bhāī, muĩ nuā̃ kāṛī ghinī thīlĩ mor bīṛī sarī galā na, mor na kāṛī ache," bailā.

duhī luka bīṛī āū kāṛī bāhar kale, sena pīle aur sena se paricay nīā̃ nūī hele. duhī jan se bīṛī kāṛī kale tārpare se mane kā̃r kārīchan? je paricay nīā̃ nūī hele. paricay mane?

A. cīn pahcān.

P. tuĩ kenar aū? tuĩ kā̃hī jaūchū? itā paricay heūche. ta senu duhī lukar paricay heūchan.

Song: tāre tāre tāre tāre re tāre tā tāre re re nāre nāre re.

keū̃ deśū̃ tuĩ ta āsīachū?
keū̃ deśū̃ tuĩ ta āsīachū?
sṭeśane rahichū re bhāī.
kāhĩ ke jāūchū?
tor paricay detū ke bābū,
paricay detū.

purubaru muĩ āsūache.
paścim ku re jāūche.
muĩ kām kā̃ sīkhīchẽ je bhāī;
dām ka neūche.
deś deś kāi būlūche re muĩ ta.
kām kāi karu.
keū̃ dīgru tuĩ āsīachū?
kāhir lāgī mote puchūchū?
keū̃ deś ke ta jībū re tuĩ ta?
nagra ke ta jībū?

mā̃ nāī mor gaõ nāī.
bāpo nāī mor thābo nāī.
muĩ jībī kito kāhĩ je bhāī
jībī kito kāhĩ?
muĩ ta kām re sīkhīchẽ
deś deś kāi būlua.
muĩ ṭhīkā kāi naūche je bhāī.
ṭhīkā kāi naū.

Glossary

ādivāsī	literally, original inhabitants; tribal; castes with tribal origins, such as the Gonds
bābū	term of address for distinguished person; title of respect
bāhak	Oriya performer who sings, drums, and dances for "each of the thirteen festivals"
bahū	daughter-in-law; often used as term of address by members of the extended family other than the mother- or father-in-law
bā̃s gīt	songs sung by cowherding Raut caste to accompaniment of large bamboo flutes
bhajan	devotional song
bhakti	religious devotion
bhāv	emotion; character or quality
bhojalī	nine-day festival celebrating the *bhojalī* goddess in her form as sprouts/seedlings
bīṛī	hand-rolled cigarettes made from leaves and cheap tobacco; many *ādivāsī* castes in Chhattisgarh make a living by picking these leaves from the jungle and rolling the cigarettes; often pronounced and transcribed *bīḍī*
burā/burī	"bad"; obscene
candainī	regional Chhattisgarhi epic whose heroine carries the same name, Candaini
celā	disciple; in performance, accompanying a lead singer/dancer
dāī	Chhattisgarhi term for mother
dāl	pulse; lentil
ḍālkhāī	festival of reversal for unmarried girls, celebrated in Phuljhar

darśan	auspicious sight; one "takes *darśan*" of a deity in worship of a *mūrti*
daśharā	festival celebrating Ram's defeat of the demon Ravan
devī	goddess
dharma	religious duty; proper action
durgā pūjā	festival honoring the goddess Durga
gānā	song
gaṇés caturthī	festival honoring the deity Ganesh, the elephant-headed god who removes obstacles
garḥ	fort
gaurā	*ādivāsī* festival celebrating the marriage of the god Shiva and the goddess Parvati
gāyak	lead singer, often accompanied by disciple or other singers
ghāṭ	bank of a river or tank where people go to bathe, wash clothes; landing place
gīt	song
holī	spring festival of reversal, during which colored water or powder is sprayed/applied on friends or passers-by
homo	Oriya girls' repartee song/game tradition
jāti	regional, endogamous caste group, in which one's position is fixed by birth
javārā	nine-day goddess festival, in which goddess is honored in form of seedlings/sprouts
kahānī	story
kathā	story; often with implications of a ritual/religious story, such as *vrat kathā* (stories told at ritual fasts)
kathānī kūhā	Oriya professional storyteller
khel	game
kissā	story, tale
kos	measure of distance, approximately two miles
kśatriya	warrior caste level/*varṇa*
lākh	100,000
laṛiyā	form of Chhattisgarhi spoken on the borders of Chhattisgarh and Orissa, highly influenced by Oriya
lok gīt	folk song
lok sāhitya	folk literature
Mahabharata	[*mahābhārat*] pan-Indian epic tradition whose central story recounts the struggle over succession to the throne of Kurukshetra, resulting in a great battle between the Pandava and Kaurava cousin-brothers; Sanskrit version attributed to sage Vyasa; Chhattisgarhi orally performed variant called *paṇḍvānī*

mahāprasād	ritual friend or friendship, formed by exchanging *prasād* from a ritual
maikā	woman's home of birth; literally, "mother's place"
majedār	amusing; pleasant; pleasing
maṇḍalī	small group; singing group
manorañjan	entertainment; amusement; recreation
mātar	festival celebrated by cowherding Raut caste
mṛdaṅg	type of drum
muṅg	type of pulse/lentil
mūrti	image; specifically, image of a deity
nācā	dance-drama
nāṭak	drama
navrātri	auspicious period of nine days, one in the spring and one in the fall, during which the goddess is worshiped
pān	betel leaf
paṇḍvānī	Chhattisgarhi performance genre of the Mahabharata (name taken from the five Pandava brothers)
pārā	neighborhood
pardeś	foreign country
pativratā	literally, one who fulfills her vows to her husband; a woman who is faithful to her husband
prasād	food offerings to deity, distributed to worshipers after *pūjā*
pūjā	ritual of worship in which the deity is served in various ways (offerings made of water, food, flowers, etc.)
purana	[*purāṇ*] a Sanskrit or regional-language religious text that records the "old stories" of ancient days; a principal source of Hindu mythology
rāg	melodic structure; tune
rāgī	literally, one who keeps the *rāg;* accompanist to lead singer
Ramayana	[*rāmāyaṇ*] pan-Indian epic tradition that recounts the life and deeds of the hero-god Ram, including his battle against the demon Ravan, who had abducted Ram's wife Sita; Sanskrit version composed by the sage Valmiki; Hindi version composed by poet Tulsidas as *Rāmcaritmānas*
Rāmcaritmānas	a Hindi (Awadhi) sixteenth-century devotional version of the Ramayana written by the poet Tulsidas
rāmlīlā	dramatic performance of Ramayana
ṛṣi/rishi	sage; ascetic
saṅgvārī	literally, companion; accompanist to lead singer
śāstra	authoritative religious text
sasurāl	woman's home/village of marriage; home/village of woman's in-laws

sat	literally, truth; honor, virtue
sevā	service; *sevā karnā,* to serve
suā nāc	parrot dance; *ādivāsī* female harvest dance and song tradition
talāb	tank; reservoir
tambūrā	stringed instrument used to accompany singer; characteristic instrument for *paṇḍvānī* performance
tapas	ascetic practice; penance
tulsī	sacred basil plant representing the goddess
tyohār	festival
vandanā	invocation
varṇa	one of four hierarchical caste levels (*brāhmaṇ, kśatriya, vaiśya, śūdra*)
vīhā gīt	wedding song
yagya	standard Hindi *yajña*; sacrifice, ritual offering

Bibliography

Abrahams, Roger D. 1976. The Complex Relations of Simple Forms. In *Folklore Genres,* edited by Dan Ben-Amos, 193–214. Austin: University of Texas Press.

Abrahams, Roger D., and Richard Bauman. 1978. Ranges of Festival Behavior. In *The Reversible World: Symbolic Inversion in Art and Society,* edited by Barbara A. Babcock. Ithaca: Cornell University Press.

Abrahams, Roger D., and Richard Bauman. 1971. Sense and Nonsense in St. Vincent: Speech Behavior and Decorum in a Caribbean Community. *American Anthropologist* 73: 762–772.

Anderson, Benedict R. O'G. 1983. *Imagined Communities: Reflections on the Origin and Spread of Nationalism.* London: Verso.

Appadurai, Arjun, Frank J. Korom, and Margaret A. Mills, eds. 1991. *Gender, Genre, and Power in South Asian Expressive Traditions.* Philadelphia: University of Pennsylvania Press.

Babb, Lawrence. 1975. *The Divine Hierarchy: Popular Hinduism in Central India.* New York: Columbia University Press.

Babcock, Barbara A., ed. 1978. *The Reversible World: Symbolic Inversion in Art and Society.* Ithaca: Cornell University Press.

Badone, Ellen. 1987. Ethnicity, Folklore, and Local Identity in Rural Brittany. *Journal of American Folklore* 100: 161–190.

Bailey, F. G. 1960. *Tribe, Caste, and Nation: A Study of Political Activity and Political Change in Highland Orissa.* Manchester: Manchester University Press.

Bakhtin, M. M. 1986. The Problem of Speech Genres. In *Speech Genres and Other Late Essays,* translated by Vern W. McGee, edited by Caryl Emerson and Michael Holquist, 60–102. Austin: University of Texas Press.

Barth, Fredrik. 1969. Pathan Identity and Its Maintenance. In *Ethnic Groups and Boundaries: The Social Organization of Cultural Difference,* edited by Fredrik Barth, 117–134. London: Allen & Unwin.

Bauman, Richard. 1992a. Contextualization, Tradition, and the Dialogue of Genres: Icelandic Legends of the *Kraftskald.* In *Rethinking Context: Language as an Interactive Phenomenon,* edited by Charles Goodwin and Alessandro Duranti, 125–146. Cambridge: Cambridge University Press.

——. 1992b. Genre. In *Folklore, Cultural Performances, and Popular Entertainments: A Communications-Centered Handbook,* edited by Richard Bauman, 53–59. New York: Oxford University Press.

——. 1986. *Story, Performance, and Event: Contextual Studies of Oral Narrative.* Cambridge: Cambridge University Press.

——. 1977. *Verbal Art as Performance.* Rowley, Mass.: Newbury House.

Bauman, Richard, and Joel Sherzer, eds. 1974 [1989, 2d edition]. *Explorations in the Ethnography of Speaking.* New York: Cambridge University Press.

Beck, Brenda E. 1982. *The Three Twins: The Telling of a South Indian Folk Epic.* Bloomington: Indiana University Press.

Ben-Amos, Dan. 1976. Analytical Categories and Ethnic Genres. In *Folklore Genres,* edited by Dan Ben-Amos, 215–242. Austin: University of Texas Press.

Blackburn, Stuart, and A. K. Ramanujan, eds. 1986. *Another Harmony: New Essays on the Folklore of India.* Berkeley: University of California Press.

Blackburn, Stuart H., and Joyce Burkhalter Flueckiger. 1989. Introduction. In *Oral Epics in India,* edited by Stuart H. Blackburn, Peter J. Claus, Joyce B. Flueckiger, and Susan S. Wadley, 1–11. Berkeley: University of California Press.

Bose, Nandini, and Pradipta Bhattacharjee. 1984. Folk Theatre: Neither Exclusive nor Esoteric. *Sunday Statesman* (New Delhi), April 22.

Briggs, Charles L. 1988. *Competence in Performance: The Creativity of Tradition in Mexicano Verbal Art.* Philadelphia: University of Pennsylvania Press.

Chadwick, Nora Kershaw, and Victor Zhirmunsky. 1969. *The Oral Epics of Central Asia.* Cambridge: Cambridge University Press.

Claus, Peter J. 1989. Behind the Text: Performance and Ideology in a Tulu Oral Tradition. In *Oral Epics in India,* edited by Stuart H. Blackburn et al., 55–74. Berkeley: University of California Press.

Coccari, Diane. 1984. The *Bir Babas* of Banaras: An Analysis of a Guardian Deity in North Indian Folk Hinduism. Ph.D. dissertation. University of Wisconsin.

Cohen, Anthony P. 1982. Belonging: The Experience of Culture. In *Belonging: Identity and Social Organization in British Rural Cultures,* edited by Anthony P. Cohen, 1–18. Manchester: Manchester University Press.

Crooke, William. [1896] 1978. *The Popular Religion and Folklore of India.* Vol. 2. Reprint, New Delhi: Munshiram Manoharlal.

Dange, A. S. 1973. An Analysis of Sex-Ratio Differentials by Regions of Madhya Pradesh. *Artha Vijnana* 14 (3): 273–286.

David, Kenneth. 1980. Hidden Powers: Cultural and Socio-economic Accounts of Jaffna Women. In *The Powers of Tamil Women,* edited by Susan S. Wadley, 93–136. Syracuse: Maxwell School of Citizenship and Public Affairs, Syracuse University.

De Lauretis, Teresa. 1987. *Technologies of Gender: Essays on Theory, Film, and Fiction.* Bloomington: Indiana University Press.

Dimmitt, Cornelia, and J. A. B. van Buitenen, ed. and trans. 1978. *Classical Hindu Mythology: A Reader in the Sanskrit Purāṇas.* Philadelphia: Temple University Press.

Doniger, Wendy, ed. 1993. *Purāṇa Perennis: Reciprocity and Transformation in Hindu and Jaina Texts.* Albany: State University of New York Press.

——. 1991. Fluid and Fixed Texts in India. In *Boundaries of the Text,* edited by Joyce Burkhalter Flueckiger and Laurie J. Sears, 31–41. Ann Arbor: Center for South and Southeast Asian Studies, University of Michigan.

Dube, Amritlal. 1963. *Tulsi ke Birva Jagay: Chattisgarh ke Kuch Lok Git* [Awakening the *tulsi* plant: some folk songs of Chhattisgarh]. Chhindwara, India: Adimjati Anusandhan.

Dube, S. C. 1963. *Field Songs of Chhattisgarh.* Chhindwara, India: Adimjati Anusandhan.

Dundes, Alan. 1983. Defining Identity through Folklore. In *Identity: Personal and Sociocultural,* edited by Anita Jacobson-Widding, 235–240. Uppsala: Acta Universitatis Upsaliensis.

Egnor, Margaret. 1980. On the Meaning of Śakti to Women in Tamil Nadu. In *The Powers of Tamil Women,* edited by Susan S. Wadley, 1–34. Syracuse: Maxwell School of Citizenship and Public Affairs, Syracuse University.

Elwin, Verrier. 1946. *Folk-songs of Chhattisgarh.* Madras: Oxford University Press.

——. 1944. *Folk-tales of Mahakoshal.* London: Oxford University Press.

Elwin, Verrier, and Shamrao Hivale. 1944. *Folk-songs of the Maikal Hills.* Madras: Oxford University Press.

Fernandez, James. 1986. *Persuasions and Performances: The Play of Tropes in Culture.* Bloomington: Indiana University Press.

Fine, Elizabeth C. 1984. *The Folklore Text: From Performance to Print.* Bloomington: Indiana University Press.

Flueckiger, Joyce Burkhalter. 1993. *Paṇḍvānī* Heroines, Chhattisgarhi Daughters: Mahabharata Performance as a Regional Folklore Genre. Paper presented at the Wisconsin Annual Conference on South Asia, November, Madison.

——. 1991a. Literacy and the Changing Concept of Text: Women's Ramayana *Maṇḍalī* in Central India. In *Boundaries of the Text: Epic Performances in South and Southeast Asia,* edited by Joyce Burkhalter Flueckiger and Laurie J. Sears, 43–60. Ann Arbor: Center for South and Southeast Asian Studies, University of Michigan.

——. 1991b. Genre and Community in the Folklore System of Chhattisgarh. In *Gender, Genre, and Power in South Asian Expressive Traditions,* edited by Arjun Appadurai et al., 181–200. Philadelphia: University of Pennsylvania Press.

——. 1989. Caste and Regional Variants of an Epic Tradition: The Lorik-Candā Epic. In *Oral Epics in India,* edited by Stuart H. Blackburn et al., 33–54. Berkeley: University of California Press.

——. 1988. "He Should Have Worn a Sari": A Failed Performance of a Chhattisgarhi Oral Epic. *The Drama Review* T117: 59–169.

——. 1987. Land of Wealth, Land of Famine: The *Suā Nāc* (Parrot Dance) of Central India. *Journal of American Folklore* 100 (395): 39–57.

——. 1983. *Bhojalī:* Song, Goddess, Friend. *Asian Folklore Studies* 42: 27–43.

Flueckiger, Joyce Burkhalter, and Laurie J. Sears, ed. 1991. *Boundaries of the Text: Epic Performances in South and Southeast Asia.* Ann Arbor: Center for South and Southeast Asian Studies, University of Michigan.

Furer-Haimendorf, Christoph von, and [in collaboration with] Elizabeth von Furer-Haimendorf. 1979. *The Gonds of Andhra Pradesh: Tradition and Change in an Indian Tribe.* London: George Allen & Unwin.

Gennep, Arnold van. 1909. *The Rites of Passage.* Translated by Monika V. Vizedom and Gabrielle L. Caffee. London: Routledge and Kegan Paul.

"Ghanshyām," Babu Mahadevprasad Singh. n.d. *Lorikāyan: Hardigarḥ kī Laṛāī* [*Lorikāyan:* The battle of Fort Hardi]. Benaras: Thakurpasad and Sons Bookseller.

Gluckman, Max. 1954. *Rituals of Rebellion in South East Africa.* Manchester: Manchester University Press.

Goffman, Erving. 1974. *Frame Analysis: An Essay on the Organization of Experience.* Cambridge: Harvard University Press.

Gold, Ann Grodzins. 1988. *Fruitful Journeys: The Ways of Rajasthani Pilgrims.* Berkeley: University of California Press.

——. 1986. Chorused Conversations in Rajasthan. Paper presented at the 15th Conference on South Asia, Madison, Wisconsin.

Goodwin, Charles, and Alessandro Duranti, eds. 1992. *Rethinking Context: Language as an Interactive Phenomenon.* Cambridge: Cambridge University Press.

Gossen, Gary. 1974. *Chamulas in the World of the Sun.* Cambridge: Harvard University Press.

Grierson, George. 1929. The Birth of Lorik. In *Studies in Honor of Charles Rockwell Lanman,* n.ed., 243–254. Cambridge: Harvard University Press.

Gumperz, John J. 1971. *Languages in Social Groups.* Stanford: Stanford University Press.

Gumperz, John J., and Dell Hymes, eds. 1972. *Directions in Sociolinguistics: The Ethnography of Communication.* New York: Holt, Rinehart and Winston.

Handelman, Don. 1990. *Models and Mirrors: Towards an Anthropology of Public Events.* New York: Cambridge University Press.

Handelman, Don, and David Shulman. In Press. *God Inside Out: Śiva's Game of Dice.* New York: Oxford University Press.

Hanks, William. 1987. Discourse Genres in a Theory of Practice. *American Ethnologist* 14 (4): 668–692.

Hansen, Kathryn. 1988. The Vīrāṅganā in North Indian History, Myth, and Popular Culture. *Economic and Political Weekly* 23 (18): 25–33.

Henry, Edward O. 1988. *Chant the Names of God: Musical Culture in Bhojpuri-Speaking India.* San Diego: San Diego State University Press.

Hiltebeitel, Alf. 1991. *The Cult of Draupadī.* Vol. 2, *On Hindu Ritual and the Goddess.* Chicago: University of Chicago Press.

——. 1988. *The Cult of Draupadī.* Vol. 1, *Mythologies: From Gingee to Kurukṣetra.* Chicago: University of Chicago Press.

Hunter, W. W. 1886. *The Imperial Gazetteer of India,* vol. 11. London: Trübner and Company.

Hymes, Dell. 1975. Breakthrough into Performance. In *Folklore: Performance and Communication,* edited by Dan Ben-Amos and Kenneth S. Goldstein, 11–74. The Hague: Mouton.

——. 1974a. Toward Ethnographies of Communication. In *Foundations in Sociolinguistics,* edited by Dell Hymes, 3–66. Philadelphia: University of Pennsylvania Press.

——. 1974b. Ways of Speaking. In *Explorations in the Ethnography of Speaking,* edited by Richard Bauman and Joel Sherzer, 433–451. London: Cambridge University Press.

Jacobson, Doranne. 1976. You Have Given Us a Goddess. In *Aspects of Changing India: Studies in Honour of G. S. Ghurye,* edited by Devadas Pillai, 315–326. Bombay: Popular Prakashan.

——. 1977. The Women of North and Central India: Goddesses and Wives. In *Women in India: Two Perspectives,* by Doranne Jacobson and Susan S. Wadley, 17–111. New Delhi: Manohar.

Jacobson, Doranne, and Susan S. Wadley. 1977. *Women in India: Two Perspectives.* Delhi: Manohar.

Jakobson, Roman. 1960. Closing Statement: Linguistics and Poetics. In *Style in Language,* edited by T. A. Sebeok, 350–373. Cambridge: MIT Press.

Jason, Heda. 1977. *Ethnopoetry: Form, Content, Function.* Bonn: Linguistica Biblica.

Jay, Edward. 1973. Bridging the Gap between Castes: Ceremonial Friendships in Chhattisgarh. *Contributions to Indian Sociology* 7: 144–158.

——. 1970. *A Tribal Village of Middle India.* Calcutta: Anthropological Survey of India.

Kavyopadhyaya, Hiralal. 1890. A Grammar of the Dialect of Chhattisgarh in the Central Province. Translated by G. A. Grierson. *Journal of the Asiatic Society of Bengal* 59: 1–153.

Khedkar, V. K. 1959. *The Divine Heritage of the Yadavas.* India: n.p.

Knipe, David. 1991. *Hinduism: Experiments in the Sacred.* New York: HarperSanFrancisco.

Lavie, Smadar, Kirin Narayan, and Renato Rosaldo, eds. 1993. *Creativity/Anthropology.* Ithaca: Cornell University Press.

Lutgendorf, Philip. 1991. *The Life of a Text: Performing the* Rāmcaritmānas *of Tulsīdās.* Berkeley: University of California Press.

McGregor, R. S. 1993. *The Oxford Hindi-English Dictionary.* Delhi: Oxford University Press.

Mandelbaum, David G. 1970. Cultural Adaptations and Models for Mobility. In *Society in India: Change and Continuity,* vol. 2, 442–467. Berkeley: University of California Press.

Menez, Hermina. 1994. Female Warriors in Philippine Oral Epics. Paper presented at conference, "Epics in the Contemporary World," April 21–23, Madison, Wisconsin.

Miller, Barbara D. 1981. *The Endangered Sex: Neglect of Female Children in Rural North India.* Ithaca: Cornell University Press.

Mills, Margaret. 1985. Sex Role Reversals, Sex Changes, and Transvestite Disguise in the Oral Tradition of a Conservative Muslim Community in Afghanistan. In *Women's Folklore, Women's Culture,* edited by Rosan Jordan and Susan Kalcik, 187–213. Philadelphia: University of Pennsylvania Press.

Nagy, Gregory. 1994. Epic as Genre. Paper presented at conference, "Epics in the Contemporary World," April 21–23, Madison, Wisconsin.

——. 1990. *Pindar's Homer: The Lyric Possession of an Epic Past.* Baltimore: Johns Hopkins University Press.

Narayana Rao, Velcheru. Unpublished ms. What Is Folklore in India?

Nelson, A. E. 1909. *Central Provinces. District Gazetteers. Raipur District.* Vol. A, *Description.* Bombay: British India Press.

Okely, Judith. 1991. Defiant Moments: Gender, Resistance, and Individuals. *Man* 26 (1): 3–22.

Pandey, S. M. 1982. *The Hindi Oral Epic Canainī.* Allahabad: Sahitya Bhawan.

——. 1979. *The Hindi Oral Epic Loriki.* Allahabad: Sahitya Bhawan.

Parmar, Shyam. 1972. *Folklore of Madhya Pradesh.* New Delhi: National Book Trust.

Raheja, Gloria Goodwin, and Ann Grodzins Gold. 1994. *Listen to the Heron's Words: Reimagining Gender and Kinship in North India.* Berkeley: University of California Press.

Ramanujan, A. K. 1986. Two Realms of Kannada Folklore. In *Another Harmony: New Essays on the Folklore of India,* edited by Stuart H. Blackburn and A. K. Ramanujan, 41–75. Berkeley: University of California Press.

Reynolds, Holly Baker. 1980. The Auspicious Married Woman. In *The Powers of Tamil Women,* edited by Susan S. Wadley, 35–60. Syracuse: Maxwell School of Citizenship and Public Affairs, Syracuse University.

Richman, Paula, ed. 1991. *Many Rāmāyaṇas: The Diversity of a Narrative Tradition in South Asia.* Berkeley: University of California Press.

Russell, R. V., and Rai Bahadur Hira Lal. [1916] 1969. *The Tribes and Castes of the Central Provinces of India.* Reprint, the Netherlands: Anthropological Publications.

Sarma, Danesvara. 1962. *Chhattīsgarḥī ke Lok Gīt* [The folk songs of Chhattisgarh]. Durg, M.P.: Chhattisgarhi Lok Sahitya Parisad.

Sax, William S. 1991. Ritual and Performance in the Pāṇḍavalīlā of Garhwal. In *Essays on the Mahābhārata,* edited by Arvind Sharma, 274–295. Leiden: E. J. Brill.

Senapati, Nilamani, and Bhabakrashna Mahanti, eds. 1971. *Orissa District Gazetteers: Sambalpur.* Cuttack: Orissa Government Press.

Sharma, Ursula M. 1980. Purdah and Public Space. In *Women in Contemporary India and South Asia,* edited by Alfred de Souza, 213–239. New Delhi: Manohar.

Sherzer, Joel. 1983. *Kuna Ways of Speaking: An Ethnographic Perspective.* Austin: University of Texas Press.

Shukla, Dayashankar. 1969. *Chhattisgarḥī Loksāhitya kā Adhyāyan* [A study of the folk literature of Chhattisgarh]. Raipur: Jyoti Prakashan.

Shulman, David. 1994. On Being Human in the Sanskrit Epic: The Riddle of Nala. *Journal of Indian Philosophy* 22: 1–29.

——. 1991. Towards a Historical Poetics of the Sanskrit Epics. *International Folklore Review:* 9–17.

Shuman, Amy. 1993. Gender and Genre. In *Feminist Theory and the Study of Folklore,* edited by Susan Tower Hollis, Linda Pershing, and M. Jane Young, 71–88. Urbana: University of Illinois Press.

Smith, John D. 1990. Worlds Apart: Orality, Literacy, and the Rajasthani Folk-*Mahābhārata. Oral Tradition* 5 (1): 3–19.

——. 1980. The Two Sanskrit Epics. In *Traditions of Heroic and Epic Poetry,* vol. 1, edited by A. T. Hatto, 48–78. London: Modern Humanities Research Association.

Sopher, David E. 1980. The Geographic Patterning of Culture in India. In *An Exploration of India: Geographical Perspectives on Society and Culture,* edited by David E. Sopher, 289–326. Ithaca: Cornell University Press.

Sweeney, Amin. 1986. *A Full Hearing: Orality and Literacy in the Malay World.* Berkeley: University of California Press.

Swynnerton, Charles. 1963. *Romantic Tales from the Punjab.* Patiala, Punjab: Department of Languages, Punjab University.

Tedlock, Dennis. 1983. *The Spoken Word and the Work of Interpretation.* Philadelphia: University of Pennsylvania Press.

Temple, R. C. [1884] 1962. *The Legends of the Punjab.* 3 vols. Reprint, Patiala, Punjab: Department of Languages, Punjab University.

Thompson, Stith. 1946. *The Folktale.* New York: Dryden.

Thompson, Stith, and Warren E. Roberts. 1960. Types of Indic Oral Tales. *FF Communications* 180.

Van Buitenen, J. A. B., trans. and ed. 1975. *The Mahābhārata.* Vol. 2. Chicago: University of Chicago Press.

Varma, Shakuntala. 1971. *Chhattisgarhi Lok Jivan aur Lok Sahitya ka Adhyayan* [An introduction to the folk life and folk literature of Chhattisgarh]. Allahabad: Rachna Prakashan.

Verma, Rajendra, ed. 1973. *Gazetteer of India. Madhya Pradesh. Raipur District.* Bhopal, M.P.: District Gazetteers Department.

Wadley, Susan S. 1991. Why Does Ram Swarup Sing? Song and Speech in the North Indian Epic Dḥolā. In *Gender, Genre, and Power in South Asian Expressive Tradition,* edited by Arjun Appadurai et al., 201–223. Philadelphia: University of Pennsylvania Press.

——. 1989. Choosing a Path: Performance Strategies in a North Indian Epic. In *Oral Epics in India,* edited by Stuart Blackburn et al., 75–101. Berkeley: University of California Press.

——. 1980. The Paradoxical Powers of Tamil Women. In *The Powers of Tamil Women,* edited by Susan S. Wadley, 153–169. Syracuse: Maxwell School of Citizenship and Public Affairs, Syracuse University.

——. 1975. Folk Literature in Karimpur. *Journal of South Asian Literature* 11: 7–17.

Weaver, Thomas F. 1968. The Farmers of Raipur. In *Developing Rural India: Plan and Practice,* edited by John W. Mellor et al., 143–229. Ithaca: Cornell University Press.

Wills, C. U. 1919. The Territorial Systems of the Rajput Kingdoms of Mediaeval Chhattisgarh. *Journal and Proceedings of the Asiatic Society of Bengal* 15: 197–262.

Index

Note: Page numbers in italic refer to illustrations.

MYTH AND POETICS

A series edited by

GREGORY NAGY

Helen of Troy and Her Shameless Phantom
by Norman Austin

The Craft of Poetic Speech in Ancient Greece
by Claude Calame
translated by Janice Orion

Masks of Dionysus
edited by Thomas W. Carpenter and Christopher A. Faraone

The Odyssey *in Athens: Myths of Cultural Origins*
by Erwin F. Cook

The Poetics of Supplication: Homer's Iliad *and* Odyssey
by Kevin Crotty

Poet and Hero in the Persian Book of Kings
by Olga M. Davidson

Gender and Genre in the Folklore of Middle India
by Joyce Burkhalter Flueckiger

The Ravenous Hyenas and the Wounded Sun: Myth and Ritual in Ancient India
by Stephanie W. Jamison

Poetry and Prophecy: The Beginnings of a Literary Tradition
edited by James Kugel

The Traffic in Praise: Pindar and the Poetics of Social Economy
by Leslie Kurke

Topographies of Hellenism: Mapping the Homeland
by Artemis Leontis

Epic Singers and Oral Tradition
by Albert Bates Lord

The Singer Resumes the Tale
by Albert Bates Lord, edited by Mary Louise Lord

The Language of Heroes: Speech and Performance in the Iliad
by Richard P. Martin

Heroic Sagas and Ballads
by Stephen A. Mitchell
The Anger of Achilles: "Mênis" in Greek Epic
by Leonard Muellner
Greek Mythology and Poetics
by Gregory Nagy
Myth and the Polis
edited by Dora C. Pozzi and John M. Wickersham
Knowing Words: Wisdom and Cunning in the Classical Traditions of China and Greece
by Lisa Raphals
Heroic Poets, Poetic Heroes: The Ethnography of Performance in an Arabic Oral Epic Tradition
by Dwight Fletcher Reynolds
Homer and the Sacred City
by Stephen Scully
Singers, Heroes, and Gods in the Odyssey
by Charles Segal
The Mute Immortals Speak: Pre-Islamic Poetry and the Poetics of Ritual
by Suzanne Pinckney Stetkevych
Phrasikleia: An Anthropology of Reading in Ancient Greece
by Jesper Svenbro
translated by Janet E. Lloyd
The Jewish Novel in the Ancient World
by Lawrence M. Wills